François Hemsterhuis and
the Writing of Philosophy

François Hemsterhuis and the Writing of Philosophy

Daniel Whistler

EDINBURGH
University Press

Edinburgh University Press is one of the leading university presses in the UK. We publish academic books and journals in our selected subject areas across the humanities and social sciences, combining cutting-edge scholarship with high editorial and production values to produce academic works of lasting importance. For more information visit our website: edinburghuniversitypress.com

© Daniel Whistler, 2022, 2024

Edinburgh University Press Ltd
The Tun – Holyrood Road
12(2f) Jackson's Entry
Edinburgh EH8 8PJ

First published in hardback by Edinburgh University Press 2022

Typeset in 10/12pt Goudy Old Style
by Cheshire Typesetting Ltd, Cuddington, Cheshire

A CIP record for this book is available from the British Library

ISBN 978 1 3995 0982 4 (hardback)
ISBN 978 1 3995 0983 1 (paperback)
ISBN 978 1 3995 0984 8 (webready PDF)
ISBN 978 1 3995 0985 5 (epub)

The right of Daniel Whistler to be identified as the author of this work has been asserted in accordance with the Copyright, Designs and Patents Act 1988, and the Copyright and Related Rights Regulations 2003 (SI No. 2498).

There will always be men destined to be subjugated by the opinions of their century, their Country, their Society. . . . One ought not to write for such Readers when one wants to live beyond one's century.

Jean-Jacques Rousseau (2018: 4)

Contents

List of Abbreviations	ix
Preface: Reasons to Read Hemsterhuis	x

Part One: Preliminaries
§1 Philosophy and Poetry ... 3
§2 Rupture ... 11

Part Two: Untimely Demands
Chapter One: Socrates and Newton ... 31
§3 'Born Greek' ... 31
§4 Geometrical Method ... 38
§5 A System of Times ... 47

Chapter Two: Analysis and Poetry ... 59
§6 'Poet-Philosophers' and 'Humble' Analysts ... 59
§7 Sentimental Certainty ... 67
§8 The Platonic Sublime ... 74
§9 The Myth of Prometheus ... 86

Part Three: A History of Organs
Chapter Three: Organs, Instruments and Insects ... 105
§10 Insectification ... 105
§11 The Plasticity of Philosophy ... 112
§12 Perfectibility ... 123
§13 The Analogy to Morality ... 134
§14 Organology and Style ... 144

Chapter Four: Writing after Materialism — 157
§15 Diderot Reads Hemsterhuis — 157
§16 Hemsterhuis Reads Diderot — 166
§17 Palingenesis and the Subversion of Materialism — 177
§18 Post-Bonnetian Style — 187

Part Four: Time-Images
Chapter Five: The Past and the Present — 203
§19 The Optimum — 203
§20 Epistolary Style — 212
§21 Genealogy — 221
§22 Irony and Anachronism — 231

Chapter Six: The Archaic and the Prophetic — 245
§23 Dreams and Shadows — 245
§24 In the Style of Hope — 255

Conclusion: Four Characters in Search of a Philosophy — 265

Bibliography — 270
Index — 287

Abbreviations

B   François Hemsterhuis, *Briefwisseling* (*Hemsterhuisiana*), 13 vols, ed. Jacob van Sluis. Berlstum: self-published, 2011–17. Citations by volume, numbered letter and page number (e.g., 2.45, 82 = volume 2, letter 45, p. 82).

EE François Hemsterhuis, *The Edinburgh Edition of the Complete Philosophical Works of François Hemsterhuis*, 3 vols, ed. and trans. Jacob van Sluis and Daniel Whistler. Edinburgh: Edinburgh University Press, 2022–. Citations by volume and page number (e.g., 2.89 = volume 2, p. 89).

IN François Hemsterhuis, *Œuvres inédits*, ed. Jacob van Sluis. Berltsum: self-published, 2021.

OP François Hemsterhuis, *Œuvres philosophiques. Edition critique*, ed. Jacob van Sluis. Leiden: Brill, 2015.

WW François Hemsterhuis, *Wijsgerige Werken*, ed. Michael John Petry. Leeuwarden: Damon, 2001.

Preface

Reasons to Read Hemsterhuis

1. Like Plato's *Symposium* before it, *Simon ou des facultés de l'âme* – the penultimate dialogue François Hemsterhuis (1721–90) completed – ends in noise, confusion and, in this case, a neighbour 'knocking on my door, howling and shouting at me with all his strength' (*EE* 2.171, *OP* 572). And, amidst this cacophony of non-philosophical voices, both the *Symposium* and *Simon* glimpse a further conversation that touches on philosophy's relation to the poetic: in the *Symposium*, Socrates, Agathon and Aristophanes invoke a poet (typically taken to refer to Plato himself) able to unite the tragic and comic arts (1962: 223c–d); in *Simon*, Socrates and Agathon examine the 'close relation between the language of philosophy and the dithyramb' (*EE* 2.171, *OP* 572). These discussions are alluded to in passing, drowned out by other noises, without being reported or performed for the reader. That is, when the two dialogues come to speak explicitly of their relation to the poetic, they break up, and the readerly desire to know more is left frustrated. Within *Simon*, Hemsterhuis is therefore faithful to a Platonic model in his refusal to methodically elucidate the poetic features of philosophy; and yet, whereas 'my Father and Teacher' Plato (B 2.45, 102) does not elsewhere comment on his own textual practices in any straightforward manner, this is not Hemsterhuis' last word on the subject. Both his final completed dialogue, *Alexis ou de l'âge d'or*, and his correspondence of the 1780s will explicitly advocate for 'the poetic interior of philosophy' as Philippe Lacoue-Labarthe and Jean-Luc Nancy have put it (1975: 155). The late Hemsterhuis, unlike the extant Plato, never again refrains from theorising his own writing of philosophy. And it is this material that forms the subject matter of this book.

One example is the following passage written to Amalie Gallitzin in April 1786:

In 1775, I had the precious happiness of making your acquaintance ... and, from then on, our frequent conversations led us to understand that, in order to familiarise men with beautiful philosophy, it was not a matter of being superficial and showing merely its shadow, as the enlightened spirits of this century believe, either in error or by necessity; but [it was a matter of] removing [this philosophy] from the weighty husks of the school which concealed it, locked it up and constrained it, so as to replace them with festoons and flowers that soften its majestic beauty to the point of attracting and no longer obfuscating the gaze. From this came those dialogues which were all born and fashioned under your gaze. (B 7.30, 86–7)[1]

Hemsterhuis here introduces the idea that in 1775 his approach to writing philosophy altered, that from 1775 onwards there is a turn towards philosophising in 'festoons and flowers' and so a concerted effort to attract the reader's gaze. Accordingly, one of my theses in this book is that Hemsterhuis' philosophy undergoes a 'poetic turn': from 1775, he increasingly experiments with dialogue, with myth, with allegory, with fake prefaces, with jokes and ironies, with personae and with tone as means to better communicate or disclose philosophical ideas. He shifts away from the epistolary style of his earlier writings to incorporate a panoply of devices that are more self-consciously and more elaborately poetic.

In the above passage, Hemsterhuis specifies that this turn arose from a desire to make philosophy more alluring – in *Alexis* he speaks of the 'honey' by which poetry disguises the 'bitter medicine' of philosophy (*EE* 2.124; *OP* 578). These images of 'honey', 'festoons and flowers' might well suggest a relegation of philosophical form to the status of mere window dressing, an ornamental afterthought to decorate an already established 'pure unit of philosophy' (Danto 1984: 7). But this impression quickly dissipates on further scrutiny. For one, *Alexis* argues, on the contrary (see §1), that poetic form furnishes the generative ground to philosophy, a moment of creativity from which truths emerge.[2] Nevertheless, it does still remain the case that,

---

[1] Translations of Hemsterhuis' texts that do not appear in the *Edinburgh Edition* are my own, and are rendered according to the translation decisions set out in the Series Preface to that edition (see *EE* 1.viii–ix), including – most noticeably – the use of 'man' to translate 'l'homme' (following the tradition of Pope's *Essay on Man*, to which Hemsterhuis belongs).

[2] It is Gallitzin herself who programmatically sets out (in relation to Plato's writing style) her and Hemsterhuis' considered position on the constitutive role of the imaginary in philosophising. She reminds him of their 'extensive' conversations concerning 'whether what Plato has written with the sole aim of presenting truths to his reader's

in addition to the numerous fundamental roles philosophical form plays in Hemsterhuis' project, it is also meant to please the reader. The fact that his 'festoons and flowers' are *also* charming is one compelling reason to carry on reading Hemsterhuis. Indeed, the origin of my own project is not primarily to be located in Hemsterhuis' status as 'the most original Dutch thinker of the eighteenth century' (Wielema 1993: 109), nor in his famous German reception history, but in my own naïve pleasure in reading him. His texts produce aesthetic effects, and it is my enjoyment of them that gave rise to this book and, with it, my overarching if implicit contention that Hemsterhuis stands as one of the great philosophical stylists of modernity and deserves, in this regard, to be mentioned in the same breath as Bruno, Shaftesbury, Diderot, Hamann, Schlegel, Kierkegaard and Nietzsche.

Such a claim is unfashionable in at least three ways. First, no one has thought to defend Hemsterhuis' philosophy in an English-language monograph since 1975 and, even then, Heinz Moenkemeyer was the very first person to think it a good idea. The anglophone world has (a few recent exceptions notwithstanding) never really found the time for Hemsterhuis' philosophy. Secondly, this is a book very much *about* untimeliness, about making productive use of an outdated past for the purpose of an unprethinkable future. It offers a speculative rendering of Rousseau's imperative (printed as the epigraph to this book) to 'live beyond one's century' through one's writing (2018: 4) – that is, to philosophise oneself *out of the present epoch* and into others. And, thirdly, it has recently become relatively unfashionable to write concertedly on philosophical textuality and philosophical style, for it is a topic that has seemingly exhausted itself both in the anglophone world (in the wake of the post-Danto 'philosophy as literature' movement) and in French theory (see, for instance, Jean-Luc Nancy's bemusement at the 'immoderate taste' of his youth for the textuality of philosophy [2002: 147–8]).

2. Beyond the pleasures afforded by Hemsterhuis' 'festoons and flowers', there are many other reasons to read him. And I will argue that one of the foremost is that Hemsterhuis *speculates about times* – and he does so precisely by means of the host of textual genres, rhetorical devices, mythic allusions

---

soul could merely be called "ornament", or whether both the truths [he presents] and their coverings do not rather form an inseparable body within his work. . . . There are authors for whom the truths they want to say and the ornaments by which they want to make [these truths] appear are two different things . . . but it is very different, in my opinion, when it comes to what has been so badly named Plato's "ornaments"' (Gallitzin 2015–17: 3.181).

and figurative effects that constitute his poetic turn. That is, by unpacking the idea of a 'poetic turn', I intend to extract a Hemsterhuis who is relatively speculative (even if sometimes uncomfortably so), a Hemsterhuis for whom philosophy is a voyage into remote epochs to discover 'unknown lands' (EE 2.45; OP 335).

In particular, I explore his speculations on time and their accompanying writing practices by way of three investigations (corresponding to Parts Two, Three and Four of the book).[3] The first investigation focuses on the absolute nature of Hemsterhuis' Platonism, that is, his attempt to inhabit all epochs simultaneously by 'doing it all' as a philosopher – by thinking geometrically as well as Socratically, by writing analytically as well as mythically and figuratively. The second investigation considers Hemsterhuis' organology, his metaphysics of pervasive, plastic organs (defined in their pre-biological sense of instruments, capacities or tools to achieve a determinate end), which emerges out of a dialogue with two rival organologies offered by Denis Diderot and Charles Bonnet. All three, I argue, take seriously the imperative to write organologically, to perform in words the plasticity of organs across epochs. Finally, the third investigation describes Hemsterhuis' post-Rousseauean art of imaging times, that is, of making different configurations of time legible in the image. His later stylistic devices, such as genealogies, fictions, ironies and remembered tales of a golden age, refuse the demand of pure presence and instead draw the reader's attention to unactualisable regions of time.

The book is therefore structured as follows. Part One introduces the book's overriding thesis by providing a reading of Hemsterhuis' last dialogue, *Alexis*, and particularly its restaging of the ancient quarrel between philosophers and poets, which concludes in the contention that 'philosophy owes much to poetry' (EE 2.143; OP 634). It further considers the various reasons previously given in the scholarship for Hemsterhuis' poetic turn, including his friendship with Gallitzin; I suggest that there are additional *reasons intrinsic to his thinking* why Hemsterhuis increasingly experiments with textual forms. Part Two specifies some of these intrinsic reasons for Hemsterhuis' poetic turn by elucidating a number of irreconcilable tendencies that structure his

---

[3] The structure of this book is therefore recursive, with each part returning to similar questions concerning the writing of philosophy (e.g., what motivates Hemsterhuis' use of dialogue or of myth?) from different angles. Moreover, it is worth noting at this point that, in order to communicate Hemsterhuis' style and to introduce his relatively unfamiliar texts to the anglophone reader, I have deployed a mosaic method of 'argument by anthology' in what follows, which directly exposes readers to how Hemsterhuis himself wrote philosophy, that is, to what Hemsterhuis' stylistic experiments actually look like.

speculative Platonism – tendencies, on the one hand, to return to a Socratic ideal that stands in judgement on modernity and, on the other hand, to celebrate the advances of geometrical method;, on the one hand, to reject the poetic in philosophical presentation in the name of 'humble' analysis and, on the other hand, to make use of aesthetically charged styles. Part Three reconstructs Hemsterhuis' writing of a history of human organs. And, following Leif Weatherby, I suggest that this history should be understood as a 'technological metaphysics', that is, a philosophising 'that is infinitely open-ended to radical possibility both in the material or empirical world and in the history of human cognition' (2016: 124). Hemsterhuis' history of organs necessitates the plasticity of knowledge, the plasticity of philosophical methodology and thus a plastic style appropriate to this distinctive practice of philosophy. The concluding Part Four looks more closely at Hemsterhuis' writing techniques themselves. I argue – with reference to Gilles Deleuze – that they constitute a set of images that 'makes perceptible, makes visible, relationships of time which cannot be seen in the represented object and do not allow themselves to be reduced to the present' (Deleuze 2013: xi). In his late dialogues, I argue, Hemsterhuis constructs 'signs that open directly onto time' (Deleuze 1989: 43): he rips time from its chronological sequence within his philosophical worlds, making perceptible to his eighteenth-century readership epochs that are not their own.

Overall, therefore, *François Hemsterhuis and the Writing of Philosophy* identifies three types of speculative reason for Hemsterhuis' poetic turn: (1) the mixing of disparate forms of philosophising on the model of Plato; (2) the telling of a history of organs in conversation with Diderot and Bonnet; and (3) the refusal of the hegemony of the present by making other times perceptible. These, I contend, are also reasons why the late Hemsterhuis is worth reading.

3. A third, more common reason why Hemsterhuis is often considered worth reading today is his German reception history. It is this romantic and idealist afterlife that now belies Jean-Louis Vieillard-Baron's suggestion that 'few authors . . . are as forgotten today' (1988: 114). Although I do not spend much time on Hemsterhuis' afterlife in Germany in this book and so keep his reception history as a whole firmly in the background, it is still worth briefly rehearsing it as one major reason why Hemsterhuis continues to be read.[4]

---

[4] Evidently, the reasons given above for reading Hemsterhuis (i.e., that he is a pleasure to read and that he speculates about times) also contribute to the reasons why he was read so avidly in Germany at the turn of the nineteenth century.

In summer 1779, Hemsterhuis' friend, Amalie Gallitzin, moved from her estate outside The Hague to Münster and, with that move, Hemsterhuis himself was forced to enter into the ambit of German letters. While he visited Germany only three times during the ensuing decade, his writings circulated widely. One can, in fact, speak of several distinct lines of transmission: the 'Düsseldorf–Münster Hemsterhuis' of Gallitzin, F. H. Jacobi and the Münster Circle; the 'Weimar Hemsterhuis' of C. M. Wieland, J. G. Herder and J. W. Goethe; the 'Tübingen Hemsterhuis' of G. W. F. Hegel, Friedrich Hölderlin and F. W. J. Schelling; the 'Jena Hemsterhuis' of Novalis and the Schlegels; and even traces of a 'Königsberg Hemsterhuis' of J. G. Hamann and Immanuel Kant.[5] In addition, there occurred numerous further interpretations of Hemsterhuis both within Germany[6] as well as outside its borders.[7]

The 'Düsseldorf–Münster Hemsterhuis' of the 1780s came about as an immediate consequence of Gallitzin's move and her resultant influence on the 'Münster Circle' of Franz von Fürstenberg, J. G. Schlosser, L. Stolberg and so on. However, it was a figure on the fringe of the group – F. H. Jacobi – who did most to proselytise Hemsterhuis in Germany. Hemsterhuis writes of his debt to Jacobi, 'It is not only the celebrity for which I owe you, but what is worth more still, the illumination' (B 12.150, 224–5). Through Jacobi, Hemsterhuis played a substantial role in the German *Spinozismusstreit* and, more specifically, a threefold role in Jacobi's own *Über die Lehre des Spinoza in Briefen an der Herrn Moses Mendelssohn*:[8] as a trigger, as a character and

---

[5] Hamann had initially praised Hemsterhuis' philosophy (he was introduced to it in 1773 by J. G. Herder) (see, e.g., 1955–75: 3.33, 3.357, 3.464) and it is through him (1955–75: 5.125, 7.255) that we learn of Kant's enthusiasm for it (and so the existence of a Königsberg strand to Hemsterhuis' reception history).

[6] For example, by Moses Mendelssohn, G. E. Lessing, Christian Garve, Jean Paul, F. D. E. Schleiermacher, Wilhelm von Humboldt, Karolina Günderrode and Wilhelm Dilthey.

[7] For example, by P. W. van Heusde, S. T. Coleridge, Maine de Biran, Victor Cousin, the Groningen School, William Hamilton, Leo Tolstoy and Benedetto Croce. Hence, despite the Germanocentric story which dominates Hemsterhuis' reception history and the scholarly prejudice that he 'did not have a noticeable influence on Dutch philosophy' (Dierik 1997: 247; Moenkemeyer 1977: 516), Hemsterhuis was read elsewhere and particularly in the Netherlands at the turn of the nineteenth century. For Hemsterhuis' influence on van Heusde, see van Bunge (2018: 188); on the Groningen School's Christianisation of Hemsterhuis' philosophy, see Wielema (1995); on de Biran's reception of him, see van Sluis (in OP 18); on Cousin's interpretation, see Moenkemeyer (1977: 519) and Boulan (1924: 58–9); S. T. Coleridge mentions Hemsterhuis (1969: 155) and William Hamilton does so in Reid (1855: 366); Leo Tolstoy discusses Hemsterhuis' aesthetics (1994: 32), as does Benedetto Croce (2017: 262).

[8] Henceforth referred to as the *Spinoza-Briefe*.

as an author (see Whistler 2022b). First, Hemsterhuis' *Aristée* – alongside Goethe's *Prometheus* – provoked Lessing to confess in Wolfenbüttel in June 1780 that 'the orthodox concepts of the Divinity are no longer for me' and that 'there is no other philosophy than the philosophy of Spinoza' (Jacobi 1994: 187). Secondly, Hemsterhuis is also a character depicted in a fictional 'battle' (1994: 202) with Spinoza, who is imagined as 'speaking to us in person [having] just finished reading the *Aristée*' (1994: 205). By means of this dialogue, Jacobi's Hemsterhuis supplies 'grounds that are sound enough to counter Spinoza's arguments against the personality and understanding of a first cause, against free will and final causes' (1994: 215). And whatever his success, Jacobi ends the dialogue 'impatient to throw myself into the arms of that sublime genius [i.e., Hemsterhuis] who said that the occasional occurrence in the soul of even one aspiration for the better, for the future and the perfect, is a better proof of the Divinity than any geometric proof' (1994: 214). Thirdly, Hemsterhuis himself also contributes a 'treatment of the theme of atheism' – the *Lettre sur l'athéisme* – as an appendix to the 1789 edition of the *Spinoza-Briefe*.[9]

In the wake of the *Spinozismusstreit*, Hemsterhuis enjoyed a widespread German readership; as Friedrich Schlegel was later to put it, 'Hemsterhuis is German because only here he found a public' (1958–2002: 18.344). Hemsterhuis' autumn 1785 tour of Germany, which included conversations with Goethe, Herder and Wieland in Weimar, was an unqualified success: J. H. Merck wrote, 'Everyone in . . . Weimar is taken with enthusiasm for Hemsterhuis' (quoted in Trunz 1971: 167), and Wieland likewise told Jacobi, 'This man is, in my estimation, among the most perfect men who has ever been; he comes close to being the Plato *of our time*' (quoted in Starnes 1987: 2.52).[10] Herder was the most passionate Hemsterhuisian: he treasured the *Lettre sur l'Homme*, for example, as containing 'a hundred of my favourite ideas', adding 'everyone has said to me that I am very similar to this man' (1977–2016: 2.240). According to Herder, Hemsterhuis' was 'an original philosophy, such as there is only once in a 100 years' (1977–2016: 3.127). His 1781 rendering of the *Lettre sur les désirs* in Wieland's *Teutsche Merkur*, post-scripted with a critical commentary, *Liebe und Selbstheit*, was to be

---

[9] This letter was not by any means Hemsterhuis' first substantial response to the *Spinozismusstreit*: for example, in correspondence with Gallitzin, he had already penned a series of letters on the concepts of belief and faith in the wake of the Jacobi–Mendelssohn debate (B 7.60–7, 157–89).

[10] Wieland had in fact been one of Hemsterhuis' earliest German admirers. In 1771, the circle of Wieland, Merck and Sophie de la Roche cultivated a communal interest in Hemsterhuis' early writings (see Starnes 1987: 1.417).

the most influential German monument to Hemsterhuis alongside Jacobi's *Spinoza-Briefe*. Likewise, J. W. Goethe had been struck by Hemsterhuis' philosophy, reading *Aristée* with Charlotte von Stein during the 1780s and, after Hemsterhuis' death in 1790, inheriting his gem collection and some unpublished manuscripts. As late as 1821, Goethe was still returning to the *Lettre sur la sculpture* as a source for his aesthetics (Trunz 1971: 134; see Trop 2022: 39–43).

Hemsterhuis' influence on Weimar is, however, merely the penultimate stage of his extraordinary reception history in Germany (see Melica 2007: 145). The final stage comprises his posthumous legacy among the next generation of German Idealists and romantics of the 1790s. It is this context to which Germaine De Staël refers in designating Hemsterhuis 'Kant's precursor' – 'the first who, in the middle of the eighteenth century, indicated in his writings the majority of the beneficent ideas on which the new German school is founded' (1814: 429–31). A. W. Schlegel will equally name Hemsterhuis a 'prophet of transcendental idealism' (1964: 3.83).

This post-Kantian Hemsterhuis was initially forged in Tübingen, where the students at the *Stift* – among them, G. W. F. Hegel, Friedrich Hölderlin and F. W. J. Schelling – encountered Hemsterhuis via Jacobi's *Spinoza-Briefe*, Herder's translation and the teaching of the Tübingen professor F. A. Boeck (Franz 2012: 80–2; Melica 2007: 148).[11] This group came to associate Hemsterhuis closely with a post-critical Platonism and, as such, his discussions of love and desire in particular were understood as 'an early precursor of *Vereinigungsphilosophie*' (Engelen 1999: 119; see also Melica 2007: 144–52). Remnants of this Kantian–Platonic Hemsterhuis survive in Hegel's *Vorlesungen über die Ästhetik*, Hölderlin's *Hyperion* and Schelling's *Fernere Darstellungen*.[12]

However, even more than in Tübingen, Hemsterhuis was central to the post-Kantian project undertaken in Jena during the 1790s. Throughout 1792, Friedrich Schlegel badgered his brother, A. W. Schlegel, for Hemsterhuis' texts (e.g., 1958–2002: 23.122, 23.134–5), until in October he confessed to having read 'all the known pieces by Hemsterhuis, excepting only the *description philosophique du caractere de feu M. Fagel*' (1958–2002: 23.140). And it was at precisely this moment that he met Novalis, whose 'favourite writers', he related to his brother, 'are Plato and Hemsterhuis' (1958–2002:

---

[11] Franz Baader was equally a later mediator of idealist appropriations of Hemsterhuis (Bonchino 2014).
[12] On these influences, see Melica (2007: 148–51), Drees (1995) and Franz (2012: 81–2), respectively.

23.40). Likewise, A. W. Schlegel describes Hemsterhuis as 'our favourite' (1964: 1.155–6) – and thus the 'Jena Hemsterhuis' was born. The high-point of this early German romantic reception is Novalis' *Hemsterhuis-Studien*, thirty-six sheets of translation and paraphrase written between 5 September and 30 November 1797, in which, as Mähl notes (in Novalis 1960–2006: 2.322), the 'boundary' between Hemsterhuis' and Novalis' own thoughts is 'not always sharply drawn'.

It is this story of Hemsterhuis' remarkable reception in German idealisms and romanticisms that has most often drawn readers back to his writings.

4. A fourth reason to read Hemsterhuis is that it has not properly been possible until now, at least not without much archival sifting. That this has now changed is due to Jacob van Sluis' efforts editing a critical edition of Hemsterhuis' publications, collecting all his unpublished fragments, and putting his complete correspondence into print for the very first time (including the 3,000 letters Hemsterhuis and Gallitzin exchanged – 'the most significant European correspondence of the eighteenth century' [Trunz 1971: x]). It is now possible to read in print everything that survives from Hemsterhuis' pen. I am very obviously indebted to van Sluis' work. For one, this book takes the newly published correspondence seriously as a philosophical document – one which not only practises but also reflects upon the playfulness, irony and occasional dissimulation that, I contend, are important Hemsterhuisian writing strategies. But, in addition, I am equally indebted to Jacob's astute comments on a draft manuscript of this book.

Lots of other people, institutions and libraries helped me enormously in writing this book. I am grateful to Carol Macdonald at Edinburgh University Press for her unwavering support, to the Alexander von Humboldt Stiftung for funding a fellowship in Münster at the start of the project, to Michael Quante, who hosted me there, to colleagues at the University of Liverpool and at Royal Holloway who supported this research, and to everyone who put up with me trying out 'my Hemsterhuis' on them. I am particularly grateful to Kirill Chepurin and to Steven Lydon for their extraordinarily helpful engagement with a draft manuscript. Most of all, though, I owe everything to Grace – this book as well as everything else. What follows is dedicated to her.

Part One
Preliminaries

§1 Philosophy and Poetry

Alexis – the last in Hemsterhuis' late sequence of dialogues, written in 1781 – restages the ancient quarrel between philosophy and poetry. Diocles undertakes to persuade Alexis (a novice convert to Socratic inquiry) not only that, despite appearances to the contrary, philosophical reasoning and poetic fable are reconcilable, but also that philosophy requires such poetry as its ground. And this is because creativity in thinking – the production of new truths and so intellectual progress – presupposes a *poietic* moment. In short, the dialogue concludes, 'Philosophy owes much to poetry' (*EE* 2.143; *OP* 634).

Plato's *Republic* had staged the quarrel by weaving together two distinct poles: (1) the explicit denunciation of *mythos* from the perspective of enlightened *logos*; and (2) the implicit performance of poetry, as dialogue and myth, within the philosophical text. *Alexis* responds by thematising both poles explicitly in its argument and concluding in favour of the latter. This conclusion additionally alludes to Rousseau's 1750 *Discours sur les sciences et les arts*, which had likewise thematised the two poles of Plato's quarrel, but conversely concluded in favour of the elimination of ornament, rhetoric and poetry from presentations of the truth. According to Rousseau, eloquence had condemned Athens to 'luxury', 'enervation' and 'vices' (2018: 10, 12); it had resulted in sophistic dissimulation under the guise of pleasing prose. Hemsterhuis will attempt to reverse Rousseau's conclusion, and he will do so – most provocatively – in an Athenian setting (equally saving Athens from Rousseau's condemnation).[1]

The dialogue begins with Alexis offering an orthodox Platonic-Rousseauian condemnation of the poets as failing to live up to the rigours

---

[1] I return in more detail to the reckoning with Rousseau's legacy in *Alexis* in §12.

of Socratic philosophy, owing to their 'lies and fables', to their ornamentation of the truth in ways 'which obscure it' like 'a stain', to their substitution of 'dreams and ruminations in place of truths' (*EE* 2.124; *OP* 576–8). What the poets fail to recognise, according to Alexis at the beginning of the dialogue, is that 'the beautiful truth is stark naked by nature', to be communicated without ornament (*EE* 2.124; *OP* 576). The dialogue ends, however, with Diocles convincing Alexis of the ineradicable poetic core to philosophising. Alexis' conversion from Rousseauianism to late Hemsterhuisianism is confirmed with the words, 'I understand for the first time what poetry is. I sense that the most profound reasoning, the wisest and most reflective march of the intellect would supply us with very few new truths, if it were not sustained, directed or pushed by this enthusiasm' (*EE* 2.142; *OP* 632). Or, as Diocles had put it earlier in the dialogue: 'It is not without reason that poetry is called the language of the Gods. . . . Without this language we would make very little progress in our sciences' (*EE* 2.140; *OP* 624).

Reason operates, in part, through poetic inspiration. This is why philosophical inquiry (even Socratic inquiry) must make use of non-logical strategies, rather than aspiring towards a neutral style-without-style. Hemsterhuis rewrites the *Republic*, such that its conclusions are rendered consistent with its own writing techniques of dialogue, myth and allegory.

1. It is therefore unsurprising that, formally, the text of *Alexis* is itself full of ornament and imagery; that is, it does not solely argue for a poetic ground to philosophy but also exemplifies it. In fact, it mixes all sorts of rhetorical devices, genres, myths and ironies. *Alexis* enthusiastically embraces stylistic experimentation, and a preliminarily list of these experiments will supply some initial evidence for my overall argument in this book.

(a) Dialogue
Dialogue is the most visible formal device that Hemsterhuis employs in *Alexis*. The eighteenth century was an age of philosophical dialogues, but Hemsterhuis manages to avoid some of its more common vices. Most obviously, he resists the temptation to transform dialogue into a monologic genre, by making one character his mouthpiece and another a pupil whose role is just to imbibe the truths on offer – 'a diatribe directed at a helpless victim' (Feyerabend 1991: 165). Although Diocles does lead the conversation and convert Alexis to his perspective, there are a number of moments when Alexis supplements Diocles, corrects Diocles and challenges Diocles. That is, Alexis makes a positive contribution to the conclusions of the dia-

logue.² As Klaus Hammacher sums up, Hemsterhuis' 'dialogue-characters are no mere representatives of philosophical positions . . . nor are they abstract elaborations of the philosophical I . . . nor just transcripts of actual dialogues . . . but forms that poetically imitate Plato in an antique garb' (2008: 592). More radically still, it is not merely Diocles who is challenged in the dialogue, but Hemsterhuis equally challenges himself: he subjects his own ideas to scrutiny. For example, when Alexis distinguishes between Socrates' and Pythagoras' philosophies in words drawn verbatim from Hemsterhuis' contemporaneous correspondence, criticising the Pythagoreans for an elitist focus on 'making a few individuals absolutely perfect'(*EE* 2.133; *OP* 604–6; see B 2.63, 190), Diocles does not merely praise this view ('this is very well observed'), he also undertakes to correct it by pointing to the valuable role played by 'the elect' in preserving 'very important pieces of knowledge' (*EE* 2.133; *OP* 606).³ Ultimately, like any good dialogue, it is left up to the reader to judge where truth lies and, on this point, the characters themselves are clear: philosophical writing has its limits and the reader must actively work to transgress them. Diocles insists,

> Although philosophy handles, with the same ease and the same precision, matters as abstract as the simplest object of geometry, it nevertheless finds less facility in the expression of ideas. . . . But in this case, it is up to the listener to remedy [this fault] by attaching to the speaker's train of thought many more words than he pronounces. (*EE* 2.145; *OP* 640)

Hemsterhuis tells his reader: any proper philosophical appreciation of his text must go far beyond it.⁴

---

[2] The clearest example of this kind of reversal occurs in *Aristée*: as soon as they speak of love, the characters swap roles in the dialogue and Aristaeus becomes the teacher with knowledge to impart (*EE* 2.78–80; *OP* 436–40).

[3] This claim is then dramatised with the introduction of the character of Hypsicles, Pythagoras' teacher.

[4] One consequence of *Alexis*' dialogue form is the attention it pays to the affective resonance of philosophical doctrines. The text does not merely exhibit ideas; it shows the types of people who have those ideas and the effects such ideas have on them and their listeners (see further §8). For example, Diocles' anger (*EE* 2.140; *OP* 624–6) is treated as a 'necessary' part of communicating the truth, so too Alexis being 'surprised and shaken' by Hypsicles' speech (*EE* 2.138; *OP* 620). In this vein, *Alexis* ends up providing an answer to the question: what does it look like to encounter a new truth? Or to put it more bluntly, *Alexis* is a conversion story: on the back of one conversion to Socratic inquiry, Alexis is further (re-)converted to poetic philosophy.

(b) Rhetorical exuberance

Alexis exhibits plenty of demonstrative rigour, but there are also asides and digressions that owe nothing to the arguments under development. At these moments, Hemsterhuis' writing betrays an exuberance that temporarily untethers the text from logic. Indeed, the dialogue's meandering is thematised in Diocles' apostrophe to memory – a superfluous rhetorical set-piece which ironically tasks the characters with getting the argument back on track (*EE* 2.132; *OP* 602). Such exuberance shines through in the various analogies the characters use, bringing together strikingly different domains and disciplines: the poet is like Pan and the philosopher like Zeus (*EE* 2.139; *OP* 622), prejudice is imagined in terms of two philosophers coming to blows (*EE* 2.130–1; *OP* 596–8) and the sciences in terms of architectural styles (*EE* 2.139; *OP* 622). These radical transitions are jarring: the reader is challenged to pass breathlessly from mythology to architectural orders to animal psychology and, in all such cases, *Alexis* can be seen to operate according to a poetic principle that variously exceeds, reinforces and disrupts its arguments – much like Le Doeuff's rendering of 'the philosophical imaginary' as the non-conceptual components of the philosophical text that are not 'extrinsic to theoretical work', but instead 'sustain something which the system cannot itself justify, but which is nevertheless needed for its proper working' (1989: 6).

(c) Fictions

One of the most distinctive features of Hemsterhuis' late dialogues is their commitment to inhabiting a coherent fictional world. *Aristée*, *Simon* and *Alexis* all belong to the same imagined world which – by means of intertextual references and an elaborate editorial framework – sustains one consistent, living background against which each dialogue appears (see §22).[5] In *Alexis* itself, a fake preface of the kind that opens both *Aristée* and *Simon* is lacking, but Hemsterhuis still makes clear that it is situated in the same world by mentioning Aristaeus (the protagonist of *Aristée*), as well as 'Diotima's beautiful speech on the faculties of the human soul' (the conclusion to the previous dialogue, *Simon*) and *Simon*'s imputed author, Phaedo of Elis (*EE* 2.123, 128; *OP* 576, 590). *Alexis* thus takes its place alongside *Aristée* and *Simon* as one more forgery, that is, a manuscript of supposed ancient origin rediscovered in the mid-eighteenth century and edited for a modern readership. *Alexis*' most visible fiction is the opening dedication

---

[5] Throughout the book, I refer to the titles of Hemsterhuis' dialogues in the original French (e.g., *Aristée*), but anglicise the names of characters (e.g., Aristaeus).

to 'wise and sacred Diotima' (*EE* 2.123; *OP* 574), which recapitulates similar dedications from *Simon* and *Aristée*. This dedication is at first blush an obvious Platonic allusion and, in this vein, helps position the dialogue in a Socratic tradition. However, any reader familiar with Hemsterhuis' previous dialogues would be aware that *Simon* and *Aristée* had been dedicated to a 'Diotima' who is explicitly distinguished by 'the editor' of these works from Socrates' teacher and assigned to a later Athenian epoch (*EE* 2.63; *OP* 390). In addition, those readers with a personal connection to Hemsterhuis would have also been able to read this dedication as a sort of in-joke – identifying 'Diotima' with Amalie Gallitzin. 'Diotima' is therefore an overdetermined fiction in *Alexis* and establishes a hierarchy of readers based on their degree of complicity – that is, on the extent to which they 'get it'.

(d) Imitation
Much of the above stands in the shadow of Plato: *Alexis* has even been dubbed 'one of the best Plato imitations of the eighteenth century' (Sonderen 2017: 44). Hemsterhuis mimics Plato in the philosophical uses to which he puts dialogue, allegory and myth, and such mimicry is not found merely at a general level, but in the very detail of *Alexis*.[6] To take one example: Alexis and Diocles rest awhile on the road outside Athens to talk philosophy (*EE* 2.123; *OP* 576), just as Socrates and Phaedrus had done. Moreover, Plato is not the only model for the dialogue: *Alexis* also reperforms d'Alembert's inquiry in the 1751 *Discours préliminaire* to the *Encyclopédie* into the interrelation between philosophy, history and poetry, 'the three orders which sustain the vast edifice of all our knowledge' (*EE* 2.139; *OP* 624; see Sonderen 2000: 129). That is, Hemsterhuis' characters implicitly contest d'Alembert's claim that history recounts facts, philosophy reflects and poetry embellishes – and they do so by insisting, on the contrary, that poetry not only 'decorates', but also 'enriches' history and philosophy, in part by making them possible in the first place (*EE* 2.139; *OP* 624).

---

[6] And like Plato, Hemsterhuis' writing is thus permeated with fictionality. As Rowe (1999: 255) puts it of Plato, 'The use of a fictional narrative form (the dialogue) will mean that any conclusions reached, by whatever method (including "rational argument"), may themselves be treated as having the status of a kind of "myth". ... A sense of the "fictionality" of human utterance, as provisional, inadequate, and at best approximating to the truth, will infect Platonic writing at its deepest level.' Indeed, McCormick has argued that this fictionalisation of philosophy is true of many seemingly sober eighteenth-century philosophical texts: he concludes that 'we have good reasons for construing at least some of these [eighteenth-century] nonfictional texts as fictions of a peculiar sort' (1987: 54).

(e) Athenian realism
The details given throughout the dialogue about persons, places and events from ancient Athens add a level of authenticity to its depiction of a Greek world. They contribute to Hemsterhuis' playful positioning of *Alexis* as a forgery by giving it the air of a genuinely antique product. Sometimes – as with the allusions to Aristaeus or to Demophon (*EE* 2.123–4; *OP* 576) – these concrete details are themselves fabulated, but at other times – as with the references to Autolycus and Strato (*EE* 2.124, 130; *OP* 576, 596) – the detail is historically accurate. Moreover, this quest for antiquarian authenticity is furthered by the philological notes that Hemsterhuis adds into *Alexis* as scholarly attestation for its veracity. These displays of erudition take on a life of their own in the footnotes, carried away by their own learned virtuosity: the note on the Cretan monument to Zeus cites obscure source after obscure source, from St Chrysostomus, St Cyril, Lactantius, Cedrenus, Sedelius, St Jerome, Epiphanus, Philostratus, Cicero, Diodorus of Sicily, Lucian, Theophilus, Minitius Felix, St Cyprien and the Scholiast of Callimachus (*EE* 2.147–8; *OP* 646–8). Whatever else Hemsterhuis' intention, manifest here is a desire to supply external corroboration for the textual details of *Alexis* and its world.[7]

(f) Recollection
Hemsterhuis follows Plato in thematising the philosophy–memory relationship: the dialogue's description of the golden age is born out of an exercise in anamnesis, recovering archaic truths passed down through the tradition. This conception of philosophy as an enterprise in recovering lost origins is personified by the figure of Hypsicles, the Phoenician priest, whose function strictly parallels that of Solon, the Egyptian priest in Plato's *Timaeus*. Both priests supplement logical argument with stories of bygone truths difficult to demonstrate through reasoning alone. Different truths, it seems, demand different types of communication. In this regard, Alexis and Diocles themselves occupy an odd temporal position: they exist in a fictional ancient Greek past, but this is a past that is not archaic enough to directly access some truths. They have come too late – and the eighteenth-century reader even more so.

(g) Figures
At the heart of *Alexis* stands the image of the 'golden age', explicitly labelled 'a figurative term' (*EE* 2.143; *OP* 634). It is a figure that shows up the limits

---

[7] See further Fresco's analysis of the Polyxena footnote in *Simon* as an 'absurdist game [of] ironic humour' (in Hemsterhuis 2007: 261–3; see also van Sluis in *OP* 731–3).

of philosophical communication – a limit-concept that Alexis compares to a 'shadow' (*EE* 2.138–9; *OP* 620–2), a mark left by what cannot itself be brought to presence in clear and distinct language. It is at this moment, of course, that poetry comes to the philosopher's aid. The story of the golden age is preposterous, strange, but also oddly compelling – and, as such, it exemplifies the very conclusions the dialogue elsewhere draws concerning the grounding function of poetry in producing new truths that outstrip the intellect. There are 'truths, beauties, sublime features felt and expressed even before they have been discussed or examined in detail by the intellect' (*EE* 2.140; *OP* 626). And these are the product of 'those happy moments of enthusiasm when . . . it is no longer the prudent, exact and determinate march of the intellect, however slow or rapid, that we follow; we take [the path] of Jupiter's lightning which strikes at the very moment it is produced'. These are, Hemsterhuis continues, moments when 'a Divinity intervenes and it is not wrong to call [them] an inspiration' (*EE* 2.142; *OP* 632). *Alexis* attempts to articulate – in both its content and its form – what it looks like to be inspired by a truth beyond the strictures of logical reasoning. In fact, this use of poetic devices to achieve what orthodox reasoning cannot even holds true for the very layout of Hemsterhuis' publications: the vignettes, diagrams and visual ornamentation that he designed constitute part of his books' communication strategy. He controlled all aesthetic elements in the production of his work, including the font, paper type, page size and engravings[8] – manifesting what Moenkemeyer calls 'an almost pedantic care for style' (1975: 26). Consequently, each of his works 'can be seen as a work of art in itself . . . beautifully designed and carefully printed and bound' to convey the 'visual appearance of his ideas' (Sonderen 2017: 41). As Grucker long ago put it, when it comes to Hemsterhuis, 'it is not just the thinker, but the writer and the artist whom we must consider' (1866: 271).

2. The reading offered above of Hemsterhuis as a poetic philosopher stands in a long line of interpretations leading back, at the very least, to Friedrich Schlegel's dictums that 'Hemsterhuis' works can be called *intellectual poems*' and that 'Hemsterhuis combined poetry and philosophy morally' (1958–2002: 2.187, 18.286; see also Cahen-Maurel 2022: 40–1). A more recent reading of Hemsterhuis along these lines is to be found in 'Le dialogue des genres' (1975) by Philippe Lacoue-Labarthe and Jean-Luc Nancy. They read *Alexis*

---

[8] All of which are explicitly commented upon in the opening to the *Lettre sur la sculpture* (*EE* 1.60; *OP* 90). This suggests a rich line of inquiry concerning Hemsterhuis' pictoral communication of philosophy, i.e., his diagrammatic thinking, which is not explored in the below, but is developed in Peter Sonderen's writings.

as a highpoint in the eighteenth-century obsession with philosophical style, and conclude that 'Hemsterhuis attempts to reveal the poetic interior of philosophy' (1975: 155). Such a claim needs to be understood in two contexts. First, *Alexis* fits snugly into those authors' overall project during the 1970s – along the lines of Derrida's prescribed 'task . . . to consider philosophy also as a "literary genre"' (1982: 294) – to chart the various solutions given to 'the question of style, of the genre of philosophy – the question of how to present and expose philosophy'. That is, they investigate the ways in which a specific philosophy 'is always a certain *how-to* of presentation and of its own exposition' (Nancy 2008: 18) – and Hemsterhuis' *Alexis* is exemplary of this in both its form and its content. On their reading, *Alexis* draws the reader towards 'the flesh of thought' (Nancy 2002: 148), towards 'the moment at which philosophy explicitly designates its own exposition as *literature*' (Nancy 2008: 18–19). In sum, the late Hemsterhuis sits alongside Hegel and the German romantics as key material for Lacoue-Labarthe's and Nancy's account of philosophy's 'will to *Darstellung*' (Nancy 2008: 128). Secondly, and more specifically, Lacoue-Labarthe and Nancy turn to *Alexis* as part of their work on 'the history of philosophical dialogue as a philosophical problem' (1975: 154). *Alexis* occupies a key moment in the history of the eighteenth-century dialogue, namely the moment it became 'the privileged mode for theoretical exposition' (1975: 151), 'the ideal of equilibrium between . . . content and exposition' (1975: 152) and so 'the very model of the union of poetry and philosophy' (1988: 88). On their reading, Hemsterhuis is a 'literary' philosopher, a philosopher who makes visible the labour of writing through which philosophical concepts come to be embodied on the page – both in his restaging of the quarrel between philosophy and poetry (the content of *Alexis*) and in the various ostentatious poetic devices that comprise the dialogue's form.

And yet, these readings of Hemsterhuis as a poetic philosopher hold good primarily for the late Hemsterhuis of *Alexis*, *Simon* and, to a lesser extent, *Sophyle* and *Aristée* too. To interpret Hemsterhuis' entire philosophy according to these categories would be to read him selectively, to neglect what he wrote prior to these dialogues. And it is for this reason I want to emphasise the idea of a 'poetic turn' in Hemsterhuis' philosophical trajectory: his discovery of 'the poetic interior of philosophy' occurs in his final publications, well after 1775. Hence, it is difficult to identify any of the writing techniques I have enumerated in this section in the 1769 *Lettre sur la sculpture*, the 1770 *Lettre sur les désirs* or the 1772 *Lettre sur l'Homme*: they are not dialogues; they lack extensive rhetorical digressions; they make no pretence to a fictional world; they do not self-consciously imitate old models in their formal structure; they do not mediate their doctrines through recollections, myths or stories;

and they do not bypass logic to generate ideas through poetic inspiration as frequently. In fact, whenever Hemsterhuis does allude to the quarrel between philosophy and poetry in his publications prior to *Alexis*, it is to expel the poets. For example, the title character of *Sophyle* insists at the beginning of that dialogue, 'No poetry or fables in philosophy, my friend; I beg you. Let's keep it simple' (*EE* 2.46; *OP* 338). *Aristée* contains a similar sentiment: 'What you are saying is very beautiful, Diocles. But do not waste time on poetry' (*EE* 2.71; *OP* 412). And while these exclamations need not be attributed to Hemsterhuis himself (since they are spoken by his characters), they do reflect sentiments in Hemsterhuis' correspondence from the period, in which 'the poet-philosophers' who 'treat philosophy in the narrative genre' and recount a 'beautiful whole ... with striking elegance' are rebuked in favour of Euclidean thinkers who 'proceed straight to the simple' and 'tell us in humble prose that there are at least some truths' (*B* 1.4, 18, 1.3, 19–20; see §6). This is a point of view seemingly opposed to the conclusions reached in *Alexis*.

This is not to say that the earlier writings are exempted from the intricacies of style. For one, their use of the epistolary form is significant (see §20). Nevertheless, something changes in the later dialogues: Hemsterhuis begins to cultivate styles far more self-consciously and elaborately. His work undergoes a poetic turn. In §2 below, I analyse in more detail this idea of a poetic turn and its implications for the idea of a rupture in his output before and after 1775 – both conceptually and in terms of the various biographical and intellectual contexts to Hemsterhuis' evolving body of thought.

§2 Rupture

Scholars tend to split Hemsterhuis' writings into 'two distinct periods ... separated by the year 1775' (Wielema 1993: 110) – the year from which his friendship with Gallitzin dates. This interpretative distinction was enshrined in the three major Hemsterhuis monographs of the early twentieth century: Bulle's *Franziskus Hemsterhuis und der deutsche Irrationalismus des 18. Jahrhunderts* separates a 'first period' from a later one on the basis of 'a new spirit which determines a new form' (1911: 6); Boulan's *François Hemsterhuis: Le Socrate hollandais* distinguishes 'two groups' of writings 'before and after 1774, the date at which he met his Diotima' (1924: 34); and Brummel's *Frans Hemsterhuis: Een philosophenleven* (1925) likewise splits Hemsterhuis' publications into two, ruptured by a period of silence in the mid-1770s. And the evidence for this break primarily consists in the different ways in which Hemsterhuis *presents philosophy* before and after 1775: it is first and foremost a 'rupture *in tone and style*' (van Sluis in *OP* 7; my emphasis). As Fresco baldly states, 'We can distinguish two periods, *mainly on formal grounds*' (1991: 73, my emphasis). There is the time of letters (the *Lettre sur la sculpture*, *Lettre sur les désirs*, *Lettre sur l'Homme et ses rapports*) and there is the time of dialogues (*Sophyle*, *Aristée*, *Simon*, *Alexis*). In fact, this interpretative schema can be traced as far back as Grucker's 1866 monograph, which is the first to articulate such a logic of rupture:

> [The dialogues] are not only superior to the earlier essays [i.e., letters] in terms of execution and conception, which might be naturally explained by the development of one's thinking; but they are different in their tone, their look, their sentiment. There is not only progress, there is transformation ... *Alexis*, *Simon* and *Aristée* are no longer [like the earlier letters] mere treatises of little originality and charm, written in an almost entirely dry and diffuse style; they are interesting, lively dialogues animated by a poetic breath, where imagination and sentiment are united in thinking to give [the texts] brilliance and warmth. (1866: 28–9)

I am using the term 'poetic turn' to designate precisely this qualitative difference in tone, look and sentiment between the letters and the dialogues.

My overarching thesis is that Hemsterhuis has good reasons for this poetic turn, that is, the motivation behind these formal changes stems directly from the evolution of his philosophical project. My aim in this section is twofold: (1) to specify this idea of a 'turn' in more detail by continuing the analyses begun in §1 and by summarising the intellectual contexts that inform it; (2) to contrast my claim that there are philosophical reasons for this poetic turn with those accounts more typically given in the literature – that is, to highlight the polemical intent of my argument in relation to existing Hemsterhuis scholarship.

1. François Hemsterhuis wrote nine works for publication between the early 1760s and the early 1780s – four as letters, four as dialogues and a short obituary of his friend, François Fagel:

> *Lettre sur une pierre antique* (published 1762)
> *Lettre sur la sculpture* (written 1765, published 1769)
> *Lettre sur les désirs* (written 1768, published 1770)
> *Lettre sur l'Homme et ses rapports* (published 1772)
> *Description philosophique du caractère de feu monsieur F. Fagel* (published 1773)

Sophyle ou de la philosophie (published 1778)

Aristée ou de la divinité (published 1779)

Simon ou des facultés de l'âme (first draft 1779–80, redrafted 1782–3, published posthumously[9])

Alexis ou de l'âge d'or (written 1781, published 1787)

To this list should be added the *Lettre de Dioclès à Diotime, sur l'athéisme*, written at the behest of F. H. Jacobi in September 1787, revised in January 1789 and printed as an appendix to the second (1789) edition of Jacobi's *Spinoza-Briefe*. Hemsterhuis also penned unpublished (and often incomplete) treatises in politics, mathematics and optics, fragments of unfinished dialogues, as well as thousands of pages of correspondence containing further elaborations of his ideas (although we now lack some 3,500 letters burned before his death and lost treatises on insect vision and the use of binocular telescopes).

At stake, in this section, is the question of what changed between the publication of Hemsterhuis' obituary of Fagel in 1773 and the publication of *Sophyle* in 1778; and, in order to begin to answer it, I want to make some introductory remarks on Hemsterhuis' work and context during this period.[10]

Of the texts written before 1775, three are most philosophically significant: the *Lettre sur la sculpture* elucidates Hemsterhuis' basic aesthetic principles – principles that, Hemsterhuis later emphasises, are 'the key to all the others' (B 3.45, 114); the closely related *Lettre sur les désirs* – another 'piece of a mosaic detached from the whole' (B 12.V9, 245) – provides the metaphysical and ethical background to this aesthetic picture; and finally the *Lettre sur l'Homme et ses rapports* is a complete exposition of Hemsterhuis' entire philosophy – from epistemology and semiotics to ethics, political philosophy and philosophy of religion. Hemsterhuis might later call it 'a small philosophy course' written for Fagel (B 7.30, 86), but it is in many ways, in Krop's words (2009a: 1172), 'the most perfect presentation of his philosophy'. However, the works I am primarily interested in are those

---

[9] An unauthorised German translation of the first version of *Simon* was published during Hemsterhuis' lifetime (by Blankenberg in 1782) and provoked him to revise the text. The first version was published in French for the first time in 1792; the second version was not published until 2001.

[10] The standard biography is Brummel (1925). In English, Moenkeymeyer (1975) provides summaries of the contents of each of the major works and the *Edinburgh Edition of the Philosophical Works of François Hemsterhuis* includes a relatively exhaustive chronology of Hemsterhuis' life, works and reception history (EE 1.xi–xviii). For a fuller version of some of the below, see Whistler (2022a).

that exemplify the poetic turn – the four dialogues (*Sophyle, Aristée, Simon, Alexis*) written in a short, creative burst between 1778 and 1781.

The content of *Sophyle* was forged as part of Hemsterhuis' and Gallitzin's 'treatises on the immaterial' developed during 1776 (*WW* 138–53; *IN* 31–8). It consists of a series of rapid-fire arguments against materialism: in Hemsterhuis' own words, it is 'a small work of philosophy in which I tried to show to messieurs the materialists from where their errors arise' (*B* 2.4, 18). The 'smallness' of *Sophyle* is a constant theme in Hemsterhuis' remarks: he envisages it acting as a gadfly to the systematic monstrosities of the materialists – as 'the most basic without comparison of all my little books' (*B* 10.4, 19), 'the ABC of all orthodox philosophy' (*B* 10.2, 15).

Aristée was sent in draft to Gallitzin in April 1777 and then to the publishers in December 1778. Unlike *Sophyle*, it covers a lot of ground: Hemsterhuis himself summarises laconically, 'The subjects it treats are order, the principal parts of morality and physics, and our relations with God' (*B* 12.92, 115). The guiding thread is the argument that a transcendent divinity is a necessary postulate from whatever perspective one considers reality. And so at stake once more are the dangers of materialism, that is, the reduction of the universe to a self-sufficient entity without need for any external principle. *Aristée* is further prefaced by a bizarre 'editor's announcement' and dedication which situate the text as a long-lost manuscript of ancient Greek provenance 'found, it has been claimed, on the Isle of Andros, during the time of the Russian [navy's] expedition to the archipelago' (*EE* 2.63; *OP* 390).

Simon – largely drafted during the early 1780s – shares its fictional framing with *Aristée*, marking it out as another ancient Greek manuscript recovered by the Russian navy. It is also an attack on materialism; specifically, it combats materialist accounts of psychology and pedagogy by means of the category of expression in aesthetic representation and moral action. However, what distinguishes *Simon* from the earlier dialogues is its formal features: it is explicitly tasked with 'speaking the language of Plato and Athens as much as possible' (*B* 2.58, 172), and, to achieve this, the dialogue's structure is far more complex than that of the others. It includes a host of fictional and historical characters, five levels of nested recollections and a series of allusions to a whole tradition of early Socratic writing. It is for these reasons that Friedrich Schlegel (1958–2002: 1.244) designated *Simon* 'Socratic poetry'.

Alexis is, according to Hamann (1955–75: 7.255), Hemsterhuis' 'last masterwork so admired by Kant', conceived in October 1779 while writing *Simon*. Hemsterhuis always thought of the two dialogues as 'wife and husband' (*B* 4.5, 23). Much of the preparatory material for the dialogue emerged from Hemsterhuis' astronomical interests in the rotation of the planets (*WW* 232–53; *IN* 127–38), as well as from a close reading of Hesiod's *Work and Days* in November 1780 (B 3.86, 199–200). *Alexis* circulated in manuscript from 1781 until Jacobi published it (and his own German translation) in Riga in 1787. I have already elucidated its principal features in §1 above.

2. In the years prior to the poetic turn of 1775, Hemsterhuis' philosophical output had been conditioned by a series of biographical moments. He had spent most of his early life in the shadow of a famous father: Tiberius Hemsterhuis, the founder of the *schola Hemsterhuisiana* in classical philology.[11] Hemsterhuis' early publications are signed 'Hemsterhuis le fils' and, as late as 1773, Herder still identifies him as '*the young* Hemsterhuis *viri dignissimi dignissimo filio*' (1977–2016: 2.287; my emphasis). But in 1740 Tiberius Hemsterhuis was called to a chair at Leiden University, and the nineteen-year-old Hemsterhuis was thrown into the middle of an 'intellectual moment' – Dutch Newtonianism. He sought out the lessons of Willem 's Gravesande and there met J. N. S. Allamand, the assistant and successor of 's Gravesande, and Johan Lulofs, with whom he collaborated on optics and insectology – two philosophers who have come to symbolise the last of the Dutch Newtonians (Krop 2009b: 1100–1).[12] Alongside experimental philosophy, Hemsterhuis studied medicine (B 1.193, 230) and experimented on freshwater polyps and their parasites in the immediate wake of Abraham Trembley's discoveries (see §17). Letters from the period capture a Hemsterhuis peering into microscopes, Hooke's *Micrographia* in hand, observing in painstaking detail the parasitic *kerona pediculus* (Van der Hoeven 1865). However, much of Hemsterhuis' time at Leiden University was spent in more practical training as a military engineer. A 'lost period' of roughly a decade follows Hemsterhuis' departure from Leiden in the late 1740s, but what is clear is that he remained active in theoretical and practical optics (Zuidervaart 2019: 139–40), and his optical work came to fruition

---

[11] Crudely put, Tiberius' *schola Hemsterhuisiana* was responsible for a shift in Dutch philology away from Latinate sources towards an appreciation of Greek texts independently of their Roman or biblical legacy (see van Sluis 1995: 80–3).

[12] In addition to Allamand and Lulofs, his most important friend from this period was Petrus Camper, 'the greatest anatomist in Europe' (B 1.141, 175; see also B 5.14, 62; van Sluis 2015). Willem Bentick was another significant ally, who gave the young Hemsterhuis access to the company of art connoisseurs (e.g., the Comte de Caylus), to the philosophical salon at Bentick's Sorgvielt estate which included Trembley (see B 12.3, 11; Marx 1976: 410) and to influential political circles (the Benticks were close to Willem III and heavily pro-English).

in 1770 when he designed the first ever achromatic binocular telescope (Zuidervaart 2019: 180).

In December 1755, Hemsterhuis entered the Dutch civil service in The Hague and rose to become First Secretary of the State's Council. From then on, the *Beamtenaristokratie* (to use Bulle's term [1911: 5]) of The Hague furnished his natural circle of acquaintances, and he was allied with a number of 'enlightened Orangists' who, as Israel explains, were 'at odds' with both 'the principles of the radical Patriots' of the 1780s and 'the religious Counter-Enlightenment' (2007: 50–1; see Wielema 1993). And it was in this society of like-minded 'enlightened Orangists' that Hemsterhuis formed his first philosophical circle – the circle within which his early works were devised and discussed (see B 2.46, 109). As always, he philosophised in company (see §7) and, during the 1760s, this company comprised other prosperous French-speaking residents of The Hague, like Fagel, the younger civil servant to whom the *Letter sur l'Homme* is addressed, and Theodor de Smeth, an Amsterdam banker, who – as someone who had been tempted by materialist, Spinozist ideas – needed to be brought back into the fold. Indeed, the overriding project of Hemsterhuis' first Hague circle seems to have been to reduce materialist and Spinozist influences in Dutch society (Israel 2007: 29).[13]

Hemsterhuis' first Hague circle dissolved with Fagel's death in 1773. The society necessary for him to philosophise dried up, only to be rekindled by a new friendship and a new circle in spring 1775 – the date of Hemsterhuis' encounter with Amalie Gallitzin, whom he will come to call his 'Diotima'.[14]

---

[13] Hemsterhuis had personally come to know many of these materialists, particularly La Mettrie and Diderot (who commented extensively on Hemsterhuis' *Lettre sur l'Homme* in 1773–4), but, instead, chose his intellectual allies from more conservative Enlightenment thinkers like d'Alembert (B 3.18, 58; 4.79, 208), Voltaire (B 10.105, 172) and Rousseau (whose *Émile* was, for the early Hemsterhuis, 'one of the best books to have appeared in quite a while' [B 12.23, 34]). Hemsterhuis belonged most clearly to this moderate Enlightenment tradition in his tendency to recognise God, but to refuse to philosophically countenance superrational revelation. As Fresco (2007: 195) bluntly puts it, 'He was no Christian and no friend of the (Calvinist) clergy'. Although there may be hints in the *Lettre sur le fatalisme* of Armenian critiques of Calvinism (Bordoli 2004: 123; Bordoli 2005: 238–40), he is always clear that he confines religion to the limits of reason and that 'I have read little of the [Church] Fathers and still less of the Reformers' (B 10.71, 125). This is one reason why it is far too simplistic to assert with Söhngen (1995: 263) that Hemsterhuis 'belonged to the movement of the Counter-Enlightenment' or, even with Hartmann (1923: 163) that he was 'a child of the Enlightenment but already its opponent on all decisive points'.

[14] For details of Gallitzin's life and work, see, for example, Brachin (1952), Sudhof (1973), Trunz (1971: 199–204).

§2 RUPTURE

From then on, in Goethe's hyperbolic words (1849: 256), Hemsterhuis 'devoted his life to the Princess as well as to his writings', and their intellectual collaborations are testament to a renewal of philosophical energy.[15] Biographically, this marks the moment of Hemsterhuis' poetic turn and the trigger for his dialogues.

Gallitzin had been raised on materialist ideas in Berlin, where she had been close to La Mettrie and d'Holbach, and these early influences account, in part, for her marriage to Dmitri Gallitzin in 1768 (Dmitri himself published a posthumous edition of Helvétius' work). However, by spring 1775 she had become estranged from materialism in general and her husband in particular, and so set out to put into practice a Rousseauian idyll with her two children at her country estate, Niethuis, 'free from the corruption and contamination of urban life' (Petry 2003a: 419). Here is how Gallitzin herself described her situation at the time:

> I was 23 years old, did not know how to do addition and all my reading extended to some novels and to Epictetus' aphorisms, when I got it into my head to be a mother to my children who were then 2 and 3. The idea that I would make myself a genuine maternal educator of boys and girls required ... all the sciences so as to be in a condition to judge which of them and in what way they were to be applied to the development of children.... During this time, Plato fell into my hands and gave me a violent passion for Socrates who did me the first and the greatest good. At the end of two years, I by chance became acquainted with Hemsterhuis, whose works I had read and tasted; he attached himself to me and I owe much to this relationship. (Quoted in Brachin 1952: 17–18)

From this time until her departure to Münster, Hemsterhuis would visit Niethuis twice a week accompanied, in Gallitzin's words, by 'our common friends, Plato, Homer, Socrates' (quoted in Gründer 1955: 86). Their ensuing collaborations were built on a mutual passion for the Socratic, on a shared commitment to the overthrow of radical materialist ideas, and on a common interest in applying psychology to education, particularly the education of Gallitzin's children.

In 1779, Gallitzin moved to Münster; Hemsterhuis visited three times over the succeeding years and *Alexis* was written while he stayed there.

---

[15] The other significant correspondent in Hemsterhuis' later years was Anna Perrenot (later, Meerman), the 'Daphne' to his 'Diocles'. She was, Hemsterhuis remarks, 'my disciple' (B 11.167, 154).

The Catholicism of the Münster Circle radicalised Gallitzin's immaterialist tendencies and she began to diverge from Hemsterhuis in her positive appreciation of faith, returning to the Catholic communion in August 1786. As a result, she would come to criticise 'Hemsterhuis' pompous Graecism', continuing that Hamann, whom she met at this later period, 'taught me more about internal dignity than all the life and works of Hemsterhuis' (quoted in Brachin 1952: 53–4).

This partial estrangement from Gallitzin is one explanation for the fact that, from the mid-1780s to his death in July 1790, Hemsterhuis' output becomes more fragmentary and abortive – often comprising nothing more than appendices or digressions to his letters to Gallitzin. As described in the Preface above, he set about cementing his German readership at this time and undertook a 1785 tour of Germany, with visits to the palace of the Duke of Gotha, with whom he renewed a conversation on binocular telescopes, the Dresden art galleries (B 12.147, 213–19; see Sonderen 2000: 203–14) and Weimar. For all intents and purposes, it is at this moment that Hemsterhuis' intellectual biography comes to an end and his reception history commences.

3. Against the backdrop of these biographical metamorphoses between 1773 and 1778, it becomes possible to pinpoint more precisely some of the changes that his philosophical doctrines likewise underwent during this period.

In fact, in one instance, Hemsterhuis openly admits that his ideas underwent radical change around 1775 – in the transformation of his moral epistemology. In the 1772 *Lettre sur l'Homme*, the faculty of the moral organ had taken centre stage as a means of accounting for the perception of value, i.e., its irreducibility to the perception of physical properties and the passivity of the subject in the process of value formation. Morality is understood on the model of sensation alone, independent of reasoning, volition and judgement in general. Being a virtuous human subject requires a sensitive, well-exercised moral organ that operates in analogy to the sense organs (see §13). There are a number of triggers (including Diderot's commentary on the *Lettre sur l'Homme*) that cause Hemsterhuis to revise this model but, in his correspondence with Gallitzin, it is her influence in particular that he stresses: 'I long considered [the moral organ to be] a simple organ, until one day at Niethuis you taught me that I must at least divide it into active and passive [components]' (B 7.92, 247). That is, he comes to see that some kind of intellectual activity is a necessary component of value formation and that, therefore, the process of forming moral judgements is a compos-

§2 RUPTURE

ite one. Hence – with the exception of *Simon* – the language of the moral organ disappears from the later dialogues; for example, *Aristée* employs the term 'moral principle' instead. Even when Hemsterhuis does revert to the term 'moral organ' in *Simon*, it is understood very differently: in analogy to the organ of the intellect (i.e., to active reasoning) rather than to the sense organs (see §13). Under Gallitzin's influence, Hemsterhuis now speaks of the moral organ as possessing 'two distinct parts' – one in which 'the soul is completely passive' and the other by which 'it judges, it modifies, it moderates, it incites, or it calms . . . sensations' (*EE* 2.116; *OP* 556). This is a very different model of moral epistemology from that given in 1772.

It seems natural to describe changes to the formal style of Hemsterhuis' texts according to a very similar model – a shift from a purely analytic conception of philosophical writing in the early 1770s to something much more complex after 1775. I have already given (in §1) some evidence for precisely this kind of interpretation. The stylistic properties of *Alexis* (its dialogic form, its recourse to myth and allegory, its rhetorical exuberance, its framing within a fictional but realistic Athenian setting, its argument by poetic figures) testify to a poeticisation of philosophical communication which, at first blush, is absent from the earlier letters.

Nevertheless, it is important to clarify ways in which this idea of a 'turn' is rather limited when it comes to interpreting Hemsterhuis' philosophical trajectory. First, Hemsterhuis' philosophy is not binary and, in particular, to reduce the four dialogues to a monolithic grouping opposed *en bloc* to the earlier letters is to simplify them; for example, the ostentatious poetic techniques of *Alexis* are muted in *Sophyle*. In consequence, reference to a 'poetic turn' demands attention to stylistic *differences between* the four dialogues as well as to their continuities.[16] Secondly, the idea of a 'turn' is not universally applicable to Hemsterhuis' philosophy. That is, the two cases of his moral epistemology and his presentation of philosophy serve as exceptions rather than the rule; otherwise, there are few abrupt reversals during the 1770s and, for the most part, what Hemsterhuis writes in the *Lettre sur la sculpture* holds good into the 1780s. It is primarily *how* he writes that is subject to transformation. Finally, the idea of a 'poetic turn' should not be so exaggerated as to imply the reversal of all Hemsterhuis' views on the communication and presentation of philosophy. One of the more jarring aspects of his switch to more dialogic, mythic and figurative ways of writing is that it is not accompanied by any explicit renunciation of his earlier statements on what good

---

[16] The same is of course true of the pre-1775 publications: they each have their own stylistic quirks.

philosophy looks like. Indeed, as I explore at length in Chapter Two, one of the difficulties in making sense of this 'turn' is that Hemsterhuis' own reflections on philosophical method do not change substantially. To take one example: throughout his life, he repeatedly professes a preference for simple, popular writing, and does sometimes write in an accessible way (e.g., in *Sophyle*); however, just as often Hemsterhuis embraces convoluted literary structures and esoteric allusions. Accounts of Hemsterhuis' poetic turn need to be sensitive to these kinds of discrepancy between theory and practice.

4. As noted at the beginning of this section, the formal differences between Hemsterhuis' early and late writings have frequently been mentioned in the literature; it is difficult, indeed, to talk about his philosophy at all without, at the very least, alluding to the switch to dialogue form. As a result, a number of reasons have traditionally been given to explain this change – out of which arise broadly three main interpretative strategies in Hemsterhuis scholarship: (1) to treat these later poetic features as merely ornamental, incidental to an unchanging doctrinal core; (2) to look for motivations for this shift that are external to the philosophy itself, for example in biography (this strategy is often complicit with the first); (3) to identify reasons intrinsic to his thinking that account for Hemsterhuis' poetic turn, that is, to trace the ways in which Hemsterhuis' stated philosophical positions necessitate (or just recommend) more elaborate modes of writing.

The first interpretative strategy has long been pervasive in the history of philosophy generally: it is used whenever an interpretation attempts to liberate some 'pure unit of philosophy' (Danto 1984: 7) from the contingencies of the text, whenever thinking is opposed to reading and writing, or whenever the literariness of a philosophical project is downplayed or ignored. Lang calls it the 'neutralist model': 'The form or structure of philosophical discourse is denied any intrinsic connection to its substance as philosophy; the relation is viewed as at most ornamental, at its least as accidental and irrelevant' (1990: 12). When it comes to Hemsterhuis, this interpretative approach is most noticeable in the lack of serious attention that has been paid to the literary elements of the dialogues: considering how bizarre Hemsterhuis' ironic attempts at forgery are in the prefaces to *Aristée* and *Simon* or how complicated his imitation of Plato becomes in *Simon*, disproportionately little ink has been spilt on them. In this vein, Fresco comments that it is 'generally thought' that Hemsterhuis' construction of a fictional world is 'just ornamental' (1995b: 93). Fresco continues that the formal features of the later dialogues are inessential, mere window-dressing behind which stands a stable analytic core. He writes of Hemsterhuis' 1775 preference for analytic over speculative methods (see §6): he 'rejects the novels of the great forgers of metaphysical systems, [and so] when he later borrows Plato's poetry, the contradiction is only apparent, for this does not concern the depths of philosophy, but just the necessity for a captivating presentation of philosophy' (in Hemsterhuis 2007: 50). This distinction between the superficial and the deep is exemplary of an entire tradition of the 'neutralist model'.

Another interpretative approach that minimises the philosophical significance of Hemsterhuis' late style is that which consigns it to the domain of the biographical. This is by far the most popular strategy in the scholarship and turns on the thesis that Hemsterhuis' poetic turn is entirely determined by his friendship with Gallitzin. Like the previous strategy, this position typically situates philosophical form outside the domain of philosophical reasons. However, it need not do so: there are also proponents of this interpretation who suggest the encounter with Gallitzin led directly to a renewal of Hemsterhuis' entire intellectual project – a renewal whose effects can be clearly seen in stylistic transformations. Appeals to Gallitzin's role in Hemsterhuis' poetic turn thus exist across a spectrum, from those positions which see the dialogues as merely formalising their conversations to those which see them as manifesting a fundamental change in philosophical vision.

The list of those who treat Gallitzin as the major – often exclusive – trigger for Hemsterhuis' poetic turn is long.[17] On one side stand those, like Vieillard-Baron, who consider such a turn a matter of altered social relations and nothing of particular doctrinal interest. They argue that the dialogue form is merely an 'aide-memoire of real conversation', rather than any highly wrought 'artifice' – a record of actual conversations held with Gallitzin transcribed as faithfully as possible onto the page. On this view, Hemsterhuis switches to dialogue for the sake of 'ease' of transcription (Vieillard-Baron 1985: 119) – and his writing of philosophy can easily be explained along the lines of Lessing's dictum, 'There's nothing better than *thinking aloud* with a friend' (2005: 185). On the other side stand those who emphasise the 'genuine two-way' process of collaboration between Hemsterhuis and Gallitzin (Petry 2003a: 421) that resulted in a new philosophical beginning. For instance, one obvious candidate for Gallitzin's influence on the poetic turn is a renewed interest in Platonic modes of writing (see Moenkemeyer 1975:

---

[17] It most obviously includes Boulan (1924: 34), Brachin (1952: 19), Moenkemeyer (1975: 97–8), Petry (2003a: 421), Sudhof (1973: 133–4), van Sluis (in OP 7), Vieillard-Baron (1985: 119) and Wielema (1993: 110).

98). Nevertheless, even in this case, commentators have insisted on restricting Gallitzin's philosophical contribution to Hemsterhuis' thought: they happily admit to Gallitzin's impact on Hemsterhuis' strategies for writing philosophy in order to save that philosophy's contents from her influence. In other words, they still imply that what matters philosophically belongs to Hemsterhuis alone.[18] In this vein, Moenkemeyer conjectures that 'most likely, the Princess had more influence on the form than the actual content of *Sophyle* and the writings which were to follow' (1975: 97) and Fresco is adamant that, doctrinally, the philosophy 'is and remained Hemsterhuis' philosophy', but what he 'essentially' learnt from Gallitzin 'is the new literary form, the dialogue' (2007: 202). At any rate, most scholars agree that 'without his Diotima, [Hemsterhuis] would have remained the writer of philosophical letters without literary worth' (Fresco 2007: 203).

The evidence for Gallitzin's influence on Hemsterhuis' dialogues is everywhere in the correspondence and cannot be gainsaid. Hemsterhuis talks of his late writings as the products of a genuine *Symphilosophie*: they are 'our children' (B 1.214, 250; 1.217, 254; 10.26, 56) of 'our marriage in friendship' (B 1.40, 76; 1.182, 221), the fruits of 'our philosophy' and 'our theory' (B 3.76, 179; 3.9, 36). *Aristée* 'carries the most marked traits of the soul of my Diotima' (B 1.201, 239), she is mother to 'our *Simon*' which 'really belongs to you' (B 8.3, 22) and *Alexis* 'is completely yours' (B 4.2, 16). After 1775, Hemsterhuis understands himself (at least in his correspondence with Gallitzin herself) as committing to paper 'our common philosophy as it is contained in our four dialogues' (B 4.35, 86) and, as such, he acknowledges her overarching influence on his thinking: 'I feel that your way of thinking and feeling has changed the path of my philosophy' (B 1.153, 188). Moreover, when it comes to the presentation of philosophy, Hemsterhuis is no less forthright: he speaks, in a passage already quoted in the Preface, of how his philosophy shed 'the weighty husks of the school which concealed it, locked it up and constrained it' and, instead, cultivated 'festoons and flowers' within 'those dialogues which were all born and fashioned under your gaze' (B 7.30, 86–7). On Hemsterhuis' account, Gallitzin shares responsibility for the dialogues: they would not have come into being 'if we

---

[18] The above change to his doctrine of moral epistemology through conversation with Gallitzin remains *exceptional* on this interpretation – Fresco calls it one of Gallitzin's 'rare contributions' to Hemsterhuis' thinking (in Hemsterhuis 2007: 126). Gallitzin herself always actively resisted any image of herself in the role of *remplissage* – that is, as 'filler' or 'padding' – 'who responds in commonplaces' to Hemsterhuis' 'sublime' thoughts (Gallitzin 2015–17: 3.192–3).

had not discussed and re-discussed a hundred time the subjects these works contain and if we had not read and reread them a hundred times piece by piece' (B 2.46, 109).

5. Hemsterhuis is very clear: the encounter with Gallitzin in 1775 was a decisive event for his philosophical development. And it is no great leap to suppose that renewed intellectual conversation, a couple of years after the loss of Fagel, likely caused Hemsterhuis to understand philosophising as a genuinely dialogic activity and so contributed in some way to his poetic turn. Nevertheless, there are two reasons why appeal to Gallitzin's friendship is still insufficient to fully explain this poetic turn, and so more is required.

First, the above explanation of the poetic turn fails to supply any kind of coherent narrative for the evolution of Hemsterhuis' philosophy itself; rather, such changes are attributed to an unanticipated rupture, resembling somewhat the advent of the moon in *Alexis*, that is, an event that disturbs equilibrium *from without*. To treat the poetic turn in this manner alone is to write off the possibility that Hemsterhuis' own intellectual development might have played some role in it. For example, commentators have typically neglected Hemsterhuis' own admissions that the *Lettre sur l'Homme* (see §15) and even *Sophyle failed* (see §8), that is, he frequently presents himself as having reached a philosophical dead-end during the mid-1770s, and they have also neglected the motivations he explicitly provides for a substantial transformation from philosophising in letters to philosophising in dialogue (e.g., B 10.93, 155). All this surely matters for an account of his poetic turn.

Secondly, the above use of Gallitzin to completely explain the poetic turn is, bluntly put, unhelpful, for it actually explains very little. It might say something about Hemsterhuis' switch from epistolary form to dialogue form after 1775, but there is much more to the turn than solely an embrace of the dialogue genre. It also includes an excess of imagery, elaborate myths, philological jokes, fake prefaces and the detailed construction of a fictional but realistic Athenian world, replete with finely wrought characters, geographies and histories. There is nothing in the mere fact of Hemsterhuis' friendship with Gallitzin that makes sense of all these other features. Moreover, appeal to Gallitzin's role in Hemsterhuis' return to Plato does not help much either, not least because – as I argue in Parts Three and Four below – there is far more to his poetic turn than just emulation of Plato. In sum, even if one accepts that Gallitzin's influence provides one good biographical reason for the poetic turn, there are, I will argue, better philosophical ones. More is needed to explain why his texts had now to be forged as long-lost ancient manuscripts, hidden behind obscure philological games and rendered into anachronistic myths.

And it is to such a task that the rest of this book is devoted. I certainly do not want to deny that working with Gallitzin was a decisive stimulus for Hemsterhuis' late philosophy and there is no reason to doubt his claims that the dialogues arose out of collaborative thinking; nevertheless, more is needed to make sense of his late writing techniques. To achieve this, each of the following three parts of this book will attempt to furnish additional, intrinsic reasons for Hemsterhuis' poetic turn.

Part Two
Untimely Demands

Hemsterhuis' reception has always advanced in waves: the sentimental Hemsterhuis of Herder and Jacobi, the prophetic Hemsterhuis of the Jena romantics, the Christian-Platonist Hemsterhuis of Meyboom, the pantheist Hemsterhuis of Dilthey, the irrationalist Hemsterhuis of Bulle, Hartmann's Hemsterhuis as 'a forerunner of the philosophy of value' (1923: 170), the Dutch-Cartesian Hemsterhuis of Hammacher, the Socratic Hemsterhuis of Fresco, Petry's and Melica's Hemsterhuis the scientist and, most recently, Israel's conservative Hemsterhuis.[1] There have indeed been many images of Hemsterhuis – and my concern in the second part of this book is with one reason for such a variety of images. I certainly do not want to suggest that there exists some fundamental, original 'image' of Hemsterhuis, nor even that one grounding principle reconciles them all. Rather, I am interested in how these partially irreconcilable interpretations spring from irreconcilable demands within Hemsterhuis' philosophy itself.

Two pairs of these competing tendencies in Hemsterhuis' texts structure the first two chapters. Chapter One takes as its subject matter the seemingly contrary tendencies, on the one hand, to return to a Socratic ideal that stands in judgement on the corrupt, ineffectual philosophising of the eighteenth century and, on the other hand, to celebrate the advances of the modern geometrical method and extend its application to all domains of human knowledge. Chapter Two is devoted to a similar (if ultimately distinct) double demand focused on the writing of philosophy – that is, the demand, on the one hand, to reject the conjectural and poetic in philosophical presentation in the name of 'humble' analysis and, on the other hand, to make use of aesthetically charged styles like myth, dialogue, metaphor and irony to effectively communicate the truth.

---

[1] On this series of attempts to determine Hemsterhuis' originality, see Morpurgo-Tagliabue (1987: 12).

By beginning with this pair of double demands, I am consciously attempting to escape (to some small extent) the very problem of the 'many images' in Hemsterhuis' reception history. That is, when it comes to the scholarship, the place where one begins does matter: the point at which one starts the exposition of Hemsterhuis' philosophy often determines in advance what that philosophy looks like. For example, Pelckmans (1987) and Petry (1985) have attacked those who begin their reconstructions with Hemsterhuis' romantic reception, for, they argue, it imposes a teleological framework that is ultimately 'a distortion of his true significance' (Petry 1985: 221). Petry will go on to consciously downplay Hemsterhuis' poetic turn and instead draw attention to his optical, astronomical and mathematical research, so as to escape a hermeneutics of anticipation. In short, there are multiple starting points – and to choose one is already to make a decision about what motivates Hemsterhuisian philosophy. My intention, therefore, is to present a series of competing points of origin, so as to get at the disparate tendencies orienting Hemsterhuis' project itself.

Moreover, the means by which Hemsterhuis himself goes about legitimating this structure of competing demands – that is, *both* the Socratic *and* the Newtonian, *both* sober analysis *and* mythic dialogue – is through continuous appeal to a Platonic prototype. Plato is so central to Hemsterhuis' philosophical self-understanding, because, he claims, Plato was able – in exemplary fashion – to affirm precisely these contrary demands in a productive manner. Hemsterhuis' Platonism rests on a vision of a thinker who lived inconsistencies constructively. Platonic philosophy succeeded because Plato remained faithful to the Socratic ideal while simultaneously incorporating geometrical reasoning, because he was committed to analytic rigour at the same time as deploying poetic modes of presentation. To write philosophy like Plato is therefore *to philosophise productively under inconsistency*.

My argument in Part Two is therefore intended as one intervention into long-running debates over the precise character of Hemsterhuis' Platonism. That is, it is relatively clear conceptually why Hemsterhuis constantly praises 'the divine Socrates' (B 3.61, 148), since the Socratic project determines (I will show) Hemsterhuis' conceptions of psychology, morality, pedagogy, irony, as well as sociability.[2] On the other hand, it has proven much

---

[2] Nevertheless, the philosophical significance of Hemsterhuis' Socratism still remains underexplored. As van Bunge helpfully observes: '[Even] Fresco refused to raise the issue *why* Socrates appealed so much to Hemsterhuis and which purposes his Philhellinism ... actually served' (2018: 182).

more difficult to pinpoint precisely what Hemsterhuis takes of substance from Plato, and so provide the exact reason for his constant praise of 'my holy Plato' (B 2.52, 143), 'Saint Plato, my Father and Teacher' (B 2.45, 102). The traditional position is best exemplified by Vieillard-Baron, for whom Hemsterhuis' philosophy 'represents a coherent rationalist Platonism' (1995: 151) and should therefore be seen in terms of its fidelity to the detail of the Platonic texts in opposition to any 'neoplatonic deformations of Plato' (1995: 154). Having conjectured, for example, that the concept of the moral organ is derived from passages in the *Alcibiades* and the *Republic* (1988: 124–7), Vieillard-Baron concludes that 'Hemsterhuis' work is a veritable revival of Platonism. It is a matter of a Plato who has been read and reflected on in Greek' (1988: 130). However, this traditional view has been challenged. In particular, Fresco has stressed Hemsterhuis' indifference to vast swathes of Platonic doctrine: the theory of the Forms is the most obvious example (1995b: 137; 1991: 80). While Hemsterhuis' 'letters abound with laudatory remarks on Plato', it is ultimately 'Socrates, not Plato, who is nearly always called the great master' (Fresco 1995b: 137), and ultimately, for Fresco, Plato has no positive contribution to make to Hemsterhuis' work other than as a conduit for Socratic philosophising. What matters is 'his being the mouthpiece of Socrates, rather than being a philosopher in his own right' (1995b: 144). Petry concludes in a similar vein, 'It is difficult to take too seriously the claim that [Hemsterhuis] was a Platonist in any very meaningful sense of the word' (2003a: 422).

In what follows, I contend that, while Fresco may well be right that Hemsterhuis is primarily interested in Plato as a disciple of Socrates, this is not – *pace* Fresco – to reduce the Hemsterhuisian Plato merely to a 'mouthpiece of Socrates'. Rather, Plato matters precisely because his philosophy, like Hemsterhuis', attempts to remain faithful to the Socratic event in the absence of Socrates. Plato, like Hemsterhuis, must reinvent philosophy anew after Socrates, creatively transforming Socratism for the demands of the present. It is because Plato was a heterodox disciple that he becomes Hemsterhuis' hero, that is, because of his ability to present philosophy as both Socratic and more than Socratic – to inhabit the competing demands of fidelity to the past and innovation in the present. This is the philosophical ideal that Hemsterhuis appropriates from the Platonic corpus.

Chapter One

Socrates and Newton

In order to have a transcendental viewpoint on antiquity, perhaps one must be pre-eminently modern. Winckelmann sensed the Greeks like a Greek. Hemsterhuis, on the contrary, . . . cast his soulful gaze simultaneously onto the old and new worlds.

Friedrich Schlegel (1958–2002: 2.211)

§3 'Born Greek'

Hemsterhuis' and Gallitzin's friendship was consecrated in 1775 in shared commitment to the Socratic ideal. Both could claim with equal legitimacy and 'in semi-religious ecstasy' (Brachin 1952: 30) that Socrates was 'my first love on this earth' (Gallitzin, quoted in Brachin 1952: 242). And their friendship blossomed during the late 1770s through a close, collaborative reading of Plato's *Symposium*, 'the most beautiful piece that ever came out of man's head' (B 2.52, 143). One of the many offspring of this collaboration was, moreover, a French translation of the *Symposium* completed by Hemsterhuis.[1] This translation work set in motion the following train of thought:

> I have been working to finish an imperfect translation of the *Symposium*. . . . I have always considered this piece not only as the most perfect description of the beauty of Greek souls, but as the most beautiful production of the human spirit. When reading it, I have always felt an analogy, such a perfect accord, such prodigious intimacy with my soul that I have become quite vain. And if I believed in metempsychosis, I would believe

---

[1] The genesis of this translation is tracked in the correspondence – see, for example, B 1.60, 102; 1.145, 181; 12.82, 106.

that, when Plato is the interpreter of his hero and master, a bit of his soul composes the essence of mine. I have said somewhere on arts and desires that a long contemplation of the most beautiful thing gives rise to disgust. ... I know only two things in the entire universe that always contradict me. It is you and Plato the interpreter. (B 1.144, 180)

For many readers of Hemsterhuis – especially German readers from the late eighteenth century – the defining feature of his philosophy was its philhellenism: in Hemsterhuis' own words, 'I feel the Greeks marvellously' (B 4.11, 38). Not only does he surpass most of his contemporaries in his knowledge of the primary Greek texts,[2] but he is always happy to show off this erudition. In his later writings, this antiquarian erudition informs his faithful recreation of an Athenian world: Socrates appears as protagonist and mouthpiece, historical figures make cameos, editorial interventions are employed to heighten the illusion of 'authentic' Greek antiquity. And outside of the publications, Hemsterhuis styles himself to Gallitzin as 'your Athenian' (B 4.4, 20).

This philhellenism rests most obviously on a detailed knowledge of the Platonic corpus. Hemsterhuis was, it appears, familiar with all of Plato's writings (Fresco 1995b: 131–2) and, in this respect, plays a significant role in the Plato renaissance then underway in northern Europe (see, e.g., Vieillard-Baron 1985: 134). That is, his knowledge of Plato's writings needs to be understood in the context of a still-prevalent neglect of them: as late as 1776, Daniel Wyttenbach observed, 'Those who read Plato are rare; those who understand him are most rare' (quoted in Fresco 1995b: 116–17; see also Rockhill 2010: 156). Evidently, Hemsterhuis' familial ties to the *schola Hemsterhuisiana* gave him a head-start; however, his philhellenism is founded on more than a renewed philological interest in the textual detail of the Platonic dialogues. He is also representative of an increasing shift

---

[2] As Fresco demonstrates, when Hemsterhuis quotes Sappho (for example), he goes back to the Greek, unlike others of the period who rely on Latin editions (1995b: 103). Furthermore, Hemsterhuis' treatment of Cicero (to which I return) is a good example of this tendency to depreciate the value of Latin sources: 'Probably Hemsterhuis knew Latin literature just as well as Greek literature; almost certainly he knew the works of Cicero nearly as well as Plato's, but there is a marked shift in his appreciation. Even when he is admiring the literary achievements of Cicero, he thinks his talents largely inferior to Plato's' (Fresco 1995b: 95). Winckelmann's relation to Hemsterhuis is often brought up in this context, and the most apt conclusions are surely Van Bunge's (2018), who sees Winckelmann's primary role *vis-à-vis* Hemsterhuis as one of preparing the ground for the latter's German reception.

away from 'the metaphysical dialogues of the last Plato, the *Sophist*, the *Parmenides*, the *Timaeus*', which had been popular in the neoplatonic traditions of sixteenth- and seventeenth-century Europe (Vieillard-Baron 1995: 153).³ Instead, he participates in a 'revival of the "aesthetic" side of Platonic philosophy' (Franz 2012: 46): 'The Plato who was now read was no longer an academic and theological monster, but the poet of graceful dialogues' (2012: 77).⁴

1. It is in this context that reading Plato felt like a homecoming for Hemsterhuis. It is 'Plato who sleeps by my side' (B 5.4, 25), he confesses. And this strong 'rapport' with Plato, his 'prodigious intimacy with my soul' described in the above quotation, is based on three grounds. That is, Hemsterhuis gives three reasons for his 'perfect accord' with the Plato of the *Symposium*: (1) Plato's ability to accurately describe the beauty of Greek souls; (2) the formal qualities of his dialogues; (3) the Socratic ideal presented therein (i.e., it is only when Plato 'is the interpreter of his hero and master' that Hemsterhuis most fully identifies with him).⁵

The Socratic ideal motivates all Hemsterhuis' thinking: he can exclaim with Erasmus, 'O sancta Socrates, ora pro nobis!' (B 7.43, 119) and take as his guiding maxim the similarly Erasmian principle: 'Think always of what Socrates would say to you' (B 5.83, 267; see also *IN* 168). Hence,

---

³ On the absence of neoplatonic influences on Hemsterhuis' philosophy, see Fresco (1991: 68–9), Vieillard-Baron (1985: 138) and Hammacher (1995b: 423). Three dissenting voices in this regard are Ayrault (1961: 1.484), Mähl (1994: 267) and Moenkemeyer (1975: 51, 116).
⁴ Indeed, Hemsterhuis explicitly criticises his predecessors for writing 'voluminous' and 'quite bad' commentaries on the *Timaeus*, instead of producing 'intellectual commentary' on the *Phaedrus*, 'which would give the reader the means to understand the rhetorical [and] the poetic' in Plato's texts (B 7.100, 266).
⁵ Although, in this section, I emphasise the Plato–Socrates relation, a third Greek thinker, Lucian, should not be forgotten. Following his father (Hammacher 1995c: 626; Fresco 1991: 788), it is Lucian whom Hemsterhuis admits to 'having most read' (B 8.3, 22) and whom (rather than Cicero) he calls Plato's true heir – 'of all the authors I know, Lucian is the only one who has perfectly felt Plato as a writer' (B 8.3, 22). Hemsterhuis writes elsewhere, 'He has been my favourite author for 40 years. He is infinitely enlightened. He is a greater dialogist than Plato. He is a finer satirist than Horace and Boileau and Pope, etc. His is a mind which is implicated in everything. He possesses nearly all styles to the greatest perfection, and in this he approaches Plato the most' (B 9.36, 82; see also B 11.35, 45). What is most important here is the reference to Lucian and Plato mixing together or assembling different styles and genres (in the original sense of 'satire'); I go on to argue in Chapter Two that *the ideal of mixed style* is one of Hemsterhuis' greatest debts to this Platonic tradition.

Hemsterhuis will always remain explicitly faithful to 'the method of my good old Socrates, my teacher and friend . . . a method that I will defend to my last drop of blood against the whole of the earth and any philosopher past, present or future' (B 1.216, 252). And he will even criticise Plato whenever the latter deviates in the slightest from such a methodological standard (e.g., B 7.43, 120).[6] Nevertheless, Plato remains, for the most part, Hemsterhuis' most trusted source for Socratic thinking; indeed, this is one reason he feels such sympathy for Plato: he is a philosopher attempting to hold onto the Socratic after Socrates' death. Likewise, Hemsterhuis is attempting to present the Socratic belatedly; he identifies with Plato as someone who also suffers the loss of the Socratic, a fellow writer who wishes to communicate a Socratic past in a benighted present. Both battle the Sophists of the day by holding onto the spirit and method of the same absent master.

Hemsterhuis is therefore one of the most vocal representatives of the 'Socratic century' (Böhm 1966: 185), one of the numerous eighteenth-century thinkers who appropriated the name 'Socrates' for their various projects, such that 'Socrates' became a kind of Proteus subject to endless transformations and reinventions during the period (Böhm 1966: 222). Socrates appears in different guises in Hemsterhuis' psychology (see §13), his philosophy of education (see §14) and his practice of irony (see §22); first and foremost, however, he is a 'moral hero' (Vieillard-Baron 1988: 120). In Socrates, Hemsterhuis saw 'nothing but the greatest faculties and the most perfect harmony' (B 7.69, 193); he is 'the greatest and most perfect of men', as opposed to Plato, who was (merely) 'the most powerful genius who has ever appeared on earth' (B 2.65, 195). That is, Socrates seems to embody an ideal for living that is prior to any philosophical doctrine and Plato's 'genius' was to have converted Socrates' life into Socratic philosophy, to have made the 'moral hero' into material for ethical theory. Nevertheless, this still might be, Hemsterhuis elsewhere insists, to grant Plato a little too much credit, for sometimes the Socrates–Plato relationship is depicted in a slightly different fashion. For example:

---

[6] This is, in fact, clearest when Hemsterhuis turns to Aristotle (instead of Plato) to make sense of political philosophy. Aristotle is 'the only great master in politics to have existed and, in this branch, more Socratic than Plato' (B 6.6, 28): when it comes to politics, it is Aristotle's *Politics*, rather than Plato's *Republic* or *Laws*, that provides the classical model to be imitated – and this is precisely because, Hemsterhuis here makes clear, of its *Socratism*. In his political philosophy, Plato strays too far from the Socratic ideal, whereas Aristotle renews it in the face of this estrangement.

Socrates created the only good and true philosophy founded on what each person feels himself to be. It was completely bare and simple, and each individual had it at his side at any moment he wanted. The prodigious Plato, who changed everything he touched into gold, embellished and enriched it so as to make it analogous to the elevation of his extraordinary soul. (B 4.86, 225)

Here, the emphasis is on Plato's embellishment of a pre-existent Socratic doctrine, on making Socratic philosophy stylistically beautiful. And this line of thinking will be investigated in Chapter Two, where it will become clear to what extent 'philosophising after Socrates' is a matter of the production of philosophical doctrine through formal devices that are broadly Platonic in origin. Moreover, the importance of Platonic writing to Hemsterhuis was already anticipated in the quotation on the *Symposium* that begins this section: it is not merely the sheer fact of Plato's stubborn fidelity to the Socratic event that Hemsterhuis lauds, it is also *the means by* which he went about reinserting the Socratic into post-Socratic debate – that is, the 'beauty' (as Hemsterhuis calls it) of Plato's philosophical presentation.

2. Hemsterhuis writes Socratically and he writes Socratically like Plato. And to do so, he takes on what Sonderen calls a Greek 'mentality' (2000: 8) and writes from the point of view of a Greek. He immerses himself in an Athenian philosophical tradition. Hemsterhuis is explicit that such a task is, in part, a matter of 'the reader or listener being prodigiously familiar with the persons, their country, their customs and their century' (B 10.71, 124). Affinity to ancient Greece requires attending to its mores, characters and language, and this comes to the fore in his repeated claims to have been 'born Greek'. In October 1780, Hemsterhuis writes to Gallitzin, 'I am Greek, and I have made a pact with their crude, but true and lasting simplicity' (B 3.76, 179) – a claim he had expanded on a few weeks earlier: 'Slavery in whatever colour it shows itself is the thing in the world I detest the most, as much for others as for myself, for I am born Greek, Platonic, Tyrannicide' (B 3.61, 147). In 1784, again in correspondence with Gallitzin, he revisits this idea: 'I am born Greek and in other centuries I would have certainly shone as an illustrious *tyrannicide*' (B 5.78, 256). And a similar assertion is made two years later as well: 'I have only ever seen or known, either personally or in their works, three people genuinely born Greek: you [Gallitzin], Goethe and me' (B 7.17, 53).

Central to this refrain is an affirmation of freedom from institutional constraint, an identification with slayers of tyrants and the martyrs of

Athenian democracy. Hemsterhuis pictures himself as a freedom-fighter, as 'unfit for servility' (Fresco 1995b: 126).[7] Furthermore, this claim to be 'born Greek' also arises from an attitude of resolute anachronism. Hemsterhuis sees himself as an *untimely* figure – a philosopher alienated from the dominant Enlightenment trends and intellectual fashions of the late eighteenth century. Raised on Greek philology, it was in the Greek language, among Greek texts and ideas, that he felt most *at home*. Hemsterhuis celebrates his 'furious inclination towards the Greeks and their genius' (B 4.80, 210), and the greatest compliment he can pay a new acquaintance is that 'not only does he know Greek, but his *soul belongs to Greece*' (B 7.78, 220; my emphasis).

This, then, is the third of those qualities that Hemsterhuis identifies in Plato's *Symposium*: Plato's ability to distil something of what it means to be Greek into his writings, to provide 'the most perfect description of the beauty of Greek souls' – to capture a Greek essence. It is a writerly ideal that Hemsterhuis prizes highly: on reading Goethe's *Iphigenie auf Tauris*, he identifies Goethe as one of the few moderns to have been 'born Greek' (as quoted above). This is not because of Goethe's ability to faithfully replicate the formal devices of Greek tragedy, it is because *Iphigenie auf Tauris* captures something of the 'tone' of classical Athens. That is, Hemsterhuis marvels how Goethe is able to 'capture so perfectly the tone of Euripides, unless there had been a time in his life when he read Greek as his own language' (B 9.22, 51).[8] This reference to speaking Greek 'as his own language' (i.e., like a native) alludes to a key Hemsterhuisian virtue, and he pays the same compliment to Gallitzin: 'In your penultimate letter you spoke Greek' (B 9.15, 35). Neither Gallitzin nor Goethe was speaking Greek in any literal sense, of course; they 'spoke Greek' while writing French or German. This is a virtue not exemplified through faultless (or even faulty) transcription of actual Greek words; it is, instead, a matter – at least, in part – of a Greek 'tone' manifest in the words, no matter what language they are written in.[9]

---

[7] For example, one of the above declarations occurs as part of a criticism of Camper's acceptance of a Fellowship at the Berlin Academy. Hemsterhuis continues, 'I have always maintained that a philosopher must avoid as much as he can these honourable associations; not from ostentation nor from a distaste for merited honours, which would be laughable and non-philosophical, but since these Societies restrict freedom of thinking, speaking and acting' (B 3.61, 147).

[8] Earlier, Hemsterhuis had described Goethe's *Iphigenie* as possessing 'a tone of naïve truth that the moderns never approach' (B 6.8, 34).

[9] Hemsterhuis is, moreover, sometimes very precise about the exact provenance of particular tones. He does not always speak generically of a 'Greek tone', but ascribes tones

Similarly, much of the late Hemsterhuis' dissatisfaction with eighteenth-century culture is bound up with a distaste for its languages, particularly the French language. He bemoans 'the thin, superficial and insipid character which so gloriously distinguishes our days from every other century, principally in the language that I have the honour to speak' (B 4.29, 74). On this basis, he contrasts the 'astonishing beauties' possessed by 'the language of the Greeks' with 'the dull, dry and ambiguous tone of the moderns' (B 4.42, 102–3). To speak Greek in modernity would be to speak an utterly alien language: it would necessarily provoke 'stupid astonishment' among contemporaries (B 2.52, 141). These appeals to the 'tone' of a language (e.g., 'the pure and celestial tone of the Greeks' [B 4.42, 103]) are attempts to articulate an underlying spirit manifest through the words on the page but irreducible to them. The spirit–letter binary has become somewhat of a hermeneutic platitude in the wake of Herder, Schleiermacher and Dilthey, and Hemsterhuis was not the first to deploy it either: some of his more obvious precursors are Montesquieu, Rousseau and even Caylus.[10] However, what I am interested in is defamiliarising this cliché of post-romantic reading practice, so as to see if we can appreciate anew the specifics of Hemsterhuis' invocation of a 'tone' that shines through words.

After acknowledging that Goethe's *Iphigenie* 'marvellously captured the tone of antiquity in general' (B 9.19, 45), Hemsterhuis goes on to specify that speaking Greek in the midst of modernity depends on meeting two conditions: (1) 'tact and genius' to replicate the appropriate tone; and (2) precise antiquarian knowledge of the ancient world. To write in an untimely fashion and to generate 'an air of antiquity' (B 1.1, 13) presuppose both conditions – the tactful divination of the appropriate tone *and* the accurate replication of factual details; both together fully constitute what it means to 'speak Greek'. Hemsterhuis is ultimately critical of Goethe for failing to meet the second condition and not attending sufficiently to erudite details: he communicates the tone of antiquity, but not its concrete details; elsewhere, he is conversely scathing of those who possess erudition without tact.[11] And

---

to specific dates, outputs or styles. This is especially clear in his conversations with Gallitzin over the revisions to *Simon* (B 2.63, 189).

[10] On Caylus' significance in this specific regard, see Sonderen (2000: 263).

[11] This latter failing is, in part, a critique of the philological mentality that Hemsterhuis had encountered in his father, who, he confesses to Gallitzin, 'wrote in all the languages of Europe and thought in none' (B 5.7, 40). Knowledge of factual particulars is a necessary but not sufficient condition for reconstructing the Greek world – and this helps distinguish the true reader from the philologist. In this vein, Hemsterhuis

ultimately, Hemsterhuis will position himself between these two extremes (tact without knowledge and knowledge without tact). He considers his own work to exhibit details that even 'the most erudite Greek antiquarian' would accept, as well as satisfying an 'Attic soul' like Gallitzin who has a true 'taste' for the Greek spirit (B 3.9, 36). On the one hand, therefore, Hemsterhuis' dialogues purport to 'speak the language of Plato and Athens' (B 2.58, 172) owing to the accuracy of their factual detail: the Greek world they conjure up is intended to be a faithful reproduction of characters, locations, customs and allusions. And, on the other hand, an authentic Greek spirit is meant to shine through these details. What is at stake in what follows, nevertheless, is how Hemsterhuis might manage to achieve this, how he can meet both conditions for speaking Greek.

§4 Geometrical Method

Hemsterhuis aspires to be faithful to the Socratic event and purports to achieve this by 'speaking Greek', that is, using Platonic formal devices to conjure a Greek tone in his texts. However, equally determinative of his philosophy is fidelity to modern geometrical method. His thinking begins from the axiom '*both* Socrates *and* Newton' – and this axiom is articulated most explicitly in *Sophyle*:

> All systems of philosophy that men have wrought so far are only loose assemblies that appealed to some individual or to his sect. . . . There are only two philosophies in the world in which truths occur and in which the mind is not corrupted: the Socratic and the Newtonian. The latter, I admit, does not merit the name system of philosophy, since it only comprises a very small branch of it, embracing just mechanics, insofar as it is applicable to pure geometry. But in the case of the Socratic, everything is within its reach. (*EE* 2.47; *OP* 342)

> continues, 'We emit only words, formulae, seeds of pedantry and ostentation, but the sublime, the sap and the essence of knowledge is identical with the soul and cannot leave it, and it is the only earth from which new truths grow' (B 3.31, 84). And yet, this criticism is also, for Hemsterhuis, an acknowledgement of the difficulty of ever moving from the letter to the spirit – not even the Athenians themselves managed it that often: 'I am persuaded that there are people who do not know a word of Greek but who are infinitely more familiar with Plato's turn of spirit and what he says and who feel infinitely better the prodigious elevation of his poetry than the thousands of Athenians who daily frequented the Stoa or the Lyceum' (B 5.8, 44).

Hemsterhuis demands that philosophy not only become Greek but become Newtonian too.[12] This double loyalty to Newton and Socrates was not particularly exceptional during the eighteenth century, particularly since neither name was exactly a rigid designator: for many, both figures were broadly construed as united in their critiques of systematisation and abstraction in the name of healthy common sense, inductive reasoning and an inclination to the practical.[13] Nonetheless, I will go on to argue in §5 that the simultaneous demands of being Greek (i.e., Socratic) and modern (i.e., Newtonian) do pull Hemsterhuis in opposite directions. As Morpurgo-Tagliabue (1987: 13) has pointed out (following Matassi [1984]), Hemsterhuis scholarship has had to live with the legacy of choosing either his moment of critique or that of sentiment, either the modern or the antique, either the Newtonian or the Socratic.

Hemsterhuis' thinking is, therefore, *also* intended to exemplify the best characteristics of Newtonian philosophising, particularly its geometrical method. It is here that the decision about where to begin reconstructing Hemsterhuis' thought is most controversial: to begin with the Socratic ideal might emphasise his counter-modern tendencies (valorising a pre-modern past in the face of the failings of the Enlightenment), but his Newtonian 'image' is very different. It is an image of a modern Hemsterhuis who celebrates (some) progress in the sciences, drives forward research in optics, animal generation and astronomy and writes on mathematical problems like indivisibility and incommensurability, as well as on 'the organs of insects' (*B* 8.83, 197). This is the Hemsterhuis who will always define his

---

[12] This sentiment is repeated in a very late letter to Gallitzin: 'It is not, my Diotima, that I want to insult those redoubtable *-isms* that so many modern philosophers adore, each in their own way. There are two heroes in *-isms* to which I adhere and defend to the last – these are Socrates in real philosophy, and Newton in all that concerns physics' (*B* 9.72, 155).

[13] In many ways, in fact, Hemsterhuis participates in a late eighteenth-century trend in which Newton the person was celebrated to disguise a gradual shift away from the rigours of Newtonianism itself. Jorink and Zuidervaart put it most helpfully: 'Increasing terminological vagueness about Dutch "Newtonianism" and the dilution of its epistemological foundation coincided with growing praise for Newton himself ... [and] reached its peak at the end of the eighteenth century.... Newton was worshipped, not only because of his scientific work, but most of all because he became an icon, onto which all kinds of values could be projected: piety, reasonableness, peacefulness and modesty.' Ultimately, 'Newton himself became even more popular than his philosophy' (2012: 48–50). See also Ducheyne (2014b: 98), Israel (2007: 23) and Jorink and Maas (2012: 8); as well as Hemsterhuis' praise for Newton outside of discussions of Newtonianism (e.g., *B* 4.93, 242; 7.79, 224).

philosophical project as contributing to 'a physics free from errors and precarious assumptions' (*EE* 2.61; *OP* 384; see also *IN* 172). For these reasons, Petry has bemoaned the scholarly tendency to marginalise this scientific Hemsterhuis. The Hemsterhuis of the Socratic ideal represents 'only one aspect of his philosophy as a whole' (1985: 212), and 'beneath the literary surface of his published letters and dialogues there was a carefully articulated vision of mathematical truth' (1995: 184–5).

1. Although, in the published passage from *Sophyle* extracted above, Hemsterhuis immediately qualifies his praise for Newtonianism by restricting its legitimate domain to 'just mechanics', elsewhere he finds its method far more universally applicable. In a letter to Gallitzin from May 1786, Hemsterhuis rehearses an epiphanic narrative in which the 'primal scene' of his philosophical maturation turns on a conversion to Newtonianism and, specifically, a realisation that Newtonian method provides the key to all domains of philosophy, not just (as *Sophyle* seems to suggest) the physical sciences. He writes,

> It came to me that we must necessarily detail with the greatest possible precision what we understand by applying the geometric spirit to general philosophy, as Newton applied geometry to mechanics, and what are the fruits we can attain by this operation in all branches of philosophy without exception. (B 7.43, 120)

In other words, Hemsterhuisian philosophy is to be understood, in part, as the retooling of all philosophy from the standpoint of Newtonianism, an investigation into the extent to which every field of philosophy can be rendered properly Newtonian. In this manner, for example, he imagines 'a psychology as certain and unbreakable as Newtonian physics is' (B 6.69, 197) or an ethics illuminated by 'the same ray of light that Newton made rebound on the visible and material universe' (B 1.26, 60–1).[14]

The demand for philosophy to become Newtonian is, of course, not particularly surprising given Hemsterhuis' intellectual biography. Raised on 's Gravesande's teachings (for whom Newton was 'prince of the mathematicians and renewer of the true philosophy' [quoted in Ducheyne 2014a:

---

[14] Thus, just as Hemsterhuis compliments Gallitzin for 'speaking Greek', he pays her the highest compliment for bringing to bear on a particular subject 'the geometric spirit with as much success as Archimedes and Newton carried geometry into physics' (B 5.40, 152–3).

§4 GEOMETRICAL METHOD   41

40]),[15] he pursued his early scientific pursuits armed with a microscope, designed optical instruments and held commerce with scientists across Europe. Indeed, a Scandinavian visitor found Hemsterhuis to be, not 'a dilettante of Plato' (as Friedrich Schlegel called him [1958–2002: 23.249]), but 'a mathematician and an astronomer ... an optician [who] invented an entirely new type of telescope' (quoted in Petry 1985: 219). Hemsterhuis himself reports that he 'worked more than fifty years on optics both theoretical and practical' (B 8.83, 197) and that 'the first letters I learnt were Euclid's figures' (B 1.209, 246). In short, Hemsterhuis was an active contributor to the broadly Newtonian scientific community of his day: his call for philosophy to become Newtonian does little more than announce his membership of this European republic of letters.

Nevertheless, the Newtonian imperative is far more than window-dressing. Hemsterhuis takes the demand to render philosophy Newtonian very seriously, and I want to contend that he epitomises an 'analogical Newtonianism' roughly similar (in one aspect, at least) to the eighteenth-century trend that Wolfe (2014) has described under this rubric.[16] Like Haller, Blumenbach, 's Gravesande and Buffon, among others, Hemsterhuis, on the one hand, refuses the 'literal project of directly transposing' Newtonian laws into other domains of scientific knowledge (Wolfe 2014: 223) but, on the other hand, still deploys Newton as a model for making sense of these domains. Newton acts as inspiration and standard for the invention of distinct yet analogous methodologies. This is not an applied Newtonianism, but Newtonianism reformulated heuristically – and such reformed Newtonianism gives rise to an effect long ago observed by Cassirer (1951): the diffusion of the experimental spirit into ethics, politics, aesthetics and philology in the mid-eighteenth century. The clearest example of Hemsterhuis' participation in this trend is his analogical reformulation of the concepts of attraction and inertia as means to conceptualise moral and erotic phenomena in the *Lettre sur les désirs*. Another striking instance is his analogical reimagining of Newtonian

---

[15] Hemsterhuis often shows fine-grained familiarity with 's Gravesande's writings – not just in the close paraphrase of Gravesande's unpublished work in a clarification to the *Lettre sur l'Homme* (EE 1.129; OP 308) but also in his correspondence (e.g., B 1.189, 226; 12.141, 202).

[16] Wolfe's category of 'analogical Newtonianism' comprises two kinds of analogy: (1) the analogical (rather than direct) use of Newtonian methods and concepts outside of the physical sciences and (2) agnosticism about the causes of natural processes and effects. It is this latter form of analogical reasoning that Wolfe takes as most important. While Hemsterhuis may sometimes exemplify this second kind of analogy (e.g., in his remarks on electricity in *Sophyle*), my focus in this section is with the first kind of analogy.

methodology in aesthetics. As Sonderen has convincingly demonstrated, Hemsterhuis holds an 'exceptional' position in the history of aesthetics in his application of 's Gravesandean principles to the aesthetic domain: 'Hemsterhuis tries to explain an aesthetic judgment by means of a hypothesis and an experiment, that is, by means of the experimental method' (1996: 324).[17] More specifically, he formulates his definition of beauty by repeating a publicly verifiable test involving the comparison of two classical vases. By describing the reactions of test-subjects to these vases, Hemsterhuis (both in the *Lettre sur la sculpture* itself [see §19] and in later iterations of the experiment [B 2.47, 119–21]) shows how aesthetic judgements naturally occur in the manner predicted. In Sonderen's words, 'The experimental method, which stems from the Newtonian tradition in physics, has moved into the metaphysical field of beauty and of art' (1996: 343). Sonderen goes on to point out that Hemsterhuis' drawings of the vases in particular act as 'the basis of a perceptual experiment'; indeed, they serve as 'both proof and outcome' (2017: 41; see also Sonderen 2000: 81–7). They act, he writes elsewhere, as 'the first aesthetic experiment in history' (1996: 213; see further Sonderen 2022: 10–13, 17–18). Ethics and aesthetics are as subject to (a reimagined version of) Newtonian method as natural philosophy itself.[18]

2. Hemsterhuis does not, therefore, divide Newtonian physics from Socratic moral philosophy, so as to create 'two distinct domains', as van Sluis puts it (in OP 12). There is no firm methodological distinction between natural philosophy (as Newtonian) and anthropological ethics (as Socratic). Rather, both Newtonian and Socratic ideals are universally applicable: Newton provides the model for psychology and ethics, just as much as Socrates does for metaphysics. *All* philosophy is to be *both* Socratic *and* Newtonian. In other words, successful thinking – in whatever domain – must be undertaken according to a geometrical method: Hemsterhuis is constantly prescribing 'a strong dose of geometry for the soul' (B 4.72, 186) or 'geometry [as] the only medicine' (B 7.6, 26).[19] This is as true of his attitude to philosophical

---

[17] This is partly what Gaiger means by Hemsterhuis' 'unusual methods' in the *Lettre sur la sculpture* (2018: 225).

[18] Petry sums this up nicely: 'The a priori "geometrical method" by means of which Newton had ordered and structured his mathematical, mechanical and optical research, was to be extended to include a systematic treatment of the feelings and the emotions, the ethical activity and the politics, the aesthetic creativeness and the religious aspirations of mankind' (1995: 195; see also Petry 1985: 229)

[19] Euclid plays an important role here, comparable to Socrates and Newton in Hemsterhuis' hagiography. See, for example, B 3.102, 231.

method in the early 1770s as it is in the 1780s, when he still apostrophises 'holy Geometry, daughter of Jupiter and mother of Truth' (B 11.95, 97; see also B 11.30, 41).[20]

Geometrical reasoning is, then, a salutary corrective to bad thinking in all its forms and, as such, has a vital pedagogical function. Hemsterhuis preaches 'a geometric education' which 'trains the intellect in all cases to follow and to undertake the path of analogy, [so as] to pass from idea to idea by intermediate ideas without breaks' (B 2.47, 114; see also B 5.54, 197). He continues,

> The habit of leaping [from idea to idea] teaches [the pupil] to fly, sustains him in the air to contemplate from a bird's eye view the vast regions of all his ideas, all his sensations and all his passions. His Olympus is there; it is from there that he sees his universe by its groupings, by its order, just as, in a glance, Jupiter sees the heroes before Troy, the depths of hell and the limits of creation. When the spirit has gained this elevation, do not doubt whether it has tact in all the arts, whether it has a creative faculty in all the sciences, whether it can bridle its own passions and govern those of others, do not doubt whether it is pleased to exist. . . . It is clear, at least, that geometrical education is the only path which [leads] to this true and real Olympus. (B 2.47, 115)

Tact, creativity, self-restraint, contentment and divine intuition are, then, some of the fruits of the geometrical spirit. Its effects go far beyond just mathematical skill. According to Hemsterhuis, these virtues result from a capacity to obtain an impersonal perspective, a dispassionate gaze on the past, present and future, as well as from a facility in reasoning syllogistically and passing from idea to idea without mistake or interruption. Through geometry, one attains 'Olympus', a god-like capacity to reason without prejudice or error, imagine creatively, judge subtly and act ethically.

If these are the effects of a geometrical education, less clear is what precisely such an education involves. Hemsterhuis is often more articulate on what geometrical method is not than what it is. In particular, he frequently

---

[20] Whatever else may change in the evolution of Hemsterhuis' philosophy, his unwavering commitment to the geometrical spirit of modernity does not. There is no turn away from Newton. That is, just as it is inaccurate to resolve the competing demands of the Socratic critique of modernity and the Newtonian affirmation of the modern by allocating them to two separates domains of philosophy, so too they cannot be understood diachronically, as if the Socratic ideal came to replace the Newtonian.

opposes the proper Newtonian use of geometrical method to its improper systematic employments. While Newton sets every idea down in its proper place without prejudice, geometric systematisers construct 'loose assemblies that appeal to some individual or to his sect' (EE 2.47; OP 340). Indeed, these modern builders of systems – who, according to Hemsterhuis, follow a Cartesian, rather than a Newtonian tradition – have stamped their 'foot onto the neck of Newton's beautiful philosophy' and transformed his 'spirit of pure geometry' into a 'slave' for metaphysics (B 1.216, 253). The modern mania for systems 'leads in the end geometrically to the pit of Tartarus' (B 7.44, 122).

In line with his strictly analogical conception of Newtonianism, this is partly a critique of the post-Cartesian mathematicisation of philosophy outside of the physical sciences. To philosophise geometrically should not involve introducing geometrical content or even geometrical operations into thinking; it is, rather, to formulate a method analogous to geometry that is nevertheless more suited to its object. Hemsterhuis is scathing of the rationalist application of geometry 'without limit or measure' into 'the arts, into metaphysics and into theology' (B 6.14, 50). Such a mistaken 'apotheosis of geometry' (B 2.47, 116) – as he calls this total mixing of philosophy and geometry – damages thinking. And the same is true of arithmetic, which is 'absurd' when applied outside of its proper domain (B 2.37, 79). In both cases, 'to mix or confuse the two disciplines is to do immeasurable damage to both' (Petry 1995: 191).[21] This is the crux of Hemsterhuis' analogical Newtonianism: while the geometrical spirit may be universal, geometry itself must remain a 'very small branch' of philosophy.

For Hemsterhuis – as so often in the eighteenth century – Spinoza serves as a foil, the paradigm of a philosopher gone wrong by failing to respect the proper limits of geometry. Spinoza refuses to recognise the analogical sensitivity needed when thinking geometrically about philosophy; he is the anti-Newton. As Hemsterhuis complains to Jacobi,

> I cannot think of this illustrious man without lamenting he did not live thirty years later. He would have seen with his own eyes, by the very pro-

---

[21] See further Petry (1995: 187–91). Hemsterhuis is here close to Nieuwentyt's critique of the employment of mathematics as an art of discovery – a critique that remained normative in the Dutch Republic throughout the eighteenth century (see Moretto 2005: 80; Petry 1985: 213). And so, it is not surprising that Hemsterhuis is very close to 's Gravesande on this issue too: like Hemsterhuis, he criticises Spinoza for 'writing everything as a mathematical system'; 'When perusing [Spinoza's] book on ethics, one thinks one is seeing a treatise on geometry, but one soon discovers how he misused this method' (quoted in Ducheyne 2014a: 39).

gress of physics, that the direct application of geometry can only be made in physics, and thus that he had confused the formulaic method of the geometers with the geometric spirit, whose application to metaphysics would have produced things more worthy of his great genius. (B 12.135, 192)

Elsewhere, he will speak of Spinoza's *Ethics* as a 'strange book' with 'its form . . . so strangely abused', penned by 'a mind so strangely spoilt by geometry' (B 7.2, 17–18).

For Hemsterhuis, to philosophise well is to philosophise geometrically, but this is not to directly transpose the methods of geometry onto philosophy. More sensitivity to the differences between geometry and philosophical thinking is required: while he recognises in Spinoza 'an admirably robust and energetic intellect', his is an intellect that lacks 'any shadow of tact': 'A tact of the least extraordinary kind would have sufficed for just sensing the difference in tone between his axioms and those of Euclid's axioms' (B 7.2, 17–18).[22] What Hemsterhuis possesses and Spinoza lacked is reflective judgement, a capacity to sense the parameters of the analogy that separates – as well as connects – geometry and the geometrical spirit.[23] And it is in this regard that he unfavourably compares Spinoza to Newton: they are 'two great geniuses' and both 'felt the necessity of carrying some geometric ray into philosophy' to institute 'some kind of marriage between philosophy and geometry'. But 'they executed this task with differing success', for Spinoza merely 'applied geometric jargon to metaphysics' – and this led directly to the 'abuse of abstractions' (B 4.86, 224–6). Nevertheless, Hemsterhuis still offers some hope here – specifically, the hope that 'he who will find a true application of the geometric spirit to the whole of philosophy will have the glory of doing with philosophy what Jupiter did with the little Pelops' (B 4.86, 224–6). That is, despite all the failings of the post-Cartesian systematisers who used mathematics to go beyond Newton, there have still been some 'admirable efforts' – efforts which 'gave the sciences a precision that they did not have before' (B 5.52, 192). Amidst all the failures, errors and distorted systems, intellectual progress has still been made – progress made possible by the tactful, nuanced deployment of a geometrical spirit within philosophy.

---

[22] It is worth noting (in light of the findings of §3) the interrelations between concepts of tact, analogy and tone established here.
[23] According to Hemsterhuis, it is this failure to think analogously (i.e., sensitively) that leads to fatalism as well. See Fresco (2003: 10).

3. According to Hemsterhuis, this geometry-inspired philosophy purged of all actual geometry is to be understood in terms of a series of methodological rules. And the formulation of such rules is, as the above implies, ultimately to go beyond Newton while remaining Newtonian, to transcend Newton's own self-limitation ('applying raw geometry to mechanical physics') so as to discover 'a true application of the geometrical spirit *to the whole of philosophy*' (B 4.86, 226; my emphasis).

These methodological rules take as their point of departure the fact that what matters in any form of geometrical reasoning is not the particular mathematical truth under discussion, but 'the *way of proceeding* towards an unknown truth' (B 2.33, 62). There are generic, domain-indifferent methods of reasoning – 'indestructible laws that all others must follow' – and they determine the 'procedures and movements' of philosophy (B 2.33, 62). They can briefly be summarised as follows:

1. The need to attain an impersonal, global view from nowhere – 'that philosophical spirit which after viewing the parts is raised up to see the whole from a bird's eye view' (B 3.8, 35) or 'a bird's eye view like Jupiter's who weighs events in his scale with tranquillity' (B 4.44, 106; see also B 2.37, 78).
2. The need to simplify or analyse ideas 'into their integral parts' (B 2.33, 61); indeed, 'the most necessary principle in our philosophy is to simplify as much as possible and in all investigation to get to the very first beginnings' (B 3.101, 230).
3. The need to be linguistically precise: geometrical training is necessary for forming 'clear and precise ideas of the words *rapport*, interrelation, proportion, finite, infinite, indefinite, and a thousand others' (B 5.52, 192).
4. The need to cultivate precision in observation: according to Hemsterhuis, the qualities required to philosophise well include '(1) seeing with the most exact precision; (2) feeling with the most exact precision; (3) having a true confidence in oneself' (B 7.24, 71).

From these four rules will result good philosophical thinking – that is, a thinking that maintains order and clarity in the progress of ideas.

For our purposes, what is particularly helpful are the conclusions that Petry draws from these types of rule for tactful geometrical reasoning:

Euclidean geometry is therefore the model for philosophy, not because its particular propositions have an unquestionable validity, or because it can provide a universal means for communicating our knowledge of natural phenomena, but because when it is viewed as a whole, the progression it involves from basic propositions to highly complex demonstrations, provides us with an abstract analogue of the comprehensive interrelatedness of all levels of knowledge of science. (1985: 230)

The geometrical method designates a way of arranging ideas to ensure facility of reasoning, exactness and precision of expression. It is a meta-method that applies to all scientific domains – an 'interdisciplinary thinking', in Petry's phrase (1995: 186). To philosophise well, for Hemsterhuis, is to think tactfully in accordance with these Newtonian metaphilosophical rules.

§5 A System of Times

At the end of the *Lettre sur l'Homme et ses rapports*, Hemsterhuis attempts to identify some 'dynamic laws of human knowledge'. However, rather than providing an ahistorical description of principles, models or conditions necessary for the production of knowledge, he offers a *history of human knowing*. That is, he historicises thinking into a series of epochs:

> The science of man, or the human mind, appears to move around perfection, like comets around the Sun, by describing very eccentric curves: it likewise has its perihelia and its aphelia. . . . In every perihelion, there has reigned a general spirit which has spread its tone or its colour over all sciences and all arts, or over all branches of human knowledge. In our perihelion, this general spirit could be defined by the spirit of geometry or the symmetrical [spirit]; in the perihelion of the Greeks, by the moral or sentimental spirit, and if I were to consider the style of the arts among the Egyptians and the ancient Etruscans, I should soon perceive that the general spirit of the previous perihelion was that of the marvellous. . . . In each perihelion there was a favourite science, more analogous to the general spirit than the other sciences, and which was perfected to the highest degree. This science – so refined and so embellished – was applied to all the others, regardless of whether it was applicable to them in this way or not. (*EE* 1.123–4; *OP* 292)

Hemsterhuis continues, 'in our perihelion' – that is, that of the Enlightenment – 'sciences will be perfect according to their degree of applicability to geometry and arithmetic'. 'Optics, mechanics, economics and astronomy' thrive in the eighteenth century, whereas 'morality, politics, and the fine arts, these tender flowers, formerly so fresh and so brilliant in the soil of Athens, fade and dry out in our arid climates'. On the contrary, among the Greeks, 'the ideas of love, gratitude, ingratitude, hate, vengeance [and] jealousy [were] almost as clear and as perfect and determinate as those of a triangle and a circle' – and this benefited ethics and the arts, but 'reduced' physics to a derivative practice of (for example) applying 'love to attraction' (*EE* 1.124; *OP* 292–4; see also *EE* 1.71; *OP* 128).

1. This theory of eccentric orbits, or system of times, determines the relation between the ancient and the modern, that is, the relation between the Socratic and the Newtonian demands described in §3 and §4.[24] Epochs are to be understood in accordance with the literal etymology of the word 'epoch' – as an orbit with two apsides, i.e., the point at which it is closest to the star around which it revolves (its perihelion) and the point at which it is furthest from it (its aphelion). There have been (and will be), Hemsterhuis is at pains to emphasise, numerous such epochs; however, from the vantage point of the eighteenth-century Dutch Republic, 'only about one and a half revolutions' are visible: the perihelion of antiquity and that of the modern Enlightenment, as well as the aphelion of the 'Dark Ages' that separate them (*EE* 1.124; *OP* 292). He speaks of the current age as 'our perihelion', but also later refers to 'our sad aphelia' (*EE* 1.124; *OP* 296; see also *B* 8.102, 233), perhaps indicating that, within the late eighteenth century, there might be discerned the seeds of a rotation back towards ignorance.

The Keplerian astronomical terminology used to articulate this cyclical theory of history is one example among many of Hemsterhuis' tendency to use scientific models outside of their proper domain. It is to be read alongside his employment of 'attraction' and 'inertia' to describe desires, as well as his account of lunar catastrophe in *Alexis*. They are all instances of Hemsterhuis' metabatic reasoning (analogously, i.e., tactfully, applying models from one scientific domain to another) and they thus complement and extend his practice of analogic Newtonianism described in §4. In other words, what these examples testify to is not the direct transposition of scientific concepts into the domain of history (or ethics), but their heuristic (i.e., sensitive and tactful) reimagining. In his commentary on the *Lettre sur l'Homme*, Diderot criticises Hemsterhuis' system of times precisely on these terms: 'All this

---

[24] It is worth noting immediately that, unlike his romantic successors, Hemsterhuis does not accord the Christ-event any explicit, orienting role in his system of times (or even in the political-theological genealogies he charts, which are explored in §21). Modernity is never understood as Christian.

has been obscured by a metaphor pushed too far' (Diderot and Hemsterhuis 1964: 471) – which is, indeed, I want to argue, an apt description of much of Hemsterhuis' late philosophical practice. Moreover, these astronomical metaphors precisely reverse the procedure that Hemsterhuis identifies in this very passage as the mark of the Greek sentimental spirit: whereas the Greeks applied ideas of love, hate, fear and indolence to physical phenomena like attraction (moving from ethics to physics), Hemsterhuis' analogical transpositions proceed in the opposite direction, that is, from physics to ethics. His transpositions are thus resolutely *modern*, anti-classical forms of metabatic reasoning. In other words, Kepler's mathematical astronomy acts as the standard (the 'favourite science') through which to understand other, ideal phenomena. The *Lettre sur l'Homme*'s system of times reflects, in short, Hemsterhuis at his most modern, implementing the very modern 'spirit of geometry' he there describes.

The content of Hemsterhuis' system of times itself is, on one level, merely a variation on the many eighteenth-century attempts to neatly distinguish modernity from antiquity.[25] Hemsterhuis' version of the quarrel of the ancients and the moderns alludes to the Pascalian binary (Pascal 1995: §21) of *esprit de finesse* and *esprit géometrique* – historicised such that the distinction between the two eras is not to be located in an opposition manifest in their products nor even in their methods of production, but rather in an altered preponderance of 'colouring' or 'general spirit', or what Hemsterhuis elsewhere dubs a 'tone of thinking' (B 2.44, 98). The spirit/letter distinction described in §3 returns to provide the conceptual framework for distinguishing the two epochs. Both ancients and moderns practise the arts and geometry; however, in modernity, art is, as it were, contaminated by a geometrical spirit, whereas, in antiquity, geometry was infected by an artistic tone.

While it seems slightly hyperbolic to claim with Moenkemeyer that the passage which opens this section marks 'a new way of solving the quarrel of the ancients and the moderns by insisting that both are capable of reaching perfection' (1975: 81) – particularly considering the evident influences of Montesquieu, Perrault and St-Evremont[26] – it is nevertheless clear that Hemsterhuis is polemicising against those, like Voltaire, who dissolve the quarrel by declaring Lockean-Newtonian philosophy to have superseded

---

[25] These attempts were as frequent in the Dutch Republic as in France or in Germany – see Van Bunge (2018: 187).
[26] On Montesquieu's influence, see Moenkemeyer (1975: 81); on Perrault's and St-Evremont's influence, see Hammacher (1971: 146–7).

Plato. Hemsterhuis opposes himself radically to the Voltairean contention that 'there is not one ancient philosopher who serves today for the instruction of the youth in enlightened nations' and that 'a man who knew all Plato and who knew only Plato would know little and know badly' (1878: 14.582; see also Rockhill 2010: 141). And this is because Hemsterhuis stresses the *equality* of perihelia: they are different, but of equal value. Each has a distinct sphere of perfection, implying that, for Hemsterhuis, such perfections are multiple and domain-dependent. Hemsterhuis is thus able to affirm *both* antiquity *and* modernity, *both* Socrates *and* Newton. His system of times is neither a narrative of progress and decline nor a fatalist recurrence of the same; rather, it sets up a series of multiple foci, teloi and forms of life that are not hierarchically arranged, but are merely different (Hammacher 1971: 145–6). Every form of historical life reaches a scientific highpoint (i.e., Socrates and Newton) from which it gradually falls away; indeed, just as Hemsterhuis' history of ancient philosophy turns on the gradual forgetting and corruption of the Socratic ideal, so too his history of the Enlightenment tells of the gradual perversion and covering over of its initial Newtonian inspiration. In the latter case, Newton's successors took his method *too far* – and so 'the geometric spirit' has ended up 'harming' political liberty and 'fogging up our sciences' (B 7.25, 74). Moreover, just as in antiquity there were those, like Plato, who, according to Hemsterhuis, fought against the inevitability of intellectual decline by attempting, in a dissolute age, to recall old models and ideals, so too this is precisely Hemsterhuis' own task at the end of the eighteenth century – to imitate Plato in the midst of the corruptions of the contemporary Enlightenment project, not only by appealing to a lost Socratic ideal, but also by appealing to a fading Newtonian inspiration as well. Hemsterhuis invokes his twin masters of Socrates and Newton precisely as lost ideals to be recovered – as exemplars of the double perihelia of antiquity and modernity in whose names he struggles against impending aphelion.

2. Hemsterhuis' project can thus be defined in terms of simultaneous fidelity to these two perihelia. However, such a project immediately encounters two problems. The first has been bubbling under the surface throughout this chapter – the possibility of being Socratic and Newtonian *at the same time*. That is, if, as the theory of perihelia implies, ancient Socratism and modern Newtonianism possess distinct perfections, how think in a way that exemplifies them both? More specifically, if the perfection of Newtonian geometry is detrimental to some forms of intellectual practice (e.g., ethics), whereas the perfection of Socratic sentiment enhances these very practices, how then

consistently take up the position of *both*? In other words, commentators like Fresco may speak in passing of Hemsterhuis' 'thinking hover[ing] between the old and the new' (1995a: 48) or of 'the peculiarity of his philosophy [as] the successful synthesis of the "esprit de géometrie" and the "esprit de finesse"' (1995a: 43), but far less attention has been paid to *how* such 'synthesis' can be achieved by Hemsterhuis' own lights. The fact that there is such a difficulty can be gleaned from a letter Gallitzin wrote to Hemsterhuis on moving to Münster:

> I am impatient to talk with you of my dear Greeks. The only fault I know at Münster is that they are not sufficiently known and celebrated, but this fault is born at bottom from a beautiful cause: Münster is the reign of the exact sciences, and the shining clarity of the sun destroys the interesting clarity of a beautiful moon. We love the moon, my dear Socrates. But the sun also has its value. Perfection would consist in reuniting them, but an exact fusion seems impossible to me. (2015–17: 4.154)

Gallitzin here articulates the problem succinctly – the seeming impossibility of fusing the sun and the moon, the 'shining clarity' of the moderns and the 'interesting clarity' of the ancients (especially given the fact that she inescapably inhabits an age in which such 'shining clarity' has obscured lunar clarity). How does one hold equally to two incommensurable spirits? Indeed, Hemsterhuis himself highlights this problem in comparing Fürstenberg to Pythagoras: both, he writes, have 'taken for their basis the singular composition of the sentimental spirit and the geometric spirit, two kinds of spirit that belong to centuries prodigiously distant from each other' (B 2.63, 190). The two spirits seem irreconcilable, so how exemplify both consistently?

Homing in on Hemsterhuis' attitude to modernity exacerbates the problem. As Hammacher points out, 'in some places, his writings clearly protest against the "geometrical spirit" of the age ... a protest against the one-sided consideration of the philosophical task through scientific cognition of physical relations' – and yet (as §4 showed at length) he still 'everywhere calls his method of philosophy "geometric"' (1971: 26). Hemsterhuis might criticise modernity, but he is no simple counter-modern figure: he is not happy in the Enlightenment, but he nevertheless belongs to it (see Bulle 1911: 11; Söhngen 1995: 264). This ambivalence towards the modern can be further discerned in Hemsterhuis' claims that, 'although our languages stand well below [the Greeks'], we have the finesse in thinking which was unknown to them' (B 5.79, 259) and that 'it is certainly not by superiority of genius that we differ from the Ancients, but by a more correct, more distinct, more symmetrical language' (B 5.54, 198). Modernity possesses some virtues, but so does antiquity: the modern geometrical spirit might have perfected precision, clarity and analytic rigour, but this is not to be considered progress (for the Greeks eminently exemplified other intellectual virtues).

Ultimately, Plato once more provides the solution to Hemsterhuis' problem, for Plato exemplifies the kind of productive ambivalence experienced by Hemsterhuis. In the scholarship, it is Vieillard-Baron who has most clearly discerned Plato's significance in this regard; he writes,

> What [Hemsterhuis] retains of Plato is essentially what he calls 'the native geometry', that is, natural reason. This reason is so important since Plato's epoch was in Hemsterhuis's eyes a 'perihelion of sentiment' and since, despite this domination of sentiment, Plato was able to discern the importance of mathematical reason. In this, Plato can be the philosopher to guide men at the end of the eighteenth century. (1995: 155)

Plato is *anomalous* – a philosopher who prefigures the modern geometrical spirit from within antiquity, who both is committed to the Socratic ideal and anticipates geometrical method.[27] He can thus act as inspiration for an eighteenth-century philosopher like Hemsterhuis who too wishes to return to a Socratic past while keeping hold of a geometrical modernity. Just as Hemsterhuis goes 'from Plato to Newton and back to Plato' (Tavani 2005: 162), so Plato goes from Socrates to geometry and back to Socrates.

However, in order to fully understand this recourse to Plato, more detail is required concerning the very possibility of such an anomalous existence, of inhabiting more than one epoch – and it is here we encounter the second problem.

3. The second problem concerns the very possibility of reviving Socratism in modernity; indeed, it concerns the very idea of a post-Newtonian thinker such as Hemsterhuis (or Goethe or Gallitzin, for that matter) being 'born Greek'. In short: how inhabit two times? How participate in a very distinct Greek form of life while living as a modern?

Hemsterhuis implicitly recognises this problem. On the one hand, he laments the lack of Greek spirit in modernity – for example, the fact that

---

[27] Thus, Hemsterhuis identifies his divergence from Gallitzin on precisely this point: 'You remain disposed to give Plato to another century' (B 2.5, 19) – that is, she renders Plato too Greek, too alien, and so fails to recognise that he was not fully at home in the Greek perihelion.

'our modern artists do not lack dexterous hands, but a Greek soul' (B 6.13, 47) and that 'no Frenchman I can think of has this sacred and pure taste for the Greeks' (B 2.36, 76). Indeed, to Fürstenberg, he worries that modernity is so different from antiquity that any 'models' to be found 'among the Ancients' are useless to us now, since 'they – closer to the simplicity of nature, freer, less subjected to prejudices – found few difficulties to vanquish compared to those to which modern times give birth' (B 12.96, 120).[28] On the other hand, Hemsterhuis still insists on his affinity with the classical world. Again and again, he draws attention to his untimeliness as a living anachronism within the Enlightenment: he exclaims to Gallitzin repeatedly, 'We belong to a century that is not our own' (e.g., B 1.90, 129). The very idea of being 'born Greek' is precisely an attempt to articulate such self-alienation, self-consciously estranging himself from modernity in order to re-enter a past Greek form of life – in order, that is, to participate in a bygone perihelion.

Hemsterhuis is thus aware of the difficulty of converting untimeliness into a positive philosophical ideal. Becoming Greek is difficult in modernity; nevertheless, he contends, it is still possible. And this possibility (the possibility of inhabiting different times intellectually) is elaborated further in Hemsterhuis' discussion of the claim introduced in §3 that he knows 'three people genuinely born Greek: you [Gallitzin], Goethe and me' (B 7.17, 53). When Gallitzin expresses puzzlement in her reply to this claim, Hemsterhuis takes it as an opportunity to develop *a doctrine of the anomaly*:

> When I spoke of a certain trio in my penultimate letter, I meant that these three persons are born with something in their minds, in their soul or in their faculties which I have not seen in other people, and by which they see, feel and envisage the arts at the same distance and from the same perspective that the Greeks did. Likewise, I have said that Hippocrates, Democritus and Archimedes were born with something in their minds, in their souls or in their faculties that I have not seen in other Ancients, and by which they have seen, felt and envisaged all the exact sciences at the same distance and from the same perspective that we do in this Newtonian century. ... My dear Diotima, it is time that prevents me from entering into this curious investigation into what is this thing in the trio which make them Greek in regard to the arts; and it annoys me

---

[28] Yet, Hemsterhuis is still more than happy to draw analogies between epochs: Aristotle is the equal of Bacon, Newton and Leibniz (B 9.18, 40–1) and Homer, Plato and Lucian compare to Newton and Huygens (B 10.25, 54).

much more that I remember, when composing *Homme et ses Rapports*, I already had formed a furious desire to clearly show why some men appear to belong, either wholly or in part, to centuries very distant from those in which they were born. I have known and I know (and you also, I think) men who are precisely from the eleventh or twelfth century and these centuries, in turn, (and this is still more astonishing) produced men who belong to our perihelion and more often still to the sentimental perihelion of the Greeks. These examples, it is true, are very rare, but it excites me still more to look for the cause of this possibility. (B 7.19, 58)

As is so often the case in Hemsterhuis' letters, the above is presented as a provocation for further reflection that never in fact takes place. However, the main lines of his thinking are clear enough. Following on from his identification of 'singular men who arise from time to time in a perihelion in which they appear as strangers' in the *Lettre sur l'Homme* (EE 1.124, OP 294), he characterises Hippocrates, for instance, as a modern living in an ancient world, whereas Hemsterhuis describes himself as an ancient living in a modern world. It is a question of 'affinities' (to return to the opening quotation in §3): one does not necessarily belong to the century in which one happens to have been born; an eighteenth-century Frisian can still possess a Greek soul, manifest a Greek spirit and think and write with a Greek tone. Hemsterhuis ascribes to himself an innate anachronistic property – something out of kilter with the times.[29] While versions of this ideal of untimeliness were relatively common (even timely) in the late eighteenth century and are but one symptom of the neoclassicism, philhellenism and Plato renaissance of the day, it still needs stressing that Hemsterhuis philosophises as an anomaly; his are untimely meditations.[30]

---

[29] Comay labels this experience of untimeliness 'trauma as a historical category' in which 'the present is never caught up to itself, [such that] we encounter history virtually, vicariously, voyeuristically – forever latecomers and precursors to our experiences, outsiders to our most intimate affairs' (2010: 4–5). This account recalls both Hemsterhuis and the German romantics and idealists who were to feel such a strong affinity to him.

[30] Hemsterhuis sometimes articulates a notion of genius in these terms. A genius is someone who produces or appreciates works valuable beyond their own epoch. For example, the true appreciation of Greek tone (or 'sublime taste for the Greeks') 'pertains neither to the finite, nor to labour, but to genius' (B 4.6, 27). More fully, he distinguishes between the 'spirited' (i.e., those who possess the spirit of the time) and the 'genius' precisely on these grounds. So, on the one hand, there are geniuses – 'Homer, Plato, Theocritus, Tasso, Montaigne, d'Alembert and Pope' – who 'at any moment... will never seem faded or superficial, neither to you nor to any century'. Geniuses escape the hegemony of the present. However, the 'spirited' author is trapped within 'a spirit of

§5 A SYSTEM OF TIMES

As we know from §3, one way in which this untimeliness manifests itself is through an unsettling *tone* – a tone alien to the present. It is through the 'colouring' of their thinking that Hippocrates, Democritus and Archimedes were exceptions, as well as Gallitzin, Goethe and Hemsterhuis himself. This notion of an alien tone is taken up again by Hemsterhuis in reflections on Plato's *Symposium*, which he characterises as the most exemplary product of the Greek perihelion:

> In *L'Homme et ses Rapports*, I speak of a general spirit, a universal tone, which reigns in all the sciences and all the arts in each perihelion of the human spirit. There is not a piece of work in the world save the *Symposium* where one sees distinctly in its vigour this tone, this ruling spirit of the Greek perihelion. (B 4.97, 253)

The sentimental spirit by which ethical ideas dominate is articulated paradigmatically in the *Symposium*. In other words, to read the *Symposium* is to access another type of perfection and, thus, when it comes to recreating a spirit foreign to the moderns – to speak Greek and be born Greek – one could do much worse than to turn back to this text, to use it as a springboard to escape the present. Tarrying with Plato – reading him, translating him and mimicking him – becomes a means of liberation, an attempt to repeat Greek 'tone' in modernity. This, then, is another reason for Hemsterhuis' obsessive rewriting of the Platonic corpus: one becomes untimely *by way of Plato*.

4. There are ancient anomalies (like Plato) and modern anomalies (like Gallitzin). And yet there is also a third kind of even more monstrous anomaly whose spectre Hemsterhuis conjures in correspondence. This is a type of philosopher, he speculates, who belongs equally to *all* epochs – that is, who is more than an ancient soul in modern times or vice versa, but a soul equally at home in any time. Hemsterhuis writes,

> To be born in a perihelion and hold by one's nature to another, either present or future, seems to be a little strange. To hold by nature to all perihelia would be much more so in my opinion, and we will discuss

the current aspect of men' and, as such, a 'spirited' work from a previous epoch exhibits 'the spirit of past lustre' that 'no longer seems genius'. Thus, Hemsterhuis concludes, 'Spirit is to lustre as the genius is to eternity' (B 3.37, 98–9). The genius frees herself from the restrictions of her time and her works flit indifferently across eras.

another time if such a monster would be possible, and if there is in the composition of man the means to lead to such monstrosity. (B 7.78, 221)

Hemsterhuis radicalises his system of times to envisage an ideal of epoch-indifference, in which a philosopher would not belong anachronistically to just one other time but would cultivate inner affinities with all times. Indeed, this is the very working out of the double demand to be *both* Socratic *and* Newtonian: the 'both . . . and . . .' logic entails equal participation in all perihelia, no matter how alien. The philosopher is to become omnitemporal: Greek, modern, Egyptian and so on – speaking all languages, mimicking all tones, thinking in all spirits and being born in all times.[31]

To this doctrine of absolute untimeliness Hemsterhuis adds three corollaries. First, he insists that this universal affinity to all times – this practice of absolute untimeliness – is a key component in intuiting new truths. He writes, for instance, 'That manner of seeing objects in other ways than other people do – this is the only and true means to make discoveries and uncover the new' (B 2.67, 200). That is, to multiply perspectives is to increase one's facility for invention. Philosophical discovery occurs through inhabiting different styles of thinking, different spirits of reflection. To belong to all past ages and to gain the capacity to inhabit all pre-existing perspectives is a means of facilitating such discovery – and so of generating the new (the *poietic* moment described in *Alexis*).

Secondly, in the above Hemsterhuis connects this becoming absolutely untimely with the figure of the monster. In line with much eighteenth-century thought (see, e.g., Ibrahim 2016), Hemsterhuis is obsessed by monsters and they haunt his writings (e.g., B 1.51, 92; 2.62, 183; 3.25, 72; 5.13, 60). He confronts them most directly in the *Lettre sur la sculpture* with the following definition: 'We call a monster any object that does not enter any known class, or that belongs to several classes at the same time, such as some unknown animal, or a centaur, a satyr, etc.' (EE 1.61; OP 94). And later in the work, he adds a historical twist, comparing unfavourably modern depictions of the monstrous with the Greeks' 'excellence in the composition of monsters': 'Look at their centaurs, their nereids, their satyrs, which are all Greek creations, and tell me whether any [other] age or any nation ever went beyond the mediocre in this genre' (EE 1.69; OP 120). The point is not

---

[31] In this vein, Hemsterhuis insists to Gallitzin that the purpose of philosophy is to cultivate 'the faculty of teaching man to fly outside of his sphere', but that this is something impossible within 'the geometrical perihelion' which at best provides the tools merely to 'clarify [the position of the human subject] within his own sphere' (B 7.96, 257).

merely that Hemsterhuis' appropriation of the monstrous as a philosophical ideal draws him, once again, close to a Greek model, but also that the philosopher is monstrous to the extent she 'belongs to several classes' – or eras – 'at the same time'. To mix all epochs is to render oneself fragmented and heterogeneous, that is, to become an intellectual monster.

Thirdly, Hemsterhuis connects this ideal of epoch-indifference with a kind of contentment and even blessedness. To become estranged from the present and indeed from any particular past is to achieve a kind of eternity – to see the world *sub specie aeternitatis* – in a manner that imitates the blessed. He writes, 'We belong to a century that is not ours, for there are holes in nature through which one can see, if one likes, the palace of the supreme God and the vast plains of eternity and happiness' (B 1.90, 129). The idea of a bird's eye view on reality central to Hemsterhuis' conception of the geometrical method (see §4) is here rendered fully diachronic, an Olympian survey of not just of all that happens to exist, but of all that has and will exist. Its ethical character is also reaffirmed: the view from nowhere becomes a view of all times and to ascend to such disinterested heights is a moral obligation. Hemsterhuis speaks of this becoming absolutely untimely not only as the intuition of something new (i.e., seeing through the cracks of modernity to something that exceeds its temporal determination), but also as a means of accessing something that is neither modern nor ancient, but everlasting. Such are the ethical stakes of untimeliness in Hemsterhuis' philosophy. It is only by overcoming the century into which one happens to have been born, it is only by estranging oneself from the prevalent trends and fashions of the age, that a kind of eternal 'happiness' is attained (see §24). Indeed, this blessedness is thus worked out in a fairly traditional way: escape from succession into eternity, release from temporal determination altogether, a flight into the beyond – but it is reinterpreted through Hemsterhuis' system of times: to achieve bliss, one must *de-present oneself*. This is an ideal that will recur throughout Hemsterhuis' philosophy – a philosophy motivated by the demand to become 'monstrous', to take the heterogeneity of epochs into oneself and so become untimely.

Chapter Two

Analysis and Poetry

> Hemsterhuis is very often a logical Homeric Hymn.
> Novalis (1960–2006: 2.462)

§6 'Poet-Philosophers' and 'Humble' Analysts

This chapter treats a second set of Hemsterhuisian demands that overlap significantly with those identified in the previous chapter, even if they ultimately remain distinct from them. In the previous chapter, my concern was Hemsterhuis' insistence on *both* Socrates *and* Newton, and, in this chapter, I am interested in a stylistic variant: *both* sober analysis *and* imaginative myth – *both* the analytic *and* the aesthetic. This is, in part, a repetition of the ancient–modern double bind of the previous chapter (insofar as analysis is aligned with the geometrical and myth with something non-Newtonian), but something also shifts in this repetition, for analysis and myth no longer strictly correspond to the two perihelia of the ancient and the modern. There are both ancient and modern writers of speculative myths (e.g., both Lucretius and Descartes), just as there are both ancient and modern analysts (e.g., both Socrates and Newton). When it comes to the communication of philosophy, Newton and Socrates no longer represent conflicting demands, but both stand on the side of analysis. It is now a matter of Socrato-Newtonian analysis, on the one hand, *and something more*, on the other – a stylistic supplement of dialogue, myth, metaphor and imagery.

To begin, it is worth returning to the problematic established at the end of §1 – that of a 'poetic turn' in Hemsterhuis' communication of philosophy. While as late as 1776 Hemsterhuis (in the guise of one of his characters) can still insist on 'no poetry or fables in philosophy' (*EE* 2.46; *OP* 338), things look very different a couple of years later: the last dialogues are filled with imagery, allegory, myth, jokes and ironic play. To get some sense of this shift, therefore, it is worth beginning with Hemsterhuis' earlier position on philosophical style from the mid-1770s – and, happily, the topic is broached in detail at the beginning of his correspondence with Gallitzin in 1775. In the first months of their friendship, Hemsterhuis provides one of his fullest statements on the writing of philosophy provoked by his and Gallitzin's shared experience reading an unnamed book by Charles Bonnet. Hemsterhuis begins by contrasting his present experience of reading the book (in 1775) with the 'many excellent things' he had initially discovered in it shortly after it had first been published. This change in judgement comes, he continues, as a result of a set of reflections he has formulated on philosophical methodology, which he lays out to Gallitzin as follows:

> I take philosophy here in terms of the way of treating it. It seems to me that there are properly two types of treatment – one could be called poetic or narrative philosophy and the other persuasive or geometric philosophy. The first was that of most of the ancient poet-philosophers, the Sophists, Descartes even and a great number of illustrious moderns. The other was that of Socrates, Aristotle, Newton and a few people of that kind. The first [group] – after having fixed a certain number of ideas in their exalted imagination – recount to us with a striking elegance what beautiful whole resulted from this procedure: it is normally a small universe which closely resembles Lucretius', born from the fortuitous play of atoms. The others – with the help of an imagination that has been tamed a little more and a reason that is well practised in sizeable, rather than small, methodological procedures – proceed straight to the simple and, from it, Euclid in hand, ascending by a few degrees at a time, they tell us in humble prose that there are at least some truths. The first have a great advantage over the others: to refute them a book must be as fat as theirs and recount exactly the opposite, whereas the latter are refuted in a few phrases, since the base of their edifices is of the most austere simplicity. (B 1.3, 18–19)

Hemsterhuis' letter is met with puzzlement on Gallitzin's part. The bulk of her reply is spent worrying over his passing reference to the Sophists as poet-philosophers, that is, in the same category as Descartes, Bonnet and Diderot, and, as part of this argument, she homes in on those later three philosophers, 'who were driven to seek the truth in good faith', even if they sometimes strayed 'beyond the true' (2015–17: 4.13–14; see Hemsterhuis

§6 'POET-PHILOSOPHERS' AND 'HUMBLE' ANALYSTS

2007: 52–3).[1] That is, while Gallitzin approves of the 'excellence' of the distinction between analysts and poets, she admits to an 'affection I still feel for what you so accurately call the poet-philosophers'. They are, she concludes, like 'those delicacies which are delicious to taste, but less necessary and easily abused', compared with the 'nourishing bread' of the analysts. And most significantly, Gallitzin assumes that Hemsterhuis will fully agree with her, that he too feels the pull of the poet-philosophers; in other words, she ultimately doubts the good faith of Hemsterhuis' initial treatment of poet-philosophers like Bonnet, and so asks him 'to communicate to me as soon as I have the honour of seeing you what your objections against Bonnet really are' (2015–17: 4.14–15).

This provokes Hemsterhuis to elaborate in a subsequent letter:

> After having read and reread the admirable letter you had the grace to write me, I recalled my own and found it lacking in a number of essentials. First of all, the false ironic tone. . . . In speaking of the poet-philosophers, I had in view the Parmenideses, Xenophaneses, Epicharmuses, Solons and Euripideses, all spirits who seem to me as admirable within their centuries as you appear to me in yours. . . . Concerning Descartes, one of the great geniuses of the modern age, he, like Leibniz, must not be judged on the novel he published. These two great men were too sane not to be slyly laughing at their own reveries that shocked the people. Hence, Madame, there are those who are not entirely unworthy of being placed besides the author in question [i.e., Bonnet]. When I say that all these men have mostly treated philosophy in the narrative genre, it is to say that they have recounted their opinions without proving their truth. But this is not all that I would say against the method of the author [Bonnet] and many other moderns. They rely too much on matter. . . . The more ground they gain by means of their purported material explanations, the less need there is for the influence of a soul, of a God, etc.; and they often perceive very acutely that their method must lead straight to the most perfect materialism and that – sometimes in good faith and sometimes with a fanatical pusillanimity – they employ palliatives to render their systems, in my opinion, still more grotesque. (B 1.4, 19–21)

---

[1] Gallitzin notes that Bonnet writes in a 'genre' in which 'there are almost solely hypotheses; and this is a problem concerning so many unknowns' (2015–17: 4.14) – which is precisely what, in a later section (§18), I take to be Hemsterhuis' ultimate problem with Bonnet's style.

On the one side, then, stands narratival or speculative philosophy – a philosophical style intent on presenting big, imaginative claims that paint a holistic vision of the universe in all its aspects – and, on the other, stands an analytic style, proceeding cautiously with geometric rigour to establish only those simple foundations that are the most certain and secure.

1. As Hemsterhuis himself notes, one of his aims in the above is to ironically invert many preconceptions about the history of philosophy. For example, while he unsurprisingly associates the speculative with pre-Socratic 'poet-philosophers' and Lucretius, he also identifies contemporary materialists, the Sophists and even Descartes and Leibniz as 'poet-philosophers' (and, therefore, as non-analytic). The analytic method itself, in its purity, is reserved solely for three named 'heroes': Socrates, Aristotle and Newton. Plato's name, we should note, is conspicuously absent from these lists.[2]

In line, then, with much eighteenth-century Newtonian prejudice, Descartes' tendency to systematise overshadows his commitment to analysis: he perverted the geometrical method for speculative ends in a way that prepared the terrain for Spinoza (see §4). Geometry becomes a kind of poetry in Descartes' writings, instead of remaining 'humble prose'. Poet-philosophers from Parmenides to Bonnet all tell stories and this is their downfall: they 'treated philosophy in the narrative genre' and so merely 'recounted their opinions without proving their truth'. And what generates some of the irony here is that it is the very Cartesian obsession with secure foundations that motivates Hemsterhuis' critique of Descartes himself and post-Cartesian systematisers. The 'edifices' of the humble prose writers, like Socrates and Newton, are 'of the most austere simplicity' – and, as such, are secured all the way down. On the other hand, the poet-philosophers justify solely 'a certain number of ideas' before proceeding to construct well beyond any limits that such meagre foundations might warrant. Ultimately, the difference is a matter of faculty psychology: the poet-philosophers construct their system from 'their exalted imagination', employing the resources of narrative to tell a story about reality – and what is valuable to them is that it conforms to aesthetic criteria (i.e., it creates a 'beautiful whole'); the analysts, however, shun such aesthetic criteria for purely logical ones: the intellect alone determines philosophical value.

Hemsterhuis is one more post-Cartesian voice to condemn imaginative extravagance and the virtues of the beautiful whole, even at the expense of

---

[2] Plato is mentioned once by Hemsterhuis within these two letters, but only in respect of his portrayal of the Sophists, not as a stylist in his own right (B 1.4, 20).

§6 'POET-PHILOSOPHERS' AND 'HUMBLE' ANALYSTS 63

abandoning Descartes himself.³ He closely follows Voltaire's *Lettres sur les Anglais*, in particular, both in the general tenor of his distinction (even if the historical lens is altered) and in dubbing Descartes' philosophy a 'novel'.⁴ In line with this broadly Voltairean tradition, Hemsterhuis valorises the pursuit of a style of 'geometry, without touching on the imagination' (B 2.14, 28); he rails against 'obscurity and equivocation' as the 'two plagues in true knowledge' (B 7.29, 82); and he insists that philosophical subjects demand a 'dignity, where all florid style, all fiction, all play of the imagination must be absolutely proscribed'. Philosophers should be exclusively 'concerned with the naked and pure truth' (B 1.41, 77).

This attitude underlies his criticisms of the perversions of the geometrical method rehearsed in §4; but it also goes on to be transformed in his writings into a far more radical, Rousseauean appeal to innate virtue and common sense – a return to the simple and straightforward in the face of reckless system construction. *Sophyle* (published a year after the above letters) is the text in which this anti-speculative moment in Hemsterhuis' trajectory is most fully on show. Socrates is presented as a thinker of good sense and destroyer of scholastic sects; he is a quintessentially anti-dogmatic thinker and 'preached philosophy itself, while others merely preached their limited philosophical systems' (*EE* 2.47; *OP* 342). Indeed, in *Sophyle* Hemsterhuis goes so far as to consider analytic style the work of neither the imagination *nor the intellect* (as in Rousseau, in *Sophyle* the intellect is corrupt and decadent): true philosophy 'is not the daughter of the mind or of the imagination'. Rather, according to *Sophyle*, it is an unmediated expression of the 'upright heart': Socrates 'taught men that it can be found in every healthy head, in any upright heart but that it is the source of universal and indestructible happiness' (*EE* 2.47; *OP* 342). Hemsterhuis draws heavily on Rousseau's Savoyard Vicar, who likewise rejects 'profound reasonings' in the name of 'good sense' and 'simplicity of heart' (1991: 266). Both Rousseau and the Hemsterhuis of *Sophyle* reject 'the jargon of metaphysics [which] has never led us to discover a single truth, and has filled philosophy with absurdities of which one is ashamed as soon as one has stripped them of their big words' (Rousseau 1991: 274; see also Rousseau 2018: 28). Hence, within *Sophyle* itself, to the question, 'What then is your philosophy?', Euthyphro

---

[3] See discussions of 's Gravesande on this topic in Jorink and Zuidervaart (2012: 34) and Ducheyne (2014a: 34–5).

[4] Voltaire writes, 'His philosophy was nothing more than an ingenious and, at the very most, probable novel' (1878: 22.131). The term 'philosophical novel' is also one that Bonnet himself employs to describe his own work. See Savioz (1948: 195).

responds, 'My philosophy, my dear Sophylus, is that of children; it is that of Socrates; it is that which is found at the bottom of our heart, of our souls, if we make the effort to seek it there' (*EE* 2.47; *OP* 342). Hemsterhuis (at least in *Sophyle*) advocates philosophy for children, a Rousseauean victory of the sincere heart over the corrupt intellect.

And it is in this vein that he elsewhere criticises the 'tone of the schools' – and, in particular, 'the tone of Wolffianism' – in favour of 'virgin good sense' (B 2.52, 141). He is even occasionally critical of his own philosophical terminology, particularly his deployment of the term 'organ', as 'a little too figurative in style' (B 2.55, 156).[5] What is particularly evident is Hemsterhuis' unease – at least, some of the time – at the imaginative in philosophy; his rejection of it in favour of the kind of naked truth he later interrogates in *Alexis*. In another letter to Gallitzin on philosophical writing, Hemsterhuis reaffirms once more this contrast between philosophising 'by means of poetic and figurative twaddle' and reasoning 'in a Euclidean manner' (B 4.68, 173). Philosophy is sometimes to be opposed to the poetic and the figurative.

2. Where the letters that begin this section go even further than the above is in their identification of the figurative with *the logic of materialism*. In other words, according to the 1775 Hemsterhuis, materialism has a style. This implies both that materialism cannot but be articulated narratively (or speculatively) and also that the narratival presentation of philosophy necessarily tends towards materialism. Poet-philosophy is the very style of materialism – or, at the very least, it might always be perverted to materialist ends. The poet-philosophers end up 'rely[ing] too much on matter', for their nonchalant attitude to certainty allows them to 'attribut[e] to matter properties which are often in contradiction to every sane physics' (B 1.4, 20). They fill up their systems with unwarranted materialist explanations: 'The more ground they gain by means of their purported material explanations, the less need there is for the influence of a soul, of a God, etc'. Poetic philosophy, on this view, 'lead[s] straight to the most perfect materialism'. Lucretius exemplifies the danger facing any philosopher who strays off the path of sober analysis: too concerned with bringing everything together under one principle of explanation (and so into a 'beautiful whole'), he ignores distinctions and generalises recklessly, passing quickly from the fact that some modifications of an object can be explained materially to argue that they all can – a speculative absolutisation of physics.

[5] Here, Hemsterhuis closely follows Diderot's criticisms of the moral organ (see §15).

§6 'POET-PHILOSOPHERS' AND 'HUMBLE' ANALYSTS

Most interesting for later sections of this book is the Bonnetian context to this diagnosis, for it is while reading Bonnet's work that Hemsterhuis draws this conclusion. And, in fact, one consistent feature of Bonnet's early reception is that he is frequently identified as a materialist or seen as some kind of 'gateway' to materialism. Rousseau, for example, will similarly label him 'a materialist' (2018: 395) and the late Bonnet himself bemoans this materialist misreading of his work. 'No, I am not a materialist' (2002: 50) is his constant refrain, and he goes so far as to correct the 'inattentive or badly disposed reader' who infers he 'inclines towards materialism' by adding asterisks to those paragraphs in his writings 'which are the most directly contrary to the language of the materialist' (2002: 49). Elsewhere in his correspondence, Hemsterhuis will describe Bonnet's Genevan disciples as degenerating into the most abject materialism, concluding that Bonnetism 'work[s] more for the materialists than the materialists themselves' (B 3.47, 120). And yet, this is all a misattribution, for Bonnet's project is explicitly designed to defend immaterialism and justify the dogmas of Christianity in the face of the Parisian materialist threat. What Hemsterhuis seems to be implicitly claiming in the letters on geometrical style is that, notwithstanding all Bonnet's protests against materialism, there is something about the way he writes philosophy that still tends towards materialism. Despite himself, Bonnet's 'philosophical novels' work against his stated ends. These claims will form the subject matter of §18.

In opposition to the poetics of materialism, analysis never generalises, and this, according to Hemsterhuis, makes it best placed to defend the existence of the soul and of God. Analysis is the style by means of which the philosopher can resist materialism. It allows space for what is different – the immaterial – in a way that speculation, narrative and the imagination do not.

3. The one insuperable obstacle that immediately faces any use of these letters to make sense of Hemsterhuis' strategies of writing is that, merely a couple of years later, he appears to renege on this commitment to analytic sobriety (at least, insofar as it is strictly opposed to mythic exuberance). The evidence for this change has been mounting over the course of the book (see §1 especially) and will continue to build. The above explanation to Gallitzin of what philosophy should look like seems to bear little resemblance to his own late philosophical writings: dialogue, myth, imagination and poetry play an increasingly constitutive role in his practice of philosophical communication. And, more explicitly, Hemsterhuis will – only two or three years later – start to speak of his dialogues as a series of 'follies

in my vast imagination' (B 3.32, 86) or 'fables' (B 3.11, 246); he will feel the need to make *Simon*, for instance, 'as pretty as possible' (B 2.55, 154), and at the end of his life will conclude that 'science and art make only one whole' (B 10.69, 120). Indeed, this is why critics often refer to the 'florid prose' (Moenkemeyer 1975: 80) of his late works, the manner in which they 'swell with the flowers and colours of poetic prophesising' (Bulle 1911: 35). The virtues of sober analysis preached in 1775 are increasingly sidelined from 1777 onwards, such that one must wonder whether, by his own lights, Hemsterhuis himself might end up a 'poet-philosopher', flirting with the dangers of materialism.[6]

And yet, these letters do already offer one clue to the possibility of reconciling the competing demands of analysis and the imaginary. For, in these letters themselves, even when expressly concerned with valorising dry and sober analysis, Hemsterhuis still does so in a ludic style. Even after being upbraided by Gallitzin for precisely this playfulness and subsequently apologising for 'the false ironic tone' of his initial epistle, he still writes playfully.[7] These letters are themselves anything but geometrical analyses that proceed slowly and soberly – in a Euclidean manner – from what is most simple to a firmly established truth. This is not to say that Hemsterhuis somehow performatively deconstructs the content of his own letter, but, rather, that his preferred analytic style does not exclude the ironic or the playful as much as appears to be the case at first blush. Rather, his geometrical method calls repeatedly for a heavy dose of irony. Here, then, is a first clue that the opposition established in these letters might partially collapse on further inspection (as Gallitzin intimates). And, in the next section, I want to consider the most influential attempt in the scholarship to show how these two poles of Hemsterhuis' style do coalesce – Klaus Hammacher's.

---

[6] It is something like this which Gallitzin already seems to hint at in her initial reply to the 1775 letters when implicitly imputing to Hemsterhuis too her own 'affection' for the 'delicacies' of the poet-philosophers.

[7] This is, moreover, a rhetorical ploy to which Hemsterhuis is repeatedly drawn in his correspondence. A decade later, he follows a series of exuberant metaphors with the following: 'You will be edified without doubt to see that I have finally submitted to your lessons and have begun this year with a simple and non-figurative style that emits raw, humble and naked truths into the heads of others' (B 10.1, 13). Many of his more playful letters to Gallitzin of this kind can be categorised as a kind of *philosophy as flirtation* – the eighteenth-century equivalent of Socratic philosophy as seduction.

§7 Sentimental Certainty

One of the most significant pieces of evidence for a poetic turn in Hemsterhuis' philosophy can be adduced from a self-critique of his earlier attempts at writing philosophy. In *Sophyle*, Hemsterhuis has his characters reflect back on the style of the *Lettre sur l'Homme* and suggest that something is lacking, something that prevents them from being convinced by it. Referring to the syllogistic arguments of the *Lettre sur l'Homme* fictively as the speech of an unnamed 'friend' containing 'various proofs of the heterogeneity of the soul and the body', Hemsterhuis uses this as an opportunity to repeat these 'three different proofs' for mind–body dualism word for word in the dialogue (*EE* 2.55; *OP* 364–6). Sophylus is persuaded by these proofs 'that the soul is another thing than the body' (*EE* 2.56; *OP* 370); however, he also confesses to 'something odd that happened to me during our friend's speech' – and he explains this oddness as follows:

> My reason follows perfectly the course of his mind. I have nothing to contradict it. It seems to me that he goes from truth to truth. But at the end his arguments repel me: I can no longer conceive them: I don't feel the truth; I don't have that intimate and perfect conviction by which it is always accompanied; and however simple his arguments may be, I tacitly fear that he has deceived me, and has strung me along with some sophisms that I failed to notice. (*EE* 2.56; *OP* 368)

The syllogistic form of argumentation is not very good at convincing: it does not make the subject 'feel the truth' and experience the 'intimate and perfect conviction' necessary for a proper experience of what is true. Syllogisms make Sophylus anxious and ultimately (and this is a strong claim to make considering it is a response to Hemsterhuis' own earlier publications) the 'arguments repel me'. This criticism is one that Hemsterhuis had perhaps internalised from various critiques of the *Lettre sur l'Homme* made by Diderot and an anonymous review in the *Journal encyclopédique* (see §15) which tended to the same conclusion: the syllogistic style of the *Lettre sur l'Homme* fails. Indeed, Euthyphro goes on to endorse Sophylus' critique of Hemsterhuis' early presentation of philosophy, emphasising that arguments of this kind merely 'stun the mind' and do not allow it to immediately 'cross the gap' between premises and conclusions (*EE* 2.56; *OP* 368–70).

Hemsterhuis dramatises his move away from syllogistic writing. And this shift is a result of the early works' inability to persuade, to induce in the reader that 'intimate and perfect conviction', that *feeling* for the truth that is a requisite of all successful argument. This is a topic to which Hemsterhuis returns at length in his next dialogue, *Aristée*.

1. More than any other of Hemsterhuis' works, *Aristée* exemplifies the conflicting demands of his philosophical project. In this text, he resolutely positions himself 'on the limit', as Bulle puts it (1911: 11), with all the ambivalences that result. It is here that he struggles most visibly with the twin demands of the geometric and the Socratic, as well as the analytic and the aesthetic. It is why, for example, Bulle – who locates the essence of Hemsterhuisian philosophy in aesthetic irrationalism – can criticise *Aristée* for 'not being free enough from rationalism' (1911: 81), whereas Moenkemeyer, for whom Hemsterhuis ultimately chooses the way of rational demonstration, worries that 'it must remain doubtful whether [*Aristée*'s] emphasis on feeling represents the "genuine" Hemsterhuis' (1975: 121). To put it another way: on the one hand, *Aristée*'s concern for the order of the cosmos places it in dialogue with a moderate Dutch Newtonian tradition (influenced strongly by Nieuwentyt) but, on the other hand, there are elements of the dialogue which, at first blush, seem to point beyond this tradition: not only the editorial preface, which acts as an elaborate philological joke (see §22), but also the following notorious passage in which Hemsterhuis appears to eschew discursive justification for God's existence to affirm, instead, the primacy of feeling. In fact, the latter passage testifies to his rigorous sifting through this very Dutch Newtonian tradition to find those elements most helpful for countering the threat of materialism; in particular, what is at stake is the utility of 's Gravesande's canonical gesture by which 'moral evidence' was accorded equal rank alongside 'mathematical evidence' as a non-syllogistic means of recognising truth.[8]

The passage reads,

> Man, Aristaeus, seems to be capable of two kinds of conviction: one is an internal sentiment, ineffaceable in a well-constituted man; the other derives from reasoning, that is, from the orderly labour of the intellect. The latter cannot exist without having the first as its sole basis; since,

---

[8] De Pater writes of 's Gravesande's contribution: 'One of the most striking results of his investigations is that he puts mathematical and moral evidence on the same level. For him both evidences are of a totally different order than whatever degree of probability.' (1995: 228). See further Hammacher (1971: 48–9; 1995a: 67) and Ducheyne (2014a: 41–2). Hemsterhuis paraphrases 's Gravesande precisely on this point: 'The conviction of sentiment is of equal value to that of the intellect' (*EE* 2.82; *OP* 448).

§7 SENTIMENTAL CERTAINTY 69

when working back to the first principles of all our knowledge, whatever their nature may be, we will arrive at axioms, that is, at the pure conviction of sentiment. ... In a well-constituted man, a simple sigh of the soul, which manifests itself from time to time towards something better, towards the future and what is perfect, is a more-than-geometric demonstration of the nature of the Divinity. ... By means of language, I can modify the intellect of another in such a way that there results for him the same geometrical and determinate conviction that I myself possess, whereas purely sentimental conviction is born in [our] essence and cannot be communicated. (*EE* 2.92; *OP* 476–8)

This passage has long been deployed as an interpretative key to Hemsterhuis' philosophy. According to Bulle, 'the perception of God [invoked in this passage] no longer has anything to do with the rational, deistic inference of his existence' (1911: 24) and, for Ayrault, it 'reads like a Pietist text where Hemsterhuis seems to enter into the lineage of anti-Cartesian Christianity' (1961: 1.485). It ultimately leads Hemsterhuis to embrace a vision of science comprising 'not ideas, but a sensation, a sentiment which is worth more than an idea' (*B* 5.92, 284–5). And it is unsurprising that the 'simple sigh of the soul' described above went on to become a perpetual refrain in Jacobi's writings, which similarly insist upon 'the concept of an immediate certainty, which not only needs no proof, but excludes all proofs absolutely'. Jacobi alludes to this 'sigh' as justification for rejecting 'the way of the syllogism' (1994: 249). For Jacobi, like Hemsterhuis, 'conviction by proofs is certainty at second hand' and 'quite another spirit must dwell in [man] than the spirit of syllogism' (1994: 347).

2. What is most striking about this passage for my purposes is Hemsterhuis' further claim that this 'purely sentimental certainty' – 'the simple sigh of the soul' – is so intimate to the essence of the human that it 'cannot be communicated'; indeed, he suggests that, insofar as any words at all can articulate such certainty, they do so merely indirectly, that is, solely through narrative, fable and myth.[9] He states that from the 'pure certainty of a simple truth' originates mythic imagery, like the 'plains beyond Acheron'

---

[9] This indirect communication is precisely dramatised elsewhere in the dialogue: when speaking of love, Aristaeus stutters and confesses, 'I cannot. I lack the words. But you feel, I hope, what I cannot express.' To which Diocles responds, 'Yes, I can feel it' (*EE* 2.79; *OP* 438). See also Alexis' comment on the golden age: 'I believe it in a certain way, but [a way] which is difficult to express' (*EE* 2.138; *OP* 618).

or Olympus (*EE* 2.92; *OP* 476). It seems plausible to conclude, then, that *Aristée*'s account of sentimental certainty provides one of the philosophical grounds motivating Hemsterhuis' poetic turn at this period; it constitutes one reason why he foregrounds mythic form in his last dialogues, despite the aversion to this mode of presentation expressed in his 1775 letters to Gallitzin on philosophical style. According to *Aristée*, mythic forms communicate the uncommunicable: they present non-discursive conviction in discourse. These kinds of poetic indirection make manifest the sentimental certainty that acts as 'the unique ground' of all geometrical reasoning (*EE* 2.92; *OP* 478) but never appears in it. Myth gets at what lies beneath philosophy as its source and principle.

The background to *Aristée*'s turn to sentimental conviction both as the ground and as an alternative to geometrical conviction is once again to be located in Hemsterhuis' critique of systematisation. One of the central concerns of his early writings is the problem of intermediary links, which, in his view, plague syllogistic reasoning: the further one passes by way of mediation from an original, self-evident axiom, the weaker the certainty that attaches to the conclusion. As Novalis summarises in his *Hemsterhuis-Studien*, 'Certainty is always in inverse proportion to distance from the *first* axiom' (1960–2006: 2.364). Or, as Hemsterhuis himself puts it in *Sophyle*: when compelled to proceed by way of intermediary links, 'the mind is astonished, stunned by the immense space between two things . . . [and] tries to vanquish the force of these mediations' (*EE* 2.56; *OP* 368–70). Mediation stupefies the mind and so hinders the pursuit of the truth. In a clarification to the *Lettre sur l'Homme*, Hemsterhuis uses the example of a triangle: the mind proceeds from the axiomatic truth that the angles on either side of two perpendicularly intersecting straight lines are right angles – by means of a series of other derived truths – to a more complex truth, such as Pythagoras' Theorem. He comments, 'By several operations of my reason I came to the truth that the square of the hypotenuse is equal to the other two squares. But being unable to link together in a single instant all of the truths through which I passed to reach it, it is far from the case that my conviction is as great as that I had of the primary simple truths I started with' (*EE* 1.128; *OP* 305–7). To reason syllogistically is to reason in a way that loses certainty: one's conviction deteriorates the further one strays from an axiom.

As the above suggests, Hemsterhuis locates the solution to this problem of diminishing certainty in simultaneity: the only way to overcome the weakness of discursive reasoning is to 'to link together in one instant all the truths I have passed to reach [the conclusion]' (*EE* 1.128; *OP* 305). That is, only the total intuition of all truths at the same time – divine intuition – would guarantee absolute conviction. A traditional distinction lurks in the background between, on the one hand, divine intuition, which simultaneously presents the axioms, conclusions and all intermediary steps, and, on the other, human reasoning, for which every step in a chain of demonstration is distanced from the others in space and time. The divine ideal of total intuition underlies the early Hemsterhuis' vision of science: 'The totality of knowledge, or science in general, is therefore composed of the sum of acquired ideas and of ideas by relation. ... If a man had the ideas of all the relations and all the combinations of these objects, he would resemble God ... and his science would be perfect' (*EE* 1.122; *OP* 288; see §19).[10]

In *Aristée*, it is this very position that has been radicalised: discursive knowledge – even if it were perfect – is necessarily insufficient, for there is still another kind of certainty which gets at the very ground of all reasoning. A supplement is required and this supplement is *a feeling*; it is sentimental certainty.[11] Such a line of thinking is crystallised in a series of letters from 1786: again, Hemsterhuis speaks of 'two species of characteristics for degrees of certainty' and specifies that the 'first' and most important (where 'knowledge = ∞') is articulated by the 'formula': 'In ourselves, *knowledge is feeling, is intimate, perfect conviction*' (B 7.65, 178). This first species of certainty is further determined as 'a present, current and intimate sensation' which constitutes the 'basis' of 'the most perfect knowledge' (B 7.62, 168). In fact, Hemsterhuis stresses in the same letter: 'This species of certainty is as much above intellectual knowledge as knowledge is above belief' and is a 'sacred principle which is divine like great poetry' (B 7.62, 168–9). A few years earlier, Hemsterhuis had given an example of the role this 'species of certainty' plays in rational inquiry. He writes,

> Do you already know the truth that you are looking for? – No, of course, except in the case where I have perfect certainty of the truth by way of tact or sentiment, but still want to have a certainty by way of the intellect. ... If it is a matter of certainty by way of intellect, then we are the masters

[10] Gallitzin inherits this ideal: successive reasoning must be transformed 'into one intuition' that produces a 'living, intuitive, rich conviction [which] differs from even the most perfect convictions that our intellect is obliged to generate successfully from one proposition to another' (quoted in Brachin 1952: 143). Brachin himself comments that this claim is 'completely in the spirit of Hemsterhuis' (Brachin 1952: 143).

[11] Hartmann dubs it a 'knowing feeling' (1923: 168) and again Rousseau's Savoyard Vicar serves as a model with his insistence that 'one may very well argue with me about this, but I sense it, and this sentiment that speaks to me is stronger than the reason combatting it' (1991: 280).

of this inquiry. We are not masters of the other certainty, since it derives necessarily from the nature of things. (B 4.77, 202–3)

The point is that sentimental certainty – which, for the late Hemsterhuis, is presupposed by all scientific inquiry – is not something to be discovered through deduction or inference; it stands outside of the inquirer's control and, when present, motivates and orients all thinking, like an inspiration.

Sentimental certainty acts as criterion and standard against which to interrogate the discursive presentation of philosophy. Those philosophers who fail to present this ground through aesthetic devices and those philosophers who diminish the geometrical certainty of an axiom through the excessive use of intermediary, syllogistic propositions are both open to criticism. And *systems* exemplify both of these failings. The system is that form of knowing in which both kinds of certainty – sentimental and geometrical – are dulled by the drive to an architectonic structure; a discursive leviathan is created at the expense of the very conditions of truth. Hemsterhuis writes in this vein in *Aristée* itself:

> [Men] have perfected their intellectual faculties and their internal sentiment has lost its vivacity. The secure and geometrical progress of the intellect has led to the determinate and precise certainty that results from it being preferred over that of sentiment, which is of infinite simplicity and hence vague and indeterminate in appearance. (*EE* 2.92; *OP* 478; see also B 4.78, 206)

The above is a very different Hemsterhuis from the one treated in §6. The 'secure and geometrical progress of the intellect' is no longer celebrated as the means to good philosophy, but is in fact an obstacle that sometimes hinders perfect certainty. Analysis obfuscates rather than reveals – and its unfettered usage in modern philosophy has weakened any claim to secure intellectual foundations because it has, at bottom, completely failed to acknowledge precisely what it is that makes these foundations so secure: *sentiment*. The predominance of analysis has problematically led to a gradual accumulation of syllogistic demonstrations that have ultimately covered over their foundations. What has been excluded, according to *Aristée* – what good philosophy requires – is a form of presentation that instead manages to disclose and acknowledge the sentimental source of truth, and this can be achieved only by a turn away from systematic presentation, to myth and imagery.

3. The above interpretation of the late Hemsterhuis' turn to the poetic was first developed in Hammacher's 1971 *Unmittelbarkeit und Kritik bei Hemsterhuis*. For Hammacher, this turn is the result of a new valorisation of sentimental forms of thinking – an 'emancipation of feeling' (1971: 23), in which it is no longer epistemically subordinate to syllogism, but gains autonomy as its own distinct form of certainty. Hence, Hammacher speaks of a 'new experience of certainty' in *Aristée* (1971: 61; see also Dierik 1997: 250) and 'a quite new valuation of feeling and its significance for philosophical cognition' (1971: 21). That is, Hammacher takes seriously Hemsterhuis' insistence on the equality between sentimental and geometrical certainty (1971: 23).

It is important to stress that, while Hammacher may at first blush appear to be perpetuating an irrationalist image of Hemsterhuis, his account of Hemsterhuisian 'feeling' is informed by early eighteenth-century debates over 'moral certainty' in the Dutch Newtonian tradition. Whereas Bulle, for instance, might speak of sentiment in *Aristée* as 'an irrational faculty which precedes all logic' (1911: 78), for Hammacher it is instead a kind of moral evidence. While the emancipation of feeling might be 'something new' in mid-eighteenth-century philosophy (1971: 123), its roots are to be located (as briefly mentioned above) variously in the work of the Royal Society, the Dutch Newtonians and even late Cartesians.

Key to my purposes is the fact that, according to Hammacher, this emancipation of feeling in *Aristée* immediately gives rise to a 'renewed question of method' (1971: 24) – that is, it gives rise to the question: what method can do justice to the certainty provided by feeling *as well as* that provided by geometrical thought? Hammacher writes, 'The discovery of "experience" and "feeling" as distinct orders of reflection poses the question of method anew for philosophy' (1971: 118), and specifically it motivates the incorporation of 'aesthetic forms of experience into philosophical argumentation' (1971: 8). The turn to the aesthetic is intended, he continues, to solve 'the fundamental tension between critique and life' (1971: 24), between the analytic, on the one hand, and the sentimental, on the other. The late Hemsterhuis' task is to present philosophy as both aesthetic and analytic at the same time.

Hence, for Hammacher's Hemsterhuis, 'conceptual determination is no longer enough' (1971: 118–19). What is required, instead, are 'arguments which demand a specific artistic method for achieving what merely scientifically-ordered arguments cannot' (1971: 7). Hemsterhuis thus makes use of a 'moral-aesthetic sensibility' that is able to 'hold onto intuitive certainty throughout the whole demonstration' (1971: 120). While syllogistic certainty gradually deteriorates as the argument of the text proceeds, the use of aesthetic devices, he argues, continuously manifests a feeling of certainty to the reader. This is why, he concludes, the late Hemsterhuis resorts to 'specific artistic methods which a purely scientific form of argument does not achieve' (1971: 7) – and myth, in particular, becomes 'the strongest means of producing that unifying, perfect inner conviction' (1971: 123). Hammacher goes on to claim that this strategy is most effective in Hemsterhuis' *Simon*: in this text, 'both aspects of thought, the aesthetic and logical, are juxtaposed without mixing' (1971: 162) and thus the dialogue stands as 'a successful example of his philosophical project. . . . Individual experience binds together logical thinking and certainty in "enthusiasm"' (1971: 165).

There is much in Hammacher's interpretation that is worth salvaging and the following sections will rely on it at many points. Nevertheless, his abstract and breezy appeal to the possibility of 'both . . . logical and aesthetic' modes of philosophical presentation seems relatively superficial. That is, it fails in particular to show precisely *how* Hemsterhuis' dialogues do actually meet these two competing demands consistently. And this is what I am interested in in what follows: how the very details of Hemsterhuis' text contribute to his strategy of philosophical communication. In other words, it will become necessary to go beyond Hammacher in describing the concrete strategies Hemsterhuis deploys to meet the conflicting demands entangled at the core of his project.

§8 The Platonic Sublime

Prior to *Alexis*, Hemsterhuis banishes poetry from philosophy while still incorporating poetry into his philosophical practice. In these earlier texts, he seems caught up in a compulsive cycle of writing out a Platonic gesture: just as Plato expelled poets from his republic without being able to banish them from the *Republic*, so too for the pre-*Alexis* Hemsterhuis in the mid-1770s. His is an ancient quarrel reimagined through a post-Newtonian lens. Plato is therefore once more the model: just as in §5 he represented a model for untimely philosophy – a philosophy which occurs belatedly in Socrates' absence and, as a result, attempts to reconcile the demands of the past and the present – so too he is the model for a philosophy struggling with the value of poetic, mythic and figurative devices. It is no shock, then, that Plato's name is so glaringly absent from Hemsterhuis' 1775 letters to Gallitzin on philosophical style, for he fits neatly into neither the group of sober analysts nor the group of poet-philosophers. Plato becomes Hemsterhuis' model because

§8 THE PLATONIC SUBLIME

he *mixes* styles: his philosophical communication is resolutely hybrid and eclectic, combining analysis with myth, dialogue, irony and narrative. The Platonic corpus is, for Hemsterhuis, the site 'where great philosophy and great poetry merge, fortify each other, decorate and ennoble each other mutually' (B 3.56, 140); and, at the end of his life, it is for that reason that Hemsterhuis explicitly defines his project as doing 'the impossible' – implementing 'a Plato in the modern idiom' (B 10.18, 40).

Reference to Hemsterhuis' imitation of Platonic style thus helps specify his response to the dual demands of the analytic and the poetic. And his most sustained reflection on the virtues of Platonic style occur in the following letter to Gallitzin, from 1786:

> In leafing through my Plato and his imitator [Cicero], I have thought about their style. . . . Great philosophy needed to be treated very differently in Plato's time than in our day. The quantity of signs (the primitive [ones], so to speak) from which we draw the exact sciences – that have since been so prodigiously perfected – gives us a precision of expression [the Greeks] did not then have. The Greeks had the advantage of using a language wholly admirable for infinitely modifying their mediocre quantity of primitive signs, but this does not help at all with the clarity of serious demonstrations. If Plato, even with all the knowledge he had of the mechanism of his language and even with his precious gift for word-choice, had written his profound philosophy the way most ancient philosophers did, the dryness and obscurity of his book would have made it forgotten for centuries. [But] Plato, son of Apollo, born poet in the supreme degree, filled his works with the most sublime poetic ideas. I think that Cicero, his imitator and copyist (as much as he could be), is mistaken in regard to Plato's stylistic aims, and he thought that this great man had mixed his divine poetry with philosophy only to embellish the material and show off his talent. . . .
>
> I think that Plato [actually] reasoned a bit like this: I must give men certainty of the most profound truths. The only means I possess is demonstration. Demonstration speaks only to the intellect, and, to the extent that these truths are abstract and profound, this intellect functions at capacity and is easily tired. The conviction which results from [such truths] has for its basis solely the retrograde progress of the intellect across truths by which I have already led it: a painful progress which demands time and the continual stimulation of attention. All intimate conviction is an absolutely simple sentiment, and since intellect – whatever rapidity it has gained through long practice – works by *succession*, it is evident

that certainty, simple sentiment, cannot pertain to the mechanism of the intellect. Therefore, this sentiment pertains to the moral. Thus, in wanting to give men certainty, I must add into the dry language of demonstration, which occupies solely the intellect, another language which pertains continually to the lively and active moral organ, so that it is, at every instant, open and ready to receive that sentiment of certainty each time the intellect has finished its job and ends its laborious regressive progress with which it is never perfectly satisfied.

I do not dare insist that Plato thought just like this, but it must have been something like this, and if ever the Parcae [Fates] oblige me again to undertake philosophy, I will eat myrtle like Matris of Thebes, so as to always have some hymn in the text to accompany the monotonous accents of geometry, to continually excite the moral and thereby to facilitate the entrance of conviction. (B 7.85, 234–6)

1. It is worth beginning by extracting a few of the key claims from this passage:

- a. A distinctive property of the ancient Greek language determines the way Greek philosophy was written: it possessed a small number of primitive signs (or distinct linguistic roots) which it 'infinitely modif[ied]' in order to generate truths, and this distinguishes it from modern philosophy, which has expanded prodigiously the number of primitive signs in use (to avoid this repetition of the same words in slightly modified form). Indeed, Hemsterhuis continues that, in order to be clear and precise, ancient philosophers were forced to make excessive use of repetition with modification, which led to 'dryness and obscurity' in their philosophies and so rendered them inaccessible.
- b. Next follows a critique of Cicero's interpretation of Platonic style: Hemsterhuis agrees with Cicero that Plato mixed 'divine poetry with philosophy', but he disagrees that this was undertaken 'only to embellish the material and show off his talent' (in line with 'the neutralist model' mentioned in §2). Plato was, in fact, intent on something more, and to write off his distinctive mode of philosophical presentation as mere ornament is to miss its substantive, even constitutive role.[12]

[12] Indeed, Hemsterhuis hardly ever mentions Cicero's name without criticising him. He may be a useful source of information about ancient philosophy, but he is a bad phi-

c. Hemsterhuis goes on to identify Plato's deployment of a 'poetic' style as ethically motivated: he makes use of poetic devices in order to communicate 'intimate certainty [as] an absolutely simple sentiment'. And syllogistic demonstration cannot accomplish this, because it is always composite, it always takes time and requires continual, error-strewn effort. Hence, 'simple sentiment' 'cannot pertain to the mechanism of the intellect': it cannot be articulated through logic, through 'the dry language of demonstration'. Rather, philosophy has need of 'another language which pertains continually to the lively and active moral organ' that eschews rationalist logic for another mode of presentation.

d. Finally, despite beginning the letter by distinguishing between modern and ancient modes of presentation, Hemsterhuis ends by enthusiastically endorsing Plato's poetic style as an important form of philosophical communication for him to emulate in the eighteenth century. Hymns should accompany 'the monotonous accents of geometry', so as to communicate sentiment, alongside geometrical truth. This is, indeed, a succinct statement of Hemsterhuis' twofold imperative: both geometry and poetry, both logical demonstration and sentimental hymns.

These points are once more emphasised in a subsequent letter to Gallitzin:

> What I really wanted to say in my penultimate letter on the subject of Plato's style is [a] that purely intellectual conviction is not absolutely perfect and that it consists only in the infinitely rapid successive contemplation of the path taken from an axiom to the perfect truth it discovers; [b] that the moral organ must be mixed in and the truths which are reached through demonstration must be united fully through that [moral] organ; [c] that a truth – even a geometric truth and no matter whether it is uninteresting or arid – affects the moral and, for an attentive soul, causes it the same kind of disturbance or stirring as one experiences in completely pure moral affections; [d] that therefore, during the demonstration of a truth, one must try to hold the moral organ spellbound so as to facilitate that concentration which constitutes absolute perfect certainty; and finally [e] that it does not seem to me impossible to so clothe a purely geometric demonstration such that, at the end of the dry and insipid operations of the intellect, the moral organ is affected in a way that our entire

losopher: 'He loves philosophy with fury, without having philosophical genius' (B 4.4, 21). *De Natura Deorum*, for instance, is 'admirable as a piece of literature and history of philosophy, but pitiable as a philosophical piece' (B 2.49, 125).

body gets goosepimples. You would be cruel, my Diotima, if you tried to impose on me the task of accommodating all of Euclid to this taste, such that for each demonstration the victorious letters Q.E.D. were bathed in tears of tenderness. This would be too demanding, but you agree, I hope, that, in all philosophy, to succeed one must speak as much to sentiment as to reason. (B 7.87, 239–40)

The key idea is the same: the requirement to devise a form of philosophical communication which speaks 'as much to sentiment as to reason', which meets the twofold demand of Hemsterhuisian philosophising – imitating Plato by writing geometrical demonstrations 'bathed in tears of tenderness'.

Hemsterhuis' argument in the above repeats much of the thinking presented in the previous section: reasoning by way of intellect falls short of the certainty of an immediate, simultaneous intuition of coexisting ideas. Discursive reasoning 'is not absolutely perfect', for it remains successive; even at its best, it is still 'only the infinitely rapid successive contemplation' of different ideas, rather than their simultaneous coexistence before the mind's eye. Hence, one of the virtues of sentimental apprehension is, according to Hemsterhuis, that – in its absolute simplicity – it approximates to a divine intuition, in which the whole is grasped all at once. And this is one reason behind Hemsterhuis' admiration for Platonic style: it manages to imitate the timelessness of sentimental apprehension in time; it manages to communicate a simultaneous coexistence of ideas by way of the apprehension of a succession of words. Hemsterhuis' Plato so arranges his texts that discursive succession points beyond itself (thereby negating itself) to hint at an eternity that is not itself presented but is intimated – 'a moving image of eternity' (1962: 37d).

And the term by which Hemsterhuis designates this formal quality of Platonic style is *the sublime* (e.g., B 4.97, 253). From Longinus he appropriates the idea that a sublime whole cannot be assembled cumulatively out of parts; it is something immediate, simultaneous and unanalysable. The sublime captures a oneness that cannot be divided, analysed or torn apart, a oneness that is incommensurable with the synthesis of the many – or, in Hemsterhuis' own words, 'the sublime as such' is the tendency 'to reach this sacred *One*' (B 8.15, 49).[13]

Plato is the most exemplary exponent of this oneness in philosophy. 'On reading the *Phaedrus*', for instance, Hemsterhuis develops a theory of the 'moral sublime' or 'the sublime of Plato's poetry', in which

[13] On Hemsterhuis' theory of the sublime, see Cahen-Maurel (2017: 264–6).

the sublime resides in the intrinsic energy of the soul or the moral. I have named it elsewhere a vague effort, an enthusiasm, or perhaps really a divine breath: a real effect of divine omnipresence. ... Neither this energy nor its object or its nourishment is expressible or representable by any of our actual signs. If a soul is gifted with such energy, put into activity or movement by either intrinsic effort or the presence of a Divinity, it has the faculty of electricizing or animating homogenous souls such that there results an activity or movement similar or homologous to its own movement. But this soul, to effectuate this operation on what is homogenous, has necessarily a need for figures, signs, gestures, words, sounds, adapted more or less to this strange operation. (B 7.92, 247–8)

He goes on to identify concrete examples of this 'moral sublime' in the *Phaedrus*' 'admirable dialogue', 'divine poetry of moral tact' and 'fine metaphors'. And this species of sublime, he adds, is to be distinguished from 'the intellectual sublime' insofar as it does not communicate anything 'determinate and expressible', but manages to communicate something seemingly incommunicable – sentimental conviction (B 7.92, 247–8). This is an energetic sublime, residing in 'the intrinsic energy of the soul' (or 'the sublime energy of the soul' [B 1.45, 82]) to express its own essence; the communication occurs indirectly by 'electricizing or animating' the same movement and the same energy in the soul to which it communicates.[14] The contents of the written words matter relatively little compared with the energy and electricity transmitted. Indeed, a violence is done to language in the moral sublime: the author must contort and mould 'figures, signs, gestures, words, sounds', so that they become 'adapted more or less to this strange operation'.[15] Language is twisted, so that it is no longer solely a conveyor of intellectual meaning, but also of essential energy from one soul to another (and this brings us back to the concepts of linguistic 'tone' and 'spirit' discussed in §3 and §5).

---

[14] Gallitzin takes up this language of 'electricizable souls' at length in her response to this letter as a way to identify those subjects susceptible to the sublime (2015–17: 3.189).

[15] Grucker conjectures, for example, that the syllogistic arguments found in *Sophyle* are meant to persuade the reader of the immortality of the soul precisely by means of this immediate sublime energy: 'These proofs have neither the precision, nor the rigour, nor the scientific authority of metaphysical proofs. But, on the contrary, they have the power of immediate persuasion, that communicative power that belongs only to sentiment'. They are 'the proofs of Plato and Descartes transposed from reason into sentiment' (1866: 224).

2. The Platonic sublime names a communicative strategy that operates by way of an energetic tone in language – an effect created through the twisting of words. Plato's own writing strategies of nested narratives, dialogue, myth and irony are not merely noted by Hemsterhuis as attempts to achieve such an effect, they are repurposed and reperformed in his own texts – in his 'masterful imitation of Platonic garb' (Hammacher 2008: 592) – so as to achieve the same effect for an eighteenth-century reader. And yet, Hemsterhuis' imitation of the Platonic model goes far beyond merely the attempted production of an energetic tone; there are many further effects that result from it. For example:

(a) Sociability
Lucian, Fontenelle, Fenelon, Diderot and others may well be sources for Hemsterhuis' turn to dialogue, but it is Plato above all who motivates it. Plato remains the essential reference point. *Simon*, in particular, 'is an explicit *emulatio* of the Platonic *Symposium*' (Fresco 1991: 78): the dialogue imitates Plato's text by beginning belatedly with a character called Hipponicus, who has been away from Athens on an expedition, calling on Simon to recall an occasion at which Socrates, Cebes, Agathon, Mnesarchus and Arisophanes were in discussion at Simon's shop.[16] Nested layers of discourse keep on proliferating, just as in the *Symposium* itself.

In §2, I detailed at length the role that Hemsterhuis' friendship with

[16] Nevertheless, despite mimicking Platonic structures, Hemsterhuis' stress on Simon, whose role in the dissemination of Socratic thought is documented by Xenophon and Diogenes Laertius, and who – whether or not he really existed (Hösle 2006: 79) – is famed to be the earliest disciple to record Socratic conversation in writing, suggests a gesture to reach beyond Plato to a more original, pristine source of Socratism, perhaps anticipating Bakhtin's anxiety that in Plato's dialogues (as opposed to earlier variants of Socratic dialogue) 'the monologism of the content begins to destroy the form of the Socratic dialogue' (1984: 110). Hemsterhuis' choice of Simon to be the eponymous character of a dialogue is, moreover, no coincidence, for, as Sellars points out, Simon 'came to be associated with a certain way of life, a specifically philosophical way of life. . . . Simon's way of life was considered to be exemplary of what it meant to be a follower of Socrates' (2003: 209). Hence, for example, Plutarch's maxim, 'Let me become Simon the Shoemaker so that I might converse with philosophers such as Socrates' (quoted in Sellars 2003: 210). In particular, Simon exemplified a form of independence (he rejected Pericles advances, as Hemsterhuis notes) that was also a model for philosophical intersubjectivity – thereby approximating to both Hemsterhuis' restoration of a primitive Socratic sociability (see §22) but also his celebration of freedom from institutional authority (as in his claim to be 'born Greek'). Simon is Hemsterhuisian in his 'independent life . . . engaging in private conversation with . . . barefoot philosophers' (2003: 214).

Gallitzin has typically been seen to play in the genesis of his late style. It is bound up with an increasing emphasis on the value of conversation and collaboration in the philosophical enterprise to the extent that, during the 1780s, Hemsterhuis will customarily speak of his publications as articulations of 'our philosophy', that is, as products of collaborative dialogue. And beneath this presumably lies a more general conviction that truth is dialogic – that, paraphrasing the *Theaetetus*, thinking is not primarily a talk which the soul has with itself, but rather a talk between kindred souls. Something of Bakhtin's characterisation of the 'Socratic notion of the dialogic nature of truth' is evident here: in opposition to systems of 'official monologism' with their 'ready-made truths' and 'naïve self-confidence' stands an intersubjective model for truth as 'born *between people* collectively searching for the truth' (1984: 110).[17]

In short, Hemsterhuis' turn to dialogue foregrounds a sociable component to philosophising. In the words of Lacoue-Labarthe and Nancy, in the eighteenth century, 'thought was placed into dialogue just like one dresses in court attire' (1975: 152). The dialogue performed a sociality of thought that is obscured in more monological genres: it maintained 'intimate relations ... with the social spirit' (1975: 152). Hemsterhuis' ideal is, as Hösle puts it (2006: 59), 'a conversational event', a piece of philosophical writing in which social and communal relationships are enacted before and with the reader.

(b) Pedagogy
In 1779, reflecting on the successes and failures of *Sophyle* as a philosophical manifesto ('the ABC of all Orthodox philosophy' [B 10.2, 15]), Hemsterhuis began to think about presenting its contents in a way that genuinely represented its core message of a philosophy of common sense, one that speaks to the uncorrupted heart, to children and to innate virtue. Philosophy, he now suggests, is in need of a catechism, a set of model questions and answers to educate non-philosophers in the concepts and methods required for attaining truths autonomously. He goes on to begin writing such a catechism for Gallitzin's children – one which will 'facilitate in the child that initial and simple operation of the intellect by which he acquires the intellectual conviction of a cause ... develop in him natural sentiments ... make him understand what this powerful thing or divinity is', and so on

---

[17] To put it another way: Hemsterhuis is one of those who insist on writing 'dialogues in the age of systems' (Duflo 2003: 42). He uses the dialogue to bolster his critique of systematisation that has been a theme in the previous sections of this book.

(B 2.29, 52).[18] And, what is more, this catechistic project was itself based on Socratic method; as Hemsterhuis puts it, 'All conclusions and all truths in the Catechism must be the natural and direct utterance of the intellect or rather, the conviction of the child himself, and for this one must have fully studied the Socratic doctrine of reminiscence that one finds in the *Phaedo*' (B 2.49, 125).

Furthermore, this abandoned experiment with catechistic form is merely the culmination of a long-standing tendency in Hemsterhuis' philosophy *to educate*. His philosophical impulse is pedagogical through and through (see §12). And this impulse is not only manifest in the early didactic letters to de Smeth and Fagel, instructing them of the dangers of Spinozism or tutoring them in good governance; but it also orients the later dialogues too. And this, of course, chimes with one of the reasons often given for Plato's own use of myth, dialogue and the figurative, that is, as pedagogical tools. Just as Hammacher identifies Hemsterhuis' 'central aim' as 'attempting to unite didacticism with philosophy by way of pictorial modes of representation' (1995a: 72–3), so too Partenie, for example, speaks of myth as 'part of Plato's complex strategy of writing aimed at luring the less philosophically inclined audience into his philosophical territory' (2009: 10).[19] The idea of making philosophy popular informs Hemsterhuis' affirmation that 'I love the simple style' (B 11.79, 84), or, as he more fully puts it,

> God willing, great philosophy may become useful and popular once more, that it quits the impertinent morgue of the peripatetics, the pedantic tone of the Ciceros and the La Rochefoucaulds, this dry air of arithmetic that hypochondriac mathematicians have given it, and that it destroys that risible phantom which carries its name and which is used by all the small teachers to ennoble their profound ignorance and their perfect nullity. (B 4.93, 244–5)

Elsewhere, Hemsterhuis is even more explicit: 'Dialogue is the true didactic genre' (B 4.93, 245); its function is to 'becalm ordinary souls, so that their weak and dulled moral organ awakens' (B 1.26, 61). The imperative first

---

[18] On Hemsterhuis' progress with the catechism, see B 2.46, 109, as well as more generally Brummel (1925: 206–7).

[19] This is of course a dialogic impulse not limited to Plato and Hemsterhuis – see, for example, Berkeley's intimation that dialogue is 'a method for rendering the sciences more easy, useful and compendious', as the full title to his *Three Dialogues between Hylas and Philonous* states (see Hirzel 1895: 2.404–5).

articulated in the *Lettre sur l'Homme* holds here: 'to make philosophical truths so palpable and so popular that the [materialists'] miserable sophisms ... no longer persuade even children. (*EE* 1.121; *OP* 286). Whatever else they are intended to achieve, the pleasing ornaments of Hemsterhuis' late myths, staged conversations, ironies and narratives seem aimed at a readership beyond the schoolmen and professional philosophers of the day.[20]

(c) Irony
And yet, it is important to emphasise that Hemsterhuis' relation to the popular is a complex one. While *Sophyle* and the unfinished catechism that follows may have been written to be accessible to everyone – a kind of 'Introduction to Non-Materialism' – the disappointment which Hemsterhuis subsequently felt at the failure of *Sophyle*'s reception seems to have also driven him in the opposite direction. The ensuing series of dialogues – *Aristée*, *Simon*, *Alexis* – do still use the figurative to access a *different* readership from 'school' philosophy, but not necessarily a wider one. This is evident in their inclusion of obscure philological jokes, of alienating ironies, of antiquarian references – all of which are intended to make sense only to an inner coterie of complicit readers. The later dialogues alienate just as much as they please. After *Sophyle* (and this will become a major theme in what follows), Hemsterhuis writes as an ironist who 'hopes to be understood – but only by people of a certain intelligence, and for that reason ... puts obstacles in the way of comprehensibility that have to be overcome' (Hösle 2006: 374).[21] He positions himself in a bind between the popular and the esoteric (and, in so doing, he emulates Plato once more); he writes for everyone and no one.

Hemsterhuis was, therefore, certainly not averse to the sceptical and ironic uses of Platonic philosophical communication. As Fresco notes (in Hemsterhuis 2007: 224; see also B 2.59. 175–7), he is one of David Hume's only eighteenth-century readers to have discerned the pervasive sceptical

---

[20] Hemsterhuis speaks of *Aristée* thus, 'I do not dare address it to the Professors who I willingly admit as judges. I am afraid that the poor language in which I am accustomed to write, not being quite familiar to them, is not particularly useful or necessary in their country for ornament and the progress of the sciences' (B 12.97, 122).

[21] To this extent, he exemplifies the Kierkegaardian definition of irony as exhibiting 'a certain superiority deriving from not wanting to be understood immediately, even though [he] wants to be understood, with the result that this figure looks down, as it were, on plain and simple talk that everyone can promptly understand' (Kierkegaard 1992: 248). Thus, Friedrich Schlegel will write of Hemsterhuis, 'The most beautiful thing about the beautiful Sanskrit of a Hemsterhuis or Plato is that only those understand it who are supposed to understand it' (1958–2002: 8.60).

irony of the *Dialogues Concerning Natural Religion*, that is, the fact that neither Cleanthes nor Philo is obviously a mouthpiece for Hume's own views, which are instead dissimulated *between* the characters.[22] Or, to put it another way: Hemsterhuis is well aware of dialogue's capacity to screen the authorial voice, to spread the authorial position across characters or even to absent it from the text altogether. Indeed, even when the authorial position is present, it can be made unconvincing or intentionally leave itself open to radical criticism. What the dialogue can stage is 'the dissimulation or dispersion of the author (or the subject of discourse) behind the figures (characters or mouthpieces) of dialogical narration' (Lacoue-Labarthe and Nancy 1975: 87). This type of philosophical play can affect the 'tone' of the text in many different ways: it can lead to an 'atmosphere of joyful relativity' (Bakhtin 1984: 107) or, equally, result in anxiety over 'the repeated failure of philosophical inquiries to be conclusive' (McCabe 2009: 45). In every case, the reader does much of the philosophical work (there is minimal *autoprosopis*). No theses are to be read 'ready-made' off the page; instead, the text demands that the reader take an active part (see §1).[23]

Moenkemeyer, for one, finds evidence of precisely the above practice of dissimulation in *Alexis*: the author uses Hypsicles 'as a mouthpiece' in order to experiment with strange, controversial conjectures, such as the idea of lunar catastrophe: 'Such personae allow the author to speak indirectly and with modesty. Using Hypsicles as a mouthpiece, Hemsterhuis was able to avoid a direct assertion of unusual ideas' (1975: 155). I will argue in the next section that the same is true of Hemsterhuis' use of the character of Diotima in *Simon*. Other examples of Hemsterhuis thinking by indirection abound throughout his late writing – and many of them have been or will be catalogued in these pages: at one end of the scale there is Socrates' avowal in *Simon* of 'premises that Hemsterhuis does not share', which might suggest that 'Hemsterhuis may here be – in a spirit of playful palinody – implicitly retracting his earlier views' (Cirulli 2015: 65; see also Mazzocut-Mis 2005: 228); at the other end there are the elaborate fictive prefaces to *Aristée* and *Simon*.

---

[22] As Hösle puts it: in this respect, 'Hume goes Plato one better' (2006: 112).

[23] And Hemsterhuis himself recognises this quality of eliciting labour from the reader in the Platonic dialogue: 'Bacon does not invite you to read him but forces you to think. Plato is the only mortal who does both to perfection' (B 2.65, 195). This distinction between thinking and reading comes straight out of Montesquieu: 'One must not always so exhaust a subject that one leaves nothing for the reader to do. It is not a question of making him read but of making him think' (1989: 186; see also Melzer 2014: 214).

(d) World-construction

Hemsterhuis' repetition of Platonic poetic devices includes the creation of characters, settings and a whole fictional world in which the philosophical conversation occurs. This has an ethical dimension, in that, in Bakhtin's words, 'the heroes of the dialogue are ideologists' (1984: 111): each character embodies and expresses a certain way of living and a certain type of thinking and the dialogue puts these embodiments of ideas into debate. What counts as philosophical success in this genre is not just cogency of argumentation, but the compelling presentation of the participants' comportment and responses. The emphasis is not only on claims and counter-claims, but the ways in which they express 'a specific attitude, a life-feeling, only against the background of which [these] arguments can be rightly understood' (Hösle 2006: 3).[24] Thinking is existentially grounded and to be interrogated in terms of how it is exemplified in the fictional world of the philosophical text.

And yet such world-construction is ultimately more than a mere ethical drama. Hemsterhuis uses his fictional world not just to test his characters, but also to communicate truths through plots, atmosphere and moods. Philosophy occurs, to quote Bakhtin once more, not just in the syllogism, but also in 'the extraordinary situation' (1984: 111). In Plato, for instance, 'the dramatic byplay at the beginning of a dialogue often creates a mood or atmosphere which suggests the general theme or at least the manner in which it will be approached' (Wolz 1970: 325) – and I will argue in §23, in particular, that the same is likewise true for Hemsterhuis' dialogues. The entire non-conceptual apparatus erected in his late work is intended, in part, to communicate an atmosphere, a background or 'imaginary' to the posited argumentation that does significant philosophical work which the foregrounded argument cannot itself undertake.

Nevertheless, there is one significant difference between the fictional worlds constructed in the ancient Socratic tradition of dialogue and their repetition in Hemsterhuis' writings. In the former, 'their starting point for understanding, evaluating and shaping reality is the living *present*'. They present a situation of ordinary Athenians talking to Socrates. Such philosophy is 'presented not in the absolute past of myth and legend, but on the plane of the present day, in a zone of immediate and even crudely familiar contact with living contemporaries' (Bakhtin 1984: 108). Those dialogues stage 'the speech of everyday life' (Hirzel 1895: 1.247). On the other hand,

---

[24] This is one reason Hemsterhuis prefers the *Symposium* to the *Phaedrus*: more details about the characters are provided to the reader – they protrude from the text as figures who are more alive, more rounded (B 5.2b, 20).

Hemsterhuis' philosophical world is intentionally constructed *as past*: the ordinary Athenians of the Socratic tradition have become legends of a bygone age – quasi-mythic figures drawn out of the lost perihelion of antiquity. Hemsterhuis constructs a world that is precisely not that of the living present, that does not take its cues from contemporary society. Rather, he imagines the atmosphere, the mores and the tone of a different epoch. In other words, the construction of a fictional world is one of the principal means by which he renders his philosophy untimely. This will be central to what follows.

§9 The Myth of Prometheus

To further identify the various formal devices used by the late Hemsterhuis, a case study will hopefully prove helpful. The case study is taken from *Simon* at the moment when it appears to imitate Plato's *Symposium* most closely: Socrates reports a conversation he had in his youth with Diotima that taught him the secrets of philosophy. However, rather than pursuing any theme from the *Symposium*, it is at this point that the text switches sources and what we hear from Diotima is, in fact, a retelling of the Prometheus myth from Plato's *Protagoras*.[25] This myth forms the philosophical climax to the dialogue, 'an inspired flight of speculation' (Moenkemeyer 1975: 143), and it is evidently the juncture in the argument at which the poetic breaks through most intensely. Here, dialogue, myth, imagery, narrative nesting and reported speech come together in one set-piece. What is more, Diotima's speech is also the moment at which a key Hemsterhuisian doctrine is introduced into the dialogue – his history of organs – and what I want to argue in this section, in transition to Part Three of this book, is that it is no coincidence that Hemsterhuis resorts to these poetic devices so openly just when he communicates his organology, for the poetic turn of his later writings is in part motivated by precisely this doctrine.

At this moment, then, Socrates embarks on a reminiscence of an occasion in his youth when he had experienced the allure of a crudely materialist psychology (Democritus is here named as representing the dangers of materi-

---

[25] The switch from the *Symposium* to the *Protagoras* is a significant one, considering the topic of the second half of the dialogue goes on to be the relation between education and virtue; after this passage, *Simon* rehearses the *Protagoras*' guiding question: can virtue be taught? In Plato's text, Protagoras' creation myth serves as justification for the position that 'all men are teachers of virtue, each one according to his ability' (1962: 327e), just as Hemsterhuis' myth is employed to defend the heavily qualified thesis that it is occasionally possible to help the young become more virtuous.

alism). But Diotima intervened to put him back on the right path and teach him the truth about the nature of human organs. He relates her creation myth – what Cahen-Maurel calls a '"psyche-gony" myth' (2022: 37) – as follows:

> Divine Diotima, I said to her, you for whom the future is present, you who have commerce with the Gods, please teach me whether our souls enjoy more organs than those we already know? Thereupon she embraced me tenderly and embarked on this speech which will never be effaced from my memory.
>
> When Jupiter had resolved to give existence to the human race, he himself created the soul of the first man, a pure essence, capable of any kind of possible sensation and capable of any kind of action. The difference between this essence and Jupiter's [essence] is that the latter senses and acts without the use of means by way of divine omnipresence, whereas the former requires means to sense and to act – and these constitute the limits of its nature. Jupiter placed this essence into the hands of Prometheus to finish the work by attaching to it those means to make it effectively living, sensitive and active. As capable of activity, [this essence] derived that indeterminate spring, that force of willpower and power to act when it has the means [to do so] from the God himself; or rather, the faculty that you call velleity adhered to [the first man's] nature. The first thing that Prometheus added to [this essence] was a receptacle for all actions, all sensations, perceptions, or ideas that were to enter it from without and be imprinted upon it; and it is this receptacle that you call imagination. In this imagination – which does not have an essence which you would call visible, audible or tangible – Prometheus made an infinite number of openings or apertures through which actions, perceptions, sensations or ideas of infinitely different kinds were to enter, and for each opening he made a kind of tube which was analogous to the kind of perception or sensation that it was to receive and transmit to the large receptacle. To receive the actions of essences as visible, he made the tube whose end is the organ that we call the eye which is analogous to light – the only vehicle which can communicate the actions of an essence as visible. To receive the actions of essences as audible, he made the tube whose end is the organ that we call the ear, which is analogous to the air – the only vehicle that can communicate the actions of an essence as audible; and so on to infinity. – Wise and sacred Diotima, I said to her, permit me to interrupt you for a moment. You say that this imagination has an infinite number of tubes and ends to receive the different actions

of essences that are outside of it, yet I know only three or four of these organs, [and] they are all material. Whence come those that are not? – My dear Socrates, she said to me, a day will come when you will receive ideas and sensations through all these tubes and ends, and then they will all seem equally material to you, because you call matter all that gives you ideas by means of the organs that you know yourself. But you are now going to ask me why you do not receive perceptions and sensations through these other openings? Remember, Socrates, that the human soul does not enjoy omnipresence like Jupiter's soul does, therefore the actions of external essences on it must be transported by means of some vehicle. The action of a visible essence is communicated by light; that of an audible essence is transported by means of vibrations of the air. Know, Socrates, that the movements of all these vehicles do not have the same velocities. The movement of air is less rapid than that of light, and there are thousands of vehicles whose vibrations have not yet arrived at the tubes that are made to receive them. See this bright star of Orion: if it had left the breast of nature only ten thousand years ago, it would be many centuries more before you could perceive its existence; and suppose that there was nothing visible except the brilliance of Orion, it would be many centuries before you would know that you have this end of perceptibility, this tube you call the eye. (*EE* 2.113–14; *OP* 548–50)

It is worth noting, to begin, that it was this passage more than almost any other in his oeuvre that caused Hemsterhuis the most trouble in drafting: in conversation with Gallitzin (who is herself, of course, Hemsterhuis' own 'Diotima'), he completely rewrote the passage to mitigate a false tone she had discerned (B 2.63, 189). Hemsterhuis pored over the minutiae of this passage to orchestrate the correct effect and communicate the right tone. It is, therefore, a key example of Hemsterhuis' efforts to 'speak Greek' – to make French words communicate an ancient tone despite themselves.

Yet, this is still not to explain *how* the specific words themselves achieve such effects and, in fact, what I want to suggest in what follows is that, once one attends more closely to the specific stylistic choices Hemsterhuis makes in the composition of this passage, a far more radical picture results – one that goes far further than mere imitation of Plato or even generalised fabrication of a Greek tone.

1. To Gallitzin, Hemsterhuis will speak of Diotima's speech in *Simon* as a 'fable' intended to introduce readers to his faculty psychology (B 3.94, 217), to elucidate the nature and function of the intellect, the imagination, the

§9 THE MYTH OF PROMETHEUS

senses and the velleity.[26] Whatever else might be true of it, this passage therefore has a particular didactic purpose – an account of his doctrine of the four mental faculties.

Nevertheless, it is also true that Hemsterhuis has no difficulty elsewhere straightforwardly explaining his entire faculty psychology in a resolutely *non*-mythic mode. For example, in the 1776 *Lettre sur les vertus et les vices*, from which much of the material in *Simon* was drawn, he repeats the whole passage demythologised. He soberly describes the velleity as 'a principle of vague activity which is to be determined by the strongest impulses that come from outside', but which is nevertheless 'not an organ, but pertains to the essence of the soul'; he describes the imagination as 'the receptacle of all ideas which come from outside, that the intellect composes and the velleity acts on'; the intellect as 'the faculty of composing, comparing and decomposing these ideas'; and finally the sense organs are, as in Diotima's speech, conceived as supplementing the simplicity of the soul, for 'since [the soul] cannot be what is outside of it, and, since to act and to enjoy, it has need of various relations with what is outside of it, it is necessary that it possesses means that mediate between it and what is outside of it. . . . All these means, of whatever nature they may be, I call *organs*' (B 1.19, 43–4). Even the more speculative material in Diotima's speech concerning the emergence of unforeseen sense organs is elsewhere described by Hemsterhuis in direct theses shorn of mythic and figurative trappings (as will be shown at length in Part Three). The point is that there is no *necessity* to use poetic devices to communicate this particular doctrine. Much of what Diotima asserts could be essentially paraphrased as follows: we are not at present using all of our capacities, and so, in future, we may be able to employ other organs,

---

[26] The unusual and idiosyncratic term 'velleity' (*velleité*) has regularly confused Hemsterhuis' readers – Diderot, for instance, told Hemsterhuis in no uncertain terms that 'this word will forever scandalise me' (Diderot and Hemsterhuis 1964: 103). It is intended to refer to the essential, indeterminate capacity for willing, i.e., willpower, which the subject possesses prior to any actualisation in concrete and determinate acts of will (for which Hemsterhuis reserves the more typical term '*volonté*'). 'Velleity' bears some resemblance to the pure matter of the *Timaeus*, which Hemsterhuis alludes to in the above passage to the extent that Prometheus acts much like the demiurge of that text. The early pages of *Simon* had been obsessed with the moment when the human is pure velleity, as it were, before Prometheus' intervention – the moment when the subject has yet to be actualised, but exists in a state of total virtuality, much like the 'dreaming spirit' of Kierkegaard's *The Concept of Anxiety*. It is this state that is depicted by Mnesarchus' sculpture which triggers the entire conversation, and it is in this state alone, the characters aver, that the external features of the human subject fully express her internal dispositions.

the capacities of which we at present know nothing. Our sensory apparatus can be ameliorated to enrich our understanding of the world. In short, there are new senses to be discovered that will generate distinctly new types of sensation.[27]

Therefore, what is going on here is not indirect communication in the strict Kierkegaardian sense: Hemsterhuis is not somehow compelled to turn to poetic forms because of the impossibility of coherent direct presentation. There is nothing paradoxical about Diotima's speech (however unpersuasive it may be), and its contents do not fundamentally resist the syllogism or need a mythic, narrative or dialogic supplement to be intelligible. Hemsterhuis does not present the unpresentable in Diotima's speech. Indeed, rather than the form of this passage being *entailed* by some kind of absurdity in its content, it is in fact primarily such a form that makes the content appear so ridiculous. Rather than mitigating, eliding or obscuring any problematic features of Hemsterhuis' doctrine, the mythic presentation *intensifies* them. This matters because Hammacher frames Hemsterhuis' poetic turn in terms of a demand to persuade or convince, but the stylistic choices Hemsterhuis makes in *Simon* seem to make his philosophical doctrine less convincing to readers. To put it bluntly: according to the myth, Prometheus seems to act as a demiurge plumber for the imagination, sawing holes and installing pipes; these tubes criss-cross the body, running from the eyes to the imagination and from the ears to the imagination. What emerges is a crude parody of the fibre physiology of the day. Of course, Hemsterhuis' doctrine shorn of its mythic dressing is already necessarily conjectural: the unprethinkable future emergence of new senses, which perceive what is currently imperceptible, cannot be asserted (since the epistemic tools we currently have at our disposal, e.g., our five senses, cannot provide the right kind of evidence for such claims). Nevertheless, Hemsterhuis' recourse to Greek polytheism, creation myths and immaterial tubes in the mind does nothing to give greater warrant to these conjectures and so persuade his readers of their plausibility. In fact, the reverse is true. *Pace* Hammacher,

---

[27] Similarly, take Nisbet's very sober description of the corresponding doctrine in Lessing's late work: 'The mental capacities of the human race may themselves evolve over time, and human reason is not a static and unchanging entity. . . . Just as our souls at present inhabit bodies equipped with five senses, so they may in former times have possessed fewer senses, just as they may in future acquire additional senses which will allow them to penetrate dimensions of the universe which are at present closed to them. Human knowledge, in other words, is relative to our present psycho-physical constitution, which is not necessarily unalterable' (2005: 144–5). This strikes me as a fairly accurate paraphrase of much of what is doctrinally at stake in Diotima's speech.

what we find in *Simon* are stylistic choices that impact detrimentally on the philosophy's persuasive power.[28]

2. This is precisely where Hemsterhuis goes beyond the Platonic model: Plato's philosophy is at times mythic and comic, but it is rarely ludicrous when it comes to the presentation of key doctrines. Conversely, scattered throughout Hemsterhuis' writing is a decidedly positive appraisal of the ridiculous – or, more specifically, an account of 'gibberish' as constitutive of philosophising.

This is his 'philofolly' (B 6.47, 136). He speaks not only of 'my lyric philosophy' (B 7.16, 50) but also of 'my eternal gibberish' (B 5.18, 77) – continuing elsewhere, 'I do not produce anything but gibberish' (B 5.15. 66).[29] He insists that his late philosophy is nonsense to all but 'perhaps two or three other people' and 'is impossible for me to translate it from now on into ordinary language' (B 10.44, 83). This feature of Hemsterhuis' philosophical self-understanding is evidently far from the popularity and accessibility of *Sophyle* (see §8) and, during the 1780s, Hemsterhuis will continue to speak of his philosophical collaborations with Gallitzin as a kind of private language, incomprehensible to the public. For example, it 'would be true gibberish to any other reader' (B 5.54, 199) and 'there is only you who could understand such gibberish' (B 7.1, 16; see also B 3.43, 109). To put it another way: the late Hemsterhuis sometimes envisages his project as esoteric; that is, the uninitiated cannot access the truths he is insinuating but will instead take his work for nonsense and lunacy. 'My dear Diotima', he writes, 'I dare write this only to you, the only person in the world, for I am certain that if someone else read this strange language, they would surely take me for mad' (B 3.17 57). And this provides one reason for his reluctance to publish at the end of his life: '[I] keep quiet on all these kinds of matters before everyone but you' (B 4.21, 60). At other times, Hemsterhuis considers this gibberish less as motivated by strategic wariness than as the product of 'a mad, childish intellect' and a 'natural monstrosity in the imagination', producing a language for 'our childish philosophy which is not found in books' (B 3.78, 184).[30]

---

[28] Nevertheless, myth does *also* retain a didactic and pedagogic function for Hemsterhuis here and elsewhere. See B 7.53, 152, as well as the educational myth Hemsterhuis penned for Gallitzin's daughter (B 12.99, 126–30).
[29] The term 'gibberish' [*galimatias*] was common in the eighteenth century to designate 'an abstract argument close to lunacy' (Ibrahim 2010: 49).
[30] The ideal of childishness, that is, fostering childish states of consciousness, is a frequent reference point in Hemsterhuis. Moreover, this tendency to childish nonsense

The point is that Hemsterhuis' philosophy revels in gibberish, and this makes it hard to assimilate him straightforwardly into a Platonic tradition of writing practices or even to speak of his poetic turn in terms of conviction and persuasion (as Hammacher does).[31] Something more is going on: he communicates in ways that are not immediately intended to persuade, but (temporarily, at least) are intended to alienate and estrange the reader from philosophical truths. Hammacher's interpretation of Hemsterhuis' poetic turn as a turn to sentimental certainty cannot be the whole story. Whatever is, in fact, going on in the myth of Prometheus, it is not making anything more certain.

Diotima's account of human physiology on the model of a series of tubes is of central importance. It resonates with Diderot's criticism of Hemsterhuis for deploying metaphors that have been pushed too far. According to Diotima, each human sense organ consists of 'openings or apertures', each connected to 'a kind of tube which was analogous to the kind of perception' being sensed. These tubes connect the apertures (the eye, the ear, etc.) with the imagination, 'a receptacle for all actions, all sensations, perceptions, or ideas' – and, through these tubes, 'the actions of essences' are communicated. The imagination itself thus has a 'physical part' (B 7.33, 93) insofar as it receives sense data from the tubes, but also an immaterial 'part' insofar as these perceptions are communicated to the intellect and will. Hemsterhuis describes this process in his correspondence less anachronistically as the way 'the soul gains its ideas and sensations from determinate modifications to its nervous system' (B 6.27, 86), where the nervous system consists of 'the delicate fibres of the sensorium which transmit ideas to our soul' (B 7.33, 93; see also B 3.33, 87–8). The term 'fibre' is presumably the eighteenth-century translation for Diotima's 'tubes': they are Hemsterhuis' preferred term in his correspondence for the organic connecting tissue in the human body (see B 8.3, 20–1). The term is widely used in the *Lettre sur l'Homme* as well:

---

and folly is not just the preserve of his friendship with Gallitzin, but was also a key element of his friendship with Camper (van Sluis 2015: 96).

[31] It is worth emphasising that, while such gibberish marks Hemsterhuis apart from how Plato and Platonists usually write, it does still remain close to elements of Platonic doctrine. Gallitzin (2015–17: 3.185, 3.192–3), in particular, develops a connection between this pursuit of gibberish and the fourth kind of madness of the *Phaedrus* by which the delirious lover of the immaterial (i.e., the philosopher) takes flight towards the immaterial realm. That is, according to Gallitzin, her and Hemsterhuis' 'philofolly' exemplifies the ascent of the philosopher 'into real being' away from 'human interests' – an ascent 'rebuked by the vulgar, who consider [the philosopher] mad and do not know that he is inspired' (Plato 1962: 249b–d).

Hemsterhuis explicitly frames his physiology around a theory of fibres, in which ideas are 'dependent on the movement of the organ's fibres' as well as 'on the movement which these fibres have imprinted upon adjoining fibres' (*EE* 1.93; *OP* 196). Even the brain is made up of fibres (*EE* 1.105; *OP* 236). To put it another way: Diotima's language of 'tubes' is a figurative rendering of the 'special fibre theory' current in eighteenth-century physiology, in which 'there is a fibre corresponding to each sense and appropriate to each kind of sensation' (Bonnet, quoted in Savioz 1948: 199) and 'all the acts of our soul correspond constantly to certain natural or acquired movements and determination of nerve fibres' (Anderson 1982: 20; see Savioz 1948: 195–6).

Versions of fibre theory were widespread at the period, and there is very little that is idiosyncratic about Hemsterhuis' recourse to it in the *Lettre sur l'Homme*: even the ideas that such fibres mediate between the material and the immaterial and that fibres for unknown senses lie dormant within the human nervous system are to be found in contemporary writings from Paris and Geneva. Charles Bonnet is Hemsterhuis' main source, for it was Bonnet who had most notoriously made use of 'special fibre theory' to construct an immaterialist psychology. As Savioz (1948: 36) puts it, 'the "psychology of fibres" begins with Bonnet'. In constructing a fibre psychology, Bonnet was drawing on the well established discourse of fibre physiology, of the kind found in Hemsterhuis' *Lettre sur l'Homme* – its prevalence indexed in Haller's axiom 'The fibre is to physiology what the line is to geometry' (1757: 1.2; see Cooper 2020). From Boerhaave through Diderot and beyond, the fibre was considered 'the basic building block of all organic structures' (Cheung 2010: 78; Ishizuka 2006: 72). Diderot had made substantial use of fibre theory to offer a materialist account of consciousness and Bonnet was responding to precisely these sorts of developments in Parisian materialism when he reappropriated the term 'fibre' for his immaterialism.[32] That is, in the middle of the eighteenth century, there arose an argument over the thesis that 'Humans think through fibres' (Cheung 2010: 68): while Diderot affirmed it without qualification, Bonnet attempted to distinguish the materials and tools of human thinking (which are made up of fibres) from the thinking agent, which is to be exempted from the fibre economy (Cheung 2010: 103).[33] It is with this kind of position Hemsterhuis

---

[32] Such repurposing of materialist tools to attack materialism is a frequent strategy within his philosophy, as I argue in §17.

[33] Bonnet's fibre theory also makes use of a notion of 'tone' or 'energy' which resonates with Hemsterhuis' employment of these concepts: as Cheung puts it, according to

is engaging in *Simon* when he describes his faculty psychology in terms of 'tubes'.

And yet, while he does often take up the fibre physiology of his day without qualm, Hemsterhuis is often extremely wary of its *extension into psychology*. He turns on fibre theorists vehemently in the *Lettre sur l'athéisme* as a post-Newtonian philosophical development equivalent to materialism insofar as it 'renders any principle other than autonomous matter useless and redundant' (*OP* 678). In his correspondence, Hemsterhuis does still speak of fibres in psychology but usually *ironically*: fibres are mentioned archly or, at the very least, non-literally (see, e.g., B 1.19, 45). As Niewöhner points out, the term 'fibre' forms part of his 'metaphorical arsenal', alongside 'the terms blood, nerves . . . vital spirits, brain, organs'; they all 'remained purely allegorical' for Hemsterhuis (1995: 390). And the reason why Hemsterhuis refuses any literal fibre psychology is the spectre of materialism: the further these kinds of concept are extended into psychology, the more human subjectivity becomes explicable in physiological terms. A literal extension of fibre theory pushes the philosopher (Bonnet included) ever further towards a materialism of the thinking subject. Niewöhner thus continues, 'Hemsterhuis chose this figurative style . . . and choose it deliberately, believing himself authorised to employ it without risk of falling into materialism' (1995: 391, 396).[34] And this is ultimately why Hemsterhuis sometimes makes use of fibre physiology as a tool, while also criticising the materialist tendencies of fibre psychology (just as he criticised the materialist tendencies of Bonnet's narratival style – see §6). What I want to suggest, therefore, is that it is precisely this ambivalence to fibre theory that is being played out in Diotima's speech.

Hemsterhuis takes an accepted eighteenth-century theory and dresses it up in the anachronistic language of tubes – a move which (to repeat) appears to somewhat weaken the persuasive power of his faculty psychology by framing it in terms sufficiently crude and naïve to make any fibre theory at all appear faintly ridiculous. This might seem counter-productive, an example of a philosopher presenting his doctrines in a way that visibly problematises them – until one recognises his long-standing wariness about the materialist

---

Bonnet, 'each fibre is a kind of key or hammer destined to produce a certain tone' (2010: 89).

[34] He continues that 'Hemsterhuis was not the only one to take this fictionality seriously' and mentions Bonnet's psychology in this context (1995: 391). I will suggest in §18 that it is, in fact, precisely on this point that Hemsterhuis is (fairly or not) most critical of Bonnet – that is, on Bonnet's failure to explicitly acknowledge the fundamental fictionality of these physiological terms that are being heuristically borrowed for psychology.

danger present in psychological extensions of fibre theory (like Bonnet's). Diotima's speech in *Simon* both presents a faculty psychology and parodies a Bonnetian faculty psychology by way of creation myth. In other words, the position made ridiculous in *Simon*'s Prometheus myth is a materialist exaggeration of Hemsterhuis' faculty psychology: he rehearses in an exaggerated and alienated fashion the manner in which such physiological language has been deployed in psychology, and he does so to mock it. Fibre theory is made ludicrous by becoming tube theory.

3. A clue to what Hemsterhuis is up to in Diotima's speech is provided by a 1787 description to Gallitzin of 'a method which I have long used, but have read about nowhere and ... which I consider as the true key to open the path that leads to what is original ... and sometimes even the true sublime'. In fact, he concludes that this method 'is the best or rather the only way to reach, the original, invention and the new'. Specifically, this method is a kind of *reductio ad ridiculum* which he describes as follows:

> Here, in a few words, is what this method consists in. When an idea occurs to us ... we must, first of all, take this idea and push it as far as it can go and even to the absurd and the extravagant. And, if during this operation of the intellect, we find anything absurd, false or bad, then we must throw away the idea without returning to it. But ordinarily, during this operation and before even reaching the absurd, we will often find either something to embellish, enrich or modify the initial idea or some other ideas that are more fecund or beautiful than the initial one and analogous to it. (B 8.13, 43–4)

The method, then, involves experiments with exaggeration – experiments in making texts ridiculous – in order to thereby squeeze new truths from them. It is a method that is most explicitly employed in *Sophyle* where Hemsterhuis exposes the absurdity of crude materialisms that reduce acts of will to a mechanical operation, concluding, 'It is not me who is being ridiculous, Sophylus, in reflecting thus; it is those who, without reflecting, hold tight to an opinion that destroys itself by its own ridiculousness' (*EE* 2.59; *OP* 380).[35] In the above passage from the correspondence, Hemsterhuis goes even further and suggests a procedure of philosophising by way of caricature. An already acquired idea is taken as far as it will go to test its value, to see

---

[35] A similar example is Hemsterhuis' treatment of 'the reasoning of the fatalist' in the 1776 *Lettre sur le fatalisme* (B 1.8, 26; see also B 9.33, 75–7).

what new ideas might emerge out of this melting pot of exaggeration. To speak of nerve fibres as 'tubes' and of creation as plumbing could well be interpreted along these lines: a process of caricaturing fibre psychology in order to test its real value for philosophy.

It is in this vein, therefore, that the myth of Prometheus should be read as simultaneously (1) a presentation of Hemsterhuis' faculty psychology, (2) an ironic exaggeration of that theory in the language of fibre psychology and (3) a critique of the materialist tendencies inherent in such an exaggeration. He makes his own organology ridiculous in order to purge it of any latent materialism. The reader is meant to recognise that what is being made ridiculous is not the doctrine as such, but any rendering of it as a literal fibre theory.

In conclusion, a number of further comments can be made on the basis of this case study that will orient the transition to Part Three. These are the implications of Hemsterhuis' stylistic choices in *Simon* that are yet to fully make sense in light of the preceding analysis.

1. Diotima's speech (as well as Socrates' questions to her) have a didactic purpose: they are meant to provoke the reader into reflecting on the possibility of new senses to come; however, they also perform the difficulty of coming to know this truth through their dialogic form. Diotima speaks as the authority 'for whom the future is present', but the reader stands in the position of the novice Socrates, for whom the future remains very much the future and, for that reason, inconceivable. The dialogic structure both gives the reader this truth and also, at the same time, withdraws it as something reserved solely for the already initiated. The text performs, in the act of reading, something of the difficulty at stake in the very doctrine itself – the difficulty of knowing anything about a radically different future. All the reader can seemingly do is sit and wait for 'a day [to] come when you will receive ideas and sensations through all these tubes'.
2. These difficulties for the reader are then compounded by the figurative nature of Diotima's mythic language.[36] The faux literalism of the crude language of tubes and openings is intended to alienate the reader, as well as distort and subvert eighteenth-century fibre theory. The myth of Prometheus functions as a reduction to the ridiculous: it both affirms an idea (the advent of new senses) and critiques a dangerous inter-

---

[36] Hemsterhuis dramatises these difficulties: at the end of Socrates' recollection, none of the other participants knows what to make of it; it goes far beyond their comprehension (*EE* 2.121; *OP* 572).

pretation of it (the materialist one). This critique is directed not only against those writers who expound a fibre theory too literally without recognising its materialist implications, but also against Hemsterhuis' own readers who lack the requisite tact and so do not discern their allegorical character.[37] The exaggeration operative in this myth is intended to jolt his readers out of literalism and into a kind of *tactful attentiveness*.

3. The myth imitates both Socrates' speech in the *Symposium* and the creation myth in the *Protagoras*. And just as in the *Symposium* Diotima's speech occurs at the culmination of a series of narrative framings, in *Simon*, too, characters remember a conversation involving Socrates that took place in the recent past and, during that conversation, Socrates himself remembers an earlier conversation with Diotima. Diotima's teachings are accessible only via a twofold act of remembrance: her myth takes place in an archaic past – a past only further thematised by the flagrant anachronisms of the myth itself. Hemsterhuis deliberately presents his doctrine as something ancient relative to the Athenian setting of his dialogue, as something belonging to an age so remote that it is no longer even a rational option for classical Athenians, let alone his late eighteenth-century readership. There is nothing particularly unique, of course, in Hemsterhuis' recourse to Greek myth, but there is something particularly obtrusive – and almost deliberately clumsy – in how excessively archaic it purports to be.

In general, then, two lines of further inquiry emerge out of this case study of the myth of Prometheus. First, there is a need to clarify the relation between Hemsterhuis' doctrine of new organs-to-come and contemporary theories subverted in the myth, particularly those, like Bonnet's and Diderot's, that extend special fibre theory into psychology. Secondly, there is a need to make sense of Hemsterhuis' system of times not only in terms of the relation of the modern to the ancient, but also – and even more pressingly – in relation to both an archaic past that can only be remembered in myth and also an unprethinkable future that furnishes material for conjecture. These two lines of inquiry determine the contents of Parts Three and Four of this book respectively.

[37] And Diotima herself is perhaps to be included among such problematic readers; indeed, Hemsterhuis implies as much when he prefaces Diotima's speech as follows: 'If you find fault with it, or if you perceive some obscurities, it would be for Diotima to clarify and to answer you, not me' (*EE* 2.112; *OP* 542). I return to this point in the Conclusion.

Part Three

A History of Organs

In one of the more provocative judgements on Hemsterhuis in recent years, Wiep van Bunge writes that 'in general, Hemsterhuis' attitude to contemporary philosophers is pretty baffling', that his oeuvre 'reveals a stunning complacency toward such crucial eighteenth-century authors as Locke, Hume, Voltaire, Diderot and a host of others' and that, with the exception of Rousseau, Hemsterhuis manifests a complete 'lack of interest in seventeenth- and eighteenth-century philosophy' (2018: 174, 176). Van Bunge is right, of course, that Rousseau is one of the most significant, if silent presences in Hemsterhuis' publications: the dialogues can be read as a response to the *Discours sur les sciences et les arts*, and *Alexis*, in particular, is – I will go on to argue – Hemsterhuis' final reckoning with Rousseau's narrative of human history in the *Discours sur l'origine et les fondements de l'inégalité parmi les hommes*.[1] Van Bunge is also right that Hemsterhuis is 'almost secretive about his sources' (2018: 180), that there is little explicit conceptual debate with any post-Newtonian philosophy in the published writings. And this is one of the reasons why Hemsterhuis' intellectual context has traditionally been reduced to the late Dutch Newtonian tradition and the nascent Münster Circle. Nevertheless, I want to contend that such a reduction does miss a number of contemporary debates in which he did intervene; and so, in this part of the book, I want to look beyond these immediate Dutch and German contexts to suggest that Hemsterhuis is a key figure in mid-eighteenth-century discussions of organology prevalent in Paris and Geneva.[2] And this

---

[1] Nevertheless, even Rousseau's influence on Hemsterhuis has often been contested. Fresco (in Hemsterhuis 2007: 228), for instance, suggests that, 'although Rousseau's ideas must have been important to Hemsterhuis, one finds scarcely any mention of him in the letters'.
[2] Lützeler (1925: 219) helpfully speaks of Hemsterhuis' 'organological vision'.

entails focusing, in Chapter Four, on Hemsterhuis' long-running conversations with Charles Bonnet and Denis Diderot.

Hemsterhuis might be more influenced by other eighteenth-century thinkers ('s Gravesande, Caylus, even Montesquieu) and he certainly does not think of Bonnet and Diderot as his 'teachers and masters', as he does Socrates and Newton; yet the imprint of their thinking is discernible in the Hemsterhuisian corpus, and my conjecture is that Hemsterhuis' history of organs – the spine of his philosophical project – is best understood precisely as a response to Bonnet's and Diderot's own organologies. Hemsterhuis came to know of Diderot's mathematical works as early as 1754 (see Petry 1985: 219, Hammacher 1971: 48) and he continued to esteem Diderot, particularly as a dramatist (e.g., B 1.124, 158, 5.96, 294). After the two met in 1773, Hemsterhuis condemns him as a materialist, but he also repeatedly qualifies this condemnation by separating Diderot out from the common run of Parisian materialists (La Mettrie, d'Holbach, etc.): 'I do not say all this to denigrate Diderot. ... He was a great spirit ... I heard excellent things and learnt a lot from him' (B 5.13, 60). Hemsterhuis' ambivalence to Bonnet has already been touched on in §6 and §9. He is generally scathing of the 'impudent arrogance' of Bonnet's school, for 'it leads without doubt to the most perfect materialism' (B 3.48, 120), and likewise he criticises the 'jumble of algebra' employed by Bonnet's disciples, which, he writes, 'is destitute of all common sense'. He continues, 'Here is the philosophy of Bonnet, Le Sage, etc. ... They work more for the materialists than the materialists themselves' (B 3.47, 119–20). And yet, Hemsterhuis still speaks of 'the great Bonnet' (B 3.47, 118), of 'the many excellent things' in his books (B 1.3, 18), and asserts that 'Bonnet is one of the most powerful brains that has existed – he has a brain whose intellect can divide and subdivide the smallest ideas with admirable dexterity. He is for ideas what Swammerdam was for insects' (B 1.216, 252). The task of Chapter Four will be to show the ways in which this qualified, contested appreciation of Diderot's and Bonnet's philosophies is cashed out in Hemsterhuis' own organological practice, particularly insofar as it impacts on the problematic of philosophical communication.

Moreover, following Leif Weatherby's recent work,[3] I will also read Diderot's, Bonnet's and, above all, Hemsterhuis' organologies both as affirmations of an ontology of relations and as forms of 'technological metaphysics'

---

[3] Weatherby makes a number of tantalising allusions to Hemsterhuis (2016: 28, 129, 214, 224, 239) and introduces his work briefly in relation to Novalis (2016: 241–2), but is constrained by his focus on German philosophies from exploring his organology fully.

(2016: 46). Organs mediate; they shape (as well as 'receive') the *rapports* out of which experience is constructed. Such a relational ontology was, indeed, one of Hemsterhuis' most influential ideas and Nassar (2013), for instance, reckons it central to his influence on Novalis. However, it is the idea of *organology as technological metaphysics* that constitutes the primary subject matter of what follows. On this point, Weatherby insists, 'Organology . . . was not "organic" in the modern [biological] sense but *technical*, functional – it provided a wide range of tools (methodological, metaphysical, literary, regulatory) to revolutionise and administer the historical and natural world' (2016: 215). And this, he argues, gives rise to 'an entirely new type of speculation' (2016: 225) – that is, doing philosophy in the organological tradition means working on one's organs, rendering them as effective as possible for philosophising. Following Novalis, the task is to generate an 'all-capable organ in philosophy' (1960–2006: 3:385; see Weatherby 2016: 233). For Weatherby, organological thinking therefore puts into practice the idea that the world, the subject and thinking itself are *malleable*: 'Organs of sense are tied to spectra of possible cognition; the sense *as organ* becomes the means to alter the nature of cognition. . . . To potentiate a sense – to make a new field of sense available – is to make a *novum* in the world, to alter or modify the world through the organ' (Weatherby 2016: 235). *Organs give thinking a history* – it is this insight and its implications that I wish to trace in the present part of the book.

My task in the next two chapters is therefore to reconstruct Hemsterhuis' organology as a technological metaphysics (Chapter Three) and to contextualise it in terms of Diderot's and Bonnet's comparable adventures in organology (Chapter Four). And, as will become increasingly apparent, both tasks are undertaken as a response to the overarching problematic of Hemsterhuis' poetic turn, for my implicit conjecture will be that Hemsterhuis stands in relation to the eighteenth-century immaterialist tradition as Diderot does to the eighteenth-century materialist tradition: both are heterodox figures within their respective traditions and that heterodoxy expresses itself first and foremost in *formal experimentation*. Both institute new ways of thinking organology, whether materialist or immaterialist, and do so by playing with writing strategies, innovating with style and rethinking philosophical communication. Specifically, I want to suggest that the particular organological content of Hemsterhuis' philosophy necessitates poetic experimentation with writing techniques in the following ways explored in the subsequent two chapters: (1) in the rapid proliferation of images; (2) in the practice of analogic predication; (3) in the figuring of the text as a prosthetic instrument (an 'organon') for enhancing perception;

(4) in the enhancement of the moral organ through a sentimental language; and (5) in the cultivation of a plastic writing that acknowledges the historical metamorphoses of truth. These strategies constitute Hemsterhuis' organological style.

Chapter Three

Organs, Instruments and Insects

Exceptional is the opinion Hemsterhuis had that there could be very many completely new and unknown senses.
                        Friedrich Schlegel (1958–2002: 18.550)

Germs of future organs – perfectibility of organs. How make something into an organ?
                        Novalis, Hemsterhuis-Studien (1960–2006: 2.368)

§10 Insectification

Hemsterhuis' *Lettre sur l'optique* serves as both his final philosophical treatise and a recollection of some of his earliest research. Sent to Gallitzin on 23 December 1788 (and handed over, after his death, into Goethe's possession), it both recalls his research from the 1740s and 1750s on 'the organs of insects and the nature of their ideas and their way of thinking' (B 8.87, 193) and stands as the culmination of 'my long work on practical optics . . . the fame of which reached Italy' (B 4.52, 127). In the final years of his life, Hemsterhuis is keen to emphasise that he had 'worked more than fifty years on optics both theoretical and practical' and that 'if I have at any time loved a science to distraction, it was above all my dear optics' (B 8.83, 197).

The argument to the 1788 letter opens as follows:

One of the most beautiful labours of man to ameliorate his composition has been without doubt that by which he has amplified and perfected his organ of sight. It seems to me interesting to determine precisely the present state of the science of optics, so as to consider, first, what paths have been taken to reach the perfection of our days; 2. What chances there are of making further progress down these paths; 3. Whether there aren't other paths still to be taken that will achieve a completely new type of perfection. (B 9.72, 156)

In the *Lettre sur l'optique*, Hemsterhuis is therefore interested in efforts to perfect the organ of sight via technological and artificial media. And these efforts will in turn serve as a model for the perfecting of every other organ. Telescopes and microscopes take on paradigmatic status not just in the optical sciences, but more generally as exemplary means for radically amplifying all of human perception.

1. The first half of the *Lettre sur l'optique* follows the sequence of tasks set out above by first considering the progress made by 'the physical part' of the science of optics (B 9.72, 156). According to Hemsterhuis, while human vision is still not yet perfect, this 'physical' aspect of the science (i.e., practical optics) has proceeded as far as it can. A new path is now needed to finally perfect sight – a path that can enhance the senses despite the exhaustion of research into the physics of light. This is what Hemsterhuis means when he speaks of 'a completely new type of perfection' that must constitute the subject matter of any future optics. And the switch in focus Hemsterhuis is anticipating away from practical optics is itself performed halfway through the letter in the following manner:

> If these considerations of optics that I have tried to express as succinctly as possible concerned only the physical part of this science, then it would have been enough to address them to opticians . . . but as what is essential in this little writing is to be found under the jurisdiction of psychology, it is completely just and natural that I expose it all to your eyes. (B 9.72, 156)

What is here programmatically announced (and performed) is a shift away from the physics of optics (as the science has been typically understood in modernity) to the study of the psychology of vision. However, it does not announce a shift away from the technics of vision *tout court* but, rather, what Hemsterhuis wishes to achieve is the utilisation of psychological analysis for technological innovation.

In this vein, the second half of the letter begins by criticising the hegemony of physics in the study of vision: 'Until now, they have undertaken the thing from the side of the organ insofar as it is absolutely what is called physical. . . . But they have not conceived vision from the side of the soul, which – without doubt – plays the greatest role in it' (B 9.72, 159). And, he continues, as soon as one starts to consider sight 'from the side of the soul', one immediately discerns a model for intellectual synthesis that has profound implications for optical advancement. This model is one that Hemsterhuis had already elaborated at the opening to the *Lettre sur la sculpture* (EE 1.62; OP 98) and it stands as the foundation of all his considerations of the psychology of sense perception. It consists in the following stages: (1) each eye records an image[1] of an external object, since 'the sole goal of all organs ... is to give the soul ... sensations of external things' (B 9.72, 162); (2) these images are then deposited in the imagination alongside images of the object received at other moments or from different senses; and (3) the soul (or synthesising intellect) draws on the requisite images from this repository to form a more rounded and complete idea of the external object. On this model, the intellect plays the role of 'correcting, completing and finalising the work' begun by the 'imperfect' faculty of vision (B 9.72, 161): it supplements each visual image with many others to attain a better conception of the object. This leads Hemsterhuis to state 'two incontestable truths' of psychological optics on which his argument is founded: 'that the soul can combine many images of the same object and that these images when combined represent the object with much more force' (B 9.72, 162). In other words, the more images of an object that are received, the more forcefully the object is represented.

This transition to psychology is additive, rather than subtractive: the psychology of vision does not replace the physics of light, but rather supplements it. Illetterati (2005: 138) helpfully emphasises the non-reductionist character of Hemsterhuis' project: 'Physics, physiology and psychology constitute different perspectives which are all fundamental to the comprehension of the phenomenon [of vision], and none of these perspectives absorb the others completely'. Hemsterhuis certainly does want to reorient optics towards psychology, but such a shift 'does not eliminate, substitute or distort physical optics and it does not even present itself as an alternative to it' (2005: 132). Thus, while Hammacher, for instance, might label Hemsterhuis' approach in this letter 'phenomenological' (1971: 35), this is too simplistic: Hemsterhuis is not in any straightforward sense anticipating (for example) Goethe's physiology of vision, which establishes itself in strict opposition to Newtonian approaches to light.[2] Instead, Hemsterhuis'

---

[1] In the *Lettre sur la sculpture*, Hemsterhuis somewhat confusingly uses the term 'idea' to refer to both visually apprehended impressions and intellectual content (see Gaiger 2018: 238). To avoid confusion, I employ the terminology of the *Lettre sur l'optique* and use 'image' to denote the former.

[2] Nevertheless, it is certainly plausible that the *Lettre sur l'optique* decisively influenced

approach is synthetic: it embeds vision within the domain of physical research at the same time as explaining it by way of faculty psychology. And yet, if Crary (1988: 5) is right that it is only with Goethe that 'a science of vision will tend to mean increasingly an interrogation of the makeup of the human subject, rather than of the mechanics of light and optical transmission', then Hemsterhuis does still stand ahead of the curve.

2. The majority of the second half of the *Lettre sur l'optique* unpacks an analogy between human vision and insect vision. As Hemsterhuis puts it in an earlier letter, the conclusion he hopes to reach is that the insect is able to see in 'a more saturated, more compact, denser, fuller way' than the human subject (B 9.60, 129). And he reaches this conclusion on the basis of two premises: (1) as already established, the quantity of images received by the mind is directly proportional to the richness of the idea subsequently formed by the intellect; and (2) according to his own early research on insect physiognomy, an insect receives many more such images than a human in any given time, for the simple reason that insects have many more eyes. Insects receive a greater quantity of visual images simultaneously. Hemsterhuis continues that it 'evidently results' from this that 'insects, gifted with so many eyes', do still form one idea of an external object (they produce 'merely one, unique idea', just as we do), but, he continues, 'it is equally evident how rich, compact and saturated this idea must be, composed out of the combination of such a great number of distinct images' (B 9.72, 163). The point is that the greater the capacity to receive images, the more are deposited in the imagination, and so the better the idea formed from them in the intellect. From a psychological perspective, the more images the better, and so the more eyes producing those images simultaneously the better.

In a prelude to the *Lettre sur l'optique*, Hemsterhuis had already drawn out the metaphysical implications of these reflections on physiognomies of vision:

> What I understand by seeing in a more saturated, more compact, denser, fuller way, I can prove completely by my [work on the] anatomy of the organ of sight and brain in insects (a work that I abandoned too early!):

Goethe's work in this area. The period when Goethe obtained the copy of Hemsterhuis' letter (1793) was one of 'radical change' to his views on vision; indeed, Petry goes so far as to claim, 'There can be little doubt, therefore, that Hemsterhuis' work on optics contributed to the change in Goethe's basic approach to the phenomena of color, and it is even possible that he precipitated it' (1985: 233–4).

there are many of these animals that see the same object as us, not in multiple, not bigger, but 3,000 or 4,000 times richer, more saturated, more compact, denser than we see it. That is, when they see the sun, for example, they see not many suns, not a bigger sun, but a sun 3,000 to 4,000 times brighter than ours. Consider now that the principal part of the organ in which sensation resides pertains necessarily to the soul, and its exterior part, its extremity and its tube, to what in physics is called matter. Consider that the different modifications of this exterior part produce such a prodigious richness in sensation. Consider that the modification of this part can be imagined in infinite ways, then it follows that the *faculty of sight* in the soul is capable by nature of a richness and a perfection well beyond all our current conceptions. Let us suppose only a very great, but finite perfection. What would we see then? Would we see into the interior of things? Would we see into their essences? (B 9.60, 129)

This passage frames a demand for *the insectification of human vision*: it is by means of becoming more insect-like that our sight will be perfected. Any future development of visual technologies requires taking seriously the proliferation of images proper to insect life – or, to put it another way, optics will be further perfected only if it makes the insect eye its model. This is Hemsterhuis' insectification imperative – the demand to maximise the quantity of simultaneous visual sensations.[3] At stake in any future optics, then, is a reorientation of technological enhancement along the lines of this imperative – and Hemsterhuis conjectures, on this basis, that consequent advances would dwarf those seen by the invention of the microscope and the telescope. That is, Hemsterhuis suggests such a reorientation might improve vision so radically that it would result in total metaphysical transparency: humans would, literally, be able to see into the very essences of things. Indeed, even a moderate improvement along these lines would, he claims, 'rejuvenate man and give him back this precious tone of innocence which sees only the true' (B 9.72, 160). As one commentator summarises, 'If one could therefore enhance the capacity of the organs, particularly the eyes, then this would signify a growth in knowledge, not simply in the sense of a quantitative increase' (Loos 1995: 333). Hemsterhuis' project of insectification by way of technological prosthesis is thus utopian in its ambition: it aims to bring about nothing short of a philosophical revolution.

---

[3] We glimpse here, once more, the extent to which the ideal of total intuition – or 'optical totality' (Blumenberg 1987: 618) – structures Hemsterhuis' thinking, a point I return to in sustained fashion in §19.

More practically, in concluding the letter, Hemsterhuis puts forward one concrete proposal for effecting an initial, moderate insectification of human vision – the manufacture of binocular technologies. He reasons as follows: telescopes artificially amplify just one retinal image at a time, and so the resultant enhancement remains constrained by the quantity of images communicated by one eye alone. On the other hand, binocular technologies allow for two visual images (i.e., from both eyes) to be enhanced *at the same time*. Binoculars respond to the insectification imperative. What is more, Hemsterhuis himself had long been at the forefront of manufacturing such binocular technologies. Not only did he design a new kind of telescope that would overcome 'the limited state of dioptrics' which, in his own words, 'almost two centuries ago ... rejected the binocular machine' (B 9.72, 160), he had these instruments made, tested them, distributed them and even wrote an instruction manual for them.[4] It is for this reason that Zuidervaart credits Hemsterhuis with being 'the first person' to 'experiment with achromatic twin telescopes' and judges his 'efforts' as key to 'the development of the achromatic *binocular* telescope' (2019: 151, 123). Similarly, Hemsterhuis' contemporaries speak of him 'carrying out important observations on the diameter of fixed stars ... by means of a binocular telescope' and of 'looking with both eyes in two different telescopes' to 'give the sensation of a wider field of vision'. An encyclopaedia article on the telescope penned by Camper in 1778 lauds the work of 'the famous and shrewd F. Hemsterhuis', who 'has again breathed new life into Galileo's telescopes and has so improved them in such a way that one cannot behold them without being awe-struck' (Stapert, Lalande and Camper, quoted in Zuidervaart 2019: 148, 155). Hemsterhuis put into practice his demand for technologies that would transmit an increasing number of enhanced images to the intellect in as short a time as possible. And the ground of these practical endeavours remained his early research on insect anatomy: human vision must approach insect vision as closely as possible.

3. Hemsterhuis' argument in the 1788 letter looks forward to the nineteenth century, since, according to Crary, 'only in the 1830s does it become

---

[4] In the 1760s, remarkably, only the Dutch Stadtholder *and Hemsterhuis* owned such achromatic binocular telescopes, and when Hemsterhuis met the Duke of Gotha in 1785 he immediately arranged for him to be sent a binocular telescope of his own design and this was 'the first astronomical instrument to be purchased for the Friedenstein Observatory' in Gotha (Zuidervaart 2019: 141, 157).

crucial for scientists to define the seeing body as essentially binocular' (1988: 25). But it also looks back to a seventeenth-century past in its coupling of a utopia of perfect vision with revolutions in metaphysics. A key source for Hemsterhuis' ambitions for the perfecting of the organ of sight was Hooke's *Micrographia*: he not only owned a copy (van Sluis 2001: 40) but emphasises its importance for his early research on insect anatomy (van der Hoeven 1865: 259).[5] Hooke's work insists that, by means of microscopic observation, 'a new visible world' is revealed to us: 'the Earth itself which lies so near us, under our feet, shows quite a new thing to us' (1665: n.p.). And this optimism in the power of new instruments to make metaphysical discoveries is established on the basis of a critique of the senses in their natural condition: just like Hemsterhuis, who contrasts the perfection of prosthetics with the 'imperfection' of the natural organs, Hooke speaks of 'artificial organs' correcting our senses' 'infirmities' (1665: n.p.). Indeed, Hemsterhuis' language of rejuvenation and returning the subject to a 'precious tone of innocence' stands extremely close to this Hookean heritage: Hooke reinterprets the Baconian project of the 'great Instauration' as one of salvation through optical instruments, which will remedy our postlapsarian epistemic faults and vices. 'New artificial instruments', he writes, act as a 'reparation' for the Fall, a compensation for 'the mischiefs, and imperfection, mankind has drawn upon itself' (1665: n.p.). As Böhme comments, 'Hooke develops a utopian future, in which all five senses are instrumentally enhanced and mechanically perfected, making unforeseen capabilities and treasures accessible' (2005: 385; see also Shapin and Schaffer 1985: 36–8).[6]

What Hemsterhuis and Hooke (and many others) are attempting to do, therefore, is innovate in optics so as to give the organ of sight *a future*. What the human is able to see – the capacities and possibilities of her field of vision – is no longer to be considered something eternally fixed; as Blumenberg writes of the telescope: 'Visibility has become a contingent fact' (1985: 370–1).[7] In this tradition, what can currently be seen does not necessarily

---

[5] Hooke's text was later translated into Latin by Camper and, in general, Camper's influence on Hemsterhuis' optics should not be overlooked: Camper's Leiden *Dissertatio optica de visu* (1746) determines much of the physiological model for vision that Hemsterhuis presupposes (see Brummel 1925: 33, Sonderen 2000: 31).
[6] Böhme adds, 'the civilising utopia of enormously enhanced senses' was 'celebrated as a release from the anthropological constraints imposed by our physiological equipment' (2005: 389).
[7] Blumenberg continues, 'Through the telescope, the contemplation of the heavens acquires a historical character: In a situation in which the cosmic horizon of experience

define the limits of human vision; this field is, instead, subject to historical change, to increasing amplification. Böhme summarises, 'For the first time, technical media of representation . . . tie the relationship between visibility and invisibility to historical stages in the technical capacity of media and no longer to ontological distinctions. This is a far-reaching epistemological turning point' (2005: 363).

Moreover, this historicisation of the sense organs further entails the plasticity of knowledge. If perception varies historically, then the empirical knowledge possible at any given time varies too. The content of philosophy is merely a function of the present, contingent capacity of our senses. And even more fundamentally, the form of philosophy also becomes subject to change: models of perception, what it is to know something and even what counts as knowledge are all equally subject to historical variation. As times change, so will the very apparatus by which (empiricist) philosophies are structured. The very organs of philosophy – and so the very notion of what philosophical practice is and can be – are themselves subject to historical alteration. In 1712, Fénelon had acknowledged the plasticity of perception in an era of prosthetic visual apparatus when he asked, 'What would we not see if we could continually refine the instruments that come to the aid of our weak and crude vision?' (1712: 40–1; see Frey 2013: 380–1). In what follows, I am going to argue that Hemsterhuis radicalises Fénelon's question by likewise asking of his readers: in what ways would we not *think* if we could continually refine such instruments?

§11 The Plasticity of Philosophy

The lessons to be drawn from the *Lettre sur l'optique*, particularly its potential radicalisation of Fénelon's question, are equally present in Hemsterhuis' earlier publications. He philosophises on the presupposition that perfecting the sense organs will result in revolutions in metaphysics and changes to philosophical practice itself. Hence, *Sophyle, ou de la philosophie* opens,

> Sophylus: Oh, philosophy is such a good thing!
> Euthyphro: Why?
> Sophylus: Why? Because it makes known the truth, it delivers us from prejudices, and it makes clear the precise limits of our knowledge.

had been constant since primeval times, the discovery of the telescope signifies a caesura, beyond which a continuous increase in the accessible reality could be anticipated' (1985: 373; see also Frey 2013: 377).

Euthyphro: I avow it; but it is still more beautiful, because it makes the universe and ourselves richer: it allows us to see unknown lands of an immense size.
Sophylus: My friend, your unknown lands are imaginary spaces, believe me. Philosophy is beautiful and good only because it destroys these fables. Its unshakeable basis is experience, and there is no truth beyond it.
Euthyphro: We agree. A philosophy based on experience is certainly the only good one; but how many types of experience there are!
Sophylus: I know just one sole kind; it is experience through our five senses. Do you know of others?
Euthyphro: To tell you the honest truth, there was a time when I had precisely the same opinion; but I have changed since. I am so changed that when I think of my small-mindedness then, I feel ashamed. (*EE* 2.45; *OP* 335–7)

Here, Hemsterhuis (taking the part of Euthyphro) argues against what he considers to be the prevailing eighteenth-century reduction of experience to sensible properties of matter (represented by Sophylus). His point is a basic one: there is more to experience than is dreamt of in sensualist philosophies.

1. This polemic against the poverty of contemporary empiricisms has three components.

First, Hemsterhuis is not pitting some variant of rationalism, natural theology or fideism against the empiricisms dominant in the mid-eighteenth century. Instead, *Sophyle* describes a contest between two empiricisms. Both sides agree that philosophy's 'unshakeable basis is experience, and there is no truth beyond it', that a 'philosophy based on experience is certainly the only good one' – and this firm commitment to empiricism is unwavering in Hemsterhuis' writings: all valuable knowledge is ultimately derived from images received from the sense organs. He is clear: 'Man's knowledge consists in ideas of things which come to us by way of the senses' and in those ideas which are born from the comparison or interrelation of what is sensed (*WW* 464; *IN* 65; see also *EE* 1.95; *OP* 206).

Euthyphro and Sophylus espouse two competing visions of empiricism, and what ultimately distinguishes them is their speculative intent. This is the second component of Hemsterhuis' alternative. Sophylus, faithful to a Lockeo-Condillacian tradition, insists that philosophy's primary purpose is critical: empiricism 'delivers us from prejudices, and it makes clear the precise limits of our knowledge'. On the contrary, Euthyphro (i.e.,

Hemsterhuis) refuses this reduction of philosophy to a critical enterprise. Philosophy should aim to enlarge the domain of knowledge, not merely circumscribe it. Empiricism thereby becomes speculative, taking the philosopher beyond the present state of knowledge into 'unknown lands'. As van Ruler puts it, Hemsterhuis 'stretches the empirical method beyond its own limits' (2005: 45): he amplifies the range of possible knowledge through new possibilities of experience. Hence, at the centre of his philosophical project lies the tenet that there are no fixed limits to possible experience: much more can be known. Part of Hemsterhuis' critique of contemporary philosophy thus consists in an attack on the stultifying ways in which empiricism has been put to use in modern thought.

Hence (and thirdly), Hemsterhuis' confidence in an alternative, ampliative empiricism depends on a prior confidence in the possibility of opening up new realms of experience. What the sense organs can *currently* perceive should not be identified with what they *will* be able to perceive, even with what they have previously been able to perceive. The *Lettre sur l'optique* articulates the warrant for this confidence: Hemsterhuis argues from analogy to early modern technological innovation; that is, if the telescope has already given rise to new experiences by enhancing the eye beyond its natural range, then, by analogy, it is the height of dogmatism to consider the capacity of the other sense organs static, to think the range of present experiences rigid and immutable. If human sense organs are as mutable as advances with the telescope suggest, then there is no reason to limit the acquisition of knowledge to just the experience of our five senses *as they are currently constituted*. As Euthyphro exclaims (and this articulates Hemsterhuis' organological project in a nutshell), 'but how many types of experience there are!'

Hemsterhuis' reworking of empiricism as ampliative is a consequence of his organology, and particularly its key tenet: as our sense organs alter, so too does cognition. And the alteration of the sense organs is to be understood in two ways: as a matter of enhancing the sense organs we possess and as a matter of developing those we currently do not. This is the dual demand that motivates Hemsterhuis' vision of what a reformed philosophy requires: (1) the cultivation of existing sense organs and (2) the activation of new ones. Both demands stem from the very same root as Hemsterhuis' pursuit of insectification in the *Lettre sur l'optique*: the multiplication of images received increases our knowledge of external objects. And this will ultimately affect Hemsterhuis' practice of philosophical writing as well: the insectification imperative entails a rapid proliferation of images in all domains of human knowing, including within the philosophical text. To help humans know better, texts must communicate as many images as possible as quickly as possible – reading becomes a matter of 'visual speed' (Sonderen 2005: 210) and instantaneous 'shock' (Cirulli 2015: 62) to effectuate absolute instantaneity and thus total transparency. In fact, I shall suggest, in Part Four, that Hemsterhuis' late dialogues are written in a way to partially resist this model of rapid data consumption, as what Cirullo (2015: 62) calls 'recalcitrant speed bumps' to 'fast philosophy'. That is, the dialogues contain strategies for both the insectification and the de-insectification of philosophical communication.

2. Hemsterhuis articulates the first demand of his organology (cultivating existing sense organs) in terms of ensuring all the organs 'find the space to develop, to extend themselves' (*EE* 2.128; *OP* 590). It is a demand to accelerate the kinds of technological innovation that have artificially enhanced the capacity of the eye, to manufacture analogous prosthetics for smell and taste, as well as the imagination, the intellect and the moral organ. I return to Hemsterhuis' demand for the enhancement of existing organs in §12. In this section, my concern is, rather, with the second demand rehearsed above – the activation of *new* senses.

The idea that new organs will generate novel types of experience is a constant theme in Hemsterhuis' work; for example, it is bluntly asserted in the *Lettre sur l'athéisme*: 'It is given to the nature of man to acquire more organs in the rest of his existence or for other organs to develop' (*OP* 680).[8] This is, moreover, an idea that taps into a long philosophical tradition according to

---

[8] As will become increasingly evident, a vagueness haunts Hemsterhuis' language of the proliferation of senses: he oscillates between a language of *new* sense organs that are to be *created* and a language of *dormant* sense organs that are to be *(re)activated*. That is, it is sometimes unclear whether 'germs of future organs' (Novalis 1960–2006: 2.368) already exist innately within us or not, whether the demand for more organs requires anamneusis or invention. Likewise, it is unclear how active the subject is supposed to be in the cultivation of new senses. On the one hand, this process is often presented as eschatological, that is, new senses *will* necessarily be revealed to humans in the fullness of time and so, at present, it is merely a case of waiting expectantly for future anthropological revolutions to occur (see, for example, Hemsterhuis' claim in the *Lettre sur l'Homme* that 'it seems that we will pass eternity in the successive contemplation of the infinite different faces of the universe' [*EE* 1.124–5; *OP* 298]). On the other hand, this mystic tendency is counterbalanced by a more humanist propensity to instruct the subject to work actively on their own self-perfecting. I explore this question of whether the subject should wait or create in §12. Ultimately, this confusion stems from Hemsterhuis' ambivalent flirtation with preformationism and catastrophism, especially Bonnet's version (as well as the ambivalence towards the new that is already present in Bonnet's doctrines themselves) – see §17, §18.

which the human is not necessarily endowed with a fixed number of senses. Epitomised in Democritus' claim that 'more [organs] exist in irrational animals, in wise men and in the gods' (Diels and Kranz 1951: A116),[9] it resurfaces in the seventeenth century's renewed emphasis on the technics of sense: Blumenberg, for example, reads in Montaigne's *Apologie de Raimon Sebond* a 'suspicion that the senses with which man is equipped will turn out to be only a contingently given selection from what is possible' (1987: 621, 627); it is present in Leibniz' reflections on the survival of the body 'according to whether its organs are differently enfolded and more or less developed' (1989: 141); and it lives on in eighteenth-century materialist arguments over the mutability of anthropological givens (e.g., Diderot's *Lettre sur les aveugles*), as well as, via Bonnet and Hemsterhuis, in the late Lessing (particularly the fragment, *Daß mehr als fünf Sinne. für den Menschen sein können*) and, subsequently, in the German romantics.[10] Within this tradition (particularly its Diderotian and post-Diderotian variants), anthropological speculation about the possibility of new organs is bound up with the becoming more mutable, more contingent and more ephemeral of philosophical knowledge.

3. The ontology underlying Hemsterhuis' doctrine of future organs is threefold: there exists (1) souls composed of both psychological and physiological organs; (2) external essences known by the mediation of organs; and (3) 'vehicles of action' or mediating organs that are external to the body and which communicate an attribute of the essence to the bodily sense organ (e.g., reflected light or 'the air put in oscillation by the movements of the [external] object' [*EE* 1.89; *OP* 184]). As a result, there exist three kinds of organs in Hemsterhuis' philosophy: (1) physiological organs, that is, the sense organs, like sight; (2) physical organs ('vehicles of action') which mediate between object and subject, for example sound waves; and

---

[9] It is unsurprising therefore that, in *Simon*, what provokes Diotima's speech on sense-mysticism (i.e., the future proliferation of organs) is Socrates' interest in Democritean physiology (*EE* 2.113; *OP* 544). Diotima responds by appropriating a key principle of Democritus' philosophy (the mutability of the number of human sense organs), while simultaneously repurposing it to attack precisely the sort of materialism for which Democritus stands as a cipher. In other words, when Socrates worries that Democritus 'is in error', Diotima responds, 'Not as much as you think' (*EE* 2.113; *OP* 544).

[10] Dierik's claim (1997: 264) that 'the possibility of a proliferation of the senses is a highly original thought, unique to Hemsterhuis' or even Schlegel's insistence on this doctrine's exceptionality (1958–2002: 18.550) must therefore be severely qualified: Hemsterhuis stands in a long tradition of sense-mysticism.

(3) psychological organs or the faculties of the mind. That is, Hemsterhuis is not only happy to designate light an organ, but he also speaks of 'the organ of the intellect' (B 1.19. 45) and is explicit that all capacities of the mind, including 'imagination, intellect, etc.' (but excluding velleity) can equally be called 'qualities, faculties or organs' (B 2.55, 156; see also WW 152; IN 38). Ultimately, with the exception of the limit-concept of 'essence', Hemsterhuis' ontology contains nothing but organs; there are organs all the way down.

Every essence can express itself in an infinite number of 'manners of being' or 'attributes'. In line with Scholastic and early modern uses of *facies*, Hemsterhuis dubs these manners of being the various 'faces of the universe', which each correspond to a particular sense organ. For example, one such 'face' is defined as follows: 'One calls the visible face of the universe, that modification, that manner of being by which certain essences are related to the organ of sight' (EE 2.52; OP 356; translation modified). Each face of an essence exhibits a different set of properties and so requires different means to be perceived; that is, each face corresponds to a particular sense organ (an extension of Diotima's special-fibre theory explored in §9 above). This one-to-one correspondence between the faces of external essences and sense organs is one of the axioms of Hemsterhuisian metaphysics. Therefore, in general, knowledge of the external world is possible only when mediated by two kinds of organ: (1) 'there must be something between [an essence] and the person and I call this the vehicle of action' (EE 2.58; OP 378), and this physical organ transmits the pertinent properties of the essence to the subject; and (2) 'it is necessary that the person has an organ analogous to this vehicle, that is, capable of receiving its action' (EE 2.58; OP 378) – that is, the subject must possess a sense organ that has some relation to the vehicle of action, in order to be able to receive an image of what is being communicated. The sense organ subsequently transmits this image through the appropriate nerve fibre to the imagination, where it is deposited. Hence, an idea of a ball is 'the result of this ball's relation to me, to my eyes, my organs, the light, and to everything that is between this ball and me' (EE 2.48; OP 344).

Hemsterhuis is therefore committed to an indirect realism: the subject does not have direct access to an external object, but still has mediated access, which – in cases where we trust our epistemic apparatus – faithfully illuminates the nature of this object. In Hemsterhuis' own words, 'I conclude from the appearance [of the object] to the being of the object' (WW 134; IN 28), for 'our simply acquired ideas don't deceive us but actually represent qualities that are essentially in the things.... We see clearly that a thing we are looking at, hearing, touching is among other things really as it appears to us' (*EE* 2.50; *OP* 350). Or, as he more bluntly puts it in *Alexis*, an idea has 'a true prototype of which it is the faithful ... impression' (*EE* 2.140; *OP* 626; see also B 8.49, 114).[11] What allows for this realist position is the absolute passivity of the subject in cognition (*EE* 1.89, 2.48, 2.57; *OP* 184, 342–4, 372): whenever the subject perceives, its soul, its organs and the vehicle of action remain the same, only the essence alters. Thus, when comparing images between two objects (e.g., a cone and a cube), we can safely infer that the difference perceived reflects an actual difference between the objects: 'Since what is between the cube and me is the same as what is between the cone and me, I conclude that the difference that I sense between the cone and the cube pertains to the true essence of the cone and the cube' (*EE* 2.51; *OP* 352).

Such a model opens up the possibility of perceiving currently imperceptible manners of being. There are, Hemsterhuis insists, other faces of the universe that do not correspond to our five material sense organs (e.g., *EE* 2.54, 2.71; *OP* 362, 414), and all of them are capable of being perceived if one were to possess the right sensory equipment and vehicles of action (*EE* 2.52; *OP* 356). The reason why the subject is currently 'ignorant of' (*EE* 2.49; *OP* 346) some of these unknown faces of the universe is therefore potentially twofold. First, the vehicle of action transmitting that face's properties could have yet to reach us, and so the corresponding organ would currently lie dormant in anticipation of a perception-to-come. Hemsterhuis raises this possibility in Diotima's speech in *Simon*, arguing – by analogy to light from Orion which takes thousands of years to reach earth – that 'the movements of all these vehicles do not have the same speed. The movement of air is less rapid than that of light and there are thousands of vehicles whose vibrations have not yet arrived at the tubes that are made to receive them' (*EE* 2.114; *OP* 548–50). Secondly, the face could be unknown at present because we lack the organ that corresponds to it: 'There is an infinite probability that there is an infinity of vehicles of action for which we have no organs' (*EE* 1.133; *OP* 315).

Hemsterhuis' faith in the existence of imperceptible properties from a strictly empiricist standpoint is, of course, troubling, and he has two responses to this anxiety. First, there is indirect evidence that there do exist

---

[11] Spruit calls this 'a strong version of realism, [for] we perceive what is really there' (2005: 51; see also van Ruler 2005: 21–2). Hemsterhuis will use this model to refute idealism as a doctrine that renders the human subject 'absurd' – 'the most absolute God within an infinitely small [domain], without creativity or power – that is, a perfect nothing' (*WW* 136; *IN* 30).

properties which are irreducible to those properties we directly perceive at present: electricity is Hemsterhuis' favourite example – a phenomenon that cannot be directly perceived, but can still be inferred to exist on the basis of its effects on other perceptible properties.[12] Secondly, Hemsterhuis' axiom of one-to-one correspondence between organs and faces of the universe entails that evidence for the contingency of the number of human sense organs also counts as evidence for imperceptible faces of the universe. Drawing on (although distinctly subverting) the canonical reasoning of Diderot's *Lettre sur les aveugles*, Hemsterhuis argues from the idea that, just because someone perceives with just four sense organs, this does not mean that the properties corresponding to a fifth sense organ simply vanish. And he concludes from this that, just because most humans are currently limited to a fixed number of sense organs, this does not rule out the existence of other senses and so the existence of currently imperceptible properties too.[13] The mutability of our sense organs implies that it might well be possible to perceive the imperceptible and so expand our cognitive powers. This is the model that provides the warrant for Euthryphro's exclamation, 'how many types of experience there are!'

4. Empiricism becomes a speculative, rather than a critical enterprise by way of the proliferation of sense organs – and this refiguring of philosophical methodology also constitutes the basis for Hemsterhuis' attack on contemporary materialisms. This is in spite of the fact that such stress on the contingency of anthropological givens was a popular materialist argumentative strategy during the mid-eighteenth century (as a means to undermine traditional metaphysical and epistemological dogmas). Hemsterhuis thus redeploys a materialist weapon against the materialists, reappropriating arguments from contingency and impermanence. I develop this thesis in Chapter Four; at present, it is important to elaborate on Hemsterhuis' intervention into debates over materialism.

To the materialist claim that material properties exhaust all that is perceptible, he responds with the following qualification: they exhaust all that is perceptible *at present* (and even then, only if the knowing subject fails

---

[12] *Sophyle* is clearest on this point (*EE* 2.53; *OP* 360). Hemsterhuis returns repeatedly to the significance of electricity for his organology in his correspondence – see B 4.33, 83; 4.77, 203; 7.62, 169.

[13] Furthermore, Hemsterhuis appeals a priori to an innate principle of perfectibility governing the evolution of the human and necessarily leading to the emergence of new senses – see §12.

to perceive moral properties – see §13). According to Hemsterhuis, the eighteenth-century definition of matter delimits present experience, not any possible experience. If new senses were to develop in the subject (or dormant senses were to reactivate), then properties foreign to what is currently taken to be material would become perceptible. Hemsterhuis is explicit: 'Matter is only a sign to express essences insofar as they have some analogy *to our current organs*' (EE 2.54; OP 362; my emphasis). As soon as 'our current organs' change, what can be perceived will change and so too will what counts as matter. Hemsterhuis does not dispute the materialist identification of matter with the entire domain of the perceptible; he merely insists on historicising them both, making both matter and what is perceptible historical variables. In *Sophyle*, for example, he argues,

> Matter seems to me impenetrable only because I have touch; if I had other means of sensation, it would have appeared to me completely differently; if it can act on me by a hundred thousand media, by a hundred thousand different organs, I would be affected by it in a hundred thousand different ways; it would have for me a hundred thousand attributes that define it? From this it follows that the number of times that I may have a different idea of matter, or rather of essence, depends on the number of my organs. (EE 2.52; OP 356)

Consequently, Hemsterhuis does not denigrate the concept of matter as such, but merely the eighteenth-century sensualist limitation of matter by the five senses as currently constituted. He rarely condemns bodily or material things in the name of some anti-material principle; he, instead, tries to enhance – even absolutise – matter to encompass much more than any eighteenth-century materialist could imagine.[14] In exactly the same way as he wishes to amplify empiricism by means of new types of experience, so too he attempts to amplify the concept of matter through the incessant addition of new types of properties. Hemsterhuis' attack on materialism does not proceed by way of the rejection or denigration of matter, but by way of relativising, historicising and therefore potentially expanding its domain. In

---

[14] I thus side with van Ruler, who insists that Hemsterhuis' arguments against materialism 'never lead to the establishment of something opposed to what is "material"' (2005: 43), against Hartmann, for whom Hemsterhuis insists that 'the world is more than matter' (1923: 165), and Fresco, who describes Hemsterhuis' 'immaterialism' as a refusal of 'the reduction of world to material without the need for further transcendence' (2007: 196).

a letter to Galliztin, he is clear on this point: he is intent on 'discarding that ridiculous barrier that separates the material from the immaterial' (B 6.55, 154).

According to Hemsterhuis, therefore, contemporary materialists are right to affirm the historical plasticity of all truths, but are wrong to exempt the concept of matter itself from this relativisation procedure: they find themselves constrained by the rigidity and consequent 'poverty of the idea we attach to the word matter' (EE 2.53; OP 358). In some ways, then, Hemsterhuis is attempting to be more radical than the materialists: to liberate materialism from the last vestiges of the permanent. He laments that since Newton 'the idea of matter [has] unnoticeably acquired a rigidity' (EE 2.58; OP 376) and argues, instead, for a *hypermaterialism* or excessive materialism: matter *exceeds* any materialist account of it. There is too much of matter to be circumscribed in thinking at present. Or, as Moenkemeyer succinctly puts it, '"Matter" is more than we know of it at any given time' (1975: 92).[15]

Sophyle contains a particularly cogent articulation of this hypermaterialism:[16]

---

[15] In this regard, the most characterisic phrase of Hemsterhuis' theoretical philosophy is 'entr'autres', paralleling the Spinozan 'quatenus' (e.g., EE 1.100, 2.49; OP 218, 348). Matter is always, *among other things*, what the subject perceives and knows of it; such perception is always and necessarily incomplete and capable of further amelioration.

[16] The major exceptions to this hypermaterialist current in *Sophyle* are the syllogistic demonstrations of the immaterial soul excerpted from the earlier *Lettre sur l'Homme* (EE 2.55; OP 364–8). These arguments are intended to prove that there is something which is not matter, which is foreign or even opposed to it. They suggest a more traditional immaterialism than what is found elsewhere in *Sophyle*. The tension between these hypermaterialist and immaterialist currents in *Sophyle* and *Lettre sur l'Homme* has been analysed in detail by Verbeek (1995) and I return to his important reading in §15. The immaterialist current is more prominent throughout Hemsterhuis' correspondence with Gallitzin, in which he does frequently set up a neat opposition between matter and soul that belies his hypermaterialist commitments elsewhere (e.g., B 1.48, 85; 2.51, 134). However, Gallitzin herself was a staunch immaterialist of the most traditional kind: she was committed to a 'perfect dualism' between spirit and matter, denigrating the body as 'an envelope that is not adapted to genius' and 'a troubling obstacle' (Brachin 1952: 143–5). Consequently, some of Hemsterhuis' terminological choices in his correspondence might well be born of accommodation. Or, one could place Hemsterhuis' use of the concept of matter whenever it is opposed to an immaterial principle in quotation marks, so as to indicate a reference to matter *as it is currently conceived*, rather than matter *as it could become* (i.e., capable of infinite expansion). He is not anti-matter, but just frustrated by the poverty of the materialist concept of matter. It is also worth noting Hemsterhuis' late suggestion that one should 'consider man from two sides: first, from all that we call *organ* in our philosophy; secondly, from the active relation between body and soul, or rather the real and active dominance that

Let us now suppose that a man deprived of the organ of touch gave the name matter to all essence which related to his organs; it is obvious that impenetrability would no longer enter into the definition of matter. Let us suppose a blind man gave the name matter to all essence that related to his organs, then extension would no longer be an attribute of matter. Let us suppose someone endowed with a hundred other types of organs, all of which have other and different relations to essence, gave the name matter to all essence insofar as it related to his organs, matter would have completely different attributes. (*EE* 2.58; *OP* 376)

On this argument, the 'definition of matter' expands to encompass more and more of what exists, such that, ultimately, Hemsterhuisian philosophy tends towards the claim that matter 'can have an infinite number of essential attributes' (*EE* 2.53; *OP* 358). Matter must be subject to a process of amplification, so that, in the end, nothing is excluded from it.[17] And this line of thought receives it paradigmatic statement in the *Lettre sur l'athéisme*, where Hemsterhuis claims that it is an 'incontestable truth':

that *matter* is only a word which designates all the real essences as they have relation with our current organs; that matter cannot have more attributes than we have organs; and that if it is given to the nature of man to acquire more organs in the rest of his existence or other organs develop there, matter (if one wants to keep this word as the sign of essences insofar as they are known) will increase its attributes proportionately. (*OP* 680)

The materialist definition of matter fails to exhaust the potential extension of the concept.[18] This potential can be realised only when the philosopher starts to rigorously think through the implications of a history of the organs, since to multiply organs (i.e., to remain faithful to the insectification imperative) is to enrich the concept of matter infinitely.

---

the former has over the latter' (B 10.102, 166). Implicit in this distinction between an organological and a dualist approach to the human is an attempt to establish hypermaterialism and immaterialism as parallel, equally valid explanatory methods.

[17] Hemsterhuis even suggests a variant of Berkeley's 'master argument' in favour of hypermaterialism *against* immaterialism: as soon as the immaterial is perceived, it becomes, by definition, 'material' (*EE* 1.110; *OP* 252). That is, it is incoherent to posit knowledge of the immaterial.

[18] Equally in his reception history, Hemsterhuis has occupied an uneasy place between immaterialism and materialism – what Trop calls 'a position of tension along an axis of materialism and immaterialism' (2022: 37).

§12 Perfectibility

Hemsterhuis' organology rests on a twofold demand: (1) the proliferation of new organs and (2) the cultivation of existing ones. The previous section described his account of the proliferation of new physiological organs; the present section is concerned with how he articulates the need to cultivate existing psychological organs or faculties. The enhancement of psychological organs – and the pedagogy of organs that informs it – constitutes the subject matter of the following.

1. Socrates exemplifies the ideal human for Hemsterhuis (see §3), and he does so for specifically organological reasons: Socrates managed to cultivate all his existing psychological organs to the highest perfection possible within humanity's current condition,[19] and for this reason he epitomises 'the most immense and richest' soul and achieves 'supreme virtue and supreme wisdom': 'all the parts' of Socrates' soul 'are equally perfect, are in complete harmony ... [His soul] has the use of all its tools [i.e., organs] at once' (B 1.19, 47). Nevertheless, Socrates stands as but one ideal organological type among many in Hemsterhuis' philosophy; for example, François Fagel is similarly transformed by Hemsterhuis into a representative of organological perfection. As Pelckmans (1987: 59) happily puts it, Hemsterhuis describes in his homage to Fagel 'a kind of utopia in a unique person', and so the text works to provoke and inspire emulation in his readers, to teach them to perfect themselves.

Hemsterhuis writes here,

> [Fagel] was endowed with several qualities which are rarely found together and almost never in such a high degree of perfection; and, from this fortunate assembly, [there] naturally arose new faculties, which distinguished him among the small number of men who can be compared to him. He had a prodigious memory. Born with a geometrical spirit, he had all his ideas clear, distinct, well determined, and a sure judgment. He possessed an admirable tact, that faculty which seems to penetrate into the essence of things and which in fact is only the effect of a quick operation of judge-

---

[19] That Socrates stands as an ideal *solely* for humanity's *current condition* is emphasised by Hemsterhuis in an extant fragment. He writes that Socrates' influence 'will last forever unless there is manifest in man some new organ which could not be manifest until now or unless there is found by a new complication of the use of different organs that are already known something which is basically equivalent to a new organ' (*IN* 168). This point is also heavily implied in the closing pages to *Simon*, where Diotima contrasts her state of perfection in which 'the future is made present' to that of Socrates – see §24.

ment, and, consequently, [he possessed] a prompt and fluent [power of] conception. He possessed that elevation of mind which never sees one thing alone, but which embraces several at the same time, along with the relations which link them – and this gives knowledge a great scope. (EE 1.137; OP 320)

For Hemsterhuis, Fagel represents a 'great soul', and this greatness is primarily manifest in the quality of his faculties, taken both individually and as a composite (as a 'fortunate assembly'). Human perfection is a function of faculty psychology.

This kind of evaluation of individuals by their organs is common: much of Hemsterhuis' later collaboration with Gallitzin consists in judging organologically their friends and acquaintances, celebrities, even mythical characters. All are subject to psychological dissection. Hemsterhuis and Gallitzin even devise both a quantitative marking rubric for each of the faculties and a diagrammatic schema for presenting these marks (a four-leaf clover containing four percentages – one for quality of intellect, one for quality of imagination, one for quality of velleity and one for quality of moral organ; see Niehaus 1998). However, they are most enthusiastic about turning this analytic psychology back onto themselves: Hemsterhuis identifies in his own mind 'the frightening and monstrous sensibility of my moral organ' (B 1.51, 92), 'my imagination which is too rich and lively' (B 1.86, 124) and 'the most grotesque memory' (B 4.12, 40).[20] And one result of this process of introspection is a set of rules for self-improvement (that also apply to Gallitzin, since 'our brains are constructed in almost exactly the same way' [B 5.2a, 14]) – rules that include keeping 'the too prodigious sensibility of your moral organ in check' and ensuring the intellect 'leads everything to the beautiful harmony of the whole' (B 1.81, 120).

This ideal of harmony stands as the central principle of Hemsterhuisian psychology. He assumes that success in perfecting each faculty separately will necessarily lead to 'the equilibrium or equal and proportionate perfection of the four faculties' (EE 2.118; OP 564). The moral psychology presented in *Simon* concludes – recalling Socrates and Fagel – that 'the richest being we can conceive of in our current state' is one in which 'every faculty of the soul is equally perfect and in complete harmony' (EE 2.118; OP 560). As well

---

[20] This forms part of Hemsterhuis' reconfiguration of Newtonianism. The best material for experimenting on is one's own faculties and so experimental method comes to be identified with an introspective attitude (i.e., philosophical method as 'experimental introspection'). See, for instance, B 3.33, 87–9.

as its intrinsic worth, there are two instrumental reasons why Hemsterhuis prizes faculty-harmony so highly. First, as he writes of Socrates, the harmonious soul 'has the use of all its tools at once' (B 1.19, 47): this recalls the insectification imperative of §10 (the more images received simultaneously, the more perfect the knowledge), for, when all organs function simultaneously at full capacity in harmonious individuals, more images enrich the imagination. In other words, Fagel and Socrates perceived, imagined, thought and willed better than everyone else – all at the same time – and this is why they ultimately have the greatest claim to wisdom. Secondly, Hemsterhuis conjectures that faculty-harmony is a condition of the proliferation of new organs: from out of Fagel's 'fortunate assembly' of existing organs, 'new faculties naturally had to emerge', and, according to *Aristée*, 'when man arrives – either by his labours or by the excellence of his nature – at the perfect harmony of the faculties which we recognise in him, other faculties – until now unknown – begin to be developed' (*EE* 2.97; *OP* 492; see also Moenkemeyer 1975: 123–4). Faculty-harmony stands as an organological ideal not only because it describes the perfect state of existing organs, but also because it facilitates the emergence of the new.

Moreover, Socrates is not just a good example of faculty-harmony, he is also represented as an ideal teacher who facilitates faculty-harmony in others. Socratic paideia is equated with a pedagogy of the organs, for Socrates 'proposed to make each man as perfect as his nature could permit' (*EE* 2.133; *OP* 604–6) and such perfection is, we have seen, defined in organological terms, in the self-perfection of the faculties. The importance of Socratic education is to be found everywhere in Hemsterhuis' writing: following Rousseau's advice to 'begin [teaching] by studying your pupils better' (1991: 34), he avers that 'the most interesting part' of 'the knowledge of man and his character ... concerns education', that is, 'to perfect myself and to perfect you' (B 1.51, 91). As Grucker glosses, 'Philosophy for Hemsterhuis was less a science than an education' (1866: 260). In *Simon*, psychology is subordinated to the purpose of 'perfecting education', and, in the correspondence, it is very often deployed to devise pedagogical strategies for Gallitzin's own children (see B 1.203, 241; 8.3, 19). Hence, Gallitzin, for one, sees their philosophical collaboration as 'nothing less than the acquisition of the necessary knowledge for the instruction and education of my children' (quoted in Brachin 1952: 154; see further Sudhof 1973: 152–64).[21]

---

[21] This point is frequently acknowledged in passing in the Hemsterhuis scholarship; see, for example, Moenkemeyer (1975: 134) and Hammacher (2008: 591). More specifically, Hemsterhuis deploys his 'clover-leaf' faculty analysis in this context, writing

Hemsterhuis was, of course, not alone at the period in foregrounding the pedagogical uses of philosophy. As Brachin (1952: 281) puts it, 'The eighteenth century was ... above all, the golden age of pedagogy'. While much separates Hemsterhuis from the Parisian materialists, he does share with them an intellectual commitment to the idea that education affects character (B 4.61, 156). What unites Hemsterhuis with a philosopher like Helvétius on this issue is their shared rejection of the idea that inborn character traits entirely determine the human – for both Hemsterhuis and the materialists, the human subject is sometimes capable of change. In *Aristée*, for example, he insists that 'the faculties of your soul and the degree of their total harmony' are things 'you have the power to perfect' (*EE* 2.95; *OP* 486).[22] And, from Friedrich Schlegel onwards, Hemsterhuis' readers have acknowledged that 'the ground of his thinking is a manifold *Bildung*' (Trunz 1971: 206; Hammacher 1995c: 614). For this reason, it is surprising that Mähl and those who follow him (e.g., Nassar) have so sharply contrasted Hemsterhuis' 'passive conception of harmony' with Novalis' 'active' conception according to which 'we must *work towards* creating harmony' (Nassar 2013: 42; see Mähl 1994: 277–82). Nassar's claim that 'while for Hemsterhuis harmony is *given* ... transformative activity, self-development and *Bildung* become central concerns in Novalis' later works' (2013: 43) seemingly overlooks the constant work needed to bring about faculty-harmony that forms the central plank of Hemsterhuisian pedagogy.[23] While

---

in *Simon*: 'In regard to education: by taking as its foundation that these four faculties constitute what is essential to the human soul in this life, you can easily study in a child these four parts separately, and come to know their value and reciprocal imperfections, and you can then modify these faculties so that, in regard to each other, there results the greatest good and the least harm possible' (*EE* 2.119; *OP* 566).

[22] Nevertheless, Hemsterhuis does still use Diotima's speech in *Simon* to distinguish his own pedagogy from that of the materialists. That is, he interrogates and ultimately puts into question the widespread thesis that 'our virtues, our vices and our failings have always appeared to me as faculties of the soul that are acquired in education and through the course of life, and not as the effect of a mixture of the faculties which pertains to the nature of the soul itself' (*EE* 2.112; *OP* 542).

[23] The Mähl quotation (1994: 280) on which Nassar's claim is based ('The unity and harmony of the universe is given, is present – here is the decisive difference between Hemsterhuis and Novalis') suggests that both Nassar and Mähl are referring to Hemsterhuis' metaphysics of order in *Aristée*, rather than *Simon*. Such a divorce of the ontological from the psychological domain seems relatively arbitrary; nevertheless, it is one that perhaps owes its origins to Novalis himself, for, as Mähl points out (in Novalis 1960–2006: 2.328), the principle of perfectibility 'on which Hemsterhuis above all insists, is not mentioned once' in the *Hemsterhuis-Studien*.

the subject might be passive in the act of knowing itself, she should work tirelessly to enhance and amplify the apparatus by which she comes to know.

2. Few philosophical concepts have a birth date as precise as the concept of perfectibility. It is coined in 1755 in Rousseau's *Discours sur l'origine et les fondements de l'inégalité parmi les hommes*:

> Nature commands every animal, and the beast obeys. Man experiences the same impression, but he recognises himself free to acquiesce or to resist; and it is mainly in the consciousness of this freedom that the spirituality of his soul exhibits itself. . . . But even if the difficulties surrounding these questions left some room for disagreement about this difference between man and animal, there is another very specific property that distinguishes between them, and about which there can be no argument, namely the faculty of perfecting oneself; a faculty which, with the aid of circumstances, successively develops all the others, and resides in us. . . . [Why is it that] man again loses through old age or other accidents all that his *perfectibility* had made him acquire, thus relapsing lower than the beast itself? It would be sad for us to be forced to agree that this distinctive and almost unlimited faculty is the source of all man's miseries; that it is the faculty which, by dint of time, draws him out of that original condition in which he would spend tranquil and innocent days; that it is the faculty which, over the centuries, causing his enlightenment and his errors, his vices and his virtues to flourish, eventually makes him his own and Nature's tyrant. (2018: 144–5)

Rousseau invents the concept of perfectibility to distinguish the human from the animal and to thereby underline the human's unique spiritual vocation. That is, the human's historicity, its 'malleability of spirit, its plasticity, the possibility of working' on itself (Lotterie 2006: xxix) succeeds where other criteria (e.g., rationality, memory, linguistic capacity) fail in specifying what is distinctive about human life. The fact that every human can improve herself (i.e., is educatable) acts as a specifically anthropological a priori, a property that cannot be located anywhere else in the natural world. It therefore constitutes, for Rousseau, the foundational principle for a new, non-Cartesian dualism that 'proves the irreducibility of thought to matter' (Salaün 2004: 205) by recourse to the human's eternal capacity for making history. Pefectibility provides a new grounding for immaterialism. As Salaün (2004: 202) puts it,

[Perfectibility] is used as a weapon, a proof capable of shoring up a dualist thesis, to resist the 'scientific' philosophy of the time and re-spiritualise 'the operations of the mind' at the very moment when the *philosophes* were trying to materialise them.

As Rousseau himself puts it, perfectibility 'raises' man 'far above nature' (2018: 145) and provides the warrant for 'those who are convinced that the divine voice called all mankind to the enlightenment and the happiness of the celestial intelligences' (2018: 209).

Perfectibility is not progress: Rousseau refuses to co-opt the human's spiritual trajectory into any kind of teleology or eschatological vision. Indeed, he attributes 'perfectibility' to humans precisely to avoid predicating 'perfection' of them. It names merely an anthropological 'potentiality, rather than an essence' (Lotterie 2006: xxii) – a regulative tendency, rather than a constitutive movement. It is a fragile and volatile condition of human development that may or may not be actualised at any given moment. In other words, perfectibility does not exclude corruptibility, but entails it as an ineffaceable danger. It gives the human a history, but not a particular history. And, importantly for my purposes, this historical capacity is articulated organologically: perfectibility is a 'metafaculty' (Binoche 2004b: 14) insofar as it constitutes 'the condition of possibility of the other faculties' (Salaün 2004: 208). Rousseau thus speaks in the passage above of this principle as 'a faculty which . . . successively develops all the others', that is, which is responsible for the enhancement of human organs. He continues, it actualises 'the other faculties which natural man had received in potentiality' (2018: 163). The principle of perfectibility gives organs a history.

Rousseau's positing of an a priori human capacity to educate and better ourselves directly informs Hemsterhuis' own stress on human educability. For Hemsterhuis too, innate in any human is the possibility of improving themselves further, and this a priori human tendency towards what is better is no bodily capacity or habit, but an inalienable property. It justifies Hemsterhuis' avowal that everyone can be perfected; this is his Socratic pedagogic universalism (Socrates 'proposed to make each man as perfect as his nature could permit'), in opposition to Pythagoras' elitism in education, which is 'an injustice and a chimera' (*EE* 2.133; *OP* 604–6; see also B 2.63, 190). Unsurprisingly, therefore, the very term 'perfectibility' frequently appears among Hemsterhuis' remarks on education (e.g., B 1.25, 59) – conceived as the power of the human to perfect herself through working on her psychological and physiological organs. The perfectible human possesses plastic organs; she can enhance her own faculties and amplify her senses. The human, for Hemsterhuis, is educatable.

Yet, Hemsterhuis' concept of perfectibility is not strictly Rousseauean, and this is unsurprising since, after 1755, the concept of perfectibility was subject to a rapid and widespread process of contestation and fragmentation. On the one side arose materialist reinterpretations of perfectibility (like Diderot's) as 'perfected instinct', transforming it from an a priori condition of human history to a physiological product of natural history (Salaün 2004: 211–17). Perfectibility was, on this account, reduced to a form of biological health. On the other side emerged with equal vehemence a teleological interpretation that reinserted perfectibility back into a story of progress – what Binoche dubs 'the reabsorption of perfectibility into becoming-perfect' (2004b: 17). For example, in Bonnet's palingenetic mutation of perfectibility, the principle is reimagined as a 'unilateral, cumulative' process of attaining always-greater perfections (see Binoche 2004b: 15) and, similarly, for Lessing and others in Germany (in the wake of Bonnet), 'the concept is infused – in opposition to Rousseau – with the idea of a natural teleology. ... Perfectibility becomes the grounding principle of nature' (Vosskamp 1992: 121). In other words, Rousseau's original inspiration for the term was immediately obscured, and Rousseau himself gradually lost interest in using it precisely because it was so 'capable of annoying reinterpretations both materialist and palingenetic' (Binoche 2004b: 13–14).

Bonnet's wresting of perfectibility away from its Rousseauean origins is particularly pertinent for reading Hemsterhuis. On the publication of Rousseau's *Discours sur l'origine et les fondements de l'inégalité* in 1755, Bonnet immediately penned a scathing reply (under the pseudonym Philopolis) attacking, among other things, the fragility of Rousseau's principle of perfectibility.[24] As Bonnet puts it,

> This perfectibility, which, for Rousseau, comprises the characteristic that essentially distinguishes man from animal, must – by the author's own logic – lead man to the point where we see him today. To wish that this weren't the outcome is to wish that man wasn't man. (1779–83: 8.333)

[24] More generally, on Bonnet's response to Rousseau, see Savioz (1948: 43–5). Although Bonnet frames this as a local debate between two Genevans (i.e., with his choice of pseudonym, Philopolis), he also sent denunciations of Rousseau to Bentick and Allamand in the Dutch Republic (Savioz 1948: 45) – both of whom were, of course, very close friends of Hemsterhuis at the time.

Bonnet attacks Rousseau's distinction between what perfectibility effects (i.e., corrupt and perverse states of affairs) and its origin innate in the essence of the human, which is characterised as good. Such a distinction is artificial: 'Must not all that results immediately from the faculties of man be said to result from his nature?' (1779–83: 8.333). That is, Bonnet suggests that to take perfectibility seriously as a 'metafaculty' entails treating all its effects as ultimately good (or perfect). This is to discard Rousseau's ambivalent pessimism in favour of a Leibnizian teleological optimism, based on the fundamental principle: 'Let the world proceed as it does and let us be sure that it proceeds as well as it can' (1779–83: 8.335).[25] In Bonnet's own constructive work, this optimism is concretised as a rational assurance 'that I am a being perfectible indefinitely', that is, that 'by continual progress' I will attain 'another state where all my faculties will be perfected' (2002: 431). The possibility of corruption, so integral to Rousseau's principle of perfectibility, is lost.

Bonnet also rejects the Rousseauean use of perfectibility to sharply distinguish the human from the animal. Bonnet naturalises perfectibility, such that it is the structuring feature of the entire organic world; that is, nature has a history too. In *La palingénésie philosophique*, for example, he is clear: 'An animal is a perfectible being, perfectible to an indefinite degree' (2002: 137). There is 'a continual progress... of all species towards a superior perfection' (2002: 155). The human still remains 'the most perfectible of all terrestrial beings' according to Bonnet (2002: 227), but this is a matter of the degree of energy or forcefulness of the species' innate principle of perfectibility. And yet, despite this naturalisation of perfectibility, Bonnet still attempts to understand it as a spiritual principle; it is just that this immaterial property pervades the natural world as a whole (2002: 393).

Hemsterhuis' principle of perfectibility owes much to Bonnet – in his teleological insistence on 'the progressive movement of the perfectibility of man' (B 7.100, 269) and in his embedding of perfectibility 'in the physical world' of the five senses (B 6.55, 154). However, just as it is not strictly Rousseauean, it is not *quite* dogmatically Bonnetian either. Hemsterhuis certainly does not make recourse to perfectibility to consolidate any kind of Leibnizian optimism, but instead constantly criticises 'the phantom of optimism' (B 4.60, 154) and Leibniz' 'satirical joke about optimism' (B 8.7, 31; see also B 7.27, 78).

---

[25] To which Rousseau responds in his reply to Philopolis: 'Simply because a thing exists it is not permissible to wish that it exist differently.... [On this basis] the most absolute quietism is the only virtue left to man' (2018: 233).

§12 PERFECTIBILITY

3. *Alexis* constitutes Hemsterhuis' final reckoning with Rousseau and Bonnet on the historicity of the human.[26] It is here that he attempts to position his principle of perfectibility amidst the competing variants in the air at the time by staging a conversion narrative that moves from Rousseau to Bonnet. *Pace* van Bunge, this is certainly one contemporaneous philosophical debate into which Hemsterhuis substantially intervenes.

The starting point is provided by Alexis' Rousseauean dogma (see §1): there is something about the human's historical development that marks it apart from the animal's lack of 'history'. In Alexis' own words, 'Man's position on the earth has changed remarkably, while animals have stayed the same'. Alexis goes on to 'conclude from the fact that men have changed immensely, while the other animals have remained in the same position' that 'there is some principle of perfectibility that adheres to the nature of man' but which is not to be found 'in other species of animals' (*EE* 2.126; *OP* 582–4). Immediately, however, Diocles (i.e., Hemsterhuis) contests this position and successfully converts Alexis away from this standard Rousseaueanism (in which perfectibility marks the opposition between human and animal). To his later question 'Are we to say then that animals are absolutely destitute of this principle?', Alexis changes his mind, rescinds his earlier response, and answers, 'It seems to me at present that we cannot do so.... It has this power of which you speak' (*EE* 2.126; *OP* 584). Diocles then summarises, 'Man and animal are endowed with the same principle' and, indeed, one can trace 'the nature and progress of your principle of perfectibility in all animals' (*EE* 2.126–7; *OP* 584, 588).

Alexis thus shifts towards a Bonnetian position in which perfectibility is naturalised. It becomes a universal feature of the organic world, rather than a uniquely anthropological distinguishing mark. The organic world is perfectible too, and so the human and the animal are not to be strictly opposed when it comes to perfectibility; instead, the principle of perfection in the human subject is distinguished by degree – it is 'richer', more 'energetic' and less 'determinate' (*EE* 2.126; *OP* 584).[27] Indeed, so close is *Alexis* to Bonnet's rendering of perfectibility as a teleological becoming-perfect of the whole organic world that Hemsterhuis has to appeal to a foreign, inorganic

---

[26] *Pace* Moenkemeyer's claim (1975: 156) that there is no trace of Rousseau in *Alexis*' account of the golden age.

[27] Hemsterhuis typically distinguishes the human from the animal in other ways than the principles of perfectibility; for example, by way of semiotic capacity or the moral organ (and so society, self-consciousness and religion), (see *EE* 1.93, 2.82; *OP* 196, 448).

body (the moon) to explain the fact that history is structured by decline, as well as progress, that is, 'the eccentric progress of [man's] perfectibility' (B 3.86, 201).[28] The coming of the moon (as a comet that is caught in the earth's gravitational pull) disrupts the equilibrium of the earth and so the happy progress of the human: 'Terror, distress, a stupid fright took the place of the sweetest tranquillity' (*EE* 2.137; *OP* 618). Left to itself, nature would have proceeded from perfection to perfection; only an external principle could have disrupted this logic.[29] This admission of a decline in human history may look Rousseauean, that is, it looks like an admission that history's movement towards perfection is fragile. But such fragility is precisely not a transcendental potential of human becoming (as it is for Rousseau), but something alien that comes from outside and disrupts the predetermined becoming-perfect of human existence. Nothing intrinsic to the human or organic nature can explain decline for Hemsterhuis, *pace* Rousseau: it must come from some kind of *lithos ex machina*.

Moreover, where Hemsterhuis is closest to Bonnet and furthest from Rousseau is in reinserting the principle of perfectibility into an eschatology. To perfect oneself is to anticipate a higher condition for the human: souls scale 'degrees of perfection' owing to the 'continual pull' they experience 'towards virtue, happiness and perfection'. They are perpetually in the process of being 'carried to another state' (B 1.19, 48). 'Man's indestructible attraction towards the future and towards something better' (*EE* 2.91; *OP* 476) is given a teleological structure in Hemsterhuis' thinking, and this not only stands in tension with Rousseau's more fragile understanding of perfectibility, but also returns us to the mystic overtones of Hemsterhuisian organology touched on in §11. Perfectibility in Hemsterhuis has two ends: the first end is that attained by Socrates and Fagel, a this-worldly ideal of faculty-harmony based on perfecting organs as currently constituted. This is the goal of Hemsterhuis' humanist pedagogical project. However, he also invokes a further end to perfectibility – one beyond the human as currently

---

[28] To put it another way: perfectibility is ultimately a 'progressive movement' (see B 7.100, 269), even if it progresses eccentrically, i.e., according to the model of Keplerian elliptical orbits (of perihelia and aphelia) set out in the *Lettre sur l'Homme*. Hemsterhuis himself admits that, while the 'movements' of perfectibility 'are not uniform', he has not got round to properly explaining its dynamic 'laws' (B 3.86, 201).

[29] See also Aristaeus' comments on 'the activity of fire' as a destructive agent of the 'organic course' of nature (*EE* 2.74; *OP* 424). In *Alexis*, Hemsterhuis repeatedly emphasises the above point by way of the anti-Rousseauean idea that 'human nature has not been bastardised' and so any suggestion of such bastardisation after the golden age has been 'merely an accidental appearance' (*EE* 2.125, 2.145; *OP* 580, 640).

defined. And this extra-terrestrial perfection is represented most visibly by the Diotima of *Simon*. She exemplifies an even higher ideal of perfection beyond the current state of the human – a perfection alluded to in the final words of her speech to Socrates:

> We have no other ladder to climb to the height at which you contemplate us. We ascended faster, and that is what gives us our advantage. . . . [Happy souls like me] devote themselves entirely to the charge of perfecting themselves. They disengage themselves from all that is earthly and perishable around them. They accelerate their development, and new organs manifest themselves. It is then that our relations to the Gods become more immediate, and that the universe manifests itself to us from several sides which are yet naught to you and other men. (*EE* 2.121; *OP* 570)

This is no perfection available in the present (for such a perfection is limited by the current number of organs the subject possesses); it is, rather, a perfection attained by transcendence and self-overcoming, a gradual divesting of the constraints of our current organs to attain something new – something more. Diotima concludes,

> When the soul is completely freed, it becomes all organ. The gap which separates the visible from the audible is filled with other sensations. All sensations are linked and together form one body, and the soul sees the universe not in God, but in the manner of the Gods. (*EE* 2.121; *OP* 570–2)

Extra-terrestrial perfection is expressly articulated in organological terms: it is a matter of *becoming entirely organ*. The human subject is perfected by becoming all organ, and to achieve this condition of all-organ is to gain a total sensation of the universe (and so the most perfect possible knowledge). Diotima, as a mystic, exemplifies this state of 'entirely organ': she has proliferated 'new organs' to the extent that 'the shining spectacle of the richness of the human soul is discovered' and the future is 'penetrated'. These organs are capable of receiving every possible sensation simultaneously – that is, Diotima not only 'insectifies' the human mind, she deifies it: she 'sees the universe not in god but in the fashion of gods' (*EE* 2.121; *OP* 572).

Of course, I have already suggested in §9 that Hemsterhuis does not always seem to fully endorse every word put into Diotima's mouth in *Simon*. That is, her speech is given to hyperbole in a way that may be intended to ironise some of its doctrines and even self-satirise Hemsterhuis' own thinking. Through

Diotima, Hemsterhuis seems happy to subject his own theories to scrutiny by means of self-critical exaggeration, a reduction to the ridiculous. This is also possibly the case here, with respect to the excessive perfections to which Diotima lays claim. That is, insofar as Diotima goes beyond a Socratic ideal, Hemsterhuis may well be suspicious of her. For example, as the dedication to *Simon* implies (*EE* 2.101; *OP* 502), her speech verges on a literal affirmation of the doctrine of palingenetic metempsychosis, a doctrine in which humans are perpetually born anew in ever higher states. Hemsterhuis certainly never lets himself get away with such claims elsewhere, and, indeed, generally he has a very ambivalent relationship to metempsychosis. While Diocles might rhapsodise in a similar vein in *Aristée* ('How many developments, how many deaths are necessary for the soul to attain the greatest perfection of which its essence is capable' [*EE* 2.98; *OP* 494]), in correspondence Hemsterhuis is quick to reject any literal interpretation of perpetual rebirth (B 1.144, 180; 7.92, 249). The extra-terrestrial perfectibility Diotima exemplifies therefore occupies an uneasy position in Hemsterhuis' philosophy (one reflected by his more general ambivalence to the palingenetic element of Bonnet's philosophy). Diotima is both the final product of a teleological conception of human historicity as entailing always-greater perfections and a mythical figure whose hyperbolic words are shot through with irony.

§13 The Analogy to Morality

The most famous (and infamous) of all Hemsterhuisian organs is the moral organ, which he introduces in the *Lettre sur l'Homme* as follows:

> When it was demonstrated that man is endowed with an organ distinct from his five other organs, it was demonstrated that essence has relations to us manifested through other means than sight, hearing, touch, etc., and I have named this means, insofar as it pertains to us, the moral organ, by which we receive all our moral sensations. (*EE* 1.131–2; *OP* 312)

Hemsterhuis' postulation of a moral organ is either seen as his 'most significant philosophical achievement' (Hammacher 1971: 78) – a 'genuinely prophetic' theory leading to a 'new treatment of morality' (Novalis 1960–2006: 3.561) – or it is written off as obscure, nonsensical or even fatuous, such as when Diderot exclaims on reading the *Lettre sur l'Homme*: 'I do not know what this moral organ is' (Diderot and Hemsterhuis 1964: 297). As Moenkemeyer summarises, 'There is nothing that has aroused as much attention or criticism as the notion of the *organe moral*' (1975: 72). What

§13 THE ANALOGY TO MORALITY

I want to argue in what follows is that, whatever its value, the moral organ must be understood as embedded within Hemsterhuis' organological project as a whole. It is merely one instance of his history of organs.

1. Hemsterhuis' doctrine of the moral organ is relatively straightforward to elucidate. There are, he claims, mind-independent moral facts that the human subject is able to perceive and that are irreducible to natural facts. Perception of these facts requires a distinct organ, an organ which is, in turn, irreducible to any other organ or configuration of organs. Again, Hemsterhuis' axiom of a one-to-one correspondence between properties and organs is central to his reasoning: where there are distinct properties, there are distinct organs (and vice versa) (see, e.g., B 2.55, 156). It follows that, on the one hand, moral value has nothing to do with volition, for values 'depend directly and uniquely on moral sensation and have no more relation to the velleity than to the faculty of sight' (B 2.64, 192). And, on the other hand, he stresses in his early work the independence of morality from rationality or any form of reasoning whatsoever: 'The intuitive or intellectual faculty must not be confused with the moral organ' (EE 1.109; OP 248). This double distinction separates Hemsterhuis both from contemporaneous moral sense theorists like Hutcheson and from the Parisian materialists. It is no surprise, then, that Diderot reacts most strongly against the ethical passages of the *Lettre sur l'Homme* (see §15).

Hemsterhuis aims to safeguard the integrity of a distinctly moral domain: 'If the moral organ is admitted as a distinct quality, just like sight and hearing are distinct qualities, then this is enough' (B 2.55, 156). He makes the case for this integrity on the basis of the absurdity of the naturalist position: any position that reduces moral facts to physical ones ends up rendering virtue dependent on the capacities of the five existing sense organs. According to the naturalist, moral judgement depends on data obtained through some amalgam of what is seen, heard and felt – and so to see, to hear or to feel worse is to be less sensitive to moral value. In other words, Hemsterhuis argues that, on the naturalist position, the blind and deaf would be ethically disabled. He complains, 'But no, [for these naturalists] the moral organ is a mixture of the visible, the audible and the tangible. Homer, the blind Homer thus had little moral sense when he sung of Heroes and Gods! And from this it is proven that Saunderson had little morality?' (B 2.53, 148). The blind Nicholas Saunderson is the hero of Diderot's *Lettre sur les aveugles*, who, for Diderot, exemplifies the cogency of the materialist position; however, Hemsterhuis appropriates him in support of a proof against the materialists – as a proof that the five physical senses have nothing to do with moral value (see Sonderen 2000: 122). As so often, Hemsterhuis turns the arguments of the materialists against themselves.

Moral properties are received from a 'face of the universe' that stands in analogy to the moral organ itself, and this face is defined as 'being-as-agent'. That is, to perceive morally is to perceive facts about the character and actions of agents and their worth. This does not merely include the value of other agents, but also one's own value. The moral organ is not just the organ of intersubjective relationships, but it is also that of self-consciousness. In Hemsterhuis' own words,

> This organ, this heart, which gives me sensations of this face of the universe, differs from our other organs principally in that it gives us a sensation of a face of which our soul, our I, forms a part; thus, for this organ, the I itself becomes an object of contemplation. (*EE* 1.104–5; *OP* 234)

The face of the universe perceived by the moral organ includes the self: through it alone, 'the I itself becomes an object of contemplation'. The other senses merely communicate 'to us relations of things outside of us', but the moral organ communicates 'our relations to things which are outside of us' (*EE* 1.104; *OP* 232). As Söhngen puts it, 'The self has, so to speak, its own organ – we become aware of ourselves, we feel our existence through this organ' (1995: 279; see also Hammacher 1971: 82–3). More particularly, what the moral organ perceives are relations of attraction and repulsion between individuals in society (and not, as is sometimes claimed, anything abstract, such as 'love' or 'the ideal'). These perceptions parallel the corresponding Newtonian physical forces of attraction and inertia, and are in fact analogous but irreducible to them. Hemsterhuis' ethics is therefore one more instance of his overall project of analogical Newtonianism (see §4).

Hemsterhuis thus gives consciousness of others and self-consciousness the same ground – the moral organ. Through the moral organ, we enter into *society*, we take our place 'in the midst of other animated beings, other acting wills' (*EE* 1.104; *OP* 232). This is an organological variation on social contract theory: the activation of the moral organ marks the subject's emergence from the state of nature. The individual considered 'absolutely isolated and ... not forming part of society' has 'no sensation of the moral face of the universe' (*EE* 1.90, 1.108; *OP* 186, 244).[30] And, in addition

---

[30] In his unpublished *Réflections*, Hemsterhuis is even more explicit: 'One man alone, isolated on earth, must be considered as deprived of this [moral] principle' (*WW* 458; *IN* 61). See also B 1.19, 45.

to socialising us, the moral organ is responsible for our self-awareness, for the fact that we reflect on our own thoughts and actions and attain self-consciousness. Indeed, Hemsterhuis goes on to add that the human subject also becomes aware of God through the moral organ (see *EE* 1.114; *OP* 264) – hence, in society, 'there are no atheists', for 'all healthy and well-adjusted men have a relatively distinct sensation of the real and necessary existence of the divinity' (*EE* 1.118; *OP* 276).

While the above elucidates much of what the moral organ is, it is also worth enumerating what it is not. The moral organ should not be equated with the unknown organs-to-come of Hemsterhuis' organology introduced in §11. This is an interpretative trap into which many fall: they identify future sense organs with the moral organ, to the extent that the latter comes to encompass all perceptions that exceed or transcend those of the five physical senses; that is, it becomes the organ of the immaterial or of the ideal in general. Nassar labels this interpretative strategy that of 'an expanded sense of the moral' (2013: 41). It is a tendency found in the reception history as early as Novalis, who designates 'moral' everything in Hemsterhuis that stands opposed to the material side of the universe (1960–2006: 2.369); Grucker aggrandises the moral organ into 'the very principle of the life of the soul' (1866: 90); and, in the twentieth century, Hartmann calls the moral organ 'the universal organ of ideal being' and 'the organ of spiritual being', explaining that it is 'a key to a whole world . . . [to] an ideal sphere, a sphere of essences' (1923: 166–8). Likewise, Walzel insists that it is 'more a spiritual than an ethical sense' (1934: 96) and even Ayrault speaks of the moral organ generically as 'the organ which opens man up to the invisible world' (1961: 1.486). Although Hemsterhuis does indeed claim that, rather like some organ still to be activated 'until now', the moral organ 'has no proper name and . . . is commonly referred to as heart, sentiment, conscience' (*EE* 1.104; *OP* 232), there is still one irrefutable reason why it cannot be identified with any of the organs-to-come: every social, self-conscious being *must already* possess an active moral organ. The moral organ functions whenever a human emerges from the state of nature.

Moreover, to incorrectly identify the moral organ with an organ-to-come is to establish a dualism between physical organs, on the one side, and 'moral' organs, on the other – an interpretative strategy that runs parallel to that which falsely opposes the immaterial to matter as such in Hemsterhuis' philosophy (see §11). Both interpretative mistakes render Hemsterhuis a binary thinker, that is, defining the moral organ by way of a break from matter as such, by way of a gesture of transcendence into the spiritual. The lessons to be drawn from Hemsterhuis' hypermaterialism in *Sophyle* hold here too: the moral organ should be placed *alongside* the eye or the imagination as one more organ in an expanded conception of material sensation. There is no hard line separating the physical organs from the 'spiritual' ones: all organs – the moral organ, as well as the organ of vision and the organ of touch – stand in analogy to each other, rather than in relations of opposition or negation. The materialist's mistake is, once more, to inadequately expand her conception of reality, in order, this time, to include *distinct* perceptions of moral relations.

2. Hemsterhuis does give an explanation for this interpretative mistake, as well as, more generally, for the widespread failure to correctly identify the moral organ. In modernity, the moral organ has fallen into disrepair, been obscured and so has been ignored by philosophers. In other words – like all organs – the moral organ has a history, and its history is one of corruption and decline. Of all the organs (physiological and psychological) the moral organ is the one most in need of perfecting, and the modern subject should focus her efforts on cultivating this organ if she desires faculty-harmony. The modern subject perceives moral properties in a less clear and vivid manner than she does audible or, particularly, visual properties. More moral sensations are needed – in line with the insectification imperative of §10 – to increase the determinacy and force of moral ideas (*EE* 1.104; *OP* 232). Moreover, according to Hemsterhuis, the decrepitude of the moral organ is a consequence of 'the limits imposed on it by a certain modification of society'. And so, he goes on to claim, while 'in the current modification of society, our organs of sight and hearing are the most exercised and least constrained', the opposite is true of the moral organ (*EE* 1.104; *OP* 230). The imperfection attributed to vision in the *Lettre sur l'optique* is here shown, from a broader perspective, to be relatively minor in relation to the radical imperfections of the moral organ. The most urgent task for Hemsterhuis' pedagogy of organs is to attend to the moral organ once more, to rectify the mistakes of modernity and to teach the modern subject how to restore it. This is the priority for his educational programme.[31]

It is here that Hemsterhuis' organology overlaps most clearly with the system of times elaborated in Chapter One. The contrast between the ancient and the modern perihelia – between the sentimental and geometrical

---

[31] Indeed, more generally, 'The greatest happiness to which it seems that man can aspire at any time resides in the increase of the perfection or sensibility of the moral organ'. He continues, 'when you have purified that organ', evil will be impossible, and you will become a 'hero... for whom virtue' is an 'emanation' of essence. It all 'depends on the degree of perfection of the moral organ' (*EE* 2.96–7; *OP* 490–2).

spirits – turns on the relative perfections of different organs. The Greeks focused on enhancing the moral organ at the expense of those organs exercised in the study of physics (particularly sight), whereas, in modernity, sight has become so dominant as to relegate the moral organ to obscurity. In modernity, 'man became completely physical' at the expense of the ethical domain (EE 1.113; OP 260). The absence of any accepted name for the moral organ (and so the peculiarity of Hemsterhuis' own use of the term) is itself evidence, he claims, of its neglect (EE 1.104; OP 232). In other words, the geometrical spirit results from disharmony of the organs, a preponderance of vision which has harmed ethical, social and religious thinking and even the vitality of self-consciousness. There is yet to appear a Newton of morality in modernity (just as no one in antiquity rose to the heights of Socratic self-reflection in the physical sciences) – and so it has fallen to Hemsterhuis himself to occupy this role. Hence, in an early letter to Gallitzin, Hemsterhuis precisely frames his project as an attempt to illuminate the moral organ 'with the same ray of light that Newton brought to the visible and material universe' (B 1.26, 60–1). What modernity lacks is a tactful physics of the moral world, which Hemsterhuis himself is aiming to provide with his account of 'the basis of all morals' as the 'counterbalance' of moral attraction and moral inertia, that is, with the formulation of 'a law ... which God has given to free and active beings, so that they love one another, so that they unite together with each other, just as he has given the laws of attraction and inertia to matter' (EE 1.81–2, 2.96; OP 160, 488). Hemsterhuis attempts to elaborate ethics (as well as aesthetics, politics and religion) in *strict analogy* to physics.[32]

It follows that the moral organ is a key component of Hemsterhuis' untimely philosophising – that is, his production of an anachronistic mode of thinking – and ultimately of his aim to inhabit all times simultaneously. To recapture the sentimental spirit of the Greeks (i.e., to emulate Socrates) is to perfect the moral organ; to conserve the geometrical spirit of the moderns is to keep on perfecting the 'physical' organs (i.e., to emulate Newton). This is one implication of the organological ideal of cultivating all organs simultaneously: faculty-harmony is the means by which to participate in all

---

[32] This is made particularly explicit in the fragment *Alexis II*: just as 'in physics' laws define the movement of bodies, so, too, willing beings are defined by 'their mutual attraction or gravitation': 'Just as there must necessarily be in solid and mobile essences a reciprocal gravitation for order to be possible, likewise in active and willing essences there must be an inclination, a mutual gravitation for morals and intellect to be possible' (WW 364; IN 117).

epochs. Such harmony entails an omnitemporal mind, one that partakes in eternity. Furthermore, it also follows that, while he makes use of advances in vision as an exemplary model for the perfecting of organs, Hemsterhuis is also critical of ocularcentrism, of the extent to which vision has assumed this paradigmatic status in modernity, that is, the extent to which the perfecting of optics dominates modern organology to the detriment of moral perfection. Advances in telescopes and microscopes should not occur at the expense of moral technologies, but in tandem with them. This, in short, captures Hemsterhuis' fundamental ambivalence towards modern science.

3. Hemsterhuis' doctrine of the moral organ is elaborated through a series of analogies:

> Just as the organ of touch exposes the universe as tangible to the individual man, just as hearing and air expose the universe as sound to him, just as sight and light expose the universe as visible to him – so what he calls heart or conscience, and society with homogeneous beings, expose the universe as moral to him. (*EE* 1.103; *OP* 230)

In particular, he stresses the analogy that holds between sight and the moral organ (i.e., between the organ most familiar to the moderns and that which is least familiar):

> The moral organ [is] infinitely curious by the very singular affinity it has with the organ of sight. I believe to have claimed, my Diotima, that a serious examination of this affinity would make us see more clearly the nature of the interior of all our organs. (*B* 8.21, 58)

In his early publications, this analogy motivates Hemsterhuis' attribution of passivity to moral reflection. That is, the passivity of the subject in perceiving the physical world holds good in moral perception too: 'I sense, thus I am passive; therefore I am' (*EE* 2.48; *OP* 344). All perceptions – whether visual or moral – necessarily presuppose the passivity of the perceiving subject. Even in his later accounts of morality in *Aristée* and *Simon*, much may change (particularly on this question of the passivity of moral judgement), but the analogy with other organs remains: the moral organ still operates 'much like the intellect works on ideas' (*EE* 2.116; *OP* 556).[33]

---

[33] The major difference between the early and late Hemsterhuis on the moral organ resides in this shift between two different meanings of 'organ' – from situating it along-

§13 THE ANALOGY TO MORALITY

In fact, analogical relations proliferate throughout Hemsterhuis' ontology, psychology, epistemology and ethics more generally. Relations between the organs themselves, between the sense organs and external objects, between the idea of an object and the object itself, between external objects, between ideas themselves, between ideas and words, between the world and God – all these are defined as analogical relations. The moral organ is just one component of an analogic ontology that goes all the way down. This is what Hammacher dubs 'Hemsterhuis' analogy-thinking' (1971: 153; 1995b: 418).[34]

For example, a fundamental analogy connects the subject to the object in knowledge, such that 'the composition of ideas represents what would effectively result from an analogous composition in things' (*EE* 2.140; *OP* 626). As a result, *Sophyle*'s argument begins with a demonstration of 'the truth of the analogy between things and ideas' (*EE* 2.51; *OP* 354). There is, furthermore, an analogical relation between the external objects themselves and between ideas themselves: 'There is between ideas the same analogy as between things' – and so 'the conclusions that I draw from reasoning [on ideas] will be equally analogous to that which I draw from reasoning on the things themselves' (*EE* 2.48; *OP* 346). Additional analogical relations exist between the external object and the vehicle of action that communicates its properties to the subject, as well as between the vehicle and the sense organ which is 'analogous to the vehicle' (*EE* 2.58; *OP* 378). When Hemsterhuis speaks of a face of the universe that is 'turned towards' the subject or that 'pertains to' it, he precisely intends to designate a series of analogies that proceed from essence to 'an organ capable of receiving its action' (*EE* 2.58; *OP* 378). Knowledge is possible only when such analogies hold. Moreover, the analogy between the moral organ and the other organs (particularly sight) is but one example of the analogic structure that holds between all organs just as analogies hold between a face of the universe and an organ (i.e., within one attribute of the universe), so too they hold across faces (i.e., transattributionally) and across organs too (i.e., transorganically). Hemsterhuis is explicit: 'Just as the tangible face [of

side the physiological sense organs (e.g., sight, hearing) in the *Lettre sur l'Homme* to situating it alongside the psychological faculties in *Simon*. It is this play on the meaning of 'organ' that warrants Hemsterhuis' return to the language of 'moral organ' in *Simon* despite the radical changes his moral epistemology undergoes in the meantime.

[34] Hammacher distinguishes the way this 'analogy thinking' is manifest in Hemsterhuis' early publications 'in derivative, analogical formulae' from its more complex and nuanced appearance in the later works (1971: 125). I explore the stylistic implications of analogy-thinking for Hemsterhuis' dialogues in subsequent sections.

the universe] is to the visible face, so too the visible face is to another face, etc.' (*EE* 1.103; *OP* 228). He continues, 'There is no more incommensurability between the moral face of the universe and the visible face than between the visible face and the audible face or between the audible face and the tangible face, etc.' (*EE* 1.103–4; *OP* 230). In other words, there is nothing exceptional about the morality–vision analogy that distinguishes it from the vision–hearing analogy or even the touch–smell analogy. And this is equally true of the analogies that hold between all these organs and the new, unknown organs about which Hemsterhuis speculates: they too are captured within this web of analogies.[35] Moreover, this proliferation of analogic relations extends much further still. To give but two more examples. First, the relation between the human and God is one of analogy, according to Hemsterhuis: an analogy exists between human faculties and divine faculties and this analogy makes possible legitimate reasoning about God's properties, even though God himself is 'infinitely above our intellect' (*EE* 2.85; *OP* 456). Secondly, an analogic relation exists between linguistic signs and the ideas to which they refer: 'signs of truth' exhibit an 'analogous [relation] to the truths they designate', and bodily gestures are also 'uniquely analogous to the ideas from which they originate' (*EE* 1.106; *OP* 236). In his *Hemsterhuis-Studien*, Novalis explicitly dubs such gestures 'analogic signs' (1960–2006: 2.365).

'Everything is analogous' (B 5.6b, 35) and analogies are everywhere (see Bulle 1911: 15). And the master concept under which all such analogic relations are subsumed is that of '*rapport*'. Hemsterhuis' philosophy is one that is always finding more and more *rapports* in the self, in the world and in science – he speaks of 'the infinitely infinite multiplicity of these *rapports*' (B 9.6, 22). This obsession with *rapports* has its roots in 's Gravesande's teaching (de Pater 1995: 235–6; see also Ducheyne 2014a: 43)[36] as well as Hemsterhuis' own reading of Newton (de Pater 1995: 236–8) and Plato (Vieillard-Barom 1988: 124–7; Funder 1912: 21);[37] it also emerges out of a late scholastic tradition found in Clauberg (Hammacher 1971: 66); and even his own father's philological methodology was established on analogic reasoning (Petry

---

[35] This is one of the reasons why none of the properties perceived by these unknown organs can be excluded from a genuinely extended – or absolute – concept of matter, on pain of arbitrariness.

[36] Although, as Hammacher points out, Hemsterhuis never resorts to analogical reasoning to prove the existence of God, as 's Gravesande often does (1971: 67).

[37] In fact, the neoplatonic axiom 'we know that in everything a cause must be analogous to its effect and the effect to its cause' (*EE* 2.59; *OP* 378) underwrites much of Hemsterhuis' analogic ontology.

§13 THE ANALOGY TO MORALITY

2003a: 426). However, Hemsterhuis' analogomania is more precisely a product of the popularisation of the concept of *rapport* in mid-eighteenth-century Francophone philosophy, particularly via Diderot and Bonnet.[38] '*Rapport*' names the structure of repetition, resemblance and also differentiation that defines the commerce between all parts of the universe, no matter how disparate and unrelated they might appear. As Hemsterhuis states at the end of *Lettre sur l'Homme*, what matters most of all in every science is the increase in the quality of our ideas of relation (*EE* 1.122; *OP* 290): the task of the knowing subject is to reveal as many of these correspondences as possible – 'seeing *rapports* when nobody had seen them before' (Moenkemeyer 1975: 111), to proliferate them in the mind as they are proliferated outside of it, to add ideas of relation onto ideas of relation.

4. Philosophers are those who recognise the most analogies, who 'train their intellect in all cases to know and to run the path of analogy' (*B* 2.47, 114–15). Hemsterhuis sometimes gives this intellectual faculty of recognising *rapports* the name 'genius' (*WW* 464; *IN* 65) or, in *Alexis*, 'enthusiasm', 'inspiration' and 'poetry' (see Cahen-Maurel 2017: 266), but mostly it is called 'tact'. We have already seen the importance of such tactful reasoning for Hemsterhuis' own philosophical practice in his extension of Newtonian methodology outside of the physical sciences, as well as in his hermeneutics of tone. Moreover, Hemsterhuisian tact will play an increasingly important role in later pages of this book. Tact is defined as a kind of 'infinitely rapid reasoning' (*B* 7.37, 104) or 'rapid intuition' (*EE* 2.142; *OP* 632) or even 'instantaneous and infinitely rapid contemplation' (*B* 4.1, 14). It is to be attributed to those minds which are able to perceive even the least evident *rapports* quickly and fluently, and which thereby exhibit a 'faculty' of 'grasping the homology between ideas that are far away from each other and very disparate in appearance, so as to bring them together' (*WW* 464; *IN* 65). Tact involves the process of encompassing 'in an instant . . . twenty or thirty ideas of extremely heterogenous things which have few relations to each other' and combining them 'into a very beautiful and luminous whole' (*B* 4.1 14).

Again, Hemsterhuis situates himself in a long philosophical tradition, reaching back to Aristotle's and Aquinas' appropriation of analogic judgement as a non-discursive, perceptual sensitivity towards experience (Burrell 1973: 89–90), through the *Encyclopédie*'s definition of Socratic method as 'the perception of subtle *rapports* between unperceived realities' (Ibrahim

---

[38] On this genealogy, see further Brummel (1925: 122) and Sonderen (2000: 144). For Bonnet in particular, *rapports* are 'primary and defining units' (Anderson 1982: 123).

2010: 101), to Bonnet, once more, who describes his methodology as 'the act of perceiving *rapports*' (quoted in Savioz 1948: 320).[39] Hemsterhuis even stands close to the romantic and idealist definition of *Witz* as a constant seeking for 'related traits in the apparently most heterogeneous material and ... combining things that are poles apart from one another' (Hegel 1999: 407). That is, for Hemsterhuis, the philosopher must sensitively search out what links together all things and all ideas – no matter what barriers appear to divide them. The philosopher must, above all, be tactful in joining up reality.

§14 Organology and Style

The preceding sections of this chapter have described the main features of Hemsterhuis' organology – that is, the twofold call to perfect our current organs and to proliferate new ones. These organological demands structure his epistemology, his metaphysics, his ethics, his philosophy of education, his philosophical methodology and even his work in optics. To conclude this chapter, I want to show how it motivates his practices of philosophical communication too, that is, why organology matters for Hemsterhuis' writing. My concern is with *organological style*. Just like in the concluding section of the previous chapter, I now proceed by way of a specific case study – Hypsicles' speech on the golden age in *Alexis*. The purpose of this case study is to identify the particular ways in which Hemsterhuis' organology impacts on how one specific passage is written.

Hypsicles' speech is introduced in *Alexis* as follow,

> Archytas used to recount to his intimate friends that when Pythagoras travelled in Phoenicia, he went to Byblos, less to contemplate the ancient ruins of this famous town which Saturn founded than to listen there to an old priest of Adonis, who was well instructed in the science of the stars and who had the reputation for being more enlightened than other men. ... He was the first to teach Pythagoras that the globe of the earth goes around the sun in a great circle over the span of a year; that the earth turns around on its axis in a day and a night from the West towards the Orient – and this, he said, is the cause of the apparent movement of all the stars from the East to the West. He taught him the causes of the change of the seasons. He explained to him the course of the planets, as well as comets,

---

[39] Bonnet continues, 'To investigate the how of a thing is to look for the secret *rapports* which link this thing with others' (quoted in Savioz 1948: 324).

whose return he predicted in the manner of the Chaldeans. Finally, when he came on to the moon, Pythagoras complained to the old man of the extravagant vanity of the Arcadians who called themselves the most ancient people on earth, since they were even older than the moon; and thereupon, the priest said to him these remarkable words: Pythagoras, it is the ignorance of your Greeks that you should complain of. (*EE* 2.133–4; *OP* 606–8)

Hypsicles (the 'old priest') goes on to relate a theodical narrative of three historical ages. There was an initial golden age before the appearance of the moon, where 'trees were always equally laden with fruit, flowers and greenery', 'language was absolutely perfect' and science was 'administered only by signs perfectly in accord with the objects that represented them'. At this period, imagination was 'so pure, so lively' as to see God everywhere, and 'all evil and all fear were absurd' (*EE* 2.136; *OP* 610–12). The golden age ended, however, with lunar catastrophe: when the moon entered the earth's orbit, it effected 'an irregular movement in the waters', leading to cloud, wind and rain, 'black vapours rose up', thunder and lightning 'criss-crossed the dark and vast vault of the sky for the first time', and 'terror, distress, a stupid fright took the place of the sweetest tranquillity' (*EE* 2.136–7; *OP* 614–16). As the effects of this lunar catastrophe waned, a post-catastrophic era dawned in which 'more tranquil moments' could be experienced: 'man began to more or less recognise himself', to 'come to terms with evils' and 'sense the beautiful and the sublime even in those objects that had been horrible to the eyes of their fathers' (*EE* 2.137; *OP* 618).

Out of this tripartite historical schema Diocles draws the following organological conclusion. Reflecting on the limitations of the human as constituted at present, he asks,

Is it not possible, my dear Alexis, to sense the large probability that we have lost senses . . . of which there no longer remains any vestige except in the more or less altered traditions of our ancient condition? Is it possible to deny all belief in Hypsicles' speech? (*EE* 2.138; *OP* 618)

The conclusion to the speech thus brings to the fore an organological lesson: that human organs are plastic (some have been lost and must be regained) and, through a pedagogy of organs, humanity will recover them and increase its perfection so as to bring about another golden age. The content of Hypsicles' speech thus turns on organology, but there is an organological style at play here too.

1. Hypsicles' teachings are situated as the primal scene of Western thinking – the ground zero from which scientific truths are then transmitted, via Pythagoras, into the Greek tradition and on into European modernity. Indeed, Hemsterhuis alludes to a number of astronomical truths that had apparently first entered Europe with Pythagoras, including those of heliocentrism and diurnal rotation (*EE* 2.134; *OP* 608). There is a sense that this moment is meant to act as *the* defining encounter that sets in motion the West's intellectual trajectory.

Hypsicles' speech on the golden age itself is sandwiched between four other discourses. First, there is Hypsicles' own crude, mythical explanation of the annual reddening of the Adonis River that flows down from Mount Liban as caused by the bleeding wound of the apparition of Adonis. Diocles and Alexis treat such 'derisory' words as little more than superstitious prejudice (*EE* 2.134; *OP* 606). Secondly, there is Hypsicles' subsequent meteorological explanation of the same phenomenon in terms of sand deposited in the river by a strong easterly wind – which is considered sufficiently scientific by the dialogue participants to be true ('This I understand!', Alexis exclaims [*EE* 2.134; *OP* 608]). Hypsicles distinguishes between these two explanations of the same phenomenon in terms of their audience: myth is for the uninitiated, science for the initiated. He then continues the latter discourse by again teaching Pythagoras (as one of the initiated) a series of fundamental astronomical truths subsequently verified in modernity (e.g., heliocentrism, the daily rotation of the earth on its axis and the inclination of the earth's axis).[40] There follows Hypsicles' speech on the golden age itself, which Hemsterhuis elsewhere describes both as a 'poetic fiction' (*B* 3.86, 199–200) and as laying claim to 'the most exact truth' (*B* 12.133, 190). And to it is appended a long editorial note (*EE* 2.149–51; *OP* 652–60) that tries to gather modern scientific evidence that might support Hypsicles' truthful fiction. This note provides 'a scientific analysis of the presuppositions for the disappearance of the first Golden Age' (Hammacher 1995a: 70; see also Melica 2005: 87). Finally, later in the dialogue, Diocles returns to Hypsicles' myth and, at Alexis' request, translates it, as far as is possible, into philosophical concepts (*EE* 2.143; *OP* 634) – a kind of logical demythologisation or rational reconstruction of Hypsicles' picture-thinking.

Two further pertinent discourses should be mentioned. First, Hesiod's original narrative of the golden age in *Work and Days* provides an initial model for the dialogue: as Alexis intimates, Hypsicles' version is intended

---

[40] Elsewhere, Hemsterhuis will speak of the Pythagoreans 'having acquired correct and true ideas of cosmology' (*EE* 1.118; *OP* 278).

as a more plausible and less absurd rendering of Hesiod's cruder myth of the golden age: 'You appear to be wanting to prove to me the truth of Hesiod's very absurd fable through the likelihood of Hypsicles' less absurd fable' (*EE* 2.138–9; *OP* 620–2). Finally, there are Hemsterhuis' own preparatory studies on the origins of the moon which he undertakes elsewhere in correspondence, in order to show – as Hypsicles does – that the moon's effects on the earth's rotation is 'the principal cause of the alteration of the natural state of this planet and our temporal maladies' (B 5.24, 99–101; see also *WW* 240–2; *IN* 132–3). This research outside of the dialogue on underlying astronomical principles is – surprisingly – quite different from what is presented in the editor's scientific note within the scholarly apparatus to *Alexis* itself. That is, while Hemsterhuis was extremely familiar with the relevant late eighteenth-century astronomical literature, he does not make reference to it at all within *Alexis*. The texts which would have been best known to his readers are eschewed in the editorial appendix in favour of more obscure and older seventeenth-century writings. As Cometa puts it, 'Hemsterhuis, in a singularly unusual footnote to *Alexis*, reconstructs an entire seventeenth-century genealogy of the astronomic interpretation of the Deluge, in which Hevelius, Eckstormius, Riccioli and Herlicius are quoted, omitting what were surely more direct sources which he undoubtedly knew and had in his library: Newton, Halley, Whiston and Maupertius' (2005: 110). Other names that go unmentioned in the editorial note in *Alexis*, but which certainly informed Hemsterhuis' understanding of lunar catastrophe, include Bailly, Boulanger and Montesquieu (see Hammacher 1995a: 70–1; Cometa 2005: 113). When writing as 'the editor', Hemsterhuis purposefully avoids a faithful transcription of his own thinking on lunar catastrophe, so as to deploy, instead, a far more arcane set of reference points. The editorial remark invents an alternative genealogy of the scientific material.[41]

In short, Hypsicles' speech is carefully arranged within a series of mythic and scientific discourses, in the middle of a spectrum extending from crude *mythos* to arcane *logos*. This seems to suggest that, while Hemsterhuis does

---

[41] This is, in part, a defence on Hemsterhuis' part against bad readings of his hypothesis of lunar catastrophe (just as the Prometheus myth of *Simon* was a way of defending against too literal readings of his fibre physiology). Hemsterhuis himself notes in this vein in his *Lettre sur la rotation des planets*, 'If ever I am advised to treat the matter of the Moon in a serious and scientific tone, I think I would be obliged to prevent as efficiently as possible the enormous abuses that our illustrious modern philosophers could make of my hypothesis' (B 5.24, 102). What 'modern philosophers' lack is, once again, *tact*: the direct presentation of scientific truths is liable to be read too literally; fictions protect the philosopher (or scientist) from bad readers.

dub it a 'poetic fiction', it is not meant to be a *crude* myth, superstition or prejudice of the kind first given by Hypsicles to explain the reddening of the Adonis River. It is meant as more than mere allegory, as Hemsterhuis' own astronomical research testifies.[42] On the other hand, however, while Hypsicles' speech might communicate 'the most exact truth', it is no purely conceptual discourse either. When Diocles later attempts to provide a philosophical translation of it, what is clearest are the limits of such a project: for example, Hypsicles' implicit conjectures about the future are lost in the reconstruction. The speech on the golden age is, then, a scientific fiction or logical myth – a mixture that partakes in both kinds of discourse, as simultaneously both 'poetic fiction' and the 'most exact truth'. In this, as so often in his oeuvre, Hemsterhuis mimics Plato, specifically the *Timaeus*' juxtaposition of Critias's myth of origins with Timaeus' relatively more scientific cosmology, which itself is labelled *both* an *eikôs logos and* an *eikôs muthos* (1962: 29d). Plato's speech has a hybrid status, and Hemsterhuis' version does too: it is even situated at an archaic point of indifference between *mythos* and *logos*, a pre-historical space before the two genres were irredeemably divided.

What is more, Hemsterhuis is able to flit between the mythic and the scientific so seamlessly precisely because of the strict analogy he has established between them: they act as a series of metaphors for each other. And it is here that the previous sections of the present chapter become crucial for identifying the operations of Hemsterhuisian writing – because analogy stands at their foundation.

2. Not only does Hemsterhuis locate analogical structures or *rapports* everywhere (§13), he also *writes* philosophy on the basis of such analogies. That is, his obsessive proliferation of analogical relations between essences, ideas, organs, faces of the universe, God and signs affect his production of philosophical texts too. As Hammacher points out (1971: 134–5), his 'analogy thinking' is ultimately bound up with an attempt to simultaneously communicate contrary ideas: the ancient and the modern, the geometrical and the poetic, the Socratic and the Newtonian, the physical and the moral. Or, to put it another way, Hemsterhuis' mania for analogy gives rise to a practice of analogic predication, and it is in this vein that he tells Gallitzin of 'the right'

---

[42] Hence, on reading Hesiod, Hemsterhuis is explicit: 'I had always believed that this state was only a poetic fiction, but although the poets have ornamented it so much, when looking at it a bit closer, we will see that this state must necessarily have existed' (B 3.86, 199–200).

§14 ORGANOLOGY AND STYLE

he possesses to transfer language figuratively or analogically across faces of the universe (for example, from the moral to the physical, and vice versa):

> Do you know what I find most pleasant in our little philosophy? It is that we have the right to bring into physics the figures that we use to express our ideas, whereas others, the brittle physicists, cannot employ the same organ without falling straight into the errors of materialism, etc. Here is the advantage of discarding that ridiculous barrier that separates the material and the immaterial. I admit that we owe all our great knowledge in physics to this barrier, but when I have built a beautiful edifice, it is to time to throw way the scaffolding which I have used and which at present obscures my beautiful architecture. (B 6.55, 154)[43]

Concepts are to be transposed trans-organically from the physical to the moral, from one face of the universe to another – and Hemsterhuis has the warrant to do this because of, on the one hand, the analogical foundations of his metaphysics and epistemology and, on the other hand, the tact or analogic sensitivity he requires of both himself and the reader to understand the figurative without flirting with dogmatism (i.e., his analogical Newtonianism). The latter is precisely what Spinoza lacked in his redeployment of geometry outside of its proper domain (§4) and it is also what Bonnet lacked in his extension of fibre physiology into psychology (§9). Hemsterhuis appeals to an analogic ontology to justify his practice of *metabasis* – taking a term out of its 'proper' domain and deploying it with equal 'right' in another.[44] The fact that *rapports* hold between all things in all domains entails that signs that hold good in one domain can be made use

---

[43] See also Trop's remarks (2022: 39) on the significance of this 'experimental blend[ing of] seemingly discrete discursive domains' for Hemsterhuis' later reception.

[44] In the *Lettre sur l'Homme*, Hemsterhuis explicitly praises Democritus, Hippocrates, Plato and Archimedes for innovations in the metabatic practice of 'applying one science to another neighbouring science' (*EE* 1.122; *OP* 290). It is, however, Hemsterhuis' mathematical treatises which demonstrate most clearly his abiding interest in transferring the conceptual apparatus of one science into another. Such metabatic 'applications of certain ideas to certain other ideas' account for 'our greatest progress in the sciences' when done tactfully and can 'reciprocally enrich both the sciences' involved; but they also account for the 'greatest absurdities' in science. Thus, Hemsterhuis reveals himself anxious to avoid 'pushing too far the application of an idea of one thing to the idea of another thing' (unconsciously mimicking Diderot's phrasing); he tries to formulate 'laws to prevent the bad effects of these arbitrary applications of one idea to another' and, ultimately, it is this worry that motivates his criticisms of Euclid's definitions at the beginning of the *Elements* (*IN* 54, 56, 59; *WW* 198, 200, 206).

of analogically in any other domain of reality whatsoever. Moral signs can be used (analogically) to make sense of physical phenomena (as the Greeks did) or signs drawn from the physical sciences can legitimately (if analogically) be deployed to make sense of moral phenomena (as Hemsterhuis himself attempts to do). Hemsterhuis speaks in this vein of the need for 'marriages' between the sciences – that is, the mixing and intermingling of scientific terms – from which 'one must expect the new, the great and the beautiful' (B 3.35, 92).

Here, then, is the Hemsterhuisian justification for what Diderot called those 'metaphors that have been pushed too far' that litter his writings (see §5). These figures pushed too far include the use of attraction and inertia to explain moral feeling, the elaboration of a system of times by way of the astronomical concepts of perihelion and aphelion and even recourse to the figure of the golden age as 'a figurative term [for] the state of some being which enjoys all the happiness of which its nature and current manner of being are capable' (EE 2.143; OP 634). In these instances, the legitimacy of the metabatic transfer of figures from (e.g.) the astronomical to the historical is guaranteed by an appeal to *rapports*. As Lützeler recognised in the 1920s, Hemsterhuis' 'tendency to mythologise' is grounded in an 'analogy between moral and physical facts' (1925: 217). Or to put it another way: the metaphysics of *rapports* makes possible a thoroughgoing philosophising through metaphor.[45]

The most extended example of such a figure pushed too far in Hemsterhuis' published writings is the lunar catastrophe of *Alexis*. Flanked by various mythic and scientific discourses, it synthesises these different genres into one composite whole. As Melica puts it, 'Hemsterhuis applies physical theories to moral-metaphysical concepts which are then exemplified via mythological metaphors' (2005: 100): he circles between three types of discourse (physical theories, moral-metaphysical concepts and mythological metaphors) to 'thicken' the resonances of his central claim. We return here to the logic of competing demands that structured Chapters One and Two: Hemsterhuis manages to do many contrary things at once (speak in both an ancient and a modern voice, write both poetry and science) and Hypsicles' speech on lunar catastrophe is one of the more arresting examples of this *art of simultaneity*.

---

[45] There is generally a strong link between this practice of analogic predication and the methodological pursuit of the ridiculous (or the comic) described in §9: Hemsterhuis pursues metaphors so far that they become gibberish and resist straightforward interpretation. A recurrent example in his correspondence is the use of the term 'placenta' to make sense of modes of thinking (e.g., B 5.12, 56).

3. Hypsicles' speech was one of Hemsterhuis' more influential myths. He relates that, on reading of lunar catastrophe in *Alexis*, Camper was nearly convinced by the new cosmological explanation of human corruption (B 4.30, 77), and Hölderlin notoriously appropriates the concept of an 'exzentrische Bahn' for an early version of *Hyperion*. However, this model of lunar catastrophe made most impression on F. W. J. Schelling, whose 1802 'further presentation' of the movements of heavenly bodies concludes as follows:

> Hemsterhuis' beautiful poetry on the end of the golden age is well-known: he looks for the ground of the altered inclination of the earth's volume in a necessary effect of the moon which he considers as a later newcomer to the earth. We are of the opinion that this idea approaches the truth to a considerable degree more than any of the others. . . . Similar sense can be made of the old tradition which shines through in the myth of Arcadia also mentioned by Hemsterhuis . . . and boasts that the age of its race reaches beyond the existence of the moon. (1856–61: 4.490–1)

Schelling is convinced by Hemsterhuis' reasoning and, indeed, what is striking here is that *Alexis* seems to act for Schelling precisely like some piece of astronomical equipment – a 'textual telescope' – that makes visible in astronomy what no amount of more literal optical technology had been able to.

Again, the analogical relations that hold between organs help make some sense of Schelling's reaction to *Alexis*. Hemsterhuis' claim in the *Lettre sur l'optique* that the telescope and microscope serve as the paradigm for all organological thinking has implications for how Hemsterhuis does philosophy: advances in optical instruments are taken as exemplary for his overarching history of organs – and this matters stylistically too. For example, the analogy between the eyes and the moral organ allows the Hemsterhuisian to posit the possibility of what Novalis aptly dubs 'moral telescopes' (see below), that is, instruments for amplifying the moral organ. Schelling seems to suggest that Hemsterhuis' own philosophical texts can sometimes be considered to act in this way – that is, as prosthetic technologies. The words of philosophy become, on this interpretation, tools or organs for facilitating new experiences, which together constitute a 'new organon'. And one precedent for this conception of a 'textual organ' is again to be found in the work of Charles Bonnet, who exemplifies a tradition of engineering philosophical texts as prosthetic instruments.

Like Hemsterhuis, Bonnet begins from 'the extreme imperfection of all our sciences and all our arts' (2002: 315) which, in turns, stems from 'the weakness or rather coarseness of our senses and the necessary imperfections of our instruments' (2002: 336). The organological imperative is therefore to manufacture better instruments to remedy this weakness. Hence, in analogy to telescope and microscope, Bonnet asks, 'Could it not be that one day these instruments will be made more perfect and new ones invented which will carry our knowledge further beyond the limit we see today?' (2002: 330–1). And it is on this basis that he begins to consider 'the mechanics of style in general and of philosophical style in particular' (2002: 12) in terms of optical instruments:

> This writing that I dedicate to the increase of the most noble pleasures of human reason will be, if you like, a kind of long-range telescope by means of which my reader will assuredly enjoy contemplating the immensity and beauty of the works of the All-Powerful. How much do I wish that the lenses of this telescope had been worked on by a better hand! I will have at least traced the construction of the instrument; more skilled opticians will perfect it. (2002: 194)

The philosophical text is understood metaphorically as an optical technology. Philosophical writing is to certain organs what the telescope is to the eye: it amplifies, proliferates and perfects sensations. To return to the opening of *Sophyle*, the task of the philosophical text is not to critically limit possible experience, but to extend its domain, to ameliorate the human capacity to know, such that, by means of the instrument of philosophy itself, the reader is able to discern more, to discover new, unknown lands.

That this kind of thinking can indeed be applied to Hemsterhuis' own project is further evidenced by some of Novalis' comments. He writes to A. W. Schlegel of 'the idea of a *moral* (in the Hemsterhuisian sense) astronomy', that is, an 'absolutely symbolic . . . physics' (1960–2006: 4.255; see also Tokarzewska 2015). And one of the ideas behind this claim seems precisely to be the analogy elucidated above: just as the organ of sight is mutable, its present condition contingent on available technologies and its future open to the possibility of radical amelioration, so too the moral organ. In two notes from the *Hemsterhuis-Studien*, Novalis makes further allusion to this kind of idea:

> Do we know – what discoveries are still vouchsafed to us on this side – ? The moral side of the universe is still more unknown and unfathomable than the heavens. *Moral arts.*

§14 ORGANOLOGY AND STYLE 153

Pythagoras' endless attempts to bring the moral organ to perfection. . . . *Are there no telescopes for this?* (1960–2006: 2.367, 2.369)

The imperative to invent 'moral arts' and moral 'telescopes' clearly follows a line of thinking I have identified in Hemsterhuis' own philosophy. The subject must manufacture instruments to perceive and think the ethical better and so, in Novalis' words, 'bring the moral organ to perfection'. These comments, I am suggesting, stand in continuity with Bonnet's treatment of the philosophical text as a type of moral telescope.

4. At the end of *Alexis*, Alexis asks Diocles to translate Hypsicles' speech into philosophical concepts, to show 'whether the golden age ... is an object capable of contemplation by your philosophy' (*EE* 2.143; *OP* 634). And Diocles obliges, insofar as he is able to. But there are limits to this translation project: Diocles cannot capture conceptually Hypsicles' invocation of a better future, but instead laments, 'All that philosophy can teach us about the different ages of perfection' excludes any future age, which instead requires 'recourse to the oracles of the Gods' (*EE* 2.146; *OP* 644). Notwithstanding this exception, for the most part Hemsterhuis seems to have been satisfied that he could still relate the basic truth of Hypsicles' 'poetic fiction' in more sober terms. And yet, this once again raises a problem first encountered in §9: if it is perfectly possible to elucidate Hypsicles' speech in more geometrical and less mythic form, why then does Hemsterhuis bother with the myth? Why conceal the cogency of the scientific argument behind an archaic, half-remembered story told by a superstitious priest?

A number of answers have, of course, already been given in the course of this book, and one in particular is important here for illuminating the specifically organological stakes of Hemsterhuisian style – the theory of the Platonic sublime described in §8. To resume: Hemsterhuis argues that philosophical writing should not 'speak only to the intellect', but ought to appeal to a 'sentiment [that] pertains to the moral'; it must 'add into the dry language of demonstration, which occupies solely the intellect, another language which pertains continually to the lively and active moral organ'.[46] One should write to exercise the moral organ, to provoke it into a state of 'openness' and 'readiness' for good perception. One should write a 'hymn' to 'continually excite the moral' alongside 'the monotonous accents of

---

[46] So, when Gallitzin accuses him 'of preferring the intellectual faculties to that sublime energy of the soul', Hemsterhuis responds, 'No accusation could be more unjust' (*B* 1.45, 82).

geometry' (B 7.84, 235–6). A philosophical text must exercise, activate and generally provoke the reader's moral organ.[47] Ultimately, all the aforementioned ways of describing philosophical style – from analogy to hyperbole – are gathered together by Hemsterhuis in his correspondence under this monikor of 'the sublime': they are all ways of conceiving the communication of truths through a language of sentiment. Hemsterhuis intends to develop a full-blown semiotics of the sublime, a catalogue of the means required 'to attain those adequate signs which could raise the intellect to the heights of sentiment'. His interest is in philosophical writing as the 'transport of sensations' (B 7.100, 267).

And what has now become clear are the organological stakes of this theory of the sublime. The most urgent educational task is the enhancement of the moral organ in modernity (see §12); it is the modern lack of attention to this organ that has led to the vices of the eighteenth century. The perfection of the moral organ will finally bring the organological ideal of faculty-harmony that much closer. Hence, philosophy must speak to that innate principle of perfectibility that calls each individual to perfect her organs further. It is for this reason, within *Alexis* itself, much is made of the pursuit of popularity and accessibility in philosophical teaching: Diocles initially refutes the idea that 'the beautiful truth is stark naked by nature' (*EE* 2.124; *OP* 576), that is, that philosophy must cultivate a neutral style that minimises rhetorical effect, by appealing to the need to make philosophy's core message of self-betterment available to all. He writes, 'If you were to compare it to some salutary but relatively bitter medicine, you would agree that, in order to swallow it, some honey or gilding is necessary' (*EE* 2.124; *OP* 578). Poetic writing 'decorates and enriches' philosophy (*EE* 2.139; *OP* 624) and it does so in order to make its 'bitter medicine' easier to swallow. Moreover, the nature of this medicine that style makes more ingestible is to be identified with the imperative to cultivate organs around which Hemsterhuis' thinking is structured. Style acts as a necessary supplement to popularise organological self-improvement.

This provides some kind of answer, then, to the problem of conceptual translatability: something is lost in the transposition of Hypsicles' speech into

---

[47] As Hemsterhuis puts it elsewhere, 'moral sentiments are the sole experiences' that ground his philosophical project, and they presuppose both the 'great art' of 'sensing purely', as well as the art of communicating them to modern subjects, since 'there are very few men who have a perfectly sensible moral organ and among this small number there are few who sense purely'. Writing must forever grapple with the interference of 'imagination, passion, prejudices, preoccupations, etc.' which disrupt the communication of purely moral sentiment (B 7.87, 239).

concepts – its moral resonance. What Hypsicles' speech does that Diocles' later rational reconstruction cannot is speak to both the intellect and the moral organ at the same time. The mythic language which Hemsterhuis intermingles with scientific truth allows him to communicate more richly in a moral register – and this is all the more pertinent considering that the lesson of the myth being communicated is precisely that of organological loss. To speak mythically (as well as scientifically at the same time) has a pedagogic end – the reawakening of obscured and unappreciated organs in the reader and the institution of a pedagogy of all the organs.

More specifically, what Hypsicles' speech is trying to communicate, beyond mere intellectual content, is the principle of perfectibility. The obligation to reflect on perfectibility is, Hemsterhuis notes in correspondence, the major lesson to be drawn from *Alexis*: the human subject must realise that 'it is impossible for man to ever return to this golden age of Hesiod', but rather the subject must 'reflect' on this myth 'to give a constant direction to the eccentric progress of his perfectibility' and so 'turn back, correct the absurd faults of his disorderly progress, and so . . . see once more on this very planet a golden age infinitely superior to those [golden ages] of the poets' (B 3.86, 200–1). The subject's tendency towards the better thus provides the conceptual foundation for talk of the golden age. But Hemsterhuis has a problem. Perfectibility as the inmost tendency of the human subject cannot be directly represented (see further §24): it can only be indirectly communicated to the human subject through the arousal of sentiment. The principle of perfectibility belongs precisely to that category of intimate, inalienable properties of human essence spoken of in *Aristée* under the rubric of 'sentimental certainty'. What Diocles' rational reconstruction specifically loses, then, is an ability to communicate the principle which stands at the very centre of the discussion, for perfectibility can be brought to the reader's mind only by way of mythic discourse, by twisting words so that they do more than merely convey conceptual meanings. Hypsicles' speech is 'sublime' insofar as it attempts to evoke the principle of perfectibility in its readers.

5. Organology has implications for the kinds of claims philosophers are able to make and the ways in which they are able to make them. Not only are organs historically variable, but so too is the practice of philosophy itself. What we know and how we come to know it is, according to Hemsterhuis, dependent on the current, contingent condition of our organs. Philosophy thereby becomes plastic, subject to radical change in the future and in the past. Hemsterhuis deliberately situates the story of the golden age in *Alexis* in an archaic past which is triply mediated through Pythagoras', Archytas' and

Diocles' reminiscences – which are themselves further mediated through the text's fictional Greek framing and contemporary editorial reconstruction. Here are truths which stand five times removed from the reader. Moreover, Hypsicles' speech tells a story about how things were radically different in the past and how they will again be radically different in the future. This is a story, therefore, that describes the radical historical change that organs have undergone at the same time as drawing attention to its own pastness and dramatising to the reader the limits of her knowledge of the past. The temporality of truths is one of the more salient themes of this passage.

In other words, one of the lessons to be drawn from both the content and the formal properties of Hypsicles' speech is that philosophical statements are contingent. This has implications for philosophical style. Any philosopher who acknowledges such plasticity must present truths in a way that likewise acknowledges their contingency and historicity. The philosopher should communicate to the reader the transient nature of philosophy. Truths are no longer timeless or static, nor as valid tomorrow as they are today or were yesterday. The transitory must thoroughly pervade philosophical writing. Thus, organological style involves the fashioning of a mode of philosophical presentation that historicises and makes contingent its own truths. It involves a plastic writing.[48]

It is this demand for organological style that will constitute the subject matter of the next chapter. By means of an extended comparison with Diderot's and Bonnet's cognate organological projects, I want to enumerate what Hemsterhuis appropriates from their modes of presentation (as well as what he contests) in order to develop his own distinctive practice of plastic writing.

---

[48] Cahen-Maurel (2022: 41) makes a helpful passing remark on Hemsterhuis' textual strategy in this context: 'The dialogue as a plastic whole becomes a central motif. Just as Hemsterhuis defended the idea of the plasticity of human psychology and physiology, here . . . we encounter the idea of a plasticity of the idea itself.'

Chapter Four
Writing after Materialism

The nation is superstitious. . . . Materialism is held in horror.
Diderot on the Dutch Republic (1975–: 24.140)

Hemsterhuis – a Dutchman, who wrote in French but was only properly esteemed by Germans – [was] so familiar with the culture of the Encyclopaedists, he accordingly dared to take the rights of speculation, ethics, art and religion away from them.
A. W. Schlegel (1964: 3.83)

§15 Diderot Reads Hemsterhuis

In June 1773, Hemsterhuis met Diderot. The latter was visiting Dmitri Gallitzin at The Hague on his way to Russia, and Hemsterhuis found an opportunity to hand over a copy of the *Lettre sur l'Homme*. When Diderot returned from Russia a year later, he gave the copy back full of annotations, remarks and suggestions, and, appended to these marginalia ('some 20,000 words that are in effect a dialogue' [Wilson 1972: 648]) – was the following message scrawled on two blank pages at the end of the book:[1]

> Reading your work has given me great pleasure. There are some very beautiful, new and subtle ideas. It is in this way that I spoke of it to Prince Gallitzin. But if you had lived two or three years in our capital, with intimate links to my friends, you would have come across a language in use, completely ready to lend itself to your ideas; and your work would have been infinitely easier and more pleasant to read. But on the other hand, it

---

[1] On the details of the Hemsterhuis–Diderot encounter, see May (in Diderot and Hemsterhuis 1964: 5–8) and Lope (1990).

would have compromised you in a quite singular way. I am thinking of the fact that being better read and understood in this country, it would have drawn upon you a violent persecution. . . . You are, in fact, one example among many others of those for whom intolerance has constrained their veracity and who have taken on the philosophy of a harlequin's dress, such that posterity alone – unsettled by their contradictions of which it does not know the cause – will be able to judge their genuine sentiments.

The Eumolpidae made Aristotle accept and then reject final causes. At one point Buffon sets down all the principles of the materialists; elsewhere he advances completely opposed principles. And what to think of Voltaire, who says with Locke that matter can think, with Toland that the world is eternal, with Tindal that freedom is a chimera, and who then confesses to a vengeful and remunerative God? Was he inconsistent? Or scared of the doctors of the Sorbonne?

I am saved by my ironic tone – the most fluent I have been able to discover – by generalities, laconism and obscurity. (Diderot and Hemsterhuis 1964: 513)

According to Diderot, Hemsterhuis philosophises in 'a harlequin's dress'; he intentionally communicates a philosophy full of 'contradictions' that pass relatively unnoticed by his contemporaries, but which – Diderot prophesises – will so 'unsettle' future readers that they will begin to discern an esoteric core lurking behind them.

The *Lettre sur l'Homme* had already been labelled obscure: in September 1772, the *Journal encyclopédique* had published a review that 'doubt[ed] that this work is accessible to a large number of readers', consigned it to 'the metaphysicians' and criticised its pretension to instruct 'all men' in its stilted jargon. The reviewer went on to contrast Hemsterhuis' presentation of 'the truth in all its austerity' with a more popular, 'ornamental' style (Anon. 1772: 360–1). Diderot reads the *Lettre sur l'Homme* in a similar vein but goes further in attributing its obscurity to an esoteric mode of writing.[2] Diderot suggests that Hemsterhuis' text appears to be trying to say something other than what its geometrical reasoning strictly demonstrates; that is, if Hemsterhuis were to speak plainly and to reveal his philosophical position in a suitable style, Diderot claims that he would open himself up to persecution from state and church. Diderot therefore groups Hemsterhuis with other radical figures of the period, including Diderot himself, who had

---

[2] On the significance of Diderot's note to Hemsterhuis in the history of philosophical esotericism, see Melzer (2014: 15–16).

been obliged to mask their ideas to avoid persecution: Hemsterhuis looks a lot like a covert radical materialist.

1. Diderot's strange rendering of Hemsterhuis into a crypto-materialist has, oddly enough, lived on in the literature. His use of the categories of concealment and dissimulation to interpret Hemsterhuis' texts is not some isolated instance, but stands at the head of a long tradition: from Diderot onwards, Hemsterhuis has regularly been figured as a practitioner of the esoteric.[3] Only a few years later, in June 1780, Lessing will spark the German *Spinozismusstreit* by naming *Aristée* an example of contemporary crypto-Spinozism. Just like Mendelssohn a few years earlier (and this was surely no coincidence) (B 4.33, 83–4; see Fresco 2003: 22–4), Lessing reads Hemsterhuis' philosophy as covertly pantheist, concealing 'an unexpressed and unambiguously heterodox view' (Strauss 1988: 186) behind its overt orthodoxy. In the nineteenth century, the image of Hemsterhuis as crypto-Spinozist was propagated by Dilthey, who described him as 'Spinoza's student', through whom 'pantheism and indirectly Spinozism enters German Idealism' (1914–2005: 15.180), as well as by Haym, who makes Hemsterhuis primarily responsible for an eruption of pantheism at the end of the eighteenth century (1870: 155). In the twentieth century, Vernière will partially defend this Spinozist reading of Hemsterhuis by identifying him as a philosopher who 'reconstitutes the Spinozist theory of being', 'stresses immanence' and 'refuses miracles' (1954: 669–70). Israel's recent interpretation of Hemsterhuisian thought as 'increasingly reveal[ing] a pantheistic tendency' (2007: 30; see also 2011: 696) repeats some of these traditional tropes.

An illuminating analysis of the esoteric Hemsterhuis is given by Theo Verbeek. Verbeek begins with the puzzle that 'Hemsterhuis made his entry into the history of philosophy under the misunderstanding that he was "Spinozist"' (1995: 258). To solve the puzzle, Verbeek draws on the distinction implicit in *Sophyle* between immaterialist and hypermaterialist argumentative strategies (see §11) to argue that some of Hemsterhuis' claims

---

[3] Hemsterhuis does obviously draw on a couple of classic strategies of writing under persecution, particularly when it is a matter of constituting and monitoring his readership. For example, one might cite 'the semi-private nature of Hemsterhuis' writings' (Petry 2003b: 421), that he shunned mass distribution in favour of controlled circulation of works among friends, or their anonymity (a couple of early works excepted) and attribution to a fictive place of publication. These were fairly common eighteenth-century practices (see van Sluis 2022: 25), but nevertheless still suggest that Hemsterhuis shared his anxiety over publication and authorship with those who were more obviously exercised by a lack of *libertas philosophandi*.

'presuppose an idea of matter which, in other places and for other reasons, is rejected by the other' tendency (1995: 253). Verbeek's intent is therefore to exploit a lack of fit between Hemsterhuis' purported aim to defend a 'theory of the immaterial' (B 1.106, 141) and his actual argumentative practice of expanding matter until it becomes absolute. In particular, Verbeek points out that the *Lettre sur l'Homme*'s and *Sophyle*'s syllogistic demonstrations of soul–body dualism presuppose 'a perfectly traditional image' of matter, but that this image is immediately subverted by Hemsterhuis' other arguments from historical plasticity; that is, the 'traditional image' turns out to be 'an aberration . . . in conflict with his own suppositions on matter' (1995: 256, 263; see also Moenkemeyer 1975: 88). For Verbeek, this leaves Hemsterhuis' whole philosophy 'vulnerable to the accusation of "Spinozism"' (1995: 256), despite the fact he was no Spinozist.[4] It provides one compelling reason why so many of his readers, from Diderot to Israel, have charged him with concealing his true views behind ineffectual syllogistic arguments.

Verbeek diagnoses the structure of all esoteric readings of Hemsterhuis: an inconsistency in the text (in this instance, between immaterialism and hypermaterialism) is said to betray a philosophical position concealed from plain sight. And this is a structure that Diderot extends to his own works and those of the Parisian materialists in general – that is, Hemsterhuis' texts look like other works from the radical Enlightenment which are determined by the logic of writing under persecution, but they do so, in this case, from an anti-materialist, anti-pantheist perspective. In other words, Hemsterhuis mimics the materialists at the same time as attacking them: he appropriates the tools of esotericism and turns them against the materialists and Spinozists who forged them.[5] His is an *esoteric reversal of esotericism*: he imitates materialist writing in order to undermine it.

---

[4] This is clear in Hemsterhuis' reactions to Lessing's charge of Spinozism (e.g., B 7.29, 85; 7.68, 192).

[5] Vernière puts it nicely: 'Hemsterhuis' originality was to begin from Spinoza and to claim to construct, through a meditation on the *Ethics*, the refutation of modern neo-Spinozism' (1954: 668). In this vein, it is worth stressing that 'esotericism is just a particular technique of communication, and different people can make use of it for totally unrelated purposes: esotericism does not designate a set of specific beliefs', but 'the practice of partly revealing and partly concealing one's beliefs, whatever they may be. It is not a philosophical doctrine, but a *form of rhetoric*, an art of writing' (Melzer 2014: 2, 69–70). There can be 'radical' esoteric writing, but there can also be 'conservative' esoteric writing, like Hemsterhuis'.

2. When Diderot reads the *Lettre sur l'Homme* in 1773–4, there is, on the one hand, much he finds consonant with his own materialism – the margins of his copy abound in remarks like 'excellent', 'very good', 'I like this idea' or even 'this is true . . . you speak exactly like us' (Diderot and Hemsterhuis 1964: 229, 283, 385, 393, 427). In particular, when Hemsterhuis sets out his organology, Diderot responds, 'All this pleases me a lot and contains nothing, but nothing at all contrary to my philosophy' (1964: 227); and when Hemsterhuis goes on to criticise revealed religion, Diderot applauds: 'Excellent proof of the stupidity of so-called revelation or the uselessness of revelation' (1964: 385). In general, Diderot emphasises 'the pleasure this reading gave me' (1964: 41). Nevertheless, there is much – especially in its form and style – that Diderot criticises in the *Lettre sur l'Homme*. This critique of the formal features of the text functions on a number of levels. At the most superficial level, it is a matter of Hemsterhuis' clumsy and occasionally inaccurate French. Diderot corrects Hemsterhuis' grammar, he marks passages as 'inelegantly written', or even more damningly as 'not French' or a 'false expression' (1964: 47, 63, 265). The implication is that Hemsterhuis writes awkwardly in his non-native tongue, without the fluency taken for granted in Parisian salons.[6]

---

[6] Two other perspectives are worth noting on this point. First, when Hemsterhuis writes of speaking Greek like a native (§5), he does not place the stress on accuracy or even elegance, but on an appropriate tone or spirit to the language. Secondly, other readers of Hemsterhuis have disagreed with Diderot's assessment – most notably Friedrich Schlegel, for whom Hemsterhuis' writing is to be lauded 'according to my feeling for the French language': 'Even though he was no Frenchman by birth', Hemsterhuis writes French 'so beautifully and harmoniously' (1958–2002: 6.346), with 'scientific rigour and brevity of expression, unity and clarity, life and grace, even with an often Platonic beauty of style' (1958–2002: 3.271). Diderot is of course more of an authority on the niceties of the French language, but one might still conjecture on the basis of the above that what he takes to be Hemsterhuis' failure to follow Parisian linguistic norms could also be read *as resistance to them*. That is, even if one were to take Diderot seriously that Hemsterhuis intentionally enters into inconsistency to indicate something that cannot be said, what Diderot seems to fail to countenance is that Hemsterhuis could be cultivating inelegance and inconsistency against the Parisian materialists: writing French badly in order to distinguish himself from those who write French well. There remains the possibility that Hemsterhuis wants to alienate the contemporary reader by a lack of fluency. I return to all these remarks in §23, but Trop (2022: 48–9) nicely sums up this more positive evaluation of Hemsterhuis' awkward French: 'Diderot senses something foreign, obscure and even scandalous in Hemsterhuis's thought; he often draws attention to the way in which the Dutch Hemsterhuis deviates from the stylistic norms of philosophical French (with Deleuze, one could say: Hemsterhuis deterritorialises standard academic French in a philosophical minor key)'.

The second level to Diderot's criticisms of the *Lettre sur l'Homme* concerns conceptual vagueness. For instance, he censures Hemsterhuis for the looseness of his concepts which lack proper definition ('It is scarcely permitted for a philosophy to employ these words, *genius, spirit, instinct, sagacity, stupidity*, without giving precise notions' [Diderot and Hemsterhuis 1964: 81]), as well as his reliance on figurative terms like 'heart': 'One must get rid of this word which works badly in a text where one speaks strictly' (1964: 239). Diderot continues, 'This abuse of the word "heart" demands a reworking of all this part of your work' (1964: 247). Diderot is most scathing when it comes to the concept of the moral organ – sceptical of the metaphorical transposition of 'organ' into the ethical domain. 'I would use another expression than *moral organ*' (1964: 329), he writes, continuing elsewhere, 'Get rid for me everywhere of this word *organ* . . . and everything will be fine' (1964: 311). More particularly, Diderot criticises it as 'a figurative expression' – a metaphor extended into the moral domain beyond its proper bounds. It is indeed one more example of his critique of 'metaphors that have been pushed too far' in Hemsterhuis' philosophy. Diderot complains of all such metaphors: 'It is the too frequent and often unnecessary use of these ways of speaking that makes your book obscure' (1964: 421). At one point in the marginal comments, Diderot laments, 'After a metaphor borrowed from painting, there is a metaphor borrowed from agriculture' (1964: 55), and this exuberance of figures leads to 'the obscurity of your style . . . which has spoiled your work in the eyes of our thinkers in Paris' (1964: 323). In short, Diderot disapproves of Hemsterhuis' practice of analogic predication.[7]

The third level at which Diderot criticises the *Lettre sur l'Homme* concerns consistency. For instance, in terms of content, he berates Hemsterhuis for reneging in the closing pages on an earlier attack on the efficacy of prayer ('But have you forgotten what you said earlier on the absurdity of prayer?' [1964: 399]). And formally he objects to features such as Hemsterhuis' 'Pindaric digression [i.e., his analogy from looking at the sun to the moral organ] that is not of the tone of your work' (1964: 293) and the lack of tonal fit in Hemsterhuis' analysis of the tensions between civil religion and the religion of the individual: 'Is this an elegy or a cruel satire? The tone is

---

[7] Similarly, when it comes to Hemsterhuis' concept of the will, Diderot is both appalled doctrinally at Hemsterhuis' use of a concept that makes no sense to him ('It seems to assume in me an act without cause' [1964: 65]), but also shocked at Hemsterhuis' strange, idiosyncratic use of *velleité*, rather than the more typical *volonté*: 'This word,' he writes, 'will forever scandalise me' (1964: 103). The scandal here is again that of Hemsterhuis' awkwardness, the alienating peculiarity of his writing. His texts take on a clumsiness that upsets any reader abiding by the canons of respectable French.

elegiac. The thing is satire' (1964: 401). Here we return to Hemsterhuis' participation in a tradition of esoteric writing: those exoteric inconsistencies identified by Diderot which provoke readers to go beyond the surface do not merely comprise doctrinal contradictions, but also formal discrepancies (discrepancies in tone, in expression, in figure). The *Lettre sur l'Homme* is 'a book that abounds in contradictions' (Strauss 1988: 176) not just doctrinally, but also stylistically, and this obscurity of style functions as a classic instance of Straussian 'writing between the lines' (Strauss 1988: 24–5).

Confusingly, Diderot's Hemsterhuis ends up being both successful at failing to communicate a consistent philosophy (as an esoteric writer), and unsuccessful at achieving this failure in a sufficiently fashionable way (because of the clumsiness of his language). Hemsterhuis is a little *too* obscure, or perhaps obscure in the wrong way. If he had spoken the contemporary jargon of Paris, then he would have fitted far more comfortably into the radical Enlightenment grouping to which Diderot wants to assign him. Hemsterhuis looks like a radical philosopher, but an odd, unfashionable, untimely one – and this is the overriding conclusion I want to draw from Diderot's commentary for the purposes of this chapter: Hemsterhuis both writes like a materialist and not like a materialist. He is, according to Diderot, nearly there, but not quite – and this is because his writing is too awkward. To be blunt: there is something about Hemsterhuis' esoteric writing that Diderot finds uncanny, unnerving, and, as a result, he is both seduced and alienated by the *Lettre sur l'Homme*.

3. From 1774 onwards, Diderot's annotated copy of the *Lettre sur l'Homme* remained in Hemsterhuis' possession, and he kept coming back to it. Two of his responses are particularly illuminating: the 1778 'Additions and Clarifications' to the *Lettre sur l'Homme* and a letter to Gallitzin from 1784.

The opening to the 'Additions and Clarifications' addresses Diderot's accusation of obscurity, as well as the similar criticisms made by the *Journal encyclopédique* review. In particular, Hemsterhuis seems to have in mind Diderot's remark that 'you have often made a particular language for yourself when the common language could have been employed' (Diderot and Hemsterhuis 1964: 325). In response, he begins the supplement to the *Lettre sur l'Homme*, 'The author has been accused quite generally of being obscure, and this accusation is not unexpected. Perhaps obscurity is a vice of style in him' (*EE* 1.127; *OP* 304). Having confessed in part to his 'vice', Hemsterhuis goes on to consider four possible reasons for it. First, he suggests that it results from the idiosyncrasy of his own 'mode of thinking', that there might be something peculiar in the way he or his reader assembles ideas that indicates that 'all minds are not composed like that of the person to whom this letter was addressed' (*EE* 1.127; *OP* 304). Such a claim resonates with Hemsterhuis' pedagogical theories, particularly as 'the person to whom this letter was addressed' was François Fagel, who is elsewhere elegised as an exemplar of faculty-harmony (§12). Hemsterhuis implies that the *Lettre sur l'Homme* was written for those who think *like the idealised Fagel*, who think with perfect faculties and, as a result, the text might feel jarring to the less than perfect. Hemsterhuis communicates to the elite in a language formed for the elite.[8]

The second reason Hemsterhuis entertains in the 'Additions and Clarifications' for the obscurity of his style is a corollary to the above – 'the ignorance of the reader' (*EE* 1.127; *OP* 304). A philosophical text fails when the reader has not sufficiently perfected her faculties to understand it. Hemsterhuis' doctrine of the moral organ is particularly pertinent: the *Lettre sur l'Homme* is the work in which he presents it most fully and so the one in which he relies on the reader's ability to recognise it in her own experience. However, this is precisely what is lacking in *modern* readers (see §13): they are the least likely to be in a position to acknowledge the cogency of Hemsterhuis' ethics. Such 'ignorance' is thus a very real danger to the success of Hemsterhuisian philosophical communication.

Thirdly – and Hemsterhuis connects this closely to 'the ignorance of the reader' – he points to 'the grandeur of the subject' and the consequent need to 'redouble one's attention' and thus cultivate a very particular reading practice (*EE* 1.127; *OP* 304). Once again, he emphasises the peculiarity of his project, the ways it goes beyond modern philosophy's customary description of a restricted physical world and so his own philosophy's extension of thinking into 'new lands'.

Finally (and here he tarries longest), Hemsterhuis suggests that 'anyone who hazards to say something new is obliged to create his own language, which few readers are interested in learning', and he goes on to call the language employed in *Lettre sur l'Homme* 'strange' and 'a little barbarous' (*EE* 1.127; *OP* 304). Hemsterhuis once more admits the force of Diderot's

---

[8] In his correspondence, Hemsterhuis sets out a programme for altering his philosophical language for those who are 'my superior', so that the minds of those who are inferior might thereby be 'enriched' (see B 1.153, 188). He also admits that his arguments will only convince 'those who possess the faculty of thinking with precision and who possess a perfectly clear and pure imagination and an intellect that is not only prompt and agile but also habituated to comparing, composing and decomposing the ideas that it finds in the imagination' (*IN* 175).

critique (i.e., that he writes in an unfashionable, clumsy manner), but refigures it into something deliberate on his part. He is, he avers, clumsy on purpose. There is something here of Hemsterhuis' positive re-evaluation of gibberish as a philosophical virtue developed in his Gallitzin correspondence (§9). To create something 'new' – something that does not repeat the fashions of the age but resists them by way of a new tone – requires the repudiation of linguistic norms, the cultivation of a 'barbarous', shocking style that flaunts them. To innovate philosophically is to write strangely, even (as in the myth of Prometheus) ridiculously.

4. In 1784, Hemsterhuis returns to Diderot's commentary in a letter to Gallitzin. He paraphrases Diderot's closing remarks before contesting them directly:

> You may remember that Diderot said in a writing he addressed to me on the subject of the *Lettre sur l'Homme* that all philosophers were guided by fear of the Sorbonne. That I had dressed truth in the habit of a harlequin so as to make it pass muster. That Buffon was saved by his retractions. That Voltaire hid behind his infinite inconsistencies. And that [Diderot] could always hide behind the finest irony he could produce. I ask you whether this man ever knew what irony was? – that irony which is so charming in the mouth of Socrates or from the pen of Lucian, that irony unknown to the French, which they forever confuse with two extremities – mordant satire or bitterness and drab pleasantry – between which it is the happy medium. (B 5.96, 294–5)

Once again, Hemsterhuis accepts without protest Diderot's characterisation of him as an esoteric thinker, concealing truths beneath elisions and contradictions, and writing in harlequin's dress. Rather, what provokes him is Diderot's self-attribution of 'the finest irony' to his own philosophical practice. Hemsterhuis criticises Diderot's claim to have mastered philosophical irony and, instead, contrasts what he takes to be 'the finest irony' (e.g., in Socrates and in Lucian) with the crude materialist variant that oscillates between 'satire' and 'drab pleasantry'. That is, Hemsterhuis stakes his own claim to irony over Diderot: proper appreciation of irony is possible only from the perspective of the Greek perihelion and so is foreign to Diderotian materialism. Hemsterhuis' untimeliness makes him a better ironist – better at those stylistic virtues Diderot prizes most highly: the mixing of philosophy with poetic genres, the use of fiction and artifice and 'giving wisdom the appearance of folly' (Diderot 1955–79: 9.126–7). Hemsterhuis implicitly sees himself as competing with Diderot in the domain of philosophical communication – and winning. He positions himself as a rival to Diderot: he is to anti-materialism what Diderot is to materialism – the inventor of new textual forms, of 'a philosophy *in image*' that functions by fictions and metaphors (Ibrahim 2010: 27–8).

More generally, both of Hemsterhuis' responses to Diderot appear to confirm the impression that Diderot's uncomfortable experience reading the *Lettre sur l'Homme* was the correct one. The text seems to have been intended to alienate, dissimulate and ironise, to scandalise fashionable inclinations with barbarisms. And yet, at the same time, Hemsterhuis also gestures towards the failure of the *Lettre sur l'Homme* as a piece of philosophical communication: it speaks exclusively to François Fagel and those constituted like him, exclusively to an elite who have already perfected their faculties. To take just one example: directly arguing for a moral organ necessarily fails, for the moral organ passes unrecognised in modernity, and so to convince a modern reader much more is needed. The inelegant language and ill-fitting form of the work do not go far enough: they prove insufficient for provoking readers out of their contemporary complacency. The 'barbarous' nature of the text must be radicalised. And this is one reason for Hemsterhuis' post-1775 poetic turn: the intensification of 'strange' and 'barbarous' philosophical forms.

§16 Hemsterhuis Reads Diderot

In December 1784, Dmitri Gallitzin procured a manuscript of Diderot's *Le Rêve de D'Alembert* and shared it with Hemsterhuis and Gallitzin. The text had been presumed lost and was not to be properly recovered until 1830; thus, Hemsterhuis was to be one of a very select group of eighteenth-century readers of Diderot's *Rêve*. His response to the work runs as follows:

> Yesterday the Prince helped me pass a quite amusing evening. He sent me a manuscript by Diderot, with the title *Rêve [de] D'Alembert*. There are 4 dialogues; the first three between d'Alembert, Mlle l'Espinasse and the doctor Bordeu, and the fourth between the woman and the doctor. If someone desired to know Diderot's entire composition, they would be satisfied with this [work], for, in this respect, it is absolutely perfect: the features of his face, the shape of his hands, of his feet, the folds of his robe came back to me exactly as if he had been in front of me. You will easily believe it when I tell you it is the most perfect dialogue, that it contains traits of genius, but much more spirit and little judgement. The tone is

serious, sad even, although it affects a gaiety that will never dwell within this sombre soul. Alembert says few things. The woman has spirit and sense, and the doctor is the author. It is the most pernicious work that I've ever seen, either among the Ancients or among the Moderns. And yet it is very interesting for a philosopher to read, and moreover our cynical friend does not say what he says in order to do evil, but because he believes it true and because he wants to be singular. But this last faculty had no need of being affected, for this will never be contested of him. In the first three dialogues, he preaches Materialism with all the force of an eloquent man, who has finesse in spirit, who has a deep knowledge of what one calls the human heart, who is a pitiable psychologist, a metaphysician as superficial as it is possible to be and who entirely lacks the geometric spirit and therefore true and sure tact. In the final [dialogue], he converses with the lady alone on the physics of what they call love. . . . All this is treated in such a serious tone that the grotesque idea with which he ends [i.e., bestiality] is insufficient to soften it or to act in a bantering tone, even though this idea is quite risible in itself. (B 5.96, 294–5)[9]

This passage reflects the ambivalence Hemsterhuis always expressed towards Diderot: he admires how the *Rêve* is written and some of the virtues of the man who writes it – but not what is written. He considers it a sincere and perfectly formed manifesto for a dangerous doctrine – simultaneously 'the most perfect dialogue' and 'the most pernicious work'.

1. Hemsterhuis never stops praising Diderot's style; indeed, he goes so far as to claim that 'Sophocles' tragedy was to Athens what Diderot's drama is to us' (B 6.8, 35). He consistently speaks highly of Diderot's dramaturgy,[10] but also his philosophical writing: all parts of the *Rêve*, he writes in a later letter to Gallitzin, 'are dialogued perfectly, and on this article our friend does not only far surpass all the moderns, but equals Plato, Menander, and Lucian himself, the greatest master of all' (B 6.37, 112). Elsewhere, Hemsterhuis dubs Rousseau and Voltaire 'Pygmies and other ephemerals next to [Diderot]' with respect to philosophical writing,

---

[9] De Booy notes that the manuscript Hemsterhuis is reading does not appear to include the opening 'Suite d'un Entretien entre D'Alembert and Diderot' and therefore must be a different manuscript from the one recovered in the nineteenth century (1956: 86, 89–90).

[10] For example, Diderot 'is an admirable dialogist and I know of no ancient nor modern who had a more profound knowledge of the theory of dramatic poetry' (B 9.22, 52).

and concludes, 'To write like that I would willingly give an arm or a leg' (B 1.124, 158).

Diderot thus stands alongside Plato and Lucian as models for philosophical writing, as a master of communication to be emulated. And evident similarities exist between the writing practices of Hemsterhuis and Diderot: Diderot also pursues a 'poetic turn' within eighteenth-century materialist philosophy, analogous to Hemsterhuis' anti-materialist poetic turn; both make a 'deliberate choice not to write a *Treatise*, a *Meditations*, a *Discourse* on metaphysics, or a *System* of nature or man', and, instead, focus on 'complicating and mixing styles, by multiplying forms of philosophy' (as Bourdin writes of Diderot [1999: 19]). Thus, Diderot insists, just like the late Hemsterhuis, that 'poetry and philosophy are two ends of the same looking glass' (1994–7: 4.704–5) – and, just like the late Hemsterhuis, all his philosophical writings exhibit a comparable 'complex theatricality' (Bourdin 1999: 33) and 'impetuous verbal excess' (Starobinski 1975: 8). Diderot exemplifies (within an opposed philosophical tradition) the same demand for 'a simultaneously poetic *and* philosophical writing' (Proust 1981: 30). Hence, whereas Hemsterhuis poeticises philosophy to strengthen his attack on contemporary materialisms, Diderot does something similar in defence of materialism: he aims, that is, to create 'materialist *fictions*' (Ibrahim 2016: 186).

At the level of detailed stylistic devices, Diderot and Hemsterhuis also have much in common. For instance, Diderot like Hemsterhuis returns to a Socratic ideal to write Platonic dialogues anew – and, in so doing, 'pushes Socrates to his limits' (Hirzel 1895: 2.416). Diderot equally turns his philosophical texts into fictional worlds inhabited by individuals who are more than the sum of the doctrines they expound – such that Hösle can write of him, 'No one since Plato has gone so deeply into the connection between character and worldview' in philosophical dialogue (2006: 113).[11] And finally, Diderot's texts are delirious both in the excess of their imagery and in their fusion of genres, motivated by 'a principle of hybridisation ... the interpenetration of all opposed tones and styles' (Starobinski 1975: 21). Mortier appeals to the concept of 'energy' to account for this delirium and it is a concept to which I return in what follows: the sheer mass of images and fictions are expressions of Diderot's intellectual energy and shatter the 'norms of decency and taste imposed on the epoch' (Mortier 1997: 82).

---

[11] The worldliness of Diderot's texts is exemplified by their tendency to 'present themselves as the continuation of a debate begun outside the text' (Bourdin 1999: 32). Diderot refuses to write from the beginning, but always commences *in media res* – within a world that takes on the appearance of pre-existing the dialogue.

2. Despite these points of stylistic resemblance, Hemsterhuis still distances himself from Diderotian style on three points; that is, there are three ways in which Hemsterhuis believes himself to have gone beyond Diderot with respect to form. First, Hemsterhuis diagnoses in Diderot's writing a disharmony of the faculties that marks all his philosophical productions. Hemsterhuis writes, 'It is certain that this famous man had some monstrosity in his composition. There was no analogy between his intellect and his imagination. . . . His judgement and tact were never sure and often false' (B 5.13, 60). Diderot's inimitable singularity (he was 'as singularly bizarre as singularly rich' [B 6.37, 114]) was born of a failure to perfect each individual organ – in particular, his imagination forever outran his intellect, resulting in chaotic arguments that sufficiently developed intellectual judgement would have remedied. The reflections on Diderot's *Rêve* which begin this section repeat such a criticism: the *Rêve* is an accurate expression of Diderot's psychological peculiarities, for it clearly demonstrates both his 'deep knowledge of what one calls the human heart' and the dominance of his fevered imagination at the expense of 'true and sure tact'.

Secondly, Hemsterhuis judges that 'there was nothing Greek in either his character or his spirit' (B 9.22, 51): Diderot compares badly to Goethe, Gallitzin and Fürstenberg, who were all 'born Greek'.[12] This criticism is one I have already aired with respect to French philosophers in general (see §5): they radicalised the modern geometrical spirit at the expense of any affinity with the sentimental spirit of the Greeks. Their resolution of the quarrel of the ancients and the moderns in favour of modernity ultimately limits their philosophy. Nevertheless, Hemsterhuis' criticism of Diderot is slightly different: while the Greek perihelion is indeed foreign to him, he 'entirely lacks the geometric spirit' too. Diderot belongs to no age: neither the modern nor the ancient. His 'monstrous' untimeliness is the inverse of Hemsterhuis' own: Diderot inhabits no times; Hemsterhuis tries to inhabit all of them.

Thirdly (and here we return to some of the material in the first limitation), Hemsterhuis discerns in Diderot's writing a transgressive energy that gives rise to chaos – a lack of regulation and order in his imaginative impulses. I turn to this criticism in more detail in §20, but pertinent here is Hemsterhuis' recourse to the category of obscurity (as a riposte to Diderot's reading of his own work): 'His style was often judged a bit obscure', Hemsterhuis writes to Gallitzin, and this is because 'his vigorous will had not that rare faculty of directing the great part of his energy towards the

---

[12] This accounts in part for what Diderot's readers identify as 'the refusal of myth' in his works (Proust 1981: 28).

voice organ from which words arise, but often many very essential parts of the idea were dispersed or diffused elsewhere to act on other organs from where arise other signs' (B 6.37, 112–13). Diderot's obscurity – the fact that his philosophical style ultimately fails – is a result of diffuse and disparate energy. Hemsterhuis reacts against the chaotic nature of Diderot's verbal exuberance to insist that any good strategy for philosophical writing needs to be ordered, that is, founded on sure judgement and, above all, tact – a feeling for those harmonious *rapports* which need to be articulated (see §13).

3. While Hemsterhuis and Diderot can be placed into constructive conversation when it comes to philosophical form and style, no such dialogue appears possible – at least at first blush – when it comes to philosophical content. The materialism espoused by Diderot is precisely what Hemsterhuis abhors and against which he spent his entire intellectual life fighting. Unsurprisingly, therefore, Hemsterhuis identifies the *Rêve* as 'the most pernicious work that I've ever seen', and is elsewhere repulsed by Diderot's materialism (e.g., B 6.37, 114; 8.48, 112–13). And yet, to reduce Hemsterhuis' and Diderot's philosophical relationship to a materialism/anti-materialism opposition is to simplify a more complex constellation of positions. The two are not as far apart in terms of both form *and content* as might initially be expected, for at the heart of both their projects stands an organology – a history of organs that renders plastic the objects of metaphysics, anthropology and epistemology, as well as philosophical practice itself. Notwithstanding the facts that Hemsterhuis' philosophy is very different from Diderot's, that it was very rarely, if at all, directly influenced by Diderot's doctrines and that Hemsterhuis did not himself acknowledge any substantial affinity between them, both still write organologies. Indeed, if Hemsterhuis could have approached the manuscript of the *Rêve* in a more open-minded manner in 1784, he might well have discovered there an organology cognate with his own. Over the rest of the chapter, I want to bring out precisely such organological affinities.

The organological principles at stake in Diderot's *Rêve* can be summarised as follows:

(a) Matter is essentially self-generating and self-organising
At the very climax of Diderot's *Rêve* – the moment at which the characters themselves comment on their speculations as 'amusing and idiotic' or 'the sort of nonsense you only hear in the madhouse' – d'Alembert cries out, 'You think there are polyps of all kinds, even human ones. . . . That is past or to come. And besides, who knows the states of affairs on other planets?'

(1974: 172–3). This allusion to the freshwater polyp will play a central role in Diderot's work: just as the polyp possesses the parthogenetic capacity to regenerate, reorganise and transform itself into new individuals, so too, he posits by analogy, does the entire natural world. The polyp's 'plastic energy capable of metamorphoses' (Ibrahim 2010: 102) is transposed onto the whole of nature.[13] In a similar vein, Diderot writes to Sophie Volland: 'It is believed that there is only one polyp; but why would the whole of nature not be of the same order?' (1994–7: 5.171). He continues in the *Rêve*: the 'extravaganza' of the polyp's hydra-like powers of regeneration 'is almost the true history of all existing and future animal species', and even the human may well in the future 'break up into myriads of minute creatures whose metamorphoses and future and final state are impossible to foresee' (1974: 172).

This is the model that informs Diderot's affirmation of the self-generation of matter – its inherent, vital creativity. And likewise, this model informs his critique of the 'vice' of traditional metaphysics: 'confounding an actively sensible matter with a brute, inert, unorganised, inanimalised matter' (1974: 163). To put it bluntly, according to Diderot, principles immanent to a dynamic, active matter are completely sufficient to explain everything that occurs in the natural world: no additional divine or transcendental principles are required. As Jouary summarises, as early as the *Pensées philosophiques* of 1746, Diderot's naturalism had been based on four founding principles: '1) nature is one; 2) matter is in movement; 3) the mineral, vegetable and animal kingdoms interpenetrate; 4) there is continuity between brute matter and living matter' (1992: 29). For our purposes, the key principle is that, in the *Rêve*'s terms, 'motion is inherent in the thing itself' (1974: 149). Matter itself fully accounts for all movement, organisation and generation – even that of organic life. This is the reason for the continuity between all forms of matter: plant, animal, rock and human are all polypic.

Such are the foundations to Diderotian materialism – and so the place where he appears most acutely opposed to Hemsterhuis' philosophy. However, what will emerge from this materialist starting point is a cognate organology.

(b) All natural forms are subject to continual metamorphosis
Since nothing external limits the process of material self-transformation, it occurs without constraints: forms are subject to perpetual revolution.

---

[13] Ibrahim continues, 'Diderot turns *Rêve* into a sort of allegorical epic of the formation of worlds and the prodigality of living nature where the polyp plays the role of the prototype of beings' (2010: 67). See further Azadpour and Whistler (2021).

Diderot writes in the *Rêve*, 'All nature is in a perpetual state of flux. . . . There is nothing clearly defined in nature' (1974: 181). This statement grounds the late Diderot's transformism, his Lucretian affirmation of the chaos of nature.[14] And the primary casualty of this view is any appeal to fixed essences: 'You poor philosophers, and you talk about essences! Drop your idea of essences' (1974: 181).[15] As Ibrahim glosses, '*morphē* is substituted for *eidos*' (1999: 4).

In consequence, there is no reason why the present should be continuous with the past or the future. Each age ends up looking very different from the others. Diderot is clear that no rule or standard restricts what might come to exist in the future or did exist in the past, for they are epochs of the most surprising transformations:

> You assume that animals were in the beginning what they are at present. How absurd! We have no more idea of what they have been in the past than we have of what they will become. The imperceptible worm wriggling in the mire is probably on its way to becoming a large animal; the huge beast whose size terrifies us is perhaps on its way to becoming a worm. Perhaps they are each a momentary production of this planet and peculiar to it. (1974: 154)

Diderot continues, 'Who know what animal species preceded us? Who knows what will follow our present ones?' (1974: 174). To put it another way: the most pressing question for the Diderotian philosopher is no longer 'why?' but 'when?' Ontogeny replaces ontology; metaphysics is a matter of emergences, not essences.

The human is no exception: these metamorphoses are as true of human forms as of any other. Hence, we do not know what the human will become at any future moment. As noted above, Diderot asserts that 'there are polyps of all kinds, even human ones', which are subject to transformations 'to

---

[14] This Lucretian element to the late Diderot's thinking is manifest in his form-indifference: 'To be born, to live and to die is merely to change forms. . . . And what does one form matter any more than another?' (1974: 182). It is at this point that Diderot finds it difficult to hold onto any fundamental process of perfectibility (why would one form be intrinsically more perfect than any other?), distinguishing his transformism from the teleological variants found in Bonnet and Hemsterhuis (see §18).

[15] In consequence, for the late Diderot, 'the species is nothing more than a transitory norm' (Curran 2001: 92) and his constant use of the category of the monstrous is intended to put into question any notion of species fixity. See further Ibrahim (2016: 170–2).

come'. He continues, the human's 'metamorphoses and future and final state are impossible to foresee' (1974: 172). That is, what it means to be human is contingent and subject to radical change: the human is plastic. This speculation on the contingency of human form is not confined to the *Rêve* alone; it appears throughout Diderot's work. In the commentary on the *Lettre sur l'Homme* (and so a passage Hemsterhuis would have known well from 1774 onwards), Diderot speculates on the contingencies of the structure of the human:

> Why is man anything but a monster more durable than any other monster? Why is the whole human species not a monstrous species? Nature exterminates an individual within a hundred years. Why would it not exterminate a species in a greater number of years? If all is *in fluxu*, as one can scarcely doubt, all beings are monstrous. (Diderot and Hemsterhuis 1964: 503)

Diderot's is a materialism without norms, and this is as true of the human as it is of any other natural object. We are all monsters both to others and to ourselves from one moment to the next.

(c) Human organs are plastic

Diderot's transformism has an epistemological correlate: if both the natural world as a whole and the human being in particular can be radically different at each moment, both what we know and how we know are subject to radical change. The act of knowing has been and will be undertaken with very different organs, which form very different kinds of ideas, which, in turn, combine in very different ways. In other words, the practice of philosophy has a history.

The *Lettre sur les aveugles* is the eighteenth century's most celebrated statement of metaphilosophical plasticity. It exploits a tacit presupposition of the empiricist tradition: knowledge (and so, ultimately, the very contents of philosophy) is contingent on the number and type of sense organs that the philosopher happens to possess. Taking the fictionalised confessions of Nicholas Saunderson as a case study, Diderot concludes,

> If ever a philosopher, blind and deaf from his birth, were to construct a man after the fashion of Descartes, I can assure you, madam, that he would put the seat of the soul at the fingers' ends, for thence the greater part of the sensations and all his knowledge are derived. (1916: 87)

For Diderot, truths, metaphysical structures, values, even languages are dependent on the sense organs that the subject happens to be using and their relative level of development. He writes, 'As to me it has always been very clear that the state of our organs and our senses has a great influence on our metaphysics and our morality, and that those ideas which seem purely intellectual are closely dependent on the conformation of our bodies' (1916: 80). As Curran summarises, 'Saunderson's monstrosity, his blindness, delivers a stinging message to Diderot's public: the conceptual "orders" on which we base our notions of humankind are both "imperfect" and "temporary"' (2001: 77). Even the very workings of the imagination are dependent on the current state of an individual's sense organs for Diderot: 'What,' he asks, 'is the imagination of a blind man?' (1916: 153).

According to Diderot, organs will transform over time; that is, humans do not have a stable number of organs. As early as the *Interprétation sur la nature*, he had been very explicit that nature works 'to extend, to restrict, to transform, to multiply, to obliterate certain organs' (1975–: 9.36). And, within the *Rêve*, Diderot envisages the possibility of future organs that at present 'have no names' – as Madame de l'Espinasse speculates: 'People who deny the possibility of a sixth sense . . . are just silly. How do they know that nature couldn't . . . give rise to some organ we don't know about?' To which Bordeu responds emphatically, 'Not only do you follow what is said, but you draw conclusions therefrom which amaze me by their rightness' (1974: 186–7).

(d) An organological philosophy acknowledges its own transience and contingency
The Diderotian philosopher must recognise herself to be one impermanent monster among many. There are three moments to this 'self-polypisation' (Curran 2001: 92) of the philosopher: a critical moment, a sceptical moment and a speculative moment. To begin, acknowledgement of the plasticity of philosophy necessitates an attack on traditional philosophical writing. Past philosophies have been 'the enemy of movement and figures' (Diderot 1975–: 16.215); they have been 'ignorant of the modality of contingency' and, instead, have 'made use of the static categories of being, manner of being, substance, qualities' (Proust 1981: 23). The Diderotian philosopher must escape from these static, necessitarian categories to introduce contingency back into the heart of the philosophical enterprise – to reshape philosophical texts around concepts of 'the accidental, the accessory, the circumstantial' (Proust 1981: 23). This is the organological imperative for Diderot.

Such an introduction of transience and contingency into philosophy requires a radical limiting of what it is possible to know at the present moment – and this is the second of the three moments. All that philosophers can aspire to write is 'the very incomplete history of an instant' (Stenger 1999: 142). In the *Rêve*, this refusal of the fixed or the continuous is articulated in terms of 'the fallacy of the ephemeral': 'that of a transient being who believes in the immutability of things'. Traditionally, philosophers have extrapolated their own image onto other times and spaces and thereby postulated a mirage of stability and analogy, much like 'Fontenelle's rose, who declared that no gardener had ever been known to die' (1974: 177). The task facing the Diderotian philosopher is to pierce such illusions, to limit philosophical knowledge within the bounds of the present and eschew fixed truths. This is the reason why Diderot's texts are full of expressions such as 'who knows . . .?', 'We have no more idea . . .', '. . . impossible to foresee' and 'How limited is our vision!' (1974: 174) – they attest to a sceptical task. Nevertheless, this scepticism is closely tied to a speculative bent in his thinking – a series of unverifiable conjectures about an unknown past and an unknown future. Diderot gets rid of knowledge to make room for conjecture. For example, he writes in the *Lettre sur les aveugles*,

> I take your word for the present state of the universe, and in return keep the liberty of thinking as I please on its ancient and primitive state, with relation to which you are as blind as myself. . . . Allow me to believe that if we went back to the origin of things and scenes and perceived matter in motion and the evolution from chaos, we should meet with a number of shapeless creatures. . . . I might affirm that [one animal] had no stomach, another no intestines. (1974: 111)

Scepticism makes possible unfettered fabulation.

Hence, the third moment in Diderot's philosophical method consists of wild fabulation about times and places (the distant past, the far-flung future, other planets) that are liberated from any illusion of knowledge. Hence, his texts become sites of imaginative excess and exuberance, as has already described in the first half of this section. Moreover, this textual practice of speculative excess is also closely linked to Diderot's picture of the natural world, for the figure of the freshwater polyp again provides a key reference point – this time as the paradigm for a new practice of philosophical writing:[16]

---

[16] On the below, see further Azadpour and Whistler (2021).

> The argument of the philosopher is only a *skeleton*, that of the orator is *a living animal. It is a species of polyp. Divide it and it will give birth to a quantity of other living animals*. It is a hydra with a hundred heads. (1955–79: 6.291–2)

Sumi (1985; 2013: 19–20) has made use of this very passage to designate Diderot's philosophical writing as 'polyp-style', and the idea has since been developed by Ibrahim (2010: 73–92). 'Polyp-style' draws, in fact, on a long tradition of Diderot research – from Starobinski (1975) to Proust (1981) and Spangler (1997) – interested in the interrelation between Diderot's remarks on the polyp and what is distinctive about his textual practice. In the above passage, the polyp stands as a cipher for vital production and organic spontaneity, that is, the need to ceaselessly sprout new, rich ideas. And this vitalist ideal of the philosophical text is opposed to the rigid, dead norms of traditional philosophy. Hence, the passage contains a call to *bring philosophy to life*. And the *Rêve* itself can be understood on the model of this polyp-style, as 'a monstrous text which would function on the biological model of the polyp' (Spangler 1997: 96).[17]

Writing polypically is one example of Diderot's commitment to organology insofar as it demands the incessant production of the new, thereby eschewing universal laws, rules or essences in favour of a shifting, plastic singularity. The philosophical text, like the polyp, must spontaneously produce the new over and over again. Moreover, such productivity both *reflects* and *is* nature: since the natural world itself is polypic in precisely this way, the best writing is that which is able to represent it accurately and to participate in it fully. Just as Diderotian nature is structured by the delirium of unprethinkable metamorphoses, so too are his texts: they are intended to teem with polypic life. And this results in that uncontrolled generation of conjecture, fabulation and imagery which has been the subject of this section.

In §18, I will directly confront some of these theses with Hemsterhuis' own organological views; however, in order to fully understand Hemsterhuis' relation to Francophone organology and its writing practices, a detour via the philosophy of Charles Bonnet is illuminating – and this is the subject of the next section.

---

[17] Likewise, Curran writes, 'The frenzied and exhilarating mood created by *Rêve*'s polyphonic world echo Diderot's view of nature itself: like the unpredictable twisting and mutation of the universe's life forms, the chain of thought in *Rêve* is subject to unexpected transformations, deviations and swerves' (2001: 80; see also Ibrahim 1999: 6).

§17 Palingenesis and the Subversion of Materialism

Hemsterhuis' earliest known text dates from December 1742. It is the first in a series of no-longer-extant letters in which the twenty-one-year-old student describes the experiments he was conducting on the freshwater polyp. He writes, for example, of 'the trickiest, final incision' in which

> one places a polyp into a dish with a little water, and, after stretching it a little, gradually pushes a scalpel [through it]. . . . When the polyp has been turned inside out, it stays in this condition with the same ease as it had in its previous state. (Quoted in van der Hoeven 1865: 258–9)

A year later, Hemsterhuis reflects once more on these experiments and explicitly 'mentions Trembley's name for the first time as the discoverer of the "miraculous properties" of polyps' (van der Hoeven 1865: 259). And the correspondence culminates in a July 1746 missive, which

> again deals with polyps and their parasites . . . that can only be seen with a magnifying glass an inch and a half thick. When seen in this way, they take on the shape of a tree. . . . When the tree expands, its rapid and pleasant movement is the most beautiful sight afforded by polyps. (van der Hoeven 1865: 260)

Hemsterhuis will later relate how 'many years ago, I conducted thousands and thousands of experiments on all kinds of polyps and on snails, etc., and it is true that all their severed parts are reborn; but I have understood the cause of this' (B 5.48, 181–2).

That Hemsterhuis stands in Abraham Trembley's debt for these experiments is evident. Trembley had been the first, as Bonnet observes, to turn the polyp 'inside out like a stocking or glove' and observe it 'keep on living, eating and multiplying' (Bonnet and Cramer 1987: 240). Trembley (1986: 83–4) had also begun to describe the polyp-lice in which Hemsterhuis seems particularly interested in his later letters. What is less clear is how Hemsterhuis had come to be involved in the international network of experimenting on polyps that Trembley had established at the beginning of the 1740s (see Ratcliffe 2004). News of Trembley's findings had quickly spread through Europe and were reported at many scientific societies during 1741; however, Trembley published his own *Mémoires pour servir à l'histoire d'un genre de polypes d'eau douce* only in 1744. The young Hemsterhuis' familiarity with these experiments from 1742 must, then, be due to a more immediate relationship with Trembley and his circle;[18] certainly, Fresco (in Hemsterhuis 2007: 12) insists on 'the capital importance' of these experiments for his intellectual development.

1. Trembley's experiments on some 'little aquatic Beings' that he found in a ditch near The Hague in June 1740 resulted in findings that were 'so unusual and so contrary to ideas generally held on the nature of animals' that they relaunched the eighteenth-century life sciences. They have been seen as signalling a turn to experimental rather than observational biology (Schiller 1974), the emergence of modern biological method (Lenhoff and Lenhoff 1986), a flashpoint for debates between materialists and vitalists (Vartanian 1950) or epigeneticists and preformationists (Roe 1981) and a

---

[18] Brummel's and Fresco's conjecture that Hemsterhuis 'assisted' or 'worked together' with Trembley at Leiden University can be discounted straightaway (Brummel 1925: 32; Fresco 1995b: 326; Fresco in Hemsterhuis 2007: 12). Trembley had departed from Leiden by 1736 and there is no evidence of him returning in the early 1740s to undertake sustained scientific work. As Lenhoff and Lenhoff note (1986: 33–4), Trembley deliberately 'worked in a setting remote from the universities and academies of Europe' so as to keep 'his physical and intellectual distance from the conflicting scientific schools of thought in the institutions'. It is therefore improbable that he would have conducted experiments at Leiden without mentioning a collaborative partner there who was engaged in verifying his results, when the *Mémoires* are elsewhere so deliberately explicit about the circumstantial details of his experiments and the other scientists who had confirmed them. A possible alternative is that, by 1742, Hemsterhuis had already cultivated a friendship with Wilhelm Bentick, at whose estate of Sorgvielt Trembley was actually conducting the experiments while tutoring the Bentick children. Hemsterhuis was certainly invited to Sorgvielt for scientific demonstrations at a later date (Zuidervaart 2019: 142) and presumably participated alongside Trembley in the intellectual salon hosted there (see §2), so he almost certainly made Trembley's acquaintance at some point (see B 2.47, 113). More likely, however, is that Hemsterhuis' experiments on the polyp were conducted to assist Allamand, whom he had certainly come to know by 1742 (see §2) and who was a formally named collaborator of Trembley's. Allamand was, Trembley writes, 'kind enough to repeat most of my experiments' and his testimony can serve as 'an excellent proof of the facts I discovered' (1986: 86). (The fact that Trembley goes on to note that Allamand discovered 'great quantities of polyps in the Province of Friesland and in the vicinity of Leiden' suggests once more that Trembley himself did not work on polyps in Leiden.) Allamand even went beyond Trembley with his skill at inverting polyps (Trembley 1986: 160–1; see Baker 1952: 74, 91) and in Leiden itself he was credited in autumn 1742 as 'one of the Gentlemen that made this discovery' (Gronovius, quoted in Baker 1952: xviii). Allamand was therefore expert in the very experiments Hemsterhuis relates in 1742 and could certainly have solicited Hemsterhuis' assistance in conducting them.

§17 PALINGENESIS AND THE SUBVERSION OF MATERIALISM 179

limit case in the classification of natural kinds (Dawson 1987). In general, what Trembley found was that 'the polyps possess the remarkable capacity to multiply as a result of being cut into sections' (1986: v): the mutilated parts of the polyp always regenerated once more into new individuals. Indeed, Trembley even managed to cut the same polyp material into fifty parts, out of which fifty healthy individual polyps grew (1986: 146).

These experiments caught the imagination of the scientific community, of philosophers and even of the public at large – and Hemsterhuis formed part of the intellectual tradition inspired by these experiments and 'the disturbing metaphysical issues' they raised (Dawson 1987: 8). These issues can be categorised into three. First, in exhibiting both plant-like and animal-like features, the polyp appeared to resist any straightforward categorisation: Trembley himself raises the possibility of freshwater polyps being a 'plant animal' (1986: 11) and Bonnet interpreted the polyp as an intermediary 'zoophyte' – he initially responds to Trembley, 'One can say that you have discovered the point of passage from the Vegetable to the Animal' (Bonnet and Trembley 1987: 138). Secondly, the hydra-like powers of regeneration exhibited by the polyp provoked a scandal: there seemed something particularly unprovidential about 'the possibility that a snip with scissors could make two animals from one' (Baker 1952: xvii). Hence, some contemporaries were encouraged to see in Trembley's research a proof of materialism – La Mettrie exclaims, for instance: 'Trembley's polyp! Does it not contain within itself the causes which produce its regeneration? . . . Matter possesses intrinsically the causes of its activity and organisation' (La Mettrie 1796: 3.164, 3.171; see also Vartanian 1950: 270–1). Finally, there was a further debate over the animal soul. By 1740, an anti-Cartesian position on animals had become widely accepted according to which they were to be attributed formative principles; however, after Trembley, it became more difficult to discern exactly how these principles could relate to the polyp, such that each of its dissected parts would equally possess a principle of individuation. And, once more, the materialist cause benefited, since the easiest solution was to eliminate altogether any kind of animate soul separate from parts of matter.

2. In opposition to the materialist interpretation of Trembley's experiments stands Charles Bonnet's philosophy. Bonnet recognised the extent to which the polyp might bolster the materialist cause; he relates how 'the materialists seized on it with avidity to justify their favourite dogma' (2002: 82). And this anxiety motivates his own attempts to reclaim it for immaterialism; as Vartanian glosses, 'His intention was to elaborate a theory of

generation which would at once account for the polyp's hydra-like powers in accordance with principles acceptable to "la saine philosophie" and would deprive materialism of a dangerous weapon' (1950: 279). That is, Bonnet worked tirelessly to reappropriate the polyp for theistic ends – not to negate or to neutralise 'the marvels, the wonders which we owe to Trembley' (Bonnet and Cramer 1987: 166) in some reactionary gesture, but rather to subvert materialist reflections for a post-polypic orthodoxy. Bonnet is clear: 'My goal was principally to show, at the very least, that the discovery of the polyp does not favour a materialist world at all' (2002: 365).

Even more than Hemsterhuis, Bonnet was both personally and professionally implicated in debates over the polyp. On the one hand, he and Trembley were 'intimate friends, as well as distant relations' (Dawson 1987: 10; see also Baker 1952: 24); on the other hand, it was his own earlier observations of aphid reproduction that laid the groundwork for Trembley's research. It was in this context that the polyp became so dear to Bonnet: 'Everything that I knew in natural history seemed like almost nothing compared to the *polyp*. It overthrew all my ideas and put my head, so to speak, into combustion' (2002: 170). The later Bonnet's vision of the natural world remained rigorously polypic in two ways. First, the polyp's intermediary status between plant and animal – as a 'zoophyte' – allows for the modelling of a genuinely linear sequence of organisms passing from the plant to the animal kingdom. As Bonnet puts it at the beginning of his *Insectologie*, polyps 'hold a middle place, and thus form points of passage or links' in the natural world – and 'this reflection gave birth to the perhaps foolhardy thought to draw up a Ladder of Natural Beings' (1745: xi). In short, Bonnet's idea of a chain of being is polypic in inspiration. Secondly, the polyp's distinctive form of generation exemplifies a palingenetic process by which all organisms evolve. Nature is full of metamorphoses up and down the chain of being – and the polyp provides the model for movement along the chain, as well as evidence for the chain itself.

3. What I am going to argue in the rest of this section and the next is that Hemsterhuis broadly follows Bonnet in this subversion of materialist doctrine for anti-materialist ends (although he goes further than Bonnet in also appropriating Diderot-like styles for such ends too). And this shared subversion of materialism is most visible in their organologies, which – just like Diderot's – are determined by this early encounter with Trembley's polyp. While there are many connections between Hemsterhuis and Bonnet that have already been explored in this book and to which I return in §18,

§17 PALINGENESIS AND THE SUBVERSION OF MATERIALISM

Hemsterhuis is most Bonnetian in his organology. To show this, what follows is a reconstruction of some of the key features of Bonnet's organology that parallels the reconstruction of Diderot's organology in §16.[19]

(a) 'Palingenesis' names the idea that everything is a recapitulation
According to Bonnet, the example of the polyp teaches us – and, on this point, he thinks all materialists would agree – that a huge number of principles of generation (or germs) correspond to a single natural form. No matter where, how or how many times one cuts up a polyp, all of its parts 'form as many new *persons*, as many new *Is*, as develop new individual wholes' (2002: 82–3). While Diderot responds to this by 'animalising everything' (Bonnet 2002: 379), that is, by making matter itself polypic, Bonnet keeps hold of the concept of an animal soul, of an immaterial generative principle, but pluralises it. Everything contains formative principles: there is no part of the polyp that does not express corresponding principles of generation or germ – or, in Bonnet's own words, 'Each molecule has a tendency to produce continually. It is, so to say, all ovary, all germ' (1762: 264).[20]

It is on this basis that Bonnet establishes his doctrine of palingenesis: it names what follows from this idea that every material point expresses multiple principles of generation and so is regenerated many times. Palingenesis asserts that all current forms exist in the middle of a long series of metamorphoses without any perceptible origin or end. Everything is always in the middle of transforming, for nature consists in nothing but 'renaissance' (2002: 125). Hence, death is a moment of transition and increase, rather than extinction – a limit that nature continually transgresses. Bonnet speaks of death as 'a kind of extraction' (2002: 204), an occasion for metamorphosis. Moreover, Bonnet makes use of this natural power of regeneration to ground a 'physics of the Resurrection' (2002: 206). That is, he supplies a naturalistic proof of the Christian dogma of the resurrection of the body, on the basis that resurrection merely names an ordinary process of natural production that Trembley's experiments had brought into view. This is, in fact, one way in which Bonnet appropriates the polyp against materialism and in favour of a new palingenetic version of theism.

---

[19] Just as, in the previous section, Diderot's late *Rêve de d'Alembert* served as the central text, in what follows, Bonnet's 1769 *La palingénésie philosophie* plays the same role.

[20] Hemsterhuis will, in fact, make a similar assertion with respect to at least some of the natural world: 'Each particle of the polyp, the tremella or the tapeworm is seed. How many plants produce their offspring through their bulbs, their roots, their stems, their leaves! The whole mineral kingdom is seed' (*EE* 1.101; *OP* 222).

(b) Bonnet affirms a variant of the materialist doctrine of perpetual transformation: new natural forms can arise at any moment
Transformism was in the air in the mid-eighteenth century: just as Diderot insisted that 'a new order' can emerge at any moment (see Cassirer 1951: 92), so too Bonnet argued that 'another order of things succeeds the first: the world is re-peopled and takes on a new face' (2002: 189). This transformism is an integral part of his doctrine of palingenesis: 'infinitely diverse orders' of germs (2002: 326) lie dormant, ready to be expressed at any moment – and, when activated, nature is radically transformed. To chart the history of the natural world is 'to behold a world completely new, a system of things of which we have now no idea' (2002: 158; see also Lovejoy 1936: 285) to the extent that Bonnet, just like Diderot, speculates fantastically on plants becoming animals and even beavers becoming playwrights (2002: 155).

This is one reason why Bonnet has often been credited with temporalising the chain of being (Lovejoy 1936) or shifting 'from a static to a dynamic concept of nature' (Bowler 1974: 160). The chain of organised bodies that exist at the present moment ruptures the chain that existed in the past, and the future will rupture it once more. When it comes to the past, Bonnet claims, 'If we could see a horse, a chicken or a snake under their first form, under the form they had at the time of creation, we would find it impossible to recognise them' (2002: 190); and, when it comes to the future, he likewise insists,

> One must not imagine that animals will have in their future state the same form, the same structure, the same parts, the same consistency, the same size as we see in their current state. They will thus be as different from what they are today as the state of our globe will differ from its present state. If we were permitted to contemplate at present this delightful scene of metamorphosis, I am convinced that we could recognise no species of animal which are today the most familiar: they too would be changed to our eyes. (2002: 139)

The past and future transgress the current limits of possible experience.

Humans are equally subject to these metamorphoses:[21] the human is 'from period to period clothed in new forms or new modalities' (2002: 189) and must 'pass through a series of apparent metamorphoses' (2002: 393).

---

[21] Bonnet's naturalism is here manifest – the embedding of the human in natural but immaterial processes: 'I have tried to study man as I have studied plants and insects' (1760: ix). See Whistler (2022c).

Future transformations will 'make man a very different being from what we know under the name man' (2002: 592). And, once again, such metamorphoses will be so extreme as to make future humans unrecognisable:

> How much would such a metamorphosis appear to us more astonishing than all those of a fable! But very probably, our surprise would be mute. ... We would in this case be much like a man who was transported to the world of Venus: even if this man possessed the whole encyclopaedic dictionary, he would probable still be incapable of describing what he discovered in that world. (2002: 314)

Each transformation is too radical to be subsumed under existing concepts: we lack 'terms of comparison' (2002: 370) and there are 'no analogues here' (2002: 139).

In sum, palingenesis makes possible a naturalistic system of times, a theory of world revolutions in which the future erupts in a way that is radically discontinuous with what has come before. Bonnetian world history comprises a series of 'new creations' that 'introduce a new order of things, completely different from what we contemplate at present' (2002: 133; see also Bowler 1974: 167). And this seems (at least at first blush) to refuse any attempt to shoehorn Bonnet's transformism into a 'continuist schema of progressive formation' (Lotterie 2006: 55; see also Anderson 1982: 25). In opposition to gradualism, Bonnet is clear: 'New revolutions are still hidden in the abyss of the future' (2002: 132).

(c) New sense organs and so new cognitive capacities emerge with each global revolution, such that philosophy will appear radically different at each moment
Like Diderot, Bonnet's anthropology is little more than an organology. Both philosophers infer directly from radical metamorphoses of nature to corresponding transformations of human organs. Moreover, both Diderot and Bonnet – as well as Hemsterhuis – frame their organologies around two criteria: the emergence of 'new organs' (2002: 164) and the enhancement and 'increase in the perfections of [existing] organs' (2002: 163). With each revolution, organisms gain 'a greater number of senses *and* more perfected senses' (2002: 353; my emphasis). The human is no exception: she participates in a universal organic process that includes the polyp, which will also 'experience new sensations and sensations of a new order' (2002: 175).

Everything is subject to radical change, including epistemic instruments. In Bonnet's own words, 'no relation' exists 'between the ideas that we acquire by our five senses' at present and 'those that we will be able to acquire by other senses' (2002: 623). Philosophy will change – and it is impossible to predict what it will become. Hence, the Bonnetian philosopher, too, must acknowledge the transience and contingency of her tools; she must replace ontology with ontogeny and remain faithful to the injunction 'At every moment, I await the discovery of a new world' (2002: 64).

As with Diderot, this refusal of the static is initially made manifest in a scepticism ('philosophical doubt is itself the path to truth' [2002: 523]) that recognises the current 'weakness or rather coarseness of our senses' (2002: 336). And as with Diderot, such a limitation of philosophical knowledge makes room for conjecture and particularly conjecture about future alterations to the type, range and perfection of empirical knowledge. Sense organs undergo revolutions (both in number and in perfection), and so too, therefore, does philosophical method. Bonnet thus belongs to the tradition of Diderot's *Lettre sur les aveugles* and plays a game of 'what if . . . ?' with the future of philosophy: 'Imagine', he suggests, 'a man who was born with a complete paralysis of three or four of the principal senses' (2002: 623) or even a 'human soul placed in the brain of an oyster', or an elephant whose 'sphere of ideas would extend further and further', whose 'associations would be strengthened by signs at the same time as they multiply and diversify' and who 'would come to contest the empire of man' (2002: 119). Bonnet equally imagines future thinkers looking back on the eighteenth century, 'smiling and seeing in these great philosophers only Hottentots' (2002: 329). What the philosopher is and what she can be has a history.[22]

(d) A major point of rupture between palingenesis and materialism lies in the introduction of a principle of perfectibility into transformism
In opposition to Diderot's Lucretian chaos, Bonnet inserts order into metamorphosis: every form that emerges is more perfect than that which preceded it; that is, perfectibility determines natural becoming.

---

[22] Like Hemsterhuis (as described in §10, §14), Bonnet makes this point by way of an analogy to optical instruments: just as 'the invention of instruments has given us all these truths', like 'the rings of Saturn, the wonders of electricity, or light, the animalcules of infusions', so 'could it not be that, one day, these instruments will be made more perfect and new ones invented which will carry our knowledge further beyond present limits?' (2002: 330–1). Bonnet reasons exactly like Hemsterhuis: just as the telescope and the microscope have prosthetically enhanced the eye, thereby increasing human knowledge in ways that would have been inconceivable to earlier generations, so the same is possible for all organs. Both Hemsterhuis and Bonnet embed a history of organs made possible by technological advances into a revolutionary organology.

Hence, while much of the above describes ways in which Bonnetian palingenesis approximates to Diderotian materialism (insofar as both philosophers construct a thoroughgoing organology out of a polypic vision of the natural world), such that Bonnet appears at times almost to be parodying transformist metaphysics from an immaterialist perspective, there remains a substantial difference between the two organologies. And this difference consists of the principle of perfectibility discussed in §12. Bonnet asserts, *pace* Diderot, 'There will be a continual progress ... of all species towards a superior perfection' (2002: 155) – or, as Lovejoy paraphrases, everything 'rises again in improved form' (1936: 286).

As §12 described, Bonnet is here in the process of transforming Rousseau's original postulate of perfectibility into a metaphysical constant, that is, into the unswerving tendency of all beings towards perfection. Everything, according to Bonnet, is always on the way to becoming perfect. Bonnet reads Rousseauean perfectibility via Leibniz, for whom 'in the whole universe, an uninterrupted and free progress always continues, through which the state of the world is always improved' (quoted in Lossky 1931: 217). Hence, the gradualist picture of the natural world that Bonnet seemingly rejected by way of a theory of global revolutions is reconstituted at the level of perfectibility (see Anderson 1982: 114). It acts as a container that restricts metamorphosis, for revolutions must always be for the better.

In fact, what appear as radically new metamorphoses in nature are not so very new at all on an ontological level; rather, they have been ordained from the beginning. God has planned the continuous becoming-perfect of all organic bodies, in one stroke, at the beginning of time, God predetermined all genesis, and so 'all parts of the universe are thus contemporaneous ... realised by one act alone' (2002: 182). On a fundamental level, there is no becoming and no transformation, because everything has already been created with a view to how it will come to be. Bonnet is explicit: 'I have posited as a fundamental principle that nothing is engendered, that everything is originally preformed, and that what we name *generation* is only the simple development of what pre-exists' (2002: 203). All principles of generation are 'as old as the universe' (2002: 326): some of them have already been expressed and others (such as Bonnet's 'germs of restitution') form another series that will be expressed in the future, but currently lie dormant.

(e) Bonnet too practises a 'polyp-style': a chain of speculations expanding outwards into a future always determined in advance
'My book forms a chain and this chain is long' (2002: 40), writes Bonnet in *La palingénésie* – and such a claim holds true for all his writings. These chains

mimic the very chain of beings he describes in the natural world: like nature itself, his writing charts a series from the simple to the complex – from the evident to the conjectural – moving sequentially from experiments on the polyp to speculations on the future dwelling place of humanity.[23] Bonnet explains this methodological approach as follows: he starts off as a 'naturalist' who 'analyses, anatomises and compares . . . proven and decisive facts', and then moves on to think through 'the series of consequences' which follow, 'linking them one to another'. He concludes, 'The whole series is quite long and demands a little more attention than a novel' (2002: 61).[24] When Bonnet succeeds at constructing a functioning chain, 'everything is so well placed . . . so well linked' and 'progress is everywhere so natural, so easy, that one could not imagine it proceeding otherwise' (2002: 54); however, when such a writing practice fails, when the initial links prove faulty, then everything falls apart. Bonnet is very clear that this is a very real danger for his project:

> [My inferences] always rest on [an] important observation. . . . I agree that if one were ever to demonstrate the falsity of this observation, the edifice I have tried to raise on that foundation would be as ruined as those [others] which I have tried to destroy. Such is the natural destiny that menaces all analytic works; if one manages to destroy its fundamental principle, to detach the master-link from the chain, then the whole work will be no more than a series of more or less erroneous propositions. (2002: 76)

The self-professed precariousness of Bonnet's methodological approach depends on the truths of its foundational links. But it also depends on a procedure of analogic conjecture – the method by which he extends these chains further and establishes new links. His writings 'often' journey 'into the region of conjecture' (2002: 60), and are able to do so because such conjecture is guaranteed by the 'great analogy I have discovered' between

---

[23] Anderson sums up this line of thought: 'Insistent repetition [in Bonnet's texts] indicates something other, I think, than a redundant literary style or the absence of an editor: it is a procedure required by Bonnet's relational view of the universe. In a world in which every particular thing is not simply a part of a harmoniously interconnected reality but, more fundamentally, derives its own identity, its locus, from the myriad relations it sustains with everything else, every part implies every other part' (Anderson 1982: 122).

[24] Here Bonnet is far from Trembley, for whom 'it is too dangerous in the subject of natural history to abandon experience and allow the imagination to lead us' (Trembley 1986: 186).

all things (2002: 80). That is, these speculations are guaranteed by the *rapports* they describe. The successful philosopher senses these *rapports* (or analogical relations) in order to speculatively transition from what is known to what is unknown. Hence, Bonnet's method is 'purely analogical' (2002: 425) and his texts proceed on the basis of 'the surest rules of analogy' (2002: 454).[25] Because 'everything is linked in the universe', because *rapports* exist between every natural object, there is a legitimate 'art of conjecture' (2002: 64; see also Savioz 1948: 84). Nevertheless, Bonnet again acknowledges that analogical conjecture is precarious: his speculations lay claim to a far weaker degree of certainty than observation or intuition. And Bonnet modifies his writing to reflect precisely this limitation: 'I have not said *I have found*, but rather *it seems to me, I conjecture, one can infer from it*. A more decisive tone would have been little suitable to the nature of my subject' (2002: 51; see also Savioz 1948: 59–60). The Bonnetian philosopher should acknowledge the relative weakness of her analogies by employing a different 'tone', one that speaks in a less 'decisive' and more hesitant voice.

Bonnet's comments on the distinctive tone of palingenetic philosophising return me to Hemsterhuis' poetic turn. In the next section, I wish to show that, notwithstanding the substantial doctrinal convergences between the two, Hemsterhuis breaks with Bonnet when it comes to the *presentation of organology*. Hemsterhuis reverts to something that resembles Diderot's more adventurous formal experiments as a better resource for capturing the transience and contingency of organological thinking. Although he expounds an anti-materialist organology founded on a principle of perfectibility, Bonnet is not radical enough for Hemsterhuis when it comes to the writing of philosophy.

§18 Post-Bonnetian Style

In the preliminary remarks to Part Three, I rehearsed some of the evidence why Hemsterhuis has traditionally been interpreted to be hostile to 'Bonnetism' (B 2.45, 103). He worries, for example, that Bonnet's example 'leads without doubt to the most perfect materialism', owing to its talk of fibres and corpuscles (B 3.48, 120; see also B 5.22, 91; 2.45, 103); he also censures Bonnet's disciples for 'the direct transformation of algebra into metaphysics' as 'destitute of common sense' (B 3.47, 119; see Hammacher 1995c: 622). Furthermore, those laws 'which search for the causes of phenomena

---

[25] Notably, Bonnet planned an unwritten treatise on the uses and abuses of analogical method. See Savioz (1948: 326).

in redundant and often absurd modifications of matter' are, according to Hemsterhuis, 'sister' to Bonnet's own laws and both sets of laws are 'daughter of that poor, small philosophy' that results from Cartesianism (B 2.45, 102). On the basis of this evidence, most readers (with the exception of Ayrault [1961: 1.489]) have concluded that there is little that unites Hemsterhuis with Bonnet. This interpretative tradition began as early as Meyboom's 1846 edition of Hemsterhuis' works, which cites an extract from a letter to Gallitzin that attests to his contempt for Swiss philosophers, like 'Bonnet, de Luc, Trembley and Le Sage', who all exemplify an 'infinitely small way of thinking in philosophy' (B 3.26, 75; Hemsterhuis 1846–50: 3.139). In Meyboom's wake, Brummel speaks of Hemsterhuis 'repeatedly expressing his aversion to a sensualist like Bonnet' (1925: 83); and contemporary scholars conclude that Hemsterhuis 'explicitly distanced himself from Bonnet' (Hammacher 1995a: 63–4), that he condemns 'the malign influence of Bonnet' (Fresco in Hemsterhuis 2007: 200) and that he 'ridicules Bonnet' (van Sluis in OP 18).

Nevertheless, Hemsterhuis' rejection of Bonnetism occurs most often in discussion of the work of Bonnet's disciples whom Hemsterhuis encountered in The Hague. His comments about Charles Bonnet himself are far more nuanced; for instance, he writes, 'Bonnet is one of the most powerful brains that has existed – he has a brain whose intellect can divide and subdivide the smallest ideas with admirable dexterity. He is for ideas what Swammerdam was for insects' (B 1.216, 252). The most important piece of evidence for some philosophical affinity between Hemsterhuis and Bonnet occurs in a letter to Gallitzin from 1780, in which Hemsterhuis relates a conversation with one of Bonnet's disciples in which he remarked: 'He will see that his hero's philosophy and my [philosophy] meet at the end of the day, and that the only difference that he will find is that [Bonnet] had begun with the tail and I with the head' (B 3.47, 118). Hemsterhuis rarely repeats himself verbatim in correspondence, except when the idea under consideration is important to him (e.g., the passages on being 'born Greek'); and, significantly, Hemsterhuis repeats the very same words to Anna Perrenot when reporting this conversation to her:

> He told me straightaway that he was the principal disciple of Bonnet and had read a lot of his works. This gave me pleasure . . . I told him that if he deigned to study my work a little, he would well see that his hero's philosophy and my [philosophy] meet each other at the end of the day, and that the only difference was that he had begun with the tail and I with the head. (B 11.30, 40)

§18 POST-BONNETIAN STYLE

In 1780 at the very least, Hemsterhuis is persuaded by the idea that the conclusions drawn in his philosophy are roughly identical to those drawn in Bonnet's. The two might reach these conclusions from contrary directions but, in the end, they say the same thing.

This remark also suggests one of the reasons for Hemsterhuis' censure of Bonnet for failing to sufficiently guard against materialist and mathematicising abuses of his work. There is something about the way Bonnet argues for his palingenetic organology that, according to Hemsterhuis, lends itself to misinterpretation, even to perversion. Hence, Hemsterhuis' refrain that Bonnet 'work[s] more for the materialists than the materialists themselves' (B 3.47, 120) and hence his criticisms of Bonnet's writings for their 'materialist' style in his 1775 letters to Gallitzin analysed in §6. The major improvement Hemsterhuis seeks over Bonnet has, by Hemsterhuis' own lights, nothing to do with doctrinal conclusions, but all to do with how much the presentation of such truths can withstand materialism. Hemsterhuis' own philosophy is intended to go beyond Bonnet's by presenting similar anti-materialist, organological conclusions in a way that foils materialist misappropriations. He wants to save Bonnet from 'Bonnetism', to purge it of all the unhelpful accretions that give succour to the materialists.

1. Bonnet cannot be classed as a major influence on Hemsterhuis' philosophy; for example, the latter is far from explicitly endorsing the notion of palingenesis, despite familiarity with it (B 7.37, 105). Nevertheless, considering Bonnet's connections to Dutch philosophy – including his closeness to members of the Sorgvielt salon, his friendship with Allamand who acted as his 'effective intermediary in the Dutch Republic' (Marx 1976: 403) and, more generally, the 'hearty welcome' his works enjoyed in the Dutch Republic (Marx 1976: 403, 411–14; Dawson 1987: 11–12, 67–8; Savioz 1948: 38), Hemsterhuis certainly knew much of Bonnet. Van der Hoeven makes Bonnet a central reference point when paraphrasing Hemsterhuis' early letters on the polyp (1865: 263); and, in the mid-1740s, both philosophers embarked on similar research programmes on insect anatomy, resulting in Bonnet's *Insectologie* and Hemsterhuis' lost treatise on insect vision. Of both philosophers it can be said that they 'came to metaphysics by way of insects' (Anderson 1982: 10).[26]

[26] Both of them thus formed part of an international project at the time *to philosophise through insects* – which earned them and those like them the epithet of 'muckworm philosophers' (Smollett, quoted in Baker 1952; 45). As Jacques Roger (1963: 238) summarises, 'Insects threw the scholars out of their ruts, refused to be placed in traditional frames of reference, ruined the most solid analogies and the most accepted laws'.

For his part, Bonnet owned a unique copy of Hemsterhuis' 1770 *Lettre sur les désirs* – the only extant manuscript copied out in a distinctive, yet unknown hand, which, according to Marx, 'leads us to suppose that the Genevan was interested in Hemsterhuis' work' (1976: 419; see also van Sluis in *OP* 38). Fresco even talks of early 'controversies between Hemsterhuis and Bonnet' (in Hemsterhuis 2007: 12).[27] Evidence for their intellectual affinity is to be found in their fibre physiologies, their recourse to *rapport* as a fundamental metaphysical idea, their teleological interpretation of the principle of perfectibility, their development of the notion of moral certainty in the wake of 's Gravesande, and even their penchant for the term 'germ'.

However, it is when it comes to organology that Hemsterhuis' doctrinal convergences with Bonnet (as well as, to a far lesser extent, with Diderot) are clearest. To demonstrate this, a set of tenets can once again be briefly extracted from Hemsterhuis' organology that correspond, often exactly, with the reconstruction of Bonnet's palingenetic organology from the previous section.

(a) For Hemsterhuis, as well as for Bonnet and for Diderot, truths are contingent on the number, type and perfection of our organs

According to Hemsterhuis, psychology is first philosophy; in this he differs from Bonnet, who typically embeds his psychology within a larger account of organic nature. That is, Bonnet foregrounds his naturalism in a way that Hemsterhuis does not, and this is another way in which Hemsterhuis' remark that Bonnet 'had begun with the tail and I with the head' holds true. And yet, the contents of their organologies share much with each other and with Diderot too. First and foremost, truths and values are dependent on both the number and the condition of the organs which a subject happens to possess at any particular time. Hence, Hemsterhuis writes, in the same tradition as Diderot's *Lettre sur les aveugles* and Bonnet's *La palingénésie*, 'When certain organs are lost to the human subject, the subject loses all idea of the faces of the universe which were turned towards them' (*EE* 1.124; *OP* 296; translation modified). And it is not just what is known that is subject to radical

---

[27] It is perhaps more prudent to say with Marx that 'The question of actual direct relations between Hemsterhuis and Bonnet gives rise to difficulty' (1976: 419). Also noteworthy is the fact that Bonnet's and Hemsterhuis' reception histories are closely linked: while it remains true that 'the significant role that Bonnet played in the intellectual life of his time' (Bohnen 1981: 363) has been neglected, a quick glance at Hemsterhuis' early German reception reveals that Bonnet's name is never far away – in Wieland's *Der Teutsche Merkur*, in Herder's arguments with Schlosser over the nature of immortality and in the *Spinozismusstreit* itself. See further Whistler (2022b, 2022c).

change, for 'it seems probable that [the soul] is already attached to several organs which will be of better service in the future' (*EE* 1.124; *OP* 296). This will result in the kinds of radical alterations to the nature of knowing itself that, according to Hemsterhuis, visual experience had already exemplified after the inventions of the telescope and the microscope.

(b) According to Hemsterhuis, the philosopher should acknowledge the plasticity of her thinking
What this reasoning makes clear to Hemsterhuis – as it does to Diderot and Bonnet as well – is that the world is always experienced as a *non-whole*; that is, it is always capable of revealing more, revealing very different features and so appearing as something else entirely. And revealing this 'more' is primarily a matter of both enhancing and proliferating sense organs. The opening to *Sophyle* is Hemsterhuis' most programmatic statement of such a position: descriptions of the world can necessarily be ameliorated as the limits of possible experience recede. The contingency of how we do philosophy allows for an ampliative empiricism that transgresses hard experiential barriers – Euthyphro gleefully talks of future philosophies 'allowing us to see unknown lands' (*EE* 2.45; *OP* 335).[28] Once the philosopher has done away with 'the fallacy of the ephemeral', philosophy can become an adventure, and the excitement of this adventure is palpable in *Sophyle*.

To put it in the terms of Chapter Three: philosophising has a history. Hemsterhuis writes in a key quotation already invoked in §11:

> Let us suppose someone endowed with a hundred other types of organs, all of which have other and different relations to essence, gave the name matter to all essence insofar as it related to his organs, matter would have completely different attributes. (*EE* 2.58; *OP* 376)

Just like Diderot and Bonnet, this passage articulates a scepticism born of the current imperfections of our organs which makes room for speculative conjec-

---

[28] Of course, Hemsterhuis' commitment to perfectibility entails that this contingency is far less radical than Diderot's, even if similar to Bonnet's. There are, more generally, two types of contingency at play here: (1) the Diderotian idea that anything can happen from one moment to the next; and (2) the sort of contingency that Blumenberg has in mind when he states that 'visibility has become a contingent fact' (1985: 370–1), that is, the idea that certain structures and limits are *not necessary*. (These two types further map onto distinctions between a radical epigenesis and preformationism and between aprovidential and providential catastrophisms.) It is the latter type that I am attributing to Hemsterhuis' philosophy.

tures about possible reconfigurations of matter in future epochs. Hemsterhuis, too, plays a game of philosophical '*what if . . .*': if our epistemic instruments can alter in all sorts of ways at any moment, what does that mean for the idea of matter? Restricting our knowledge of matter ends up liberating all sorts of imaginative possibilities for what matter could become. Hemsterhuis thereby associates himself with a tradition of philosophical 'whatifery' running through the mid-eighteenth century for which the injunctions 'let us suppose . . .' and 'imagine that . . .', etc., are crucial philosophical tools.

And, as with Bonnet and Diderot, this organological plasticity is made possible by a more general account of the human as malleable: what the human is alters radically both in the past and in the future. In one of his most startlingly palingenetic statements, Hemsterhuis claims, 'It is no absurdity to imagine that man will change species on the surface of the earth' (*EE* 2.74; *OP* 424). Hemsterhuis even extends this kind of speculation to the natural world on occasion: 'It seems probable, from [the anatomy] of some insects, there are animals which enjoy an organ we do not have that is turned towards a face of the universe unknown to us' (*EE* 1.105; *OP* 234). These remarks could have come straight out of Bonnet's *La palingénésie*; they serve as the implicit foundation of his more explicit claims about organs and also hint at a more all-encompassing metaphysical vision of transformism.

(c) Hemsterhuis even occasionally follows Bonnet in grounding his transformism in a theory of global revolution

Hemsterhuis speculates in *Alexis*, 'The human species could well have lost in some ancient revolution either some organ . . . or some vehicle of sensation' (*EE* 2.142–3; *OP* 632; translation modified). Catastrophism was, of course, a common motif of much eighteenth-century thinking and Hemsterhuis is drawing on many sources when he speaks of an 'ancient revolution'; nevertheless, as Cometa notes, 'Hemsterhuis' text belongs to a tradition that perceives the catastrophe as an occasion of palingenesis' (2005: 114). Mähl also notes an 'orientation towards palingenesis' in *Alexis* (1994: 270). That is, there is something distinctly Bonnetian about the connection Hemsterhuis establishes between natural revolution and a history of organs. Once again, a background assumption fleetingly appears: Hemsterhuis' organology presupposes wholesale alterations in the structure of nature.[29]

---

[29] In correspondence, Hemsterhuis also speculates on the 'successive developments' of living forms among inhabitants of other planets, just as Bonnet and Diderot do (B 5.30, 122). Furthermore, while not developed in an organological context, a key influence on Hemsterhuis on catastrophe was presumably his lifelong friend, Camper,

§18 POST-BONNETIAN STYLE   193

Alexis talks about death along the lines of palingenetic principles as well. Just as Bonnet sees in death an occasion for transformation rather than extinction, so Hemsterhuis writes that inhabitants of the golden age correctly saw death 'as one of the continual and ordinary developments of [their] essence', a trigger for an 'acceleration' of metamorphosis. But the modern individual has lost this palingenetic insight and now wrongly considers death 'to cut human existence into two parts': 'present life' and 'a vague, doubtful and, at the very most, possible eternity' (*EE* 2.145; *OP* 640–2). The fundamental truth about death obscured in modernity is a palingenetic one.

(d) Like Bonnet but unlike Diderot, metamorphoses are not chaotic, but grounded in a principle which guarantees the greater perfections of what is to come
Further evidence for Hemsterhuis' proximity to palingenesis is to be found in his appropriation of Bonnetian perfectibility, as already discussed in §12. Hemsterhuis opposes both Diderot's Lucretian rejection of perfectibility and Rousseau's restrictive use of it as a postulate; instead, like Bonnet, he advocates a teleological metaphysics; that is, his version of perfectibility rests on the idea that every future state will necessarily be more perfect than what has come before. Both Hemsterhuis and Bonnet confidently anticipate future enhancements to the human, who will achieve 'perfection well beyond all our current conceptions' (*B* 9.60, 129). Just like Bonnet, Hemsterhuis grounds his organology in a transformism of global revolutions that is guaranteed by a robust principle of perfectibility.

2. The above is one way of making sense of Hemsterhuis' claim that, even though he and Bonnet take different approaches, both reach the same conclusions. Nevertheless, even if Bonnet gets to the correct destination, he takes the wrong route, according to Hemsterhuis: his philosophy still leaves itself open to materialist appropriation, to the threat of bad readers of the kind Hemsterhuis laments in the 'Additions and Clarifications' to the *Lettre sur l'Homme* and Bonnet himself bemoans as 'inattentive or badly disposed readers' who fail to notice his claims that are 'directly contrary to the language of the materialist' (2002: 49). It is in order to obstruct these 'badly disposed readers' that Hemsterhuis breaks with Bonnet on the *communication* of organology. Bonnet merely tries to resist materialist esoteric writing

who himself undertook a very public conversion to a radical catastrophism, including extinction events, during the 1780s. As Kant relates, according to the late Camper, 'natural revolutions... submerged the plant and animal kingdoms before human beings ever existed.' (1996: 305)

by way of a reversal of esoteric concepts, for example by reappropriating the polyp for orthodoxy. Hemsterhuis, however, resists materialist esoteric writing with an *esoteric* reversal of esoteric style, for example by reappropriating esoteric writing practices already deployed by the materialists for antimaterialist ends. Bonnet writes in a way too likely to be misunderstood by the bad reader; Hemsterhuis fights against this tendency by learning lessons from those who have written under persecution.

In general, there are three ways in which Hemsterhuis attempts to improve upon Bonnet's writing of philosophy. The first is a direct response to the above. A connection seems to exist between the monologic nature of Bonnet's texts and their subsequent perversion for the materialist cause – and thus, by disrupting any monologic tendencies in his own philosophy, Hemsterhuis hopes to avoid this consequence, to resist the materialist corruption of organology. Hence, as part of a pervasive, even hyperbolic use of poetic devices, Hemsterhuis fills his texts with 'metaphors that have been pushed too far', myths that render his own doctrines ridiculous and dialogues that put into question the very arguments they make – all of which are writing techniques deployed in the esoteric tradition from Plato to Diderot. Like Plato and Diderot, Hemsterhuis places the concepts he uses under erasure, unsaying them at the same time as saying them through figuration, mythologisation and dialogue. The myth of Prometheus analysed in §9 is the most obvious example of this strategy: Diotima's earnest presentation of a Bonnet-inspired palingenesis flirts with parody and the ridiculous and so problematises any assent the reader might have been inclined to give it. Hemsterhuis manages to occupy a position simultaneously close to and distant from materialism in a way that imitates Bonnet, but still succeeds by virtue of its more faltering, self-ironising voice.

The second way in which Hemsterhuis breaks with Bonnet over the communication of organology turns on the practice of analogical predication. Just like Hemsterhuis, Bonnet's ontology is analogic, that is, structured around *rapports*. Everything is analogically connected as part of a chain of being leading from the simplest elements in organic nature to the most complex, and this 'great analogy' provides the warrant for Bonnet's own chains of analogic reasoning. Moreover, as rehearsed in §17, Bonnet himself frets over the limitations of such chain construction, anxious about its lack of syllogistic rigour and weakening the language of his conclusions accordingly. Hemsterhuis, too, constructs an analogic ontology that informs his philosophical writing. His early letters (particularly the *Lettre sur l'Homme*) are very close to Bonnet in their long chains of inferences. However, from 1775 onwards, he attacks such a method: analogies should not merely ascend up a speculative ladder unidirectionally. Hemsterhuis explicitly criticises these chains of conjecture in the 1775 letters to Gallitzin on philosophical style (§6): Bonnet's works are the latest example of a long tradition of narratival philosophy in which conjecture has been piled on top of conjecture.[30] Philosophies become 'novels' that transport the reader further and further from the fundamental truths on which they are grounded. Likewise, Hemsterhuis attacks arguments that lose demonstrative certainty by moving too far from their initial axioms – his rehearsal of this critique in *Sophyle* (§7) indicates a desire to free his own philosophical writing from Bonnetian form. Thus, when Sophylus complains that the author's 'arguments repel me... I don't feel the truth... I tacitly fear that he has deceived me, and has strung me along with some sophisms that I failed to notice' (*EE* 2.56; *OP* 368), these criticisms have purchase on both the pre-1775 Hemsterhuis *and Bonnet.*

Hemsterhuis' most explicit criticisms of the kind of discursive chains paradigmatic of Bonnet's style are to be found, however, in a 1783 letter to Fürstenberg in which he worries about the 'the risk of losing precious links in a chain', for such links 'often exist only for an instant and can then no longer be found'. He goes on, moreover, to point out that the sturdiness of these chains is dependent in part on considerations of genre. That is, in 'a geometry, a physics, a jurisprudence, the whole chain which constitutes the science is composed of homogenous material' and each link is bolstered by 'weighty and grave reason' – and so the chain holds up for most readers. However, Hemsterhuis continues, when the text takes the form of an encyclopaedia or another genre that crosses multiple, 'excessively composite' domains of inquiry (as both Bonnet's and Hemsterhuis' own early works aspire to do – see §20), then the links are no longer bolstered by reason but are instead dependent on 'the rapid dexterity of tact'. The chain therefore becomes 'volatile' and 'the organ of the imagination too crude to conserve for a few moments the delicate and transitory impressions of tact' (B 12.128, 178–9). Such is very precisely the difficulty with Bonnet's style: it attempts to operate tactfully, identifying *rapports* across the faces of the universe, but this process does not stick. Bonnet, like Spinoza, ultimately lacks the requisite tact. The analogies cannot be glued together through long, unanchored chains of discourse.

Bonnet himself is very aware of this precise difficulty and writes of his reader needing 'a rare degree of attention to follow... my chain of facts and consequences and to comprehend the totality of its principles and their immediate and mediate results'. He continues, 'Despite the extreme clarity with which I

---

[30] As I pointed out in §6, it is Gallitzin who articulates this anxiety most clearly: Bonnet writes in a 'genre' in which 'there are almost solely hypotheses; and this is a problem concerning so many unknowns' (Gallitzin 2015–17: 4.14).

have tried to permeate my book, despite these natural chains of truths, I have not always been understood well' (2002: 58). Hemsterhuis takes up Bonnet's self-critique, but he radicalises it by seeking out an alternative – a way to avoid the sequential presentation of analogies in favour of an absolute simultaneity of ideas. Hemsterhuis' poetic turn is, in part, a reaction to the failings of Bonnet's chains of analogies. For example, the appeal to sentimental certainty and its demand for mythic writing in *Aristée* is precisely meant to overcome the deficiencies of the chain-method. The philosophical text must be something more than a mere one-dimensional march from secure axiom to conjectural conclusion. It is for this reason that Hemsterhuis' late analogic texts are structured more like a web (an image of which Hemsterhuis, like Diderot, was fond [*EE* 2.46; *OP* 336; see Cahen-Maurel 2022: 35–6]) than a chain: the reader should move like a spider dancing across it in all directions, as opposed to a climber precariously scaling even greater heights.

Finally, Hemsterhuis' late philosophy can also be read as a response to the assertoric mode in which Bonnet speculates about past and future eras radically different from our own. Again, Bonnet appears to do the bare minimum when adjusting his style to the demands of organology: he still *asserts* and thereby obscures the 'problematic' (in the Kantian sense) nature of his conjectures beyond the limits of currently possible experience.[31] To put it another way, Bonnet's texts still fall foul of Diderot's 'fallacy of the ephemeral', the vice which all organological thinking ought to avoid. His categories remain those of the immutable even when he speaks of the transient, and so they fail to sufficiently acknowledge the plasticity of the philosophical enterprise. The task facing Hemsterhuis, therefore, is to devise a way of writing philosophy that fully acknowledges its own history, that is thoroughly permeated by its own transience and the problematic status of its conjectures. The task is to write *more Diderot-like*, to take the communication of organology seriously by experimenting with genres and by fabulating in different voices and tones. The late Hemsterhuis' imperative is to achieve for anti-materialist organology what Diderot had elsewhere achieved for materialist organology – to write in a way that is adequate to the temporal becoming of philosophising. And it is this encounter between writing and time that forms the subject matter of the final part of this book.

---

[31] Moenkemeyer puts it nicely: unlike Bonnet, Hemsterhuis 'insinuated rather than affirmed an increase of knowledge along new lines after death' (1975: 85).

Part Four
Time-Images

Hemsterhuis scholars have often been wary to make too much of Rousseau's influence. Hemsterhuis mentions Rousseau's name but once in his mature published and unpublished writings and even then amidst a long list of names (B 1.124, 158); the publication of Rousseau's confessional writings in 1782 makes no impact on Hemsterhuis' correspondence of the time and his library contained only one Rousseau volume published after 1765 (van Sluis 2001: 49, 114, 120, 139). Nevertheless, the young Hemsterhuis adored *Émile* (B 12.23, 34) and this has given rise to an alternative tradition of scholarship that has been less guarded in perceiving Rousseau's influence in Hemsterhuis works (e.g., Gobbers 1963: 200–1), and, indeed, my argument in previous sections (§1, §13) has been that *Alexis*, in particular, is engaged in a rigorous conversation with the early Rousseau. It is from this point that the final part of the book begins and, more specifically, it begins from the following claim: Hemsterhuis also emulates Rousseau in his attempt to write philosophy *as an outsider*, to take up a perspective external to the here-and-now.[1]

This strategy of writing as an outsider is threefold. First, it is present in *Simon*'s anecdote of the Scythian who comes to Athens from an 'uncivilised' outside to judge Greek culture: it is, Socrates relates, 'necessary to be a Scythian to judge the nature [of the arts]', for only an outsider can see them 'as a whole' and discern 'the constitution of their nature' (*EE* 2.109; *OP* 532). This reversal of the enlightened–barbarian binary (in which a sup-

---

[1] Both Hemsterhuis and Rousseau implicitly take up the *Urtext* for such outsider-philosophy – the opening to the *Apology*. Here Socrates presents himself as 'a stranger to the manner of speaking' of the powerful, that is, an outsider who speaks a language that flouts convention (and rejects 'embroidered and stylised phrases') but is also resolutely popular (using 'the same kind of language as I am accustomed to use in the marketplace') (Plato 1962: 17a–18a).

posed 'barbarian' takes up a master-position within 'civilisation') is common in the Francophone eighteenth century (e.g., Voltaire, Montesquieu) and structures Rousseau's first *Discours sur les sciences et les arts*, which speaks, just like Hemsterhuis, of 'inhabitants of some distant lands' arriving in Europe to judge the arts and, in this context, even praises the Scythians (2018: 3, 9, 11; see also Moenkemeyer 1975: 137–9). In a similar fashion to his embrace of 'barbarous language' in response to Diderot's enlightened materialism, Hemsterhuis follows Rousseau in interrogating the value of enlightenment from a viewpoint that 'clash[es] head on with all that is today admired by men' (Rousseau 2018: 4).

In addition to the creation of a geographical outside, the story of the Scythian – as with so much of the dialogues – attests to Hemsterhuis' obsession with the production of chronological outsides. According to the terms of Chapter One, Hemsterhuis constructs a Greek world in his writings as a means to become untimely, to alienate himself from the present. The late Hemsterhuis philosophises in the past often because of its difference from the present. *Alexis*, in particular, invokes a 'comparison ... between the men of the golden age and the present corruption of these same men and the awful disorder of their society' (*EE* 2.125; *OP* 580). And again, this resonates with Rousseau's project in the second *Discours* to disrupt, relativise and thereby escape the hegemony of the present by excavating images of an alternative past. That is, Rousseau's description of 'primitive man ... in the first embryo of the species' (2018: 137) is intended to emphasise 'the immense distance' that separates the origin from the present (2018: 191) – and Hemsterhuis follows Rousseau in weaponising the archaic against the here-and-now.

Finally, Hemsterhuis is at his most Rousseauean in drawing attention to a principle of becoming, which structures human history (perfectibility), which exceeds any actualisation in the present, and which is always more than any single presentation of it can encompass. This is the second type of temporal image to be found in the *Discours sur l'origine de l'inegalité*: as well as images of a radically different past, it contains images of a virtuality that resists reduction to any single moment. Rousseau writes,

> It is in this *slow succession* of things that [the reader] will see the solution to an infinite number of problems of ethics and of politics which philosophers are unable to solve. He will sense that, since the mankind of one age is not the mankind of another age, the reason why Diogenes did not find a man is that he was looking among his contemporaries for the man of a time that was no more. (2018: 191; my emphasis)

The perfectible human is always different, always pushing *beyond* what is given, and Hemsterhuis and Rousseau are united in a shared attempt to communicate '*the progress* of this principle' (B 3.86, 200; my emphasis) – that is, to make perceptible a principle of becoming. Hemsterhuis practises a post-Rousseauean art of imaging time, both imagining a primitive origin of temporality and imagining the very movement of time passing itself.

It is this third outsider-writing strategy with which the final part of my book culminates. For twenty-first-century readers, this attempt to communicate a tendency that exceeds any single moment is now most familiar through a Bergsonian tradition and its working out in Gilles Deleuze's philosophy. The early Deleuze, indeed, returns to Rousseau as a philosopher of virtual genesis, whose principle of perfectibility 'must be understood as a genetic element, heavy with potential, with virtualities' (2014: 10) and whose *Discours sur l'origine de l'inegalité* is a work dedicated to the description of 'a law of development of virtualities' (2014: 9). This is what Deleuze will describe a couple of years later as 'Proust's problem': 'that we do not recompose the past with various presents, but that we place ourselves directly in the past itself', in 'the being of the past in itself' (2008: 38). And it is a problem with which, I want to suggest, Hemsterhuis was also engaged; in particular, I want to take as a rough heuristic for the following pages the taxonomy of time-images Deleuze supplies in *Cinema II* – images devised 'to make perceptible, to make visible, relationships of time which ... do not allow themselves to be reduced to the present' (2013: xi). There is something Hemsterhuisian in Deleuze's interest in showing up 'the falsest obviousness' of the idea that the 'image is in the present, necessarily in the present' (2013: 37–8). The taxonomy of *Cinema II* includes, for instance, a *recollection-image* that excavates 'a whole temporal "panorama" [of] images of a past in general' (2013: 57); an *archaic-image* that 'affirm[s] a pure power of time which overflows all memory' (2013: 50); a *world-image* that digs up 'a universe of prehistory' and so 'gives a world to the image, surrounds it with an atmosphere of world' (2013: 64, 121); and a *crystal-image* that fuses the present and the past into a saturated moment, as in the experience of *déjà vu* (2013: 82).

What these images have in common is that they 'open directly onto time', mobilise 'virtual regions of the past' and so compel the viewer to 'jump' out of the present (2013: 43, 104). And what I want to argue in the final chapters of this book is that broadly similar things can be said of the writing techniques in Hemsterhuis' dialogues. They are likewise composed of sequences of time-images which rip the temporal from its chronological sequence and reconfigure it in archaic philosophical worlds. These images make perceptible to Hemsterhuis' eighteenth-century readers epochs that are not their own. And so, the main thrust of what follows is to detail the specific kinds of time-images employed by Hemsterhuis, such as flashbacks, prophecies, recollections, dreams, genealogies, myths of alternative pasts, fictions of prehistoric golden ages, and reimagined Athenian worlds. In all such instances, Hemsterhuis is cultivating the ideal of untimeliness provisionally described in Chapter One, performing his system of times in his writings and estranging his reader from the present; and he is also pursuing the organological project of Part Three by describing radically different pasts and futures to challenge the philosopher's sense of permanence. Hemsterhuis' time-images form part of his restructuring of the philosophical text around ideals of historicity and mutability; they help make philosophical writing plastic.

What orients this final part of the book is therefore the idea that Hemsterhuis' texts *present without making present*, that they make perceptible worlds irreducible to the present that are, nevertheless, still presented within the text.

Chapter Five

The Past and the Present

I would give so very much for a conversation with Hemsterhuis: he is your Plato but his century does not understand him.

Jean de Müller to Goethe
(quoted in Brachin 1952: 52)

For Hemsterhuis, philosophy is dead.

Poritzky (1926: 103)

§19 The Optimum

The present chapter describes some of the ways in which Hemsterhuis attempts to make time perceptible in his writing, and it proceeds by setting up a contrast between the function of the present in the early and the late Hemsterhuis' practices of philosophical communication. Before 1775, Hemsterhuis' writing is structured according to a model of *optimal form* – a model which privileges intuitive over discursive reasoning, which is hostile to temporal and historical succession, and which calls, instead, for simultaneity in thinking, i.e., the coexistence of as many ideas as possible. It is a model of the all-at-once. After 1775, Hemsterhuis begins to write in a way that is open to history and succession *as well as optimal form*. The dialogues stage a conflict between the present and the past – not just a quarrel between the ancient perihelion and the modern perihelion, but between historicity and presentism, between the virtual and the actual.

In the last of his published dialogues, *Alexis*, Hemsterhuis returns to a principle that had served as 'a leitmotif across his work . . . a genuine guiding thread' (Boulan 1924: 66) – the ideal of the *optimum*. He writes,

> The ideas of many existent or possible things can be reconciled such that they are almost coexistent in the mind for some moments, [and] it is

certain that the intellect will perceive most of the relations between these ideas, which let themselves be grasped with the utmost facility – that is, relations which constitute for us the richest, truest and simplest beauty. . . . Hence, my dear Alexis, it is the faculty of bringing together the most and the best ideas which gives birth to the beautiful and the sublime, and which, so to speak, shows great truths by intuition to those souls which thereby appear to us to have the most intimate relationships with the Divinity. (*EE* 2.141; *OP* 628)

Hemsterhuis describes an epistemic ideal that consists in making coexist as many ideas as possible so as to intuit their *rapports*. In the much earlier *Lettre sur la sculpture*, Hemsterhuis names this model 'the optimum' and defines it as bringing to mind 'a great number of ideas in the smallest space of time possible' (*EE* 1.65; *OP* 108). The ideal of the optimum recalls many topics from earlier in this book: it motivates Hemsterhuis' critique of syllogistic reasoning (where ideas come one after another) and turn to sentimental certainty (as instantaneous and intuitive); it motivates his invocation of a Platonic sublime (as transporting the subject beyond mediation); it motivates his insectification imperative (which demands ever more coexistent perceptions); and it motivates his theory of tact (as sensitive attention by which the mind 'perceives most of the relations between . . . ideas' [*EE* 2.141; *OP* 628]). There are ultimately few Hemsterhuisian ideas not determined by the ideal of the optimum.

With all these invocations of the optimum, Hemsterhuis draws on an early-modern – often Cartesian – tradition that aspires to a certainty born of holding both the premise and the conclusion to an argument equally in mind *at the same time*. Descartes' eleventh rule in the *Regulae* sets the precedent here: one of the conditions of an intuition is that 'it must be one simultaneous whole without succession', since, on the basis of such a 'simultaneous conception', 'our knowledge becomes much more certain, and our mental capacity is enormously increased' (1985–91: 1.37). In line with this tradition, Hemsterhuis identifies the advantages of intuitive simultaneity in the twin virtues of *celeritas* and *facilitas*: the more quickly and fluently the intellect passes from idea to idea, the more certain the truth it comprehends (see d'Acunto 2005: 10). Indeed, in the passage above, Hemsterhuis indicates more generally that these virtues are conditions of 'the richest, truest and simplest beauty', of perceiving 'great truths by intuition' and 'the most intimate relationships with the Divinity'. And in the correspondence he further identifies this optimum, 'the principle of the maximum of ideas and the minimum of time', as 'important for the psychological part of our philosophy' (*B* 4.61, 157).

§19 THE OPTIMUM

The aim of the present section is to elucidate just how ubiquitous the ideal of the optimum is in Hemsterhuis' early philosophy, that is, to show just how much the optimum matters for the Hemsterhuis *who writes letters*. On this basis, I go on to suggest in §20 that his early epistolary style is a deliberate attempt to perform such an ideal textually, that there is a unity of form and content in these early works, since Hemsterhuis both describes an epistemic demand for the maximum of ideas in the minimum of time and also meets this demand himself by writing letters.

1. The *Lettre sur la sculpture* is the first of the early writings to thematise the optimum. It takes as its task the demonstration that the optimum grounds artistic production and appreciation, that is, that it is the very criterion of beauty. As Hemsterhuis himself summarises, 'The soul judges as the most beautiful what it can form an idea of in the shortest space of time' (*EE* 1.63; *OP* 102).

As mentioned in §4, Hemsterhuis argues to this conclusion by way of an aesthetic experiment, set out as follows:

> I drew two vases ... [and] showed them to several people, and, among others, to someone of very good sense, but who did not even have a mediocre knowledge of the arts. When I asked them which vase was the most beautiful, everyone replied to me that it was vase A, and when I asked why to the [person of good sense], he replied, after some reflection, that he was more strongly affected by vase A than by vase B. (*EE* 1.63; *OP* 98)

He then goes on to analyse this idea of being 'more strongly affected' in terms of 'intensity' (or the 'number of visible points' registered by the eye [*EE* 1.63; *OP* 100], i.e., 'the amount of visual information' [Sonderen 1996: 323–4]) and 'duration', concluding,

> In vases A and B, the intensity is supposed to be the same – that is, the visible quantity is equal in both cases; consequently, vase A acted with more velocity on the soul of this person than vase B – that is, he was able to link the visible points together in A in a smaller space of time than in B; or what comes back to the same: he obtained an idea of A as a whole more rapidly than of B as a whole. (*EE* 1.63; *OP* 98–100)

Vase A and vase B contain the same amount of visual information, but vase A conveys it 'in a smaller space of time', and so affects the viewer more strongly, provokes greater pleasure and is thus to be judged more beautiful.

Beauty is, in Sonderen's paraphrase, a matter of 'visual speed' (Sonderen 2005: 210): 'The senses must experience [the vase] effortlessly and in a single moment: it is when they do so that we call it beautiful' (Sonderen 1996: 330).[1] In other words, the more beautiful vase is the one that most closely approximates to the optimum by generating ideas in the least amount of time; so Hemsterhuis concludes, 'The beautiful in all arts must give us the greatest possible number of ideas in the shortest possible space of time' (EE 1.65; OP 108).

Hemsterhuis goes on to employ this aesthetic optimum as the criterion by which to further evaluate artworks, genres, styles and epochs in art history. For example, it justifies what Hemsterhuis sees as the worth of preliminary artistic sketches that 'possess much more of that divine vivacity of the first conceived idea than finished works that have cost so much time' (EE 1.64; OP 106). That is, sketches are products of inspiration – the production of an idea in the shortest possible time. The aesthetic optimum also explains why two very different ways of treating a subject might be equally beautiful: one artwork might display 'finesse and fluency of outline', thereby minimising the time required to intuit it; another might, on the contrary, increase the number of ideas being intuited, as Michelangelo did in Hemsterhuis' opinion. Michelangelo 'wished to obtain the *optimum* by augmenting the *maximum* of the quantity of ideas . . . rather than by diminishing the *minimum* of time employed' (EE 1.65; OP 108). Moreover, the aesthetic optimum can further be used to distinguish the virtues of painting from those of sculpture: the relative ease by which paint can be manipulated suggests it more easily achieves the optimum by way of proliferating ideas, whereas conversely the less malleable nature of sculpture suggests the need to foreground the minimum of time taken to experience ideas (EE 1.72; OP 130).

Hemsterhuis' notion of aesthetic experience thus comprises a pleasure gained from linking together a series of images into a complete whole as quickly and as easily as possible. In his own words, beautiful artworks 'are great wholes whose parts are so artistically composed that the soul can link them together instantly and without effort' (EE 1.64; OP 104). And this lack of effort is ultimately the most significant feature of Hemsterhuis' definition of the beautiful (as opposed to the property of *unitas in varietas* on which critics more often tarry).[2] This facility of forming wholes is a kind of visual

---

[1] On the other hand, ugliness is a matter of perceptive slowness, often caused by 'recalcitrant speed bumps' in the perceived object (Cirulli 2015: 62).

[2] Sonderen (1996: 317) provides the decisive corrective on this point.

skill which corresponds, within the aesthetic domain, to tact, i.e., the art of making connections as quickly and fluently as possible.

The aesthetic optimum is implicated in a tendency to eliminate time that dominates Hemsterhuis' early psychology. He concludes from his definition of beauty that 'it seems incontestable that there is something in our soul which loathes all relation to what we call succession' (*EE* 1.67; *OP* 114). The soul, he implies, is naturally averse to time and searches out experiences in which time is most extinguished. Cirulli describes this aspect of Hemsterhuis' aesthetics well: 'It is the almost instantaneous apprehension that gives the spectator the ecstatic (though deceptive) feeling that she has perceived the object in *no* time' (2015: 60). The beautiful object provides an 'illusion of arrested time, and this illusion rests on the ease with which the visual media may be instantaneously comprehended' (2015: 67); so, judgements of beauty are pleasurable because, through them, the soul fleetingly approximates to timeless eternity – they 'short-circuit (if briefly) the feeling of existential time' (2015: 66; see further Tavani 2005: 156–82; Gaiger 2018: 246–8). This is ultimately an organological issue: one of the conditions of artistic beauty is the perfection of vision along the lines of the insectification imperative set out in the *Lettre sur l'optique* (§10), that is, to supply the mind with a greater quantity of retinal images at a greater rate. Better aesthetic judgements require sense organs which pass more information to the mind more quickly, until any temporal lag between initial contact with the other and comprehension of it seems to disappear – that is, until the very mediation which organs instantiate between mind and world is overcome. For the early Hemsterhuis, the end of organology lies in organs that negate themselves – and this comprises the theme of the *Lettre sur les désirs*.

2. The *Lettre sur les désirs* is framed as a 'continuation and clarification' (*EE* 1.79; *OP* 92) of the project of the *Lettre sur la sculpture*,[3] building on its conclusions as follows:

> I have proven to you . . . that the soul always seeks the greatest possible number of ideas in the smallest possible space of time, and that what prevents it from being satisfied in this respect lies in the necessity by which it is compelled to use organs and media, and to act by way of a succession of time and parts. (*EE* 1.79; *OP* 152)

---

[3] Hence, Friedrich Schlegel's comment that 'Hemsterhuis' aesthetics is moral-philosophical and his morals are thoroughly aesthetic' (1958–2002: 18.116).

In the *Lettre sur les désirs*, this model will become a universal structure for how the soul operates. The basic impulse of all life approximates to the ideal of the optimum; indeed, Hemsterhuis will even conjecture that the production of maximum variety in a minimum of time is an innate goal of the universe itself. Moreover, this model is once more a matter of the elimination of time, of approximating to an eternity in which succession no longer holds. And so, the sense organs are again accorded a problematic status: the soul both requires them, but also desires their supersession. However, where the *Lettre sur les désirs* goes beyond the *Lettre sur la sculpture* is in understanding the soul's desire for the elimination of mediation in terms of a *will to unite* with the desired other. Ultimately, the only way to do away with any mediation separating subject and object is for the two to fuse together, or, as Hemsterhuis himself writes, the soul desires to 'be intimately united to this object, or rather it will make a single whole with this object without any duality' (*EE* 1.87; *OP* 176). Hemsterhuis is self-consciously Aristophanic on this point: desire is always a desire to become one with the beloved, so that all distinction between object and subject disappears. As Herder paraphrases, 'Hemsterhuis demonstrated that love *unites* beings and that all *longing*, all *desire*, *strives* only for this *union*, as the only possible *pleasure of separated beings*. Every deep longing for sensual and spiritual pleasure, every desire for friendship and love thirsts for union with the object of desire' (1993: 112).

Hemsterhuis argues for this position by establishing, in Bulle's phrase, 'the natural laws of the soul' (1911: 33), conceived in analogy to the Newtonian forces of attraction and inertia. It results in a kind of physics of the ideal or, perhaps better, a scientific analysis of the irreducibly social forces by which humans interact. And this becomes clearest in the central example given in the text:

> When we enter into a group of several people, all unknown to us, there is ordinarily one to whom we address ourselves, at whose side we stay, and with whom we carry on a conversation in preference to all the others. The reason for choosing this person is in the principle of the greatest number of ideas in the smallest space of time; and that of affinity, in the principle of the attractive force. (*EE* 1.83; *OP* 162–4)

The subject unites with this new friend who 'thinks the same' and so, Hemsterhuis concludes, 'homogeneity is [here] manifest' (*EE* 1.83; *OP* 164). Just as in the vase experiment, so too in friendship: the intellect encounters few alien features that resist the quick and easy assimilation of ideas; its attraction to the object of its desire meets few obstacles. Moreover, this ideal force of attraction will go on to serve as the basis for moral judgements in *Aristée*: Hemsterhuis speaks of the 'tendency towards a union of essence with beings' as 'a faculty' from whose nature derive 'the laws which . . . constitute morality' (*EE* 2.81, 2.96; *OP* 444, 490).[4] Indeed, in *Aristée* (under Gallitzin's influence), Hemsterhuis accounts for the attractive force felt in desire in terms of a feeling of empathy: desire is motivated by the 'principle by which an individual identifies himself with another essence in some way, by which he senses what she senses, and [by which] he can contemplate himself from the centre of another individual' (*EE* 2.82; *OP* 446–8). To fuse with the desired object is to take up its perspective and thus to gain a fully empathetic, and so moral understanding of it and oneself; hence, the more one is attracted to the other, the more one understands its point of view empathetically and the better a moral subject one becomes. Such an empathetic stepping outside of oneself and into another's perspective allows the subject to 'see himself from outside and judge himself as others would judge him' (*EE* 2.82; *OP* 448). And such empathy is once more a matter of 'exquisite tact', 'extreme sensitivity' or the intuition of the *rapports* by which another individual is conditioned (*EE* 1.80, 1.85; *OP* 156, 166). In the social sphere, tact is defined as sensitive attention to the *rapports* between subjects and is attained only by those who organologically enhance 'the number, liveliness and tenacity of the sensations that it has of interrelations between the essences of certain things' (*EE* 2.81; *OP* 444–6).

For the early Hemsterhuis, the sense organs both make possible this social tact (it is ascribed only to those who sense 'in proportion to the quantity and finesse of [their] sensibility' [*EE* 2.82; *OP* 444–6; translation modified]), but nevertheless they also keep getting in the way of it. Perfect friendship, perfect love and perfect knowledge of the other – all grounded in union with the other through empathy – depend on eradicating the mediation of organs, for union is only possible without mediation and, by definition, organs are what mediate between subject and object. Hemsterhuis writes, 'in the current state in which the soul is found, it is almost impossible to reach this union *except by means of organs*' (*EE* 1.80; *OP* 154; my emphasis). And this ultimately means that the *Lettre sur les désirs* ends tragically: organs mediate and so precisely cannot attain the desired immediate connection; the ideal of the social optimum is too much for organ-laden humans, who

---

[4] Hemsterhuis will pick this up in correspondence: 'The same source whence derives religion, friendship, love and all desires [is] this universal attraction of souls from which morality is born' (*B* 3.113, 246).

can only approximate to it as 'the hyperbola to its asymptote' (*EE* 1.87; *OP* 178).

3. The *Lettre sur la sculpture* treats optimal aesthetic experience; the *Lettre sur les désirs* treats a social optimum identified with empathetic understanding; and the *Lettre sur l'Homme* treats, for the most part, a scientific optimum, that is, the ways in which the ideal of the optimum structure human knowledge.

§12 already noted how pursuit of the greatest number of ideas in the shortest possible time was exemplified by Hemsterhuis' version of François Fagel (to whom the *Lettre sur l'Homme* is dedicated). Fagel is appropriated by Hemsterhuis as an exemplar of the optimum, since his 'elevation of mind [could] never see[s] one thing alone, but embrace[d] several at the same time, along with the relations which link them', as opposed to amateurs, who 'lack . . . this velocity in linking together parts'. Fagel 'made a judgment in an instant which he would never take back', and so was able to form 'that sublime whole which constitutes true science' (*EE* 1.137–9; *OP* 320–6). He achieved for science what the ideal aesthetic critic does for art: the fluent and rapid composition of ideas into a whole. To put it another way, Hemsterhuis' Fagel epitomises what the *Lettre sur l'Homme* designates as 'genius' – someone who 'senses . . . relations in the same instant'. The genius works by 'intuitive . . . logic', that is, she intuits 'without regard to any intermediate relation', without the need to pass successively from truth to truth (*EE* 1.91–2; *OP* 190–2). Hemsterhuis is even more explicit on the connection between the optimum and scientific practice in the concluding pages to the *Lettre sur l'Homme*: 'The science or knowledge of man' comprises, in part, ideas of relation 'derived from the coexistence' of simple ideas such that 'the intuitive faculty can embrace [them all] at once'. Hence, 'science would be perfect' and the knowing subject would 'resemble God', if all simple ideas could be held together at once and the subject could simultaneously comprehend 'ideas of all the relations and all the combinations of these objects' (*EE* 1.122; *OP* 288–90). This is Hemsterhuis' most comprehensive vision of the optimum. Just as, in the *Lettre sur la sculpture*, aesthetic experience was possible on the condition of the suppression of the time taken to intuit and just as, in the *Lettre sur les désirs*, the soul naturally desired eternity, so too scientific knowledge in the *Lettre sur l'Homme* contributes to a timeless edifice of ideas – a structure of knowing indifferent to the passing of time. The ideal philosopher knows everything *in a moment*.

All three variants of the ideal of the optimum in the early Hemsterhuis therefore rest on the possibility of the coexistence of ideas. He is clear,

'What constitutes the degree of perfection in intelligences is the greater or lesser quantity of coexisting ideas that these intelligences can supply and submit to their intuitive faculty. An absolutely perfect intelligence could make ... many ideas coexist' (*EE* 1.91; *OP* 190). And he labels this perfection 'absolute coexistence' (*EE* 1.91; *OP* 190).[5] As Novalis paraphrases, 'An intelligence is the more perfect, the more coexisting ideas it can survey' (1960–2006: 2.364). To put it another way: the optimal philosopher is the one who thinks without time, who renders her mental space an eternal present. On reading the *Lettre sur l'Homme*, Diderot, for one, professed himself suspicious of such claims; for Diderot, simultaneous attention to multiple ideas is impossible. He repeatedly reacts to Hemsterhuis' epistemology with incredulity: 'I declare to you that there is not a man on the surface of the earth capable of having coexistent [ideas of] *rapports*' (Diderot and Hemsterhuis 1964: 77, 457). And yet, Diderot neglects the extent to which so much of the *Lettre sur l'Homme* is precisely intended as a reply to this very question of the possibility of coexistence and as an enumeration of the conditions needed to instantiate it.[6]

These conditions are, for the most part, *semiotic*. Hemsterhuis' theory of the sign, which dominates the early pages of the *Lettre sur l'Homme*, is intended to explain the possibility of the coexistence of ideas. And it is here, moreover, that the model of the optimum becomes most explicitly pertinent to the theme of philosophical communication: for the early Hemsterhuis, the philosopher must make use of those signs that facilitate the most possible simultaneous ideas, those signs that express the maximum of ideas in a minimum of time.

Hemsterhuis' semiotics arises out of a distinction between 'primitive ideas' which 'completely evaporate with the absence of the object' and recollective signs that can be recalled without its presence (*EE* 1.90; *OP* 186). This maps onto a further distinction between those ideas over which the subject has no control but which are determined by external circumstance and those ideas over which she has mastery. As Hemsterhuis puts it, 'A being which has the faculty of receiving ideas, thinking, reasoning or planning must have signs which are not the objects, but which correspond to the objects and of which he is perfectly the master' (*EE* 1.90; *OP* 188). Thus, it is this second kind

---

[5] Conversely, imperfection is 'when I cannot make every part of a demonstration coexist in my intellect' and so 'it ceases to be one for me' (B 9.72, 154). This is what Sophylus experiences in the passage that opens §7.
[6] On the Dutch Newtonian context to Hemsterhuis' defence of the coexistence of ideas, see Ducheyne (2014b: 105).

of sign that defines the human: the human is a master of signs. Moreover, it is in this second kind of sign that Hemsterhuis also locates the capacity to bring ideas into coexistence; that is, he identifies the faculty of mastery over signs with 'the intuitive faculty' or 'reason' (*EE* 1.90; *OP* 188–90) and claims that 'the being which joins this intuitive faculty to the ability to recall ideas by means of signs can make this faculty act upon as many objects at the same time as can be made, in some way, to coexist in appearance by means of ideas' (*EE* 1.91; *OP* 188–90). In short, while 'primitive signs' overwhelm the mind and tyrannise reason, recollective signs possess 'a lot less clarity', can be tamed without causing 'confusion' or 'disorder' and so can exist alongside each other without demanding full attention (*EE* 1.92; *OP* 192–4). The capacity of comparison depends on this – and so too the possibility of good philosophy. Good philosophy comprises ordered, recollective signs offered up to reason simultaneously. Hemsterhuis' semiotics, therefore, makes possible an image of thinking faithful to Descartes' notion of intuition as a practice of seeing the whole simultaneously (see Tavani 2005: 196). Indeed, in *Lettre sur l'Homme*, Hemsterhuis provides, as it were, the semiotic working out of *Regulae* XI. Just as it is for Descartes, to be a philosopher is to practise the twin virtues of *celeritas* and *facilitas*.

And what I want to suggest in the next section is that the early Hemsterhuis' choice of the epistolary genre for communicating his philosophy is motivated by precisely this Cartesian ideal of intuitive simultaneity. Letters approximate (as much as any genre can) to the scientific optimum, to conveying a maximum of theoretical ideas in a minimum of time.

§20 Epistolary Style

In the wake of his visit to Weimar in autumn 1785, Hemsterhuis embarked on a reading programme of contemporary German authors: Goethe, Herder, Jacobi, Kant and so on. And this, in turn, led to a series of reflections in 1789 on Goethe's *Die Leiden des jungen Werthers*:

> Reading Werther's letters has led me to reflect on this abrupt and interrupted epistolary style so much in vogue today. It is true that when well done, it can sometimes supply a happy and bold sketch, but never a perfect description. The thinking of man does not work thus and cannot work thus; it is more regular ... I have never been able to understand how the German, the French and the Swiss have all ended up borrowing this, in my opinion, absurd epistolary style from the English and transported it into their languages, which are much less suited to it than the

§20 EPISTOLARY STYLE 213

English language. Sometimes you have used this style in your letters, but never – that I know of – when it was not good for something and when your phrase-fragments could not be linked together with the most perfect ease by the mind of your reader. Note that if these fragments themselves do not naturally fill the gaps that separate them, [the author] becomes obscure and so often gives way, despite himself, to the most absurd equivocations which then rely uniquely on the reader's mind. I believe that whoever first said that a letter is an imitation of a dialogue uttered a great falsehood. (B 10.93, 155)

The closing sentence is telling: letters are not dialogues; the two are incommensurable genres with very different advantages and disadvantages. And it is hard not to read this assertion in the context of Hemsterhuis' own post-1775 poetic turn (see Morpurgo-Tagliabue 1987: 39).[7] Moreover, it is likewise hard not to read the preceding criticisms of epistolary style as furnishing some of the reasons for this earlier turn away from letters as the most appropriate medium for philosophising. According to Hemsterhuis, conveying human thinking in letters is 'absurd', because the letter does not present the process of thinking faithfully: 'the abrupt and interrupted epistolary style' obscures more than it reveals the workings of the mind. And therefore, the reader of a letter must work harder to fight against obscurity and equivocation. By the time of these reflections in 1789, Hemsterhuis has seemingly overcome his earlier inclination for epistolary style.

1. And yet, these late reflections on *Werther* still offer some clues as to why the early Hemsterhuis might have valued letters highly as a vehicle for philosophising.[8] One benefit to writing in letters, he implies, is that they 'can sometimes supply a happy and bold sketch'. This allusion to the sketch immediately recalls the *Lettre sur la sculpture*, which lauds artistic sketches as more beautiful than the finished artwork, partly because they are

---

[7] In other words, Hemsterhuis might single out the French, the Swiss and the Germans, as well as the English as proponents of epistolary style – but, in so doing, he effaces a strong tradition of epistolary writing in the eighteenth-century Dutch Republic, of which his own early letters are some of the most famous monuments. See Krop (2005: 209).

[8] There were certainly biographical reasons why it so happened that Hemsterhuis' first publications took the form of letters – they were occasional pieces solicited in correspondence, addressed to a particular recipient under a specific set of circumstances; but my interest here is in *additional*, intrinsically philosophical reasons for the adoption and subsequent repudiation of the epistolary style.

products of an instant, rather than of protracted labour, and partly because they make the viewer work more efficiently in rapidly constituting the represented whole. 'Initial sketches', Hemsterhuis writes, 'most please the man of genius and the true connoisseur' owing to their 'divine vivacity' and to the onus they put on the viewer to 'instantly finish and complete what was merely sketched out' (*EE* 1.64; *OP* 106). The effortlessness of the sketch provokes an instantaneous appreciation by the viewer – the type of experience that epitomises the *aesthetic optimum*. Sketches communicate the most ideas in the shortest possible time – they offer the viewer an opportunity for rapid consumption. Indeed, it is precisely this rapidity valued by the early Hemsterhuis as conducive to beauty which is subsequently condemned by the Hemsterhuis of 1789 as 'abrupt' and 'interrupted'.

The 1789 passage thus suggests one major reason for the early Hemsterhuis' use of the epistolary style to communicate philosophy: letters epitomise *optimal form*. Indeed, the sketch-like quality of the early works themselves is something to which Sonderen has recently drawn attention: he considers Hemsterhuis' early letters to be 'essentially intended as sketches', provoking the reader to engage with, enhance and complete them – that is, they are 'invitations to co-think ... what has merely been drafted'. Sonderen continues, 'Hemsterhuis' philosophical practice does not aim at producing and imposing a full-fledged, rounded theory on the world, but, instead, proposes to function more as an artistic sketch that requires the look of the other for completion. His philosophical workshop functions as a space where things and ideas are tried out' (2022: 4). Rather than providing fully articulated systems, Hemsterhuis publishes epistolary sketches of ideas. And the *Lettre sur l'Homme* provides the clearest example of the link between the letter, the sketch and the optimum implied here: not only does it describe the scientific optimum, it also performs it.

On the one hand, this is evident from the sheer number of ideas the *Lettre sur l'Homme* tries to communicate. Hemsterhuis later notes that '*L'Homme et ses rapports* contains basically all that I know and every great truth of which I am intimately persuaded in my consciousness' (B 1.166, 200) – hence, Brummel's worry that the text contains 'too many issues' to make it anything but 'an ill-fitting whole' (1925: 157–8) and Moenkemeyer's complaint that 'too many heterogenous themes are crowded into' it (1975: 87). The *Lettre sur l'Homme* functions as a kind of subjective encyclopaedia[9]

---

[9] Both the Hemsterhuisian letter and the encyclopaedia are wholes made out of an inventory of heterogeneous ideas; they both value speed in consuming diverse subjects (over monomania), and both practise a writerly art of 'linking between the most

that manages both to 'paint the author and his state' and to say everything that needs saying 'promptly and distinctly'.[10] On the other hand, the text also attempts to incorporate this mass of ideas into an easily consumable whole. As van Sluis observes (in OP 39), it is remarkable that Hemsterhuis decided to compose a 25,000-word treatise without any break in the text: he included no chapters, subheadings or even visual breaks; the *Lettre sur l'Homme* consists of an uninterrupted series of compressed ideas – what Pelckmans dubs 'an inventory punctuated by "succesivement", "ensuite", "à la fin"' (1987: 20). Hence, the form of this letter approximates to something like *unitas in varietas*; that is, it crams as many ideas as possible into one seamless whole. Hemsterhuis deliberately chooses to traverse as many ideas as quickly as possible – and, for this reason, the *Lettre sur l'Homme* is his most complete text in terms of content (covering ideas as disparate as prayer and musical harmony) and also tries to present this content *all-at-once*, without division or dispersion. Friedrich Schlegel dubs it Hemsterhuis' tendency to the 'small essay in the grand style' (1958–2002: 18.223).

The early Hemsterhuis writes with the aim of generating a unified, condensed – even compressed – whole that surveys the whole of science, and so performs the very optimum it is trying to describe. It presupposes that such a 'happy and bold sketch' of the sciences is the most appropriate form of philosophical communication, and is therefore reliant on readerly virtues of *celeritas* and *facilitas*. The *Lettre sur l'Homme* is intended as a quickly consumable work of philosophy – intellectual fast-food for the skilled amateur (like Hemsterhuis' Fagel).

2. The *Lettre sur l'Homme* itself describes this optimal reading practice under the rubric of genius (*EE* 1.91–2; *OP* 192). The genius-reader consumes as

---

disparate two thoughts', as Ibrahim writes of Diderot (2010: 118). Indeed, Diderot's definition of the encyclopaedic genre as that which 'gathers together the pieces of knowledge scattered over the surface of the earth' by 'finding the best links' between them, so as to make its readers 'happier and more virtuous' (d'Alembert and Diderot 2021: 5.634) is an equally good description of the *Lettre sur l'Homme*, especially when d'Alembert's supplement that it does so 'in the smallest space possible' is also factored in (2021: 1.xv). The one exception that makes Hemsterhuis' letter a *subjective* encyclopaedia is that it situates the reader within a conversation between author and addressee.

[10] That is, more fully, Hemsterhuis writes: first, 'I have been struck by all the beauty demanded by epistolary style. It paints the author and his state. And variety burns there, for each paragraph is separate, being modified by each interruption' (B 6.59, 166); and secondly, 'The goal of letters is to say promptly and distinctly what they have to say' (B 4.91, 235).

many ideas as possible as quickly as possible; she need not work too hard at philosophy, since she can effortlessly and rapidly hold together in almost 'absolute coexistence' (*EE* 1.90; *OP* 190) the ideas necessary for an intuitive grasp of the truth – 'perceiving in an instant the extreme terms of a relation' (d'Acunto 2005: 15). As the Fagel obituary made clear, the *Lettre sur l'Homme* was expressly written for an idealised genius-reader of precisely this type and is structured as such – something Hemsterhuis himself later acknowledged in the 'Additions and Clarifications'. There he admits (see §15) that one limitation of his letter is that only those who read optimally will understand it. And he returns to this worry in correspondence: while 'epistolary style and the dialogue are without comparison the best for richly expressing ideas', they possess 'one fault' – they speak a particular 'language analogous to the mind of the [addressed] friend or to the minds of the interlocuters', and this is a different language from 'what the public demand' (B 5.69, 236).[11] The *Lettre sur l'Homme* was not written for the common reader, who can only lament, with Brummel and Moenkemeyer, its compressed, heterogeneous themes.[12]

As the 'Additions and Clarifications' acknowledge, what epistolary style risks most is the vice of obscurity. And elsewhere Hemsterhuis addresses this link between obscurity and compression directly in a response he makes to Diderot's commentary (briefly mentioned in §15). When diagnosing the chaotic obscurity of Diderot's *Rêve* as symptomatic of a lack of properly ordered energy, Hemsterhuis notes,

> [Diderot was] born an admirable mime or pantomime, and it is this latter faculty which has prevented him from being placed among the greatest writers. I said this to him one day and will never forget it. He had read me something he had just finished. He asked me what I thought of his style. I told the truth by praising it in many parts, but I added that he could not be ignorant of the fact that his style was often judged a bit obscure. He said

---

[11] Elsewhere, Hemsterhuis stresses this limitation. For example, he writes to Gallitzin, following up the series of reflections on *Werther* that begin this section: 'I wanted to know whether you did not find this abrupt style – found in *Werther* and the English novels that are so extravagant and outside of nature as they appear to me to be – above all in letters. The epistolary style is, I believe, only the description of the natural movement of each intellect in its imagination. Each individual has their own, and it can only alter with due cause' (B 10.96, 159).

[12] Of course, this is not to claim that the actual recipients of Hemsterhuis' early letters (de Smeth, the real Fagel) were geniuses, but just that Hemsterhuis' idealised reader of the letters is one.

to me that he knew, but that he did not feel the truth of this. Then I said to him that his obscurity was not of that kind which derives from wanting to utter ideas in the fewest possible words, and in the smallest space of time, as one sees in Thucydides, Tacitus or Lucian, but of a more really harmful kind; that he was too good a mime by nature; that when he had a beautiful and great idea that he wanted to express forcefully, his vigorous velleity had not that rare faculty of directing the great part of his energy towards the voice organ from which words arise, but that often many very essential parts of the idea were dispersed or diffused elsewhere, and act on other organs from where arise other signs. . . . Hence, his written expressions sometimes have real hiatuses that no mortal reader could fill. . . . I was quite as much astonished as charmed to hear our Diderot with a truly respectable tranquillity and modesty say: I have never thought this, but believe that you are telling the truth. The famous man did not think at this moment how many articles of our system he agreed with by this response. (B 6.37, 112–13)[13]

While Diderot had branded the *Lettre sur l'Homme* obscure, Hemsterhuis retorts that, in fact, Diderot's own style is much more obscure – and this is a product of a dispersion of linguistic energy in his texts. Diderot might have been a great orator, a great conversationalist and great actor, but his writing suffered as a result. In general, the dissipation of energy in Diderot's writings results in a loss of meaning: 'hiatuses' and 'jumps' litter his text, such that 'whole parts of the original idea are lost [and] cannot be reconstructed' (Sonderen 1996: 332).

For present purposes, what is key is that the passage establishes two models for obscurity, for this loss of meaning through hiatuses and jumps. The first model, associated with Tacitus and Lucian, is 'epigrammatic': it is born from a desire to present too many ideas in too few words. Diderot's obscurity, however, is of a different kind: it results from a failure to transmit linguistic energy to the reader in an orderly fashion. I return to the question of energetic obscurity in §23; what matters for present concerns is the first model, of epigrammatic obscurity. And this is because conveying too many ideas in too few words is precisely the danger run by any aspirant to optimal form – to compress ideas a little too much is to force the reader to do too much hermeneutic work in supplying what is missing. This is a concern that is very evident in the passage on Goethe's *Werther* that begins this section: the elisions that are natural to letters tend to generate an obscurity which it

---

[13] For a full analysis of this passage, see Sonderen (2000: 70–3).

falls to the reader to remedy. With 'abrupt' styles, the reader is asked to work too hard, to furnish all the gaping transitions from idea to idea.

Significantly, Hemsterhuis will criticise his own early publications in very similar terms. He writes to Gallitzin, 'In my small works, I feel that I have often tried to be too laconic and have sometimes neglected the intermediary demonstrations that were very necessary to be clear' (B 5.69, 236). This fault is born, he admits elsewhere, of an overwhelming desire to 'make the demonstration so concise that you will have no fear of the distraction of turning the page' (B 9.72, 154). In other words, by his own lights, Hemsterhuis flirts with epigrammatic obscurity in the name of rapid, fluid comprehension: he might, he thinks, sometimes rely too heavily on the genius of his reader to do the philosophical work for him, since the tendency to over-compression renders the text a dense, compact and crystalline instant. To put it another way: the *successive* presentation of ideas one after another is typically taken as a necessary feature of any text and especially one that aspires to clarity, for it ensures an orderly communication of transitions between ideas; hence, any communication strategy that desires to eliminate (or at least minimise) such succession in the name of simultaneity has to reckon with a correlate loss of clarity.[14] And it is for this reason that the late Hemsterhuis appears to conclude that writing letters is not always the best strategy. Optimal form is not always the most appropriate vehicle for philosophising.

3. Optimal form values 'presence' in two senses. The first is the sense that all ideas are to be thought simultaneously in the present instant; that is, they must be retrieved from the past to be made present. Secondly, in the related sense of total actualisation, all ideas are to be brought to mind, such that none are left latent or virtual, nothing remains unexpressed. Everything is to be brought *to presence in the present*. And this double sense of presence in turn informs the early Hemsterhuis' model of the idealised genius-reader, who makes ideas coexist and so works with a synchronic, spatialised model of knowing. Every idea is equally *present* to her, such that scientific change, development and history fade into the background. The genius-reader takes

---

[14] There is also a materialist danger here. Part of materialism's allure is how easily it explains everything. Hemsterhuis notes, materialism 'perfectly explains every event in the universe without exception, with an ease worthy of an enlightened century like ours' (B 8.48, 112–13). The virtues of *celeritas* and *facilitas* are associated with the materialists – and so a philosophy that resists them must deploy these same virtues far more circumspectly.

up a timeless vantage point (see §4), from which, the early Hemsterhuis seems to assume, she surveys everything worth surveying: nothing valuable is excluded from the genius' instantaneous snapshot of the sum of ideas. Even Hemsterhuis' preferred phrasing of the ideal of the optimum – 'the greatest number of ideas in the shortest possible *space* of time' – emphasises the reduction of the diachronic to the synchronic (see Matazzi 2004: 193; 2005: 143–6). Time is one more spatial relation: the philosopher takes up a bird's eye view from which each idea gains value only in its interrelations within a synchronic whole (see Hammacher 1971: 43).

The post-1775 Hemsterhuis is less sure of this model. For example, the opening to *Simon* is one place where he submits it to critical interrogation. When Mnesarchus is asked by Socrates to justify the pre-eminence he accords sculpture among the arts, he responds as follows:

> My art, Socrates, is without a doubt the most perfect of all the arts, since it speaks to two senses at once, to touch and to vision. It is the most perfect because it perfectly represents everything that can be represented. It is the most perfect since it is the only one of the arts that can master time by making one happy moment eternal and rendering it visible from all sides and into all centuries. And I believe, Socrates, that this is enough to paint the perfection of the art of sculpture and its pre-eminence above all other arts. (*EE* 2.108; *OP* 526)

This speech faithfully rehearses the early Hemsterhuis' reasoning in the *Lettre sur la sculpture*. Just as the *Lettre sur la sculpture* finds the beauty of sculptures in their expression of an aesthetic optimum, Mnesarchus, as a sculptor, approximates to optimal form by presenting, in one instant, 'everything that can be represented'. He masters time by reducing it to one static 'happy moment' that still manages to communicate a great number of ideas 'from all sides and into all centuries'. And yet, rather than this statement receiving unanimous agreement in *Simon* (as one might expect of Hemsterhuis' professed views), Socrates makes clear his dissatisfaction with it. In particular, Socrates questions Mnesarchus' axiom that sculpture 'perfectly represents everything that can be represented'. The problem, Socrates responds, is that Mnesarchus' emphasis on the 'happy moment' is exclusory: by taming time into a present instant, sculptors cannot represent any movement, becoming or history, that is, anything that resists being represented in a single moment. If, as Mnesarchus claims, sculptures approach optimal form, they thereby fail to represent everything that cannot be made manifest all at once. Socrates considers this a serious problem:

> Why do you always want to give movement to your figures, to make them speak, to inspire them with soul and life, if making the moment eternal was not an imperfection? Your art is obliged by its nature to annihilate movement: the succession of actions; and ultimately everything that designates the continuous energy of an active being, and to reduce this movement, this succession, this life, to rest and to inertia. (*EE* 2.108; *OP* 528)

Socrates puts into question the conclusions to the *Lettre sur la sculpture*;[15] he doubts whether a form of artistic expression structured solely on the model of the aesthetic optimum could adequately represent anything of temporal succession. For the Socrates of *Simon*, an art of the instant is imperfect, an impoverishment of expression.

Socrates' focus in this passage on what resists representation motivates much of the rest of *Simon*. A generalised anxiety pervades the dialogue over what cannot be brought to expression but must remain concealed. This is not just an aesthetic worry, but a moral and pedagogical one: if 'there are things in man which cannot be expressed by any art, because they are not perceivable in any way whatsoever from without' (*EE* 2.105; *OP* 516), then it is impossible to judge an individual's psychological state from her words or actions (as Hemsterhuis and Gallitzin try to do) or to know how best to correct her and set her on the right path. If there are things 'found at the bottom of [humans'] souls' that cannot be expressed in 'physiognomies and attitudes', then the pessimistic remark Aristophanes makes at the very beginning of the dialogue holds true: Prometheus 'made man all wrong ... hid the most essential parts of man ... [and] gave the light of day to' the superficial (*EE* 2.103–4; *OP* 508).[16] It is such passages that lead Lacoue-

---

[15] In the very same passage, he additionally puts another key tenet of the *Lettre sur la sculpture* into question (see Cirulli 2015: 65; Mazzocut-Mis 2005: 228). To the early Hemsterhuis' claim that sculpture 'satisfies two senses at one and the same time, touch and sight' as repeated by Mnesarchus above (*EE* 1.72; *OP* 114; see *EE* 2.108; *OP* 528), Socrates now responds categorically that 'it does not speak to touch' (*EE* 2.108; *OP* 528). The Hemsterhuis of *Simon* is intent on subjecting his earlier views to critical scrutiny through the persona of Socrates.

[16] As Sonderen helpfully elucidates (2000: 177–81), Hemsterhuis' concern with expression in *Simon* is in part a response to Lavater's physiognomical project, which itself rests on the presupposition that the external traits of an individual faithfully express her inner character (see B 3.61, 148). There is, of course, also a Rousseauean edge to this crisis of expression: for Rousseau, too, 'to be and to appear [are] two entirely different things' and one must reject anything that posits that 'the outward countenance is always the image of the heart's dispositions' (2018: 7, 175).

Labarthe and Nancy (1975) to situate Hemsterhuis' work within a late eighteenth-century 'crisis of expression'. For Hemsterhuis himself, what is at stake in these anxieties is, at bottom, the status of what is incapable of swift, easy consumption, that is, what is lost in the becoming-present of ideas. And what I want to suggest is that this concern is widespread in Hemsterhuis' thinking after 1775.

Nevertheless, this passage from *Simon* is no knock-down argument against the ideal of the optimum. Socrates' reservations are aired, considered, and then the conversation moves on without conclusion. Socrates' worries remain provisional – a set of questions rather than judgements. And this is for a couple of reasons. First, the later Hemsterhuis cannot in any way be said to abandon the ideal of the optimum: it plays a decisive doctrinal role in *Aristée* and *Alexis*; at most, all that can be proposed is that, after 1775, Hemsterhuis begins to *relativise* the ideal of the optimum, such that it is no longer the *sole* principle determining his philosophical project. The virtues of *celeritas* and *facilitas* now exist *alongside* other virtues of untimeliness and plasticity. There is no radical turn. Secondly, Hemsterhuis does not supply an argument against the value of the optimum in *Simon*, because the optimum is not susceptible to this kind of refutation. Optimal form is consistent with the coming-to-presence of any idea whatsoever – even the idea of its own falsity – so long as that idea *is presented*. An explicit, syllogistic refutation of the optimum is itself a performance of the optimum, insofar as it is complicit in making as many ideas as possible present to the mind in the shortest possible time. Both the assertion of optimal form and its rejection are to be included among those 'as many ideas as possible'. Therefore, to be effective, refutations ought not to be turned into ideas for swift, effortless consumption – other strategies are required, other ways of doing philosophy. And this experiment with slower, less consumable alternatives informs the late Hemsterhuis' texts.

§21 Genealogy

One of the most visible ways by which Hemsterhuis relativises the present and stresses the historicity of truth is through telling genealogical stories, where 'genealogy' is, broadly, understood as a critical 'knowledge of the conditions and circumstances out of which [ideas] grew, under which they evolved and changed' (Nietzsche 1969: 9). Many of this kind of story are familiar already from the previous sections: Hemsterhuis' story of the loss of sentimental spirit, his history of organs, and so on. From his earliest publications onwards, Hemsterhuis embeds his research into beauty, desire and knowledge within a historical narrative.

1. The *Lettre sur l'athéisme* is exemplary. Hemsterhuis was caught up in the German *Spinozismusstreit* from the outset: *Aristée* was one of the texts to trigger Lessing's confession of Spinozism at Wolfenbüttel in 1780 and Jacobi's 'Letter to Hemsterhuis' dominates the first half of his *Spinoza-Briefe*. Hemsterhuis' initial reception of Jacobi's polemic was relatively positive (e.g., B 8.47, 111; 12.150, 225) and this encouraged Jacobi to write to Gallitzin with the request 'that you and others might think about *how the concept of atheism could be philosophically and precisely determined* . . . [in particular] you could move Hemsterhuis to likewise think about the philosophical determination of the concept of atheism' (quoted in Trunz 1971: 52). Hemsterhuis responded by interpreting this plea for a precise, philosophical determination as a request for a genealogy. The history of atheism that he pens in 1787 (and revises in 1789) concludes as follows:

> The first atheism born of a reason still too little enlightened is soon destroyed by serious contemplation of a moral world. The second, which is really only an incredulity which is often reasonable and which easily degenerates into indifference, is cured only in the breast of true philosophy. But with respect to the last [atheism], this gigantic son of our proud folly, it will only ever be cured after man has familiarised himself with this incontestable truth: that *matter* is only a word which designates all the real essences as they have relation with our current organs. (OP 680)

It is striking that in response to Jacobi's request for a philosophical determination of atheism Hemsterhuis tells a story. And this impression is compounded by the fact that he also refuses to engage directly with any of Jacobi's own theses from the *Spinoza-Briefe*, ignores his identification of pantheism, fatalism and atheism, and even refuses to name Spinoza once.[17] There is something, in fact, almost playful to Hemsterhuis' *Lettre sur l'athéisme* – a response to Jacobi and an intervention in the *Spinozismusstreit* that avoids engaging with any of their most obvious concerns.

Instead, the basic thesis defended in the *Lettre sur l'athéisme* is that atheism is not a fixed label whose manifestations remain constant across the ages.[18] It is historically mutable and dependent on intellectual and social

---

[17] In fact, despite arguing against Spinoza from his very earliest publications onwards, Hemsterhuis never mentions Spinoza in print (B 10.16, 37; see Israel 2007: 31) – continuing a long-standing eighteenth-century tradition of combatting Spinozism through omission (see Bell 1984).

[18] On the below, see further Whistler (2022b).

contexts. Hence, Hemsterhuis identifies the above three kinds of atheism as products of three specific contexts: a primitive atheism in which 'divinity becomes superfluous' (*OP* 668), which is indexed to ancient societies and is due to an optimism in the explanatory power of the physical senses; a second 'very natural incredulity', linked to Roman and medieval forms of life, which emerges as a response to the 'infinite abuses' of mixing religion and politics, 'mixtures which often turn divinity into such an absurd monster that it destroys itself' (*OP* 670); and finally, a 'third atheism, born from the vanity of the triumphant intellect' identified with contemporary materialisms which 'give to the entirety of the universe a charming homogeneity, the simplicity of which renders useless and superfluous all other principles than autonomous matter' (*OP* 678). Ultimately, this more recent and philosophically sophisticated manifestation of atheism is a theoretical repetition of the first: it marks a return to its childlike optimism. That is, Hemsterhuis implies that, despite the eighteenth century's pretension to have attained maturity, its philosophers end up behaving like naïve children – it is not the theists who need to grow up, but the atheists (Fresco 2003: 19).

Jacobi was sufficiently pleased with Hemsterhuis' *Lettre sur l'athéisme* to include it in the 1789 edition of the *Spinoza-Briefe*, despite his worry (in Hemsterhuis' own paraphrase) that, 'without naming' Spinoza, the letter seemed 'a little thin, dubious or too vague' (*B* 10.20, 43). And yet, Hemsterhuis' letter can itself be read as a mild rebuke to Jacobi's own position set out in the *Spinoza-Briefe*: Hemsterhuis implicitly argues that 'Spinozism' is no ahistorical category capable of accounting for any manifestation of philosophical atheism whatsoever. Where Jacobi defines atheism in terms of a stable conceptual link to Spinoza, Hemsterhuis tells a story of *many atheisms*. For Hemsterhuis, Spinoza's atheism is one very specific product of the post-Cartesian Dutch Republic: Spinoza was born at a time when all 'ardent imagination[s] were fully liberated from their chains', when each philosopher felt, in the wake of the Cartesian revolution, 'set free and . . . found nothing obscure or impossible'. Spinoza functioned as the logical next step after Descartes, for 'the same effort that before could compose a universe out of matter could now make a God' (*OP* 672). In his correspondence, Hemsterhuis goes even further in emphasising the need to study the particular Dutch intellectual context of the period to make sense of Spinoza: 'One must excavate in Holland to have a rounded idea of the system of the too-famous Spinoza. The Dutch have lived with him, have been his disciples, his protectors, his admirers' (*B* 10.20, 42–3; see also Hammacher 2003: 35–6). Krop summarises nicely, 'By relating Spinozism to its particular Dutch context, [Hemsterhuis] reduced the philosophy of Spinoza to an essentially historical phenomenon' (2005: 189).[19] Spinoza is a manifestation of a particular time and place – he cannot become a symbol of anything more universal: Jacobi abuses the category of Spinozism by failing to respect its historical specificity.

2. The *Lettre sur l'athéisme* furnishes just one of a multitude of Hemsterhuisian genealogies. For example, correlate with his history of atheism, Hemsterhuis elsewhere provides a history of religious ways of life 'as they have been modified in Europe over the centuries' (B 4.6, 27).[20] He tells a familiar post-Reformation story in which Christianity's original inspiration is gradually lost under the accretions of priestcraft, politics and theology. As a result, 'it is almost impossible to represent the Christian religion in all its purity' (*EE* 1.116; *OP* 272). What is less typical in Hemsterhuis' genealogy of religious corruption is the role he accords the moral organ. Hemsterhuis' 'axiom' when philosophising on religion 'is and always will be that religion derives from the relation of the individual to God' (B 7.67, 187), and he continues elsewhere, 'this relation is only manifested by the moral organ' (*EE* 1.113; *OP* 262). From this perspective, 'no man is an atheist' in society (*EE* 1.118; *OP* 276), but there are merely those who, through a process of corruption, diminish their moral organ to the extent that it has 'extremely weak ... sensations of the real and necessary existence of the divinity' (*EE* 1.118; *OP* 276). Hence, the historical mutability of religion 'depends on the degree of perfection of the moral organ' (*EE* 1.114; *OP* 264). This is unsurprising in the light of Hemsterhuis' organology, but what remains to be noted is his attention to political structures as the main explanatory factor

---

[19] Hemsterhuis' relativisation of Spinoza as a product of a specific time and place was itself, moreover, a typical Dutch response to the scandal of Spinozism. In Hennert's contemporaneous work, for instance, 'Spinozism is presented ... as a historical phenomenon to be understood by philosophers, instead of merely as a set of radical ideas with dangerous implications' (Petry 2003b: 428). As a result, both Hemsterhuis and Hennert end up partially saving Spinoza at the expense of contemporary materialists (Israel 2007: 26–9; Krop 2005: 186) – separating out a 'sanitised' Spinozism which is of mainly historical interest from the philosophies of Diderot, d'Holbach and so on, which remain a contemporary threat. (These methods are, however, not limited to the Dutch context – as Zammito points out, Mendelssohn's strategy in this regard was 'not to affirm Spinoza's philosophical positions, but to historicise them' [2003: 352].)

[20] Hemsterhuis often affirms 'the utility and value of history' (B 5.2a, 15) for subjecting religious truths to criticism. He writes, 'The truth of a revelation that the all-powerful God designed to give me seventeen centuries ago for my salvation should be subjected to the same processes which I must use to work out the truth or falsity of some fact that Herodotus reports' (B 4.80, 212).

in a genealogy of religion. That is, he constructs a political theology, which tells the story of the 'relations between the modification of religion and the constitution of the state' (B 4.50, 123), for, he continues, the form of the state determines whether each individual's moral organ will be cultivated or suppressed. On the one hand, some 'mixture of religion with civil virtue' is valuable insofar as it guarantees oaths and martial virtue (e.g., B 4.80, 210; EE 1.117; OP 274); however, on the other hand, legal structures can end up supplanting the role of religious feeling and rendering it redundant – and this is what Hemsterhuis considers to be the story of modernity. Laws are originally instituted as a means to foster the moral organ, but ultimately the means becomes the end. Hemsterhuis writes of the encroachment of legislation: 'The moral organ is gradually annihilated to the extent that men's activity becomes circumscribed, determined and administered by laws' (EE 1.113; OP 262).[21]

It is on this basis that Hemsterhuis launches a critique of the modern system of laws. Take, for example, the following lament against the legal system:

> When you see man, who you know so well, who is so good by nature, who formerly had as his despot and master the all-powerful God and the laws that derived from his essence – laws which were sufficient to form the only society of which he is capable – when you see him transform himself into a citizen, become a slave, in all the force of the term, to a fantastic collective being, to a bizarre assemblage forged by our follies and our misfortunes, quit virtue, love, duty (things which belong uniquely to man as such and have nothing in common with the citizen as such), should you not conclude that this strange metamorphosis, this baroque phenomenon, is the sinister effect of some serious physical accident rather than of an apple and a snake? (B 7.81, 228; see also Wielema 1993: 111)

Hemsterhuis' criticisms of legislative society are continued in attacks on particular legal institutions like property (EE 2.115; OP 552), prison (B 3.18, 59), marriage (B 11.156, 144) and patriotism (B 4.41, 99). During the political tumult of the 1780s, this 'doggedly pessimistic and sceptical' political philosophy (Israel 2007: 31) is further radicalised: society

---

[21] Social structures are both the problem and the solution to the rectification of the moral organ: 'Only in social and political activity can man's moral faculty be fully developed. Instead of politics using people, people should start using politics as a means of moral self-perfection, as in the Greek city states' (Wielema 1993: 115).

becomes 'the most absurd and grotesque machine that the madness of men could imagine' (B 3.60, 145), the product of 'an imbecilic, blind and corrupted mankind' (B 7.73, 209) and governed by 'the Devil of the Orthodox' (B 8.75, 179).

In sum, Hemsterhuis uses genealogy to criticise the present dispensation of things: what exists now need not be the case; it is merely one contingent product of specific historical conditions.[22] To put it in the terms of this book, genealogical method challenges the fallacy of the ephemeral and traces metamorphoses of forms of life from epoch to epoch.

3. Two related Hemsterhuisian genealogies are pertinent at this point: the genealogy of sociability from the *Lettre sur les désirs* and the genealogy of language sketched in the *Réflexions sur la République des Provinces-Unies*.

In the *Lettre sur les désirs*, Hemsterhuis tells a story of different forms of comportment and intersubjectivity – a story which elucidates the models of social interaction possible within different social structures.[23] Specifically, Hemsterhuis' narrative again revolves around a critique of the becoming-legislative of modern society: to the modern axiom that 'mores are always the result of laws', Hemsterhuis gives the historicist riposte 'Not always' (B 12.69, 92).

In particular, Hemsterhuis avers that modern modes of sociability arise as part of a story that begins in post-Roman Europe. After the decline of antiquity,

> From our old chivalry was born the point of honour which gave birth to a kind of ceremonial between man and man. A singular monstrosity: a bizarre composite of Asian splendour and the Christian spirit of humility, which in truth meant that the masses, whom it enveloped like an atmosphere, insulted each other less, but also saw each other through a cloud. (EE 1.85; OP 170)

---

[22] Again, it is worth emphasising that this is not a narrative of decline in any straightforward sense: all societies – as imperfect, artificial creations – end up betraying the ideals of human intersubjectivity.

[23] As Nassar points out, this elaboration of the history of intersubjectivity was one of Hemsterhuis' more influential narratives; for example, 'Through Hemsterhuis, it seems, Novalis begins to develop a communal consciousness' (2013: 41). In fact, the Jena romantics' experiments in sociability by means of which they 'pushed the art of reciprocal philosophical communication to new, higher levels' (Kneller 2014: 110–11) are markedly Hemsterhuisian.

This post-chivalric form of social comportment regulated all relations between individuals through the mediation of the 'ceremonial'. And this 'ceremonial' created an artificial distance between all subjects, which, on the one hand, dulled the unpredictability of fortune and chance encounters and, on the other hand, created a rigid social structure in which each individual took up a pre-assigned position. As Novalis summarises in his *Hemsterhuis-Studien*, 'Etiquette is the death of all free humanity' (1960–2006: 2.362). The story of the emergence of modernity is, in part, a story of attempted liberation from this ceremonial yoke: 'Men become more enlightened' when they 'throw off this type of politeness, like a defensive weapon whose weight is a hindrance' (*EE* 1.85; *OP* 170). Enlightened maturity was achieved through overcoming chivalric sociability and developing new forms of intersubjective comportment. But modernity's failing, according to Hemsterhuis, is to have not completed this task: its overthrow of the ceremonial has been partial, at best. And this is because the modern legislative state replicates chivalric politesse in a new guise: it, too, regulates social relations so as to minimise the vicissitudes of fortune, replacing individual encounters with generic structures. Hence, Hemsterhuis writes to Gallitzin,

> The time of chivalry [was an age] in which a ridiculous mixture of religion, fanaticism, love and debauchery gave birth to absurdities, many of which existed for a long time, *and also* to the stupidities of our own day which evidently belong to the spirit of novels and chivalry. (B 4.58, 149; my emphasis)

Hence, Hemsterhuis will go on to discern the survival of ceremonial intersubjectivity in 'the relative place that men and women have occupied in society', which, he continues, is 'extremely absurd' (B 4.58, 148). But such particular structural inequalities are not the main point; the chivalric ceremonial lives on in the very omnipotence of structures themselves.

Hemsterhuis tells his eighteenth-century readers: we have never been modern. The history of sociability reveals a failure of the Enlightenment, its inability to live up to its own project of superseding the past. And it is therefore no surprise that Hemsterhuis' solution is to turn to an alternative mode of sociability, a pre-chivalric form of comportment that forms part of a different story – the Socratic (see §22).

4. Hemsterhuis' fragmentary *Réflexions* are intended to establish the principles of political history. And central to this account of the development of nations is an analysis of language. And this is because, in Hemsterhuis'

words, 'the condition of [a people's] language is the most perfect image of [the condition] of a people's intellectual faculties' (*WW* 466; *IN* 66). As he explains to Gallitzin, 'In the *Réflexions sur la République* I have tried to test the possibility of a theory by which one could judge the beauty, richness or polish of a language without understanding one single word of it, as long as one knows well the history of the people who speak it' (*B* 4.21, 60). The history of a language is manifest in political history and political history can be read off the history of a language, for the evolution of a nation depends on the frequent communication of its subjects necessitated by their geographical proximity. And so, Hemsterhuis writes, 'The continual communication of ideas gives birth to a great common imagination: a great common treasury of ideas, which by the rich nature of man could be placed easily in each of the best-composed heads' (*WW* 458; *IN* 62). This is what ultimately binds a nation together, according to Hemsterhuis – a common stock of signs. Each nation is therefore to be distinguished by its particular 'common treasury' of signs and, as a consequence, Hemsterhuis' political analysis requires 'penetrating into [a nation's] most ancient' form of life 'to see it in its infancy', in order to chart diachronic linguistic changes that are symptomatic of political changes (*WW* 468; *IN* 68).

Languages, Hemsterhuis continues, are of two types – those that are naturally rich and contain a wealth of primitive signs (identified by their quantity of roots) and those that are artificially rich and contain a wealth of complex terms as a result of 'augmenting ideas of relation' (*WW* 464; *IN* 66). Languages that are naturally rich are associated by Hemsterhuis with the virtue of energy and languages that are artificially rich with the virtue of precision: 'The perfection of a language consists in the *energy* or in the *precision* with which it expresses even the lightest nuances and the most delicate of ideas and sensations' (*WW* 466; *IN* 66; my emphases). And this, he insists, is a political distinction; for example, the difference between energy and precision supplies the means to differentiate monarchies from republics: on the one hand lies the flattering nuance of monarchical language and, on the other, the 'energetic and victorious persuasive clarity' of a republican (*WW* 466; *IN* 67). Hemsterhuis' primary example is his own nation: the Dutch have a language relatively poor in primitive roots, but rich in combinations, since their very political existence has been a matter of increasingly complex interrelations and 'infinite complication' (*B* 12.149, 221; see also *WW* 456; *IN* 60). More generally, a recurring theme in Hemsterhuis' system of times is the association of linguistic precision with post-Newtonian modernity; indeed, in his letters on the Platonic sublime (§8), Hemsterhuis draws a distinction between the Greek and modern languages based solely on the 'precision of expression' which has been 'prodigiously perfected' in modern languages through increasing their 'quantity' of relational 'signs', but which the Greeks 'did not then have' (B 7.85, 234).[24]

As always, therefore, while Hemsterhuis values equally both forms of linguistic perfection and works towards a synthesis of linguistic precision and linguistic energy, he sees his most pressing task to be a work of compensation, a rebalancing that will reclaim the natural perfection of linguistic energy to the same extent as post-Newtonians have invested in the artificial perfection of linguistic precision. Hemsterhuis therefore prioritises 'the energy of my language' (B 5.6b, 34–5) – he worries over the 'loss of tone or energy' that results when the soul 'thinks either for too long or too deeply' (B 3.33, 88) and praises 'the true and energetic language of the golden age' (B 6.30, 97). In short, Hemsterhuis labours to maximise linguistic energy in an age of linguistic precision. I return to this in §23.

5. Hemsterhuis was not alone among eighteenth-century philosophers in undertaking genealogy. The genetic explanations proffered by those practising analytic or regressive methodologies often verged on genealogical projects: to trace complex ideas back to simple ideas or to reduce abstract notions to sense impressions is frequently to turn to the past. The most visible of these genealogies stands at the head of d'Alembert's *Discours préliminaire* to the *Encyclopédie*: d'Alembert begins by charting 'the genealogy and filiation of our ideas, the causes that gave birth to them and the characteristics which distinguish them'. His story is one of beginnings, 'ascending to the origin and generation of our ideas' and then descending back into the various branches of science – such that the *Encyclopédie* itself comes to be modelled as a 'genealogical tree' (d'Alembert and Diderot 2021: 1.i–ii, 1.xiv). D'Alembert's is thus a vindicatory form of genealogy:[25] he tells a story to strengthen the legitimacy of the present disposition of the sciences, to show that what currently exists is the 'natural' conclusion to a rational process.

However, the eighteenth century also housed more critical types of genealogy, and the paradigmatic example of this more subversive form is Rousseau's *Discours sur l'inégalité*. A critical genealogy can be defined in terms of its 'historical problematization of the present' (Koopman 2013: 2), its dissolu-

---

[24] However, compare this with his remarks on the 'refined' and 'tender nuances' of the Greek language in the *Lettre sur la sculpture* (EE 1.83; OP 166).
[25] On 'vindicatory' and 'subversive' types of genealogy, see Koopman (2013: 58–60), as well as Geuss' distinction (1994: 274–7) between critical genealogy and 'tracing a pedigree'.

tion of 'standards of truth that have been posited as timeless and universal' (Kretsdemas 2017: 2) and its liberation of the reader through the realisation that things could have been otherwise (see Nehemas 1985: 112). In this vein, Rousseau's aim in the second *Discours* is, as Neuhouser summarises, 'to "denaturalize" a host of social conditions whose legitimacy we tend to accept unreflectively precisely because we view those arrangements as "eternal givens" . . . to disrupt our unreflective "consent" to . . . what we take to be a "natural" social order' (2012: 385). When we turn back to Hemsterhuis, it is evident that his writings offer examples of both vindicatory and critical genealogies; but what I have been emphasising in this section is the significant role played by post-Rousseauean critical genealogy in his philosophy. Hemsterhuis tells historical stories to denaturalise the present, to dissolve givens and to jolt the reader into imagining alternative presents and futures. From this genealogical perspective, the present is just one contingent historical moment among others – a moment that might not have been and will be subject to transformation in the future. To this extent, Hemsterhuis' practice of genealogy resists optimal form in the name of untimeliness and plasticity; it posits historicity against the hegemony of the present.

Nevertheless, genealogical reasoning is not a particularly successful mode of resistance to optimal form. Genealogies tell stories about the past; they represent this past and make it present to the reader. The genealogical still actualises the past in the present: each past phenomenon is rendered one more idea coexisting alongside others. Genealogy functions by making explicit the *rapports* that hold between the present and the past, and so contributes to an aspiration to the 'absolute coexistence' of ideas. Something different is needed to rigorously resit optimal form. And a clue to this something different is offered by the history of sociability that Hemsterhuis tells, for he does not merely describe different modes of intersubjectivity but performs them in his writing as well. The very structure of Hemsterhuis' dialogues and the comportment of the characters within them attest to a different way of resisting optimal form – one that does not rely on anything directly talked about (which can always be appropriated as information, as ideas for consumption), but comprises the unthematised but no less salient ways in which characters go about conversing. Here Hemsterhuis contests the modern legislative regulation of social relations most effectively, for, unlike genealogical stories, which make the past present to consciousness and susceptible to comparison, these formal structures appear *as past* and remain *as past*. And, in a very similar vein, one can likewise point to Hemsterhuis' aspiration to write energetic prose in an age of precision mentioned above: this practice also contests optimal form in a performative register. To write in this way is (as §3 made clear) not a matter of the actual words on the page, but the tone expressed in them. When Hemsterhuis contorts French to his own ends, he renders it alien to itself without necessarily giving material for any new ideas.[26] And it is to these performative practices of subversion I now turn in the following sections.

§22 Irony and Anachronism

The final section of this chapter comprises, like many of the final sections in previous chapters, a dedicated case study – in this instance, of the extended prefaces to *Aristée* and *Simon*.[27] My task is to enumerate the various theoretical functions performed by these opening fictions. For it is here that the antagonism staged in the dialogues between the present and the past – between optimal form, on the one hand, and untimeliness and plasticity, on the other – is most visible. The prefaces oscillate abruptly between different temporal perspectives, thereby producing a series of ironies that shifts the ground from under the reader's feet and estranges her from secure footing in the present. While the early letters did already include short prefaces, it is with the entrance of a fictional editor in *Aristée* that the prefaces begin to do significant theoretical work.

The preface to *Aristée* reads,

> Since no one today is ignorant of philosophy and since the study of morals has attained a point of perfection and refinement that astonishes, we pride ourselves on contributing to the amusement of the public by offering them this small metaphysico-moral work.
>
> The manuscript was found, it has been claimed, on the island of Andros, at the time of the Russian expedition in the archipelago. The Greek text is extremely corrupt; this has obliged the translator, who is little versed in critique, to occasionally give only the outline of the reasoning, and – so as to make it intelligible to everyone – often to substitute the terms of our physico-geometry for the indecipherable jargon of the physics of the Ancients. We thought it best to alert our savants to this, so they would not ascribe to the Greeks knowledge whose discovery or creation does not belong to them.

---

[26] This practice is, in fact, strictly analogous to speaking like a republican in a language determined by monarchical social structures (see above).

[27] Technically, Hemsterhuis designates each of these preambles an 'avertissement de l'éditeur', but I refer to them here more loosely as 'prefaces'.

We owe it to our century's public prurience to excuse some crude expressions to be found in this small piece: we humbly beg the public ... to reflect on the fact that centuries owe each other some indulgence and that, if it were decent or commonsensical to conceive of a century more perfect than our own, we ourselves in all our perfection would have need, as it were, of some bounty on its part.

Concerning the author of this writing, he seems to have belonged to the school of Socrates. We see in the work some characteristics – even if they are weak – of the good sense of this philosopher, of the poetry of Plato and of the exactitude of Aristotle. He seems to be Athenian and from the era of Demetrius of Phalerum. ... The work is addressed to Diotima. We know that Diotima was that sacred and prodigious woman from whom Socates confessed to have learnt all that he knew on the nature of friendship and who flourished around the LXXXII Olympiad. However, to confound her with the one who is spoken of here would suppose her to be at least 140 years old. (*EE* 2.63; *OP* 388–90)

In the preface to *Simon*, the same themes recur. The preface begins with a mock apology for 'having the effrontery to ... once more for your amusement present some profound metaphysics' (*EE* 2.100; *OP* 498). It traces a fake manuscript history that both parallels *Aristée's* ('it is to the same Russians and to the same archipelago to which we owe *Aristaeus* that we are indebted for this small and singular work') and sheds light on *Aristée's* own history ('our conjectures about the Diotima to which *Aristaeus* was addressed were very felicitous') (*EE* 2.101; *OP* 500). It provides historical context concerning the eponymous character, Simon: 'You know that Simon was a leather merchant who lived in the Piraeus next to Telecles the weaver ...' (*EE* 2.100; *OP* 498). It speculates on the original Greek authorship of the dialogue: while the first version of the dialogue notes that 'Diogenes Laertius has conserved for us the titles' of Simon's dialogues 'but none bears that of *Simon*', the second version of the text[28] adds more constructively: 'It seems much more probable that the dialogue in question here only bears the title of Simon because he is the main actor, and that the real author of this writing is Phaedo of Elis' (*EE* 2.100; *OP* 500). The preface includes a series of erudite references, including a note on the proper translation of Σκυτοτόμος, a short biography of the Athenian general Charmus and allusions to relatively obscure Greek authors such as Cleidemus, Theon of Alexandria and Olympiodorus (*EE* 2.100–1; *OP* 500).

---

[28] That is, the 1782–3 revisions of the text that had originally been drafted in 1779–80. See §2.

§22 IRONY AND ANACHRONISM

It also foregrounds the role of the editor: on the one hand, this editor writes that 'we leave the text as it is, correcting in the notes only small flagrant faults which would impede an attentive reader'; and, on the other hand, he admits to a lack of philosophical expertise:

> As for the content of the work, Socrates's purpose or Diotima's reasoning, I can tell you nothing. I have studied each sentence with care, but I have not read the work in the spirit required to understand its full meaning. I am a brave translator, a great antiquarian and a hardy critic, but for psychology one has need of algebra, which I do not possess. I am told, however, that this is a theory which could serve to perfect men. That being said, the redundancy and uselessness of such a doctrine in your century of perfection means I am merely left with the unfortunate service of having offered you an antiquity. (EE 2.101; OP 502)

Simon, like *Aristée* before it, also includes a fictional dedication, now identified as being written by Diocles, who was the first to rediscover and edit the text in antiquity, before it was lost again. This dedication (like *Aristée*'s [EE 2.64; OP 392]) is addressed to 'wise and sacred Diotima'; it speaks of 'restoring in this writing what it might have lost over the course of more than a century'; and it praises 'the philosophy that you have formed for your own happiness and for that of others' (EE 2.101; OP 502). These dedications connect *Aristée* and *Simon* to the later *Alexis*, which lacks their extended prefaces, but opens with a similar dedication to 'wise and sacred Diotima' and recounts the dialogue's purported origins in ancient Athens (EE 2.123; OP 574). The three dedications mark *Alexis* as belonging to the same fictional world as *Aristée* and *Simon*.

1. These prefaces and dedications turn *Aristée*, *Simon* and *Alexis* into *forgeries*. They attempt (however playfully) to pass the dialogues off as something they are not – as antique texts with Greek authors, Athenian origins and convoluted manuscript histories. *Aristée* is ascribed to an unknown Athenian author writing between 317 to 307 BC (the period when Demetrius of Phalerum was in power); *Simon* is initially ascribed to the fourth-century Simon, before, in the second version of the text, being definitively attributed to the fourth-century Phaedo of Elis; and *Alexis* appears to have been written later, according to Hemsterhuis' fictional world, possibly by the Diocles who had first edited *Simon*.

The sheer intricacy of the effort Hemsterhuis puts in to making the late dialogues forgeries positions them in a similar space to Macpherson's

Ossian cycle and other fakes of the era: Hemsterhuis follows them in, as Grafton puts it, 'the free invention of whole new pasts . . . lavishing space and imagination on the origins and settings of their creations' (1990: 28, 56). However, unlike Macpherson's text, no one has ever admitted to being taken in by the fabulated manuscript histories of Hemsterhuis' dialogues. There is something fundamentally *unserious* about them: whatever else they are intended to accomplish, they are certainly also intended as a series of philological jokes. They are meant to amuse the reader and establish complicity with those 'in on the joke'. This playfulness is corroborated by the fact that the trappings of forgeries were also appropriated by late eighteenth-century novels (e.g., Goethe's *Werther*) to teasingly test the boundary between truths and fictions. And, in this vein, Hemsterhuis' prefaces are intended to warn the reader that what follows is no earnest system, but a ludic text that requires an appropriately playful, almost novelistic reading practice – hence, Hemsterhuis' references in correspondence to the prefaces as 'follies' or 'mad' (B 3.13, 45; 3.9, 37) and to their 'levity' (B 3.13, 45–6). And yet, these prefaces equally seem to want to be taken seriously: they consist of concerted exercises in antiquarian erudition. Even relatively small details such as 'the altar that Charmus dedicated to love at the entrance of the academy' (*EE* 2.101; *OP* 500; translation modified) was, as Hemsterhuis testifies in correspondence, based on extensive scholarly reconstruction of Pausanias' *Description of Greece* (B 3.9, 38). Despite the jokes, the reader is surely meant to feel the force of Hemsterhuis' knowledge as something impressive, as something that confers authority on the world constructed in the text.[29]

Moreover, these playful but erudite prefaces and dedications are of a piece with the dialogues that follow: their experiments with fictions and novelistic forms are as paradigmatic of the post-1775 poetic turn as anything that occurs within the rest of the dialogues. *Simon* furnishes the most obvious example: the preface and dedication merely extend the nested narratives and framing devices present elsewhere in the text, multiplying stories, reminiscences and conversations. That is, the doctrinal crux of the dialogue, Diotima's Prometheus myth, is reported from memory by Socrates to a group gathered at Simon's shop; Socrates' speech is later reported by Simon him-

---

[29] This tension between the serious and non-serious in the prefaces is confirmed in a letter to Anna Perrenot explaining the conceit of *Simon*: the letter begins with a series of erudite details about 'the locale of Athens at the time of Socrates and Aristophanes' which 'must be known' to appreciate the dialogue properly, but ends by admitting that 'this little work, as a whole, is only a pure fiction' (B 11.164, 151–2).

§22 IRONY AND ANACHRONISM   235

self to Hipponicus and then, according to the preface, written down by Phaedo. The preface adds that this text was subsequently recovered, edited and supplemented in late antiquity with a dedication that itself refers back to an archaic past when Charmus dedicated the temple altar to Aphrodite. The dialogue was then lost again and discovered for a second time by the Russian navy during its 1769 expedition to the Aegean archipelago and was ultimately edited, corrected and translated, with the addition of a preface, by an eighteenth-century 'editor'.

2. There are therefore three basic functions performed by the prefaces:

   (a) *as joke* – the prefaces play with the categories of truth and fiction by selling themselves as forgeries and so alert the reader to the kind of levity required to read the ensuing text properly;
   (b) *as exercise in erudition* – the prefaces equally make a case for the historical precision of Hemsterhuis' rendering of an Athenian world, and so bestow authority on the text's antiquarian details;
   (c) *as propadeutic* – the prefaces radicalise the poetic turn already underway elsewhere in the dialogues and so immerse the reader from the beginning in modes of fabulation characteristic of the late Hemsterhuis.

Nevertheless, this is to omit the most significant function performed by these prefaces: they situate Hemsterhuis' philosophy in the past, as an *anachronism*. As Morpurgo-Tagliabue phrases it (1987: 40), the effect of these prefaces is to render the whole of the late Hemsterhuis' output 'a singular speculative anachronism'. They implicitly tell the reader that the arguments and concepts that follow should not be expected to engage with contemporary debates, but, instead, arise out of a long dead philosophical past. It is here, then, that Hemsterhuis most visibly pursues a goal of *becoming untimely*.

The prefaces communicate the untimeliness of Hemsterhuis' philosophy primarily by means of a series of contrasts between the 'small' and 'crude' nature of the dialogues themselves and the 'century of perfection' in which they have been published, that is, by means of an ironic critique of a hubristic, enlightened present in the name of an unassuming past. This critique of the present, it should be noted, is absent from the short preludes that preface the pre-1775 publications: they emphasise, on the contrary, *the fit* between Hemsterhuis' philosophy and the times, announcing a publication possessing 'a philosophical tone that conforms sufficiently to the taste of the age' (*EE* 1.78; *OP* 150). By the end of the 1770s, however, Hemsterhuis' attitude towards 'the taste of the age' was such that it could no longer be reconciled with his philosophical project. In his correspondence, he laments that 'the character of this century is of such thinness and weakness that it astonishes me as much as it does you' (B 11.218, 188), that it is 'rich in that bounty of stupidity with which . . . it replaced the virtues of the ancients' (B 10.7, 22), that it is a 'perverse century' (B 6.56, 158) and 'a devil of a century' (B 8.101, 232). A clear, unironised statement of this position is found in a letter to Gallitzin from August 1780: 'Those who say that our century is one of philosophy know very little of both philosophy and the century' (B 3.58, 144).

Hemsterhuis never allows himself to be this explicit in the prefaces themselves; instead, he insinuates his criticisms ironically. The editor flatters eighteenth-century Europe as an era of 'perfection and refinement' in which philosophy has reached its apex and therefore come to an end: the ethics and metaphysics needed as a crutch by earlier civilisations have now reached a condition of 'redundancy and uselessness' – as a mere 'antiquity'. Thus, on the one hand, Enlightenment philosophy is called 'serious' and 'profound' and, on the other hand, the dialogues are depreciated as 'small' and superfluous. And it is on this basis that *Aristée* differentiates the obscure 'indecipherable jargon' of the ancients from 'the terms of our physico-geometry', which are 'intelligible to everyone'. Throughout, Hemsterhuis' method is always the same: he estranges his work from present modes of thought by a twofold rhetorical gesture – *auxesis*, or the excessive inflation of the object of critique (eighteenth-century philosophy) and *meiosis*, or the radical deflation of the critiquing subject (Hemsterhuis). This production of auxetic–meiotic contrasts defines what van Sluis refers to as Hemsterhuis' 'characteristic irony' (in OP 729), what Fresco dubs his 'talent for self-irony' (1995a: 105) and what Moenkemeyer calls the 'ironic detachment of the late dialogues' (1975: 109).

And this ironic dialectic of *auxesis* and *meiosis* is precisely Socratic in origin.[30] Socrates' comportment to his contemporaries likewise comprises an ironic mixture of excessive flattery and self-depreciation; this is one of the fundamental features of Socratic irony. Thus, in the *Symposium* (to take one example from many), Socrates responds to Agathon's encomium: 'How can I or anyone else not be left feeling that he has nothing to say, when he has to follow a discourse of such beauty and variety! . . . As I reflected that I would not be able to give a speech myself anywhere near as fine, I almost turned tail with shame' (Plato 1962: 198b). Socrates then proceeds

---

[30] It is also a radicalised form of the kind of humility common to early modern scientific treatises – as Blumenberg notes (1985: 362), 'tactical and economic "understatement" rules the early history of modern sciences'.

to destroy the foundations of Agathon's speech. Moreover, the Socratic provenance of Hemsterhuis' ironic dialectic also accounts for its striking resemblance to Kierkegaard's offering of crumbs and fragments that do 'not make the slightest pretension to share in the philosophical movement of the day' and resist 'the idea of . . . any sort of epoch-making significance' (1962: 3–4). Hemsterhuis – like Socrates before him and Kierkegaard after him – envisages himself a gadfly nipping at the ankles of contemporary intellectual goliaths. But where Hemsterhuis' prefaces go beyond a strict repetition of this Socratic model is by tying this practice of irony *to time*: he uses it to establish an opposition to the present and thereby position *Aristée*, *Simon* and *Alexis* on the side of the past.[31]

3. In addition to the above ironic contrasts which run through the prefaces, *Simon* establishes a further opposition between the fictional editor of the dialogue (purportedly the author of these prefaces) – a 'brave translator, a great antiquarian and a hardy critic' who is unable to 'read the work in the spirit required to understand its full meaning' – and those readers (as well as Hemsterhuis himself) who possess the requisite psychological and metaphysical insight to read them properly ('to understand its full meaning'), owing to their proper mathematical training (i.e., sufficient 'algebra').

This contrast is odd. On the one hand, the editor's claim that the dialogue transposes algebra into psychological investigation (i.e., the use of models from the natural sciences to make sense of mental phenomena) refers, according to Hemsterhuis' system of times (§5), to a distinctively modern practice and so jars with the pretence that the philosophy espoused in *Simon* is of ancient Greek provenance. On the other hand, the editor is right that this kind of transposition is a very important component of Hemsterhuis' modern project, which makes use of mathematics to analyse psychological facul-

---

[31] Kierkegaard's version of Socratic irony, it should be noted, does exploit its potential for anachronism in a way consonant with Hemsterhuis' practice. For Kierkegaard, the ironist 'becomes alien to the whole world to which he belongs' (1992: 196) and 'a riddle to the contemporary age, in which he lives as a stranger and a foreigner' (1992: 246). He continues, 'The ironist has stepped out of line with his age, has turned around and faced it' (1992: 261), and so his writing functions 'much like an antediluvian fossil reminding us of another kind of life that doubt has eroded' (1992: 103). In other words, Hemsterhuis is an ally of Kierkegaard in resisting what will become a Hegelian image of philosophy as 'its own time apprehended in thoughts', limited to the comprehension of what is actual (Hegel 2008: 15). In fact, when Hegel continues, 'It is just as absurd to fancy that a philosophy can transcend its contemporary world as it is to fancy that an individual can overleap his own age, jump over Rhodes' (2008: 15), this can be read as a critical commentary on the entire Hemsterhuisian project outlined in this book.

ties. The character of the editor seems to misunderstand what distinguishes modernity from antiquity, yet simultaneously seems to correctly identify the key to properly understanding the text. This is an instance of the kind of 'ironic self-entanglement' which Friedlander attributes to Plato's texts (1970: 143). The point appears to be that the editor is so constrained by the horizon of the present, so unable to 'speak Greek' like a native in the Hemsterhuisian sense, that he even misconstrues basic characteristics of the Greek perihelion that distinguish it from modernity. As the editor himself emphasises, he cannot appreciate the proper 'tone' of *Simon* and should thus be categorised as one bad eighteenth-century reader among many, stuck in the wrong perihelion without the hermeneutic sensitivity (i.e., tact) necessary to participate in another epoch. The editor is trapped in and by the present. As well as an exercise in antiquarian erudition, these prefaces are therefore also a critique of it in the guise of the editor and his arid reconstruction of everything but what matters – the spirit of the work. The editor's constant allusions to names and places ultimately testify to a philological impotence, to a failure to read properly and pass beyond the scholarly exterior of Greek life. As elucidated in §3, Hemsterhuis insists on two conditions for immersion in the Greek world: (1) tact to replicate the appropriate tone and (2) precise antiquarian knowledge – and the editor meets only the second of them. To put it another way: the classical philologist comes out of the prefaces badly.[32]

Moreover, by representing the editor as a bad, contemporary reader, Hemsterhuis strengthens his own claim (as the implicit author) to be doing more than mere philology, that is, to be writing in an authentically Greek tone as well. Hemsterhuis considers himself able to transcend the present in a way that the character of the editor does not. And this holds, in turn, for an ideal reader too, who is meant to be provoked by all of this to pass beyond the prejudices of an eighteenth-century perception of the Greek world to achieve complete immersion in another time. One of the functions of the prefaces, therefore, is to encourage an appropriate reading of the dialogues by initially staging an example of a bad reading. Readers of *Aristée* and *Simon* are invited to do better than the editor.

Moreover, this provocation to read better is also accomplished through a dialectic of complicity and estrangement running through the prefaces. This

---

[32] Elsewhere, Hemsterhuis will talk of his father (the foremost Dutch philologist of the previous generation) as uninterested in the art of reading: he speaks of his own difficulties in reading as 'the fault is my father's, who preferred to see me think than read' (B 6.30, 97). To put it bluntly, in the prefaces Hemsterhuis parodies a voice like his father's.

is visible in the fluctuation of possessive pronouns: sometimes the reader addressed in the preface is associated with the present in opposition to the editor, as with '*your* century of perfection'; sometimes both the editor and the reader are associated with modernity, as with 'our physico-geometry'. In both cases, the reader who is explicitly addressed by the editor is taken to be complicit in present modes of thinking (even more so than the editor). In consequence, this gesture partly involves differentiating between an esoteric reader and an exoteric reader (much in the way that Diderot speaks of the *Lettre sur l'Homme* – see §15). On the one hand, there are the uninitiated, those unable to get outside of their era and become untimely – they lack access to the dialogue's genuine 'tone' and are therefore identified with the bad reader (the 'you') addressed in the prefaces. On the other hand, there are the initiated readers, who are not explicitly represented in the text at all, who 'get it' and so appreciate the irony of the editor's claims.[33] They are complicit in (and even supposed to emulate) Hemsterhuis' own writing techniques. In short, the prefaces attempt to generate (or at least identify) a readerly elite – 'the people of great spirit', mentioned by Hemsterhuis in correspondence, who 'esteem each other mutually' and disdain 'the approbation of the vile populace' (B 12.46, 63).

What characterises the esoteric reader is encapsulated in the fundamental maxim of Hemsterhuisian hermeneutics, articulated in the preface to *Aristée*:

> We humbly beg the public ... to reflect on the fact that centuries owe each other some indulgence and that, if it were decent or commonsensical to conceive of a century more perfect than our own, we ourselves in all our perfection would have need, as it were, of some bounty on its part.

Perfections, Hemsterhuis argues in his system of times (see §5), are various and of equal value. Antiquity might appear relatively imperfect set against modernity's geometrical triumphs, but this is compensated by antiquity's sentimental perfections. No solution to the quarrel between the ancients and the moderns is acceptable that resorts to models of mere progress or decline. And from this basis arises the above maxim: Show 'bounty' to other epochs, judge them charitably. Moreover, this maxim thematises once more the limitations of the early Hemsterhuis' ideal of the optimum. The perfections celebrated as unsurpassable by the eighteenth century are perfections of total actualisation, of an absolute encyclopaedia that aspires to

---

[33] Hemsterhuis writes in passing to Gallitzin that, in order to understand 'the true character of Socrates' and Plato's irony ... one must have exquisite tact' (B 6.19, 64).

the simultaneous making-present of every scientific idea. The eighteenth century appears unsurpassable to the extent that every possible combination of every existing idea is collated into a divine-like intuition. Hemsterhuisian irony contests this. By contrasting the unassuming smallness and redundancy of the dialogues to the comprehensiveness of the absolute encyclopaedia, Hemsterhuis hopes that complicit readers will join in laughing at such pretensions.

And yet, these complicit readers are absent from the text. Unlike the bad readers addressed by the editor, they are neither spoken of nor spoken to; the true reader remains concealed. And this absence is essential to the functioning of Hemsterhuisian irony, for it foregrounds irony's esotericism and indirection. That is, in line with classical understandings of irony as referring to the unsaid by contrary names (see Vlastos 1991: 26–8), Hemsterhuis opposes the optimum from a position that goes unrepresented in the textual economy of the prefaces. Irony in *Aristée* and *Simon* operates, as Kierkegaard puts it, such that the 'exterior suggests something quite different from [the] interior' (1992: 212) – a theme subsequently taken up within *Simon* itself in its anxiety over the crisis of expression: the whole dialogue is a reflection on the ironic dissonance between exoteric surfaces and esoteric depths (see §20). Those who are in on the joke do not come to presence but stand unsaid above the text. In other words, this practice of irony resists optimal form in a way that other critical practices, like genealogy, do not: insofar as it does not actualise or thematise its referent, it resists without explicitly bringing ideas to mind. Instead, irony silently insinuates alternatives. Hemsterhuisian irony is therefore an exemplary, unrepresentable instance of the thesis that the optimum is not everything, that there is more to philosophising than bringing to presence the maximum of ideas in the shortest possible time.

4. As has become abundantly clear, Hemsterhuis identifies this strategy of resistance to the optimum with one particular instance of philosophising – *the Socratic*. Reinventions of Socratic irony in the eighteenth century were as common as idealisations of Socrates himself (see §3); nevertheless, what Friedrich Schlegel is hinting at when he asserts that Hemsterhuis 'was the only genuine Socratic of his age' (1958–2002: 18.6) and what Fresco discerns with his claim that 'Hemsterhuis' "Socratism" was entirely his own, viz. different from that of his contemporaries and friends' (Fresco 1991: 71) is the richness of Hemsterhuis' reimagining of Socratic irony. In addition to the *auxesis–meiosis* dialectic described above, Hemsterhuisian irony is also constituted *as a mode of sociability* and *as an imposture*.

Sociability is one relatively distinctive feature of Hemsterhuis' practice of irony. For example, whereas Hamann treats Socratic irony as a tool for turning away from the intersubjective in the name of inward 'sensibility' (1967: 167), whereas Gallitzin turns Socratic irony into a sceptical retreat into 'our ignorance, our fragility and our weakness' (quoted in Brachin 1952: 165) and whereas Kierkegaard will transform Socratic irony into the 'annihilating enthusiasm of negativity' that 'allows nothing whatever to endure' (1992: 175, 40), Hemsterhuis' recovers Socratic irony as primarily *outward-facing* and *upbuilding*. It aspires to form a community of like-minded readers on the model of what Melzer calls 'pedagogical esotericism' (2014: 3–4). Hemsterhuis' Socrates educates others into a community of autonomous individuals founded on tact, as opposed to modern legislative states that inaugurate civil society through generic structures.[34] For Hemsterhuis, 'amical irony' (Gourinot 1986: 353) is the ideal of intersubjectivity and education – an alternative vision of social comportment to what was on offer in his genealogy of modern sociability rehearsed in the *Lettre sur les désirs* (see §21).

Part of what is at stake here is Hemsterhuis' refusal to reduce Socratic irony solely to the epistemological paradox of knowing that one knows nothing. Instead, Hemsterhuis sees Socrates' claim to only know that he knows nothing as but one instance among many of a meiotic practice, a habit of self-depreciation that is, at bottom, a social attitude, not an epistemic one. He therefore eschews any interpretation of irony that renders it primarily sceptical, negating or even a manifestation of epistemic humility, such as Hamann's, for which 'all of Socrates' ideas ... were nothing more than expectorations and secretions of his ignorance' (1967: 167). Hemsterhuis implies that the above is a skewed, partial picture of Socratic irony – an argument which Nightingale (1995: 114, 118–19) has repeated in a contemporary context when chastising 'recent investigations of Socratic irony' which 'have centred on the philosopher's disavowal of knowledge' and which have consequently neglected 'as central to Socrates' ironic technique ... Socrates' habit of heaping praise upon undeserving people'. Nightingale concludes,

---

[34] Hence, Socrates was 'the greatest master in education that will ever be' not merely because he 'taught Plato philosophy', but because 'he taught him that he was Plato, what he would never have known his whole life without his divine teacher.... It was the only secret, the only method, the only goal of Socrates' philosophy' (B 7.47, 128). And Socrates achieved this by means of irony. Hemsterhuis' representations of Socrates are not like Kierkegaard's isolated rebel who lived his 'whole life [in] protest' (Kierkegaard 1992: 218), but more like Vlastos' version of Socrates as 'even-keeled, light-hearted, jocular, cheerfully and obstinately sane' (1991: 39).

what has thereby been missed is the role of Socratic irony in promoting 'a cooperative dialectical quest' in the face of 'hubristic self-assertion'.

In Hemsterhuis scholarship, there has been a corresponding overemphasis on Hemsterhuis' use of Socratic irony to motivate a turn inwards, a retreat into psychological introspection along the lines of the Delphic 'know thyself'. This is understandable, for Hemsterhuis' most celebrated invocation of Socrates at the opening to *Sophyle* is precisely to this end: Socratic philosophy is that 'which is found at the bottom of our heart, of our souls, if we make the effort to seek it there' (*EE* 2.47; *OP* 342; see also *EE* 2.95; *OP* 486). Thus, Van Bunge, for example, discerns in Hemsterhuis' Socratism a symptom of 'the essentially introspective nature of [his] philosophical project' (2018: 188) and Cahen-Maurel reduces Hemsterhuis' appeal to Socrates to an 'imperative for introspection', an 'appeal to turn our gaze within' (2022: 25–6). Both think of Hemsterhuis' use of Socrates along the lines of Kierkegaard's Socrates, who 'encloses himself within himself' (1992: 168–9), or Hamann's, who turns 'to a truth in the inward being, to a wisdom in the secret heart' (1967: 175). However, for the most part, Socrates appears in Hemsterhuis' dialogues as someone constantly talking to others, questioning others, teaching others – that is, a philosopher *in dialogue*. Far from bolstering an image of philosophy as private and solitary, Socratic irony is primarily intended by Hemsterhuis as an ideal mode of comportment for reforming society and fostering a community of tactful subjects ('a special way of dealing person to person', as Kierkegaard will later phrase it [1992: 266]). Hemsterhuis does not use Socrates to escape society, but to mend it.

The other significant component of Hemsterhuis' understanding of Socratic irony is his commitment to *imposture* as a means to achieve this communal upbuilding of tactful subjects. Hemsterhuis returns to one of the original Greek meanings of irony as 'the intention to deceive', which, as Vlastos points out in a contemporary context (1991: 23), is 'so alien to our word for irony, but normal in its Greek ancestor'. Hemsterhuis' Socratic irony operates 'by a feint or dissimulation' (Gourinot 1986: 347), what Thrasymachus calls Socrates' 'habitual shamming' (Plato 1962: 337a; translation modified) – and, on this point, Hemsterhuis' forgeries are not far away at all from Hamann's 'pious frauds' (1967: 139) or Kierkegaard's pseudonymous indirection. This is evident in the lack of fit or disunity between the contents of the late Hemsterhuis' philosophical texts (which still promulgate the ideal of the optimum) and their ironic forms. There exists a formal dissonance which the reader experiences as one of Strauss's 'awakening stumbling blocks' (1988: 36); that is, the discrepancy functions as an initiation into an esoteric community: the ironic forgeries, fictions and deceits of the prefaces build up more suitable readers through deception. Hemsterhuis sets traps for the complacent reader and, by avoiding them, the alert reader learns and enters a community of 'insiders' for whom his 'gibberish' is intended. These readers begin to see the present from an alienated perspective, much like the Scythian of *Simon* who judges Greek art from outside; indeed, this Scythian exemplifies the very ideal reader that the late Hemsterhuis hopes to cultivate.

5. In sum, the prefaces to *Aristée* and *Simon* are ultimately about how to read the texts that follow; they encourage what Hemsterhuis sees as appropriate reading practices and warn against inappropriate ones. And, according to Hemsterhuis, to read his philosophy properly is to undergo a series of initiatory trials, to submit oneself to alienation and to become untimely. It is no surprise therefore that, on several occasions during the 1780s, Hemsterhuis reflects on the difficulty of reading. For example, in 1784, he complains of the contemporary 'evil of not being able to read' brought on by the 'style of our days . . . the style of the spirit of the century', and, in response, he calls for writers of 'the truly great style . . . addressed to high and divine souls' who can 'make one feel' and possess 'richness of imagination', 'ardour of intellect' and 'a wise and strong soul' (B 5.14, 64). Likewise, at the end of his life, Hemsterhuis bemoans 'finding myself so utterly misunderstood' by his new German audience and continues to Gallitzin,

> I have made some very profound reflections on what it is *to read* and *reading* and, moreover, on what it is to have claimed to have spoken intelligibly to the public. The result was that I returned to my old opinion that the talent of *reading* is infinitely rarer than that of *writing*. (B 10.20, 43)

Chapter Six

The Archaic and the Prophetic

There are wishes and desires which are so little suited to the conditions of our earthly life that we could surely suppose a state in which they gain powerful wings, take to some element by which they are lifted up and [discover] some island where they could come to rest.
                    Novalis, Hemsterhuis-Studien (1960–2006: 2.373)

§23 Dreams and Shadows

The previous chapter described ways in which the late Hemsterhuis holds the present and the past at a distance from each other, as well as the ways in which these disjunctions place the reader within a digressive loop, as it were, moving away from the present and into an alternative past. In other words, it showed how Hemsterhuis criticises the present by shifting to another era and to another tone, generating an outside from which to hold the present to account.

Such a holding-apart of the present and the past in a critical relationship is, however, but one of the time-images at work in the dialogues. In this final chapter, I want to elucidate three more such images, that is, three further configurations of modes of time in Hemsterhuis' dialogues. These are, it must be admitted, marginal images which exist at the fringes of Hemsterhuis' philosophy, which appear fleetingly within the dialogues and which are accordingly far less visible than Hemsterhuis' strategies of 'critique by anachronism'; nevertheless, all three do significant philosophical work and they can be enumerated as follows: (1) the condensation of the past into the present, so that the two forms of time come together in the shortest possible loop, instead of the longer loops described in the previous chapter; (2) the staging of a past world absolved from relation to the present, that is, a sterile, absolute world cut off from presentation; (3) the premonition of perpetual becoming into the future which exceeds any past or present moment. This third time-image forms the subject matter of §24; the present section traces the initial condensation-image and the world-image in Hemsterhuis' post-1775 dialogues.

1. One of the ways to begin outlining these three marginal time-images is through Hemsterhuis' scattered remarks on dreams, for he speaks of three kinds of dream experience that very roughly map onto the above three textual images.

Hemsterhuis returns to dreams again and again. Sleep, he claims, is a 'fundamentally different . . . manner of being' than being awake, and 'if I ask myself which of these two situations seems the most analogous, the most natural to the essence of the soul, the response must be that it is the state of sleep' (B 5.60, 210–11). What happens to the mind in sleep is, therefore, a privileged domain of philosophical investigation, since it can shed light more directly on the nature of the soul than any inquiry into the conscious mind. The mind is more itself (i.e., it reveals more of itself) in dreams – or, as Hemsterhuis himself puts it, the human subject is 'perhaps a more fundamental thinker in dreams than when awake' (B 9.67, 143; see also Pelckmans 1987: 40–2; Vieillard-Baron 1995: 168). This claim is already implicit in the *Lettre sur l'Homme*, which includes an extended section on 'comparing the clarity of the true day with that of the [dream] day just left behind', so as to exhibit the 'immense' difference between the two. Dreams are important to the philosopher because, Hemsterhuis there enumerates, of their discovery of 'geometrical truths that had been sought for in vain when awake', their moral improvement of the self ('in dreams, man is commonly more resolute and more determined than when awake') and their presentation of 'the perfect picture of [the subject's] moral character' (EE 1.92; OP 194). In dreams, the mind comes into its own, because it is no longer determined by anything external (i.e., by contingent encounters with foreign objects) and so all that remains are 'internal faculties in which reside the cause of the genuine passions and all the activity of the soul': the sense organs are inoperative, 'the imagination remains the same', the intellect 'has much to gain in sleep' and the moral organ 'shows itself more purely and distinctly in a state of sleep' (B 6.27, 86).[1] Hence, Hemsterhuis concludes, 'A tranquil and serious inquiry into the nature of dreams of all kinds would be the surest means, in my opinion, to arrive at a solid and luminous psychology, which in its turn

---

[1] This experience approaches the early Hemsterhuis' organological ideal of a state free from the mediation of the sense organs (see §19).

would illuminate many branches of physiology' (B 8.1, 13; see also B 6.38, 115; 8.11, 41).

It is for these reasons that, from the mid-1780s onwards, Hemsterhuis frequently promises Gallitzin 'a long letter on dreams' and 'burns with desire to finish my observations on dreams' (B 7.63, 172; 8.90, 212); however, the closest he gets to such a dedicated letter is a series of reflections penned in 1789 in response to a reading of J. C. Hennings' *Von den Träumen und Nachtwandlern*. After pointing out that 'sleep and waking supply the only case where one can compare the soul with itself, and therefore the only one where one can claim to find something in relation to its nature', he continues that Hennings

> fails to speak of two experiences [in dreams] which are without comparison the richest and most fecund – that is: (1) an experience that involves the absolute absurd, and (2) an experience which is as common as it is difficult to explain – that one sees in sleep everything present with its past, and everything exterior with its interior, just like when awake. For example, when I am awake and enter my house in which I have lived for many years, I do not only have the idea and the conviction of all the modifications of this house which are currently available to see, but also many of those that are not currently visible. I know that in a certain room there is a window missing, there is a broken board, that in a certain corner some tool is to be found, etc., and I recall on what occasion and at what time my house acquired these different modifications. In my dreams I will likewise enter a house, which often does not resemble any I have ever seen waking, and yet I will often have the same perfect knowledge of many of its unseen internal modifications and their history – and all this in exactly the same way as when awake. For the first of these two experiences I do not doubt that I know the cause. . . . But for the second experience I confess to you, my Diotima, that until now it has given me torture and that its cause seems to me of all the problems proposed the most difficult and perhaps the most important. However, I sometimes feel vaguely that this prodigious problem is not indissoluble, even for man. (B 9.3, 16)

In an earlier letter to Gallitzin, Hemsterhuis had also drawn attention to a third dream phenomenon – a kind of hypnotic state, a presentiment, or what Hemsterhuis himself calls 'the simulacrum of a truth'. This state reveals

> one of the most majestic properties of the soul that I know – that is, it often acts without conviction, it often uses organs that it does not know,

since the vehicles of sensation that are analogous to them have not yet arrived, and which therefore cannot yet give the soul a language or necessary signs, for it needs distinct and determinate ideas and sensations of this new, unknown category. (B 7.35, 100)

This third dream experience occupies a special position in Hemsterhuis' history of organs: it represents a moment when new organs appear before their time, as it were, and function in advance of themselves, thereby providing an anticipation of the very different experiences possible to human subjects in the future.

Hemsterhuis thus elucidates three types of dream in the above passages: there is an uncanny dream in which 'one sees in sleep everything present with its past' and about whose cause he is uncertain; there is an absurd dream, of whose cause he has long been sure; and there is a premonition dream, which fleetingly makes present future experiences. In the rest of this section, I want to use the first two types of dream to think about Hemsterhuis' philosophical writing, before turning to the third type in the final section of this book.

2. When we enter a familiar house awake, we are aware not only of what is currently being perceived, but also of past ideas associated with long-unoccupied rooms and long-hidden nooks. To enter a house when dreaming, Hemsterhuis continues, is to experience a hallucinatory repetition of this saturation of the present by the past. This is not a matter of specific memories (even false memories), but of an indeterminate sense of there being some unrecalled memory, a pure form of recollection without content that haunts the present moment. Instead of recalling actual ideas from the past, the subject is immersed in a virtual, unactualisable memory-atmosphere. The past obtrudes into the present as an indeterminate feeling of pastness. This type of dream thus has the structure of a *déjà vu*, according to which 'the image has to be present and past, still present and already past, at one and at the same time' (Deleuze 2013: 82). The present 'crystallises with its own virtual image [and] puts the actual image beside a kind of immediate, symmetrical, consecutive or even simultaneous double' of the past (2013: 71–2). And this contraction of the pure form of the past into the present is a very different configuration of time from those explored in the previous chapter. The actualised now is precisely not estranged from an absent past, but instead flooded with an all-too-present past, an overwhelming presence of the non-present.

The late Hemsterhuis is no surrealist: even if he does experiment with a practice that resembles automatic writing (see B 5.7, 39), he does not deliberately cultivate a dream-writing. Nevertheless, there exists a minor

Hemsterhuis who – as mentioned in earlier chapters – does make use of the ridiculous, insist on the barbarous and revel in gibberish. Niewöhner (1995: 395) even notes that Hemsterhuisian dreams and Hemsterhuisian writing rest on the same double operation: the 'fabulation of an object' by means of 'the misuse of signs in a figurative space'. It is for these sorts of reason that I am suggesting that Hemsterhuis' analysis of dreams provides an illuminating theoretical framework for explaining his more marginal strategies of philosophical communication.

In this case, Hemsterhuis' description of a dream experience of *déjà vu* corresponds to what Pelckmans (1987: 50) identifies as 'a strange sentiment of déjà-lu' experienced by the reader of Hemsterhuis' late texts. These texts are doubled: they evoke a lost past at the very moment they come to presence. Or to put it more bluntly still: the dialogues are saturated by a virtual (i.e., fictional) past that accompanies every idea or argument communicated to the reader. This 'déjà-lu' is, indeed, one of the fundamental structures of Hemsterhuis' entire philosophical project – to write simultaneously as modern and as ancient, to render his philosophy both past and present at the same time. Thus, for example, this 'sentiment of déjà-lu' is one name for the intended effect of Hemsterhuis' practice of the Platonic sublime (§8): each word in the dialogues is intended to express a precise modern concept and simultaneously evoke a non-conceptual feeling characteristic of the sentimental spirit – intended, that is, to mix 'simple sentiment' with 'the dry language of demonstration', or 'divine poetry with philosophy' (B 7.85, 235–6).[2] To put it another way, this is to write energetically in an age of precision (see §21), to 'speak Greek' by turning French against itself.[3]

---

[2] Even more precisely Hemsterhuis stages the tension between rationality and memory in an unpublished fragment: 'Memory is properly the tenacity with which ideas remain in place within the imagination. If the intellect is lively and prodigiously exercised, it will continually displace, recompose and decompose these ideas, and by this operation it will do all it must to destroy this tenacity and therefore [destroy] memory. However, we must remark that by the intellect's labour ideas are infinitely perfected, polished and finished off and imagination will present isolated ideas with much more precision, although they will have less of the reciprocity between them that they initially had on entry. It follows that the man who possesses the most intellect must ordinarily be he who possesses the least memory' (*IN* 166). In other words, memory is not reason and to appeal to it something very different is needed, in analogy to the model of the Platonic sublime.

[3] Hemsterhuis implicitly opposes himself to Diderot on this point: Diderot, according to Hemsterhuis (see §21), was also an energetic writer, but a disordered one, that is, his energy was 'dispersed or diffused elsewhere'. Thus, where contemporary commentators might attribute to Diderot's energetic writing a 'power to express simultaneously a multitude' of ideas (Sumi 1985: 20, 31; see also Ibrahim 2010: 81–2; Mortier 1997),

Hemsterhuis often speaks of the labour of contorting French in this way (e.g., B 9.26, 59–60). And Plato is once again his great model in this endeavour, for Plato likewise tried to contort Greek to make it speak geometrically. Hemsterhuis writes, 'The proudest, wisest, most agile and most delicate intellect that has ever existed on this earth had to work hard day and night to find' in Greek 'signs perfectly *adequate* to these surprising ideas'. And it is this labour of marrying the past and the present in which Hemsterhuis sees himself engaged: 'What then would be the work of a man who began to look for the same quantity of equivalent signs to Plato's primitive signs in a much poorer language!' (B 5.8, 43). This subversion of French's artificial perfections for an alien end (the energetic) is, moreover, something long recognised by Hemsterhuis' readers – as Georg Forster noted in 1791, 'All [Hemsterhuis'] work is written in French, but this language is reformed, as it were, to his own ends, for he forces his own style upon it' (1791: 1.707; see also Hammacher 1971: 6). Hemsterhuis' reform of language is an untimely one, 'forcing' French to speak the virtues of the past and the present at the same time.

Therefore, when Hemsterhuis speaks to Gallitzin of 'bathing' all of his demonstrations 'in tears of tenderness' (B 7.87, 240), he is precisely gesturing towards an experience comparable to that dream-state in which 'one sees in sleep everything present with its past'. The feeling of pastness must, the late Hemsterhuis insists, saturate his ideas as their virtual, hallucinatory double. Hemsterhuis wants his reader to enter his philosophical texts with the uncanny feeling of having been there before.

3. Hemsterhuis mentions the further category of dreams of 'the absurd' only in passing in his late letters, but this, however, is not the result of a lack of interest, but of having already exhausted their philosophical significance. His comment in the above letter that 'I do not doubt that I know the cause' of such a dream experience is an allusion back to the *Lettre sur l'Homme*'s distinction between ideas experienced in dreams, on the one hand, and ideas produced either by the presence of an external object or by voluntarily bringing a sign to mind, on the other (EE 1.92–3; OP 192–4). In the absurd dream, the mind is cut off from external reality – both cut off from the stimulus of sense impressions and cut off from the ordered reproduction of such reality by the conscious mind. Instead, the mind generates a series of ideas free from external determination which appear (to the conscious

---

Hemsterhuis disagrees, for it is only his own writing that can accomplish this: Diderot's is a failure to properly transmit linguistic energy to the reader, whereas Hemsterhuis considers himself able to capture this energy in an orderly way.

mind) as 'absurd'. This dream experience obeys the laws of the slumbering mind, rather than the waking laws of the empirically determined mind – an unconscious variant of the Spinozan ideal of a 'spiritual automaton'. The absurdity of such dreams is caused, according to Hemsterhuis, by their lack of relation to anything that has come to pass, their production of an independent dream world.

Moreover, Hemsterhuis associates this liberation of the mind into an absolute dream world with a specific experience of linguistic signs. The 'strange combinations' of ideas out of which these absurd dreams arise might, at first blush, seem to render them 'perfectly inexpressible', such that 'the richest imagination could not supply adequate signs to trace them' (B 6.27, 87). But, Hemsterhuis continues elsewhere, there is in fact a kind of language proper to these dreams – one in which there occurs 'a frightful disorder in the signs employed' (B 7.35, 100); that is, Hemsterhuis suggests that there is the possibility of expressing absurd dreams in some way – through disorder, through a derangement of semiotic norms and through a flouting of linguistic good taste. To articulate dreams is, once again, to make one's language 'barbarous'.

A correspondence between the above absolute dream world and Hemsterhuisian writing practices is further suggested by Jean Paul's remarks on Hemsterhuis in his 1804 *Vorschule der Ästhetik*. Jean Paul initially subjects Hemsterhuis' elaboration of an aesthetic optimum to criticism (1973: 24; see also Trop 2022: 42), before then turning to the later work and supplementing this critique with the following comments:

> [The stylist] digs only for bodies, not for spirits. [But] the poetic soul shows itself, like ours, only to the whole body, not in the single toes and fingers it animates, which a collector of specimens would tear off and hold out to view with the words: See how the spider's leg is twitching! ... There can be philosophic works, like some by Hemsterhuis and Lessing, which inspire us with philosophical spirit without disposing their matter in separate philosophical paragraphs. (1973: 42)

The comparison to Lessing builds on a contrast that had already been presented a few pages earlier:

> Even [Lessing's] most ingenious conceptions had to be confined in a coffin of Wolffian formulas. Without, of course, being like Plato, Leibniz, or Hemsterhuis, the creator of a philosophical world, he was nevertheless the prophetic son of a creator. (1973: 33)

Hemsterhuis creates 'a philosophical world'. And this, according to Jean Paul, is a matter of imbuing 'the spirit of a whole book' (1973: 15) with a unity and singularity that cannot be analysed into parts. The Greek tone of Hemsterhuis' dialogues is, he implies, located in the textual whole and cannot be found in any discrete paragraph, particular allusion or syllogistic chain. Of course, such an analysis retrospectively imposes romantic categories back onto Hemsterhuis' corpus: for one, Hemsterhuis is very clear that the minutiae of his texts – the specific allusions and discrete details – matter too. Thus, while the late Hemsterhuis does, in a similar vein to Jean Paul, criticise 'the grammarian-philologists' who dissect the sublime instead of feeling it (B 7.96, 257), he is equally critical of the kind of polemic for holism and against erudition that Jean Paul articulates when, for example, he evaluates Goethe's *Iphigenie auf Tauris*. As rehearsed in §3, Goethe wrongly prioritises pure tact for the Greek past over a corresponding mastery of antiquarian detail – and so presumably, by extension, does Jean Paul. So, while 'the editor' to Hemsterhuis' prefaces does possess a passing resemblance to Jean Paul's 'stylicist', a fundamental difference separates them: according to Hemsterhuis, the editor's viewpoint is not incorrect, but merely one-sided.

Nevertheless, there is still one feature of Jean Paul's remarks that I wish to recover, for it does illuminate something of Hemsterhuis' writing strategies. And that is his invocation of the concept of philosophical worlds, which I want to suggest exist cut off from temporal progress in much the same way as Hemsterhuis' 'absurd' dream experience exists cut off from the external world. This gets at a key feature of the dialogues: each of them takes place in the same fictional world which exceeds them and, indeed, exceeds any particular allusion to people, places or events. All the texts can offer is a series of snapshots of this fictional background out of which characters and arguments temporarily protrude. It is to this background that readers refer when they speak of the 'Athenian *couleur locale*' (Moenkemeyer 1975: 94), 'archaeological décor' (Pelckmans 1987: 18) or 'Greek milieu' (Hammacher 1995b: 407) of the dialogues – an anachronistic atmosphere or 'imaginary' which does not directly contribute to the philosophical arguments, but which is still *at work*. Specifically, this background functions as the 'tone' or 'spirit' of the work, which can now be more precisely defined as a textual, unthematised horizon within which and out of which the arguments emerge. Hemsterhuis' philosophical world is a virtual structure of his texts – unactualisable and therefore resistant to optimal form.

A passage from *Alexis* alludes to the significance of this virtual horizon (without, of course, itself being able to name it directly). At the end of Hypsicles' story of a lost archaic golden age, Alexis responds,

I confess to you that the priest's speech, along with your reflections, have surprised and shaken me. Yes, I believe it in a certain way, but [a way] which is difficult to express. – I believe in his golden age in his speech, as I would believe in the existence of a body which I had never seen, seeing only the shape of its well-defined shadow. (*EE* 2.138; *OP* 620)

Hypsicles' golden age is intended to suggest an analogy to the reader, which runs something like as follows:

golden age : Alexis :: fictional Athens : eighteenth-century reader

The archaic nature of the golden age stands in relation to Alexis' fictional viewpoint in much the same way as the world of Hemsterhuis' dialogues is meant to stand in relation to its readers' viewpoint. To put it another way: the golden age itself is something radically 'past' not just for Hemsterhuis' readers, but for the Greek characters of the dialogues themselves. It exists as *doubly past* from the perspective of the eighteenth-century present and, as a consequence, its relation to the present can only be indirect.

Such is the significance of Alexis' 'shadow': the golden age cannot be directly perceived but can only be inferred from its 'shadow'. What matters, Alexis continues, is not 'whether [the storyteller] gives true shadows of true things', nor even whether such a shadow 'could be but a production of art'; rather, its function – as either fact or fiction, original or fake – is to make manifest something that is directly unrepresentable (*EE* 2.138; *OP* 620). Only the shadow of the golden age is accessible to present-day thinking, that is, it is an archaic past that cannot itself come to consciousness, for only its effects are actual. It is unverifiable, but with real effects. Moreover, this type of phenomenon elsewhere fascinates Hemsterhuis: *Sophyle* describes magnetic 'iron filings', whose properties are revealed only by their 'emissions' as well as an invisible 'immense block of the purest crystal', which becomes perceptible only when another block collides with it. In both these cases, it is a matter of 'knowing how an essence, which has no analogy at all to our organs' can appear to the subject through effects 'that do have an analogy to our organs' (*EE* 2.53–4, 59; *OP* 360, 364, 378). This is, indeed, the very structure by which Hemsterhuis regularly speaks of mind–body interaction. And what I am suggesting is that the archaic narratives (the discursive 'shadows') of Hemsterhuis' dialogues are the textual equivalents of these effects. They are the traces that allow one to make inferences to eras, organs and forms of experience that are not accessible to the present. As a result, these archaic narratives play a hugely significant role in Hemsterhuis' development of an organological style: by way of their effects, they allude to other forms of existence, other constitutions of the human and thus other visions of knowing than what can currently be represented. Hemsterhuis thus preserves the *difference* of past modes of life (and consequently the plasticity of human and natural structures).

The golden age is an archaic virtual world. This archaic world is thus absolved of all direct relation to the present and to the actual – as Lacoue-Labarthe and Nancy helpfully gloss, the past and the present 'effectuate no exchange' between past and present, but instead take on the form of 'the *pastness* of an impossible distribution . . . the figure of an impossible accord' (1975: 148). This is why such worlds are analogous to the absurd dream experience Hemsterhuis relates: they evoke a 'pastness' which remains withdrawn, which does not touch the present directly and so which exists as a self-sufficient, sterile absolute, independent of other modes of time. Hemsterhuis creates a world that, in part, differentiates itself from the present by means of resolute *indifference* to that present. Or, more prosaically, in Grucker's words, 'Reading Hemsterhuis' writings where everything breathes in antiquity and nothing seems to betray the traces of the eighteenth century, one could believe that they are completely foreign to the movement of ideas and intellectual struggles of his epoch' (1866: 269). The past of Hemsterhuis' archaic narratives does not open directly onto the now but remains closed off – as 'text-asylums', discursive performances of a Rousseauean flight into isolation (see Philipsen 1992: 73–8).

Moreover, this withdrawal from any relation to the present is discernible not just in Hemsterhuis' texts, but in his mode of living as well – he constructs asylums, sheltered from the demands of the present. Niethuis (the country estate at which his friendship with Gallitzin was forged) is the most obvious example: it comes to signify a retreat within which Gallitzin and Hemsterhuis worked to protect her children against the corruptions of eighteenth-century thinking. Jacobi thus describes its purpose as follows:

> The princess believed she must isolate her children from the century in which they lived, so as to give them the habits and principles of a completely different epoch and give them thus the power to one day force humanity to take its first steps towards the amelioration of its current state. (Quoted in Brachin 1952: 358)

In these safe refuges – whether real or textual – the reader-pupil is meant to learn 'a tone of thinking' (B 2.44, 98) incommensurable with the present and, in so doing, commence an education in becoming untimely.

§24 In the Style of Hope

On 4 October 1779, Hemsterhuis commences a playful letter to Gallitzin with reference to a lottery in The Hague they had recently been playing. Hemsterhuis confesses to his desire to keep on playing notwithstanding their previous losses ('when we lose, we must keep on going to win'), and continues,

> Who knows? Perhaps! Let's see! This is not the style of geometry, it's that of hope. Hope! you most precious gift of the heavens – when I think of you, I wish to know your source. [Hope] is not the opposite of fear. Fear always has some determinate object. Hope can be vague and smile at the whole universe. It is a sensation which derives from the very nature of the soul. It is to souls what embalming chemicals are to the body: they preserve them from putrefaction. (B 2.49, 128)

Although the tone of Hemsterhuis' remarks may be flippant, what he writes of hope cuts to the core of his late philosophy. And I want to argue that some of this late philosophy is written not in the style of geometry, but in the style of hope, that is, as an attempt to orient the reader optimistically towards the future and ultimately towards eternity. This section therefore transitions from the indicative mood of Hemsterhuis' early writings and the subjunctive mood of his myths and fictions to an optative mood in which he speaks of the future: I suggest, in fact, that while Hemsterhuis may continually write of the past, his real interest is in the future. He writes so much about origins in order to open up alternative futures to his readers.

1. *Aristée*'s invocation of sentimental certainty (§7) is left underdetermined in the dialogue itself: further inquiry into the precise nature of this feeling was needed. And so, in the mid-1780s, Hemsterhuis pursued the idea that sentimental certainty is not a unitary category, but rather that there are multiple types of sentimental certainties, which he then set about classifying. They can, for instance, be classified according to the 'character' of the knowing subject (B 7.3, 19) or whether the truth in question is experienced directly or merely 'read or recounted' (B 4.60, 163). Primarily, however, what accounts for differences between sentimental certainties is the temporality of the truth in question: the subject feels differently 'according to the different ways the past, present and future affect them' (B 7.3, 19; see also *IN* 166). Hence, Hemsterhuis remarks that, when 'recalling a past good', he

himself experiences 'extraordinary charms' absent from his considerations of past or future pleasures, and concludes, there is always 'a singular and very great difference between the tone of the pleasure of a past good that one recalls, the tone of the pleasure of a present good that one enjoys and that of the pleasure of a future good for which one hopes' (B 7.3, 19–20). The difference between sentimental convictions is therefore a matter of 'tone', and elsewhere Hemsterhuis will expand on this:

> The sensation of past pleasure or happiness, the sensation of a present pleasure or happiness and the sensation of a future pleasure or happiness are three extremely agreeable sensations, of course, but the nature, tone or colour of these three sensations are prodigiously different, and so much so that one can compare them as little as one can compare the audible to the visible, or the visible to the moral . . . these differences of which I speak are not differences of energy, nor of degree of intensity, but a total difference of nature, tone, colour, etc. (B 2.45, 105)

Feelings for the past, for the present and for the future are irreducible to each other, because they are coloured by very different tones. And my task is to describe the specific 'tone' of future truths in contrast to the present truths and past truths already described above. As Hemsterhuis himself puts it, 'Let us look at future truths, [for] man is capable of sensations of future truths, accompanied not by belief, but by the most intimate conviction' (B 7.60, 159–60; see also Melica 2004: 29).

This conviction accompanying future truths is ultimately a matter of presentiment and prophecy. Hemsterhuis often speaks satirically in his correspondence of his 'famous talent for prophecies', his 'quality as physician-prophet' and his tendency 'to act the prophet a little' (B 9.71, 153; 7.97, 258; 10.84, 182; see also Mähl 1994: 271). And there is more to such statements than mere self-ironisation, for he is not afraid to speculate about the future in his philosophical works: *Simon*, for instance – via the character of Diotima – has much to say about novel organological futures. On occasion, Hemsterhuis speaks in a prophetic voice.

And this tendency 'to act the prophet a little' is grounded in a psychological analysis of the figure of the prophet.[4] That is, Hemsterhuis speaks of how prophetic 'talent' is developed by way of cultivating 'those rare and

---

[4] Generally, Hemsterhuis will claim that the source of 'having a presentiment' or knowing the future, which 'pertains to a higher principle', 'has been the object of my investigations for a long time' (B 7.65, 179).

sublime moments when the soul – completely absorbed in its own joys – renders the imagination inactive and stops it from adding to the present, so as to glimpse a richer and more embellished future' (EE 2.91; OP 474). Likewise, the dream experience of presentiment described in §23 supplies 'ideas and sensations of [a] new, unknown category' (B 7.35, 100). And, elsewhere in correspondence with Gallitzin, Hemsterhuis writes of souls that are so 'healthy, rich and robust . . . that they acquire the force to be able to penetrate into their own essence, develop their faculties, have a real presentiment of a future category, and to sow and harvest in this life the nourishment that belongs to another state' (B 5.12, 56). Hemsterhuis seriously countenances the possibility of intuiting the future when the mind is in a state in which the sense organs become inoperative, the imagination 'inactive' and the mind withdraws into itself – whether in sleep, in self-absorption or in introspection. This results in a loss of empirical sensation and what remains is a condensation of the mind's faculties that owes nothing to the external world. In such a state, the mind cuts itself off from 'any concern with the present' and achieves a kind of ataraxia (corresponding to the text-asylums invoked in §23). Immersed in itself, it becomes absolute and conducive to presentiment, that is, to a feeling for the future.

To put it another way, while the subject might 'lack the data' from external perception to warrant any certainty about future states of affairs and 'the state of men in future worlds', data is forthcoming *from within*. Hemsterhuis tells Gallitzin,

> I am persuaded that we carry some of this data in our own breast, which can be accessed through some happy accident or through hard work. I tell you truly, my Diotima, I have moments when I feel such data ready to appear, just as you feel a geometric truth long before you have the conviction that the intellect gives. Man, who has made such progress in physics, is still a child in psychology and metaphysics. Let him enter into himself, let him experiment tranquilly on all that happens within him, on his own sensations, let him combine them, and you will see whether a multitude of such data does not appear. (B 3.87, 202)

The precise structure of this internal conviction is illuminated by the analogy Hemsterhuis gives in the above passage – that of feeling the conclusion to a geometrical proof long before discursive certainty is forthcoming. The idea recalls the paradox of inquiry from Book X of Augustine's *Confessions*: an indeterminate yet immediate anticipation of a truth that is yet to be discursively acknowledged. Certainty about future truths is to be defined as *conviction in advance*.[5]

This is once more a matter of tact, of sensing analogies with the future. Tact has already played a number of roles in my reconstruction of Hemsterhuis' philosophy as an activity of the intellect leaping synchronously from idea to idea. This is 'optimal' tact: the quicker the intellect makes these leaps, the quicker an idea of the whole is formed. Tact has named precisely the swift and flexible form of judgement that Hemsterhuis idealises in his early work: it helps bring all ideas, no matter how disparate, into instantaneous coexistence. Yet, in Hemsterhuis' later philosophy, tact goes on to additionally designate a mental operation distinct from the workings of the intellect as well as all the other faculties (considered individually). Tact still jumps between ideas to discover new *rapports*, but it now does so *in advance* of the intellect. It is pre-rational, the capacity to discern a truth before reasoning catches up. In his *Hemsterhuis-Studien* Novalis calls this 'tact in the extraordinary sense' (1960–2006: 2.373) as opposed to the tact of 'infinitely rapid reasoning' (B 7.37, 104). And Hemsterhuis himself opposes pre-rational tact to 'analysis and synthesis', as well as to 'reasoning and geometry', and, instead, he associates it with 'sentiment' and the 'foreseeing' or 'presentiment' of a truth (B 4.81, 213; 7.57, 151; 7.65, 179). For the Hemsterhuis of the 1780s, 'tact in the extraordinary sense' has more to do with good sense, enthusiasm, the condensation of the imagination and moral intuition than discursive reasoning (e.g., B 8.51, 119; 10.1, 13). It is for this reason that, after writing *Alexis*, he becomes increasingly interested in the distinctive workings of this kind of tact and promises Gallitzin 'a little treatise on tact', for, he continues, it is 'the faculty which makes men feel God in his works: it is the faculty of true philosophers' (B 5.98, 305; 10.88, 148). Moreover, this turn to pre-rational tact precisely marks a point in Hemsterhuis' philosophical

---

[5] Moreover, just as in *Aristée* Hemsterhuis had used the idea of the 'sigh' to describe the communication of sentimental certainty (*EE* 2.92; *OP* 476–8), so too, in correspondence with Gallitzin, the sigh functions as the paradigm for communicating conviction in advance. He laments that 'until the present, a *sigh* has been a very vague and indeterminate sign for us' and insufficient attention has been paid to sighs of hope, of fear, of desire and of 'repose in the breast of the divinity'. He goes on to foretell a future 'science of sighs', which will allow them to take their place alongside other linguistic signs as bearers of determinate meanings: 'In terms of the progressive movement of the perfectibility of man, there is the sense that with time the sigh, the laugh, the cry, etc., will be specified and by this means enrich the treasure of its signs in a prodigious way' (B 7.100, 267–9). The communication of future truths rests partly on ongoing scientific work in gradually transforming the sigh into a linguistically viable sign.

trajectory where he goes beyond the ideal of the harmony of the faculties to that of their union. And this is because 'tact in the extraordinary sense' presupposes, according to Hemsterhuis, not just one or two faculties working in tandem and not even the harmonious interplay of all the faculties together, but a successful *fusing* of these faculties into one. Tact, he writes, is 'the instantaneous effect of a rapid operation of all our faculties together' (B 5.92, 284–5) and, in this vein, he distinguishes between the subject of discursive reasoning who is merely 'the number 4, a collection of 4 unities' (i.e., she possesses the four distinct faculties of intellect, imagination, the velleity and the moral organ) and 'the man of tact [who] is the quaternity, the true result of a perfect composition' (B 5.71, 240).[6] This is the context for Hemsterhuis' introduction of the concept of personality into *Alexis* (EE 2.131; OP 600): with the advent of 'tact in the extraordinary sense' comes a shift away from treating the subject in terms of interacting faculties and towards a principle of their unity, that is, personality, which acts as the ground for the late Hemsterhuis' model for 'the positive epiphany of a new truth' that occurs in advance of reason (Cahen-Maurel 2017: 263).

2. The above turn to this model of pre-rational epiphany in Hemsterhuis' epistemology occurs in *Alexis* alongside a corresponding thematisation of the principle of perfectibility. Just as 'tact in the extraordinary sense' moves in advance of reason, so too 'the cries of my perfectibility always go ahead of me' (B 11.39, 48) and call the subject ever forwards. What *Alexis* attempts to communicate is a human 'inclination', specifically an 'inclination towards perfection and happiness' (B 6.9, 38). This inclination is a virtual power that cannot be reduced to its expression in any specific moment in time, but which always exceeds the present instant. The problem of communication at stake in *Alexis* is a throwback to Mnesarchus' problem in *Simon*, that is, how to express time in art (§20). According to the principle of perfectibility, the human is always pushing *beyond*, always surpassing the present – in Hemsterhuis' own words, 'there is in the nature of man a principle of perfectibility which appears to have no limit' and to represent it would be to represent 'the progress of this principle' (B 3.86, 200). At stake, therefore, is a writing of philosophy that captures the inexorable forward momentum of the human subject through history and that, therefore, relativises all past and present instantiations of this principle as but one stepping-stone towards something better.

---

[6] See Hemsterhuis' account of the conceptual distinction between a unity and an aggregate in B 8.15, 48.

The communication of perfectibility is thus, in part, a problem of communicating a virtual tendency (as summarised in Hemsterhuis' question, 'How do you [depict] in the sleeping lion ... the vigour and vehemence of its activity?' [EE 2.107; OP 524]), but it is also a problem of making another subject discern a principle that is too intimate to be communicated – as briefly described in §14. Perfectibility is unshareable, for it resides 'within the individual, constituted by internal forces' and so it 'is absolutely impossible that one individual can give it to another' (B 5.27, 110). Each must work on their own principle, for perfectibility is a 'singular principle that adheres to [man's] nature' [B 8.1, 14]) and, as such, is too intimate, too indeterminate, too essential to be articulated in discourse. No direct communication is possible.

It is to solve these kinds of problems that Hemsterhuis turns to 'the style of hope' in his final writings. Where direct statements fail to communicate perfectibility, a hopeful tone succeeds in conveying some of its movement. Hope is a central concept for the late Hemsterhuis: it 'derives from the nature of the soul itself' (B 2.49, 128) as 'an indestructible instinct that pertains to essence' (B 8.55, 128), it is linked to prophecy (B 3.107, 241) and it is always to be found when the principle of perfectibility is at work. Hope is indeed the name for the affect that corresponds to the workings of such perfectibility, since it, too, 'has for its goal the absolute, although indeterminate best' (EE 2.144; OP 636) and it, too, expresses 'the great indeterminate principle which agitates' the human (EE 2.145; OP 638). Hope designates the pull of the soul towards the better, 'the natural progress of the soul that proceeds always ahead of us into eternity' (B 11.143, 134).

Hemsterhuis conveys this hopeful tone in *Alexis* by telling stories – or, more precisely, by retelling Hesiod's stories. Hypsicles' narrative of the golden age is intended to communicate to the reader, among other things, an indeterminate sense of momentum towards a future good. What seems at first blush to be a pessimistic story about an archaic past gone wrong (i.e., lost through lunar catastrophe) turns out to be a narrative about how things can be different and about how the present is transitory. It therefore opens up the possibility of a better future, emphasising the contingencies and impermanence of any settled state. Hemsterhuis redeploys Hesiod's material to attack the fallacy of the ephemeral: everything, it implies, is in transition and 'man is merely a bird of passage' (WW 456; IN 61). 'The golden age of Hesiod and Hypsicles' in which 'man was absolutely perfect' is mutable (EE 2.145; OP 640) and what really matters is not Hypsicles' presentation of the golden age itself, but the fact that human and natural history is subject to a 'great catastrophe of the globe' both in the past and in the future (*EE* 2.145; *OP* 642). The revolutions that human history has already undergone show that such revolutions are again possible: if they have happened before, they can again. There is the suggestion of the future possibility of a third age, beyond gold or silver, in which the subject will gain a 'happy simplicity' and 'recognise the homogeneity of man's eternal existence' (*EE* 2.146; *OP* 642).

Notably, when first speaking to Gallitzin of his study of Hesiod in November 1780 and rehearsing the material that would go on to comprise *Alexis*, Hemsterhuis makes some of these points explicit. He writes,

> Here is what follows [from Hesiod's myth], my Diotima. If man, who is only an animal on earth, has in him a principle which by his nature has already led him infinitely beyond the golden age, that is, beyond his happiness and his perfection as an inhabitant of the earth, and even into an absurd state in comparison to the state which pertains to man as animal, it is completely evident that the existence of man on this earth is only transitory and that by his nature he belongs to something else entirely. (B 3.86, 200–1)

Perfectibility has a future as well as a past. Hemsterhuis goes on to comment that, first, the invocation of an archaic past is never reactionary, for 'it is impossible for man to ever return to this golden age of Hesiod'; that, secondly, narratives of the golden age help readers orient their future better and 'give a constant direction to the eccentric progress of his perfectibility'; and that, thirdly, the present is not enough, for 'the perfectibility of man, which has no limits in his nature, finds itself in imperfection' and one must postulate a future 'golden age infinitely superior to those of the poets' (B 3.86, 200–1). Hypsicles' story about a distant past is meant as consolation for a bright future.

The closing lines of *Simon* say something similar. Diotima recovers an archaic past ('the remotest of times') that has been lost ('man has not been able to keep the Goddess's precious gift in its entirety') (*EE* 2.116; *OP* 554). Nevertheless, the point of the story is that such a golden age still exists *in germ*: the human subject 'has conserved the germ of [this blessed state] which, when cultivated with care, produces the same fruit' (*EE* 2.116; *OP* 554). The golden age endures virtually, even in the present, thereby opening up once more a perspective of radical transformation: more is possible and will always be possible. In sum, Hesiod serves as one of the late Hemsterhuis' more significant models for philosophical style because his myths provide the material for philosophising in the style of hope, for articulating an innate dynamic, yet indeterminate tendency towards the better. Hesiod helps Hemsterhuis find the suitable way of talking about a past that is ultimately about the future.

3. While these stories indirectly provoke the reader to reflect on a bright future, there are additionally exceptional, extraordinary moments at the edges of the dialogues when the future is directly presented, moments when figures of prophetic authority speak freely.[7] The Diotima of *Simon* is exemplary: she talks of a very different future inhabited by very different humans who 'appear higher than the rest of mortals' by possessing an infinite number of sense organs that correspond to the infinite faces of the universe. For these future humans, 'new organs manifest themselves', 'the gap which separates the visible from the audible is filled with other sensations' and so 'all sensations are linked and together form one'; that is, the human subject 'becomes all organ'. Such a perfect individual 'sees the universe . . . in the manner of the Gods' (*EE* 2.121; *OP* 570–2). At these moments in Hemsterhuis' dialogues, the future comes to presence.

Therefore, sometimes Hemsterhuis overcomes any residual reticence he might retain for conjectural philosophy and describes the future mythically. Diotima does something unique in Hemsterhuis' philosophical world: she moves freely between past, present and future ages, weaving together archaic golden ages, elenchus and prophecy, or recollection, analysis and hope. What the reader experiences at such moments is the making-present of all times, the constitution of a new kind of optimum in which the present no longer predominates. Diotima exemplifies an *omnitemporal optimum*, inhabiting all epochs equally and indifferently, as Hemsterhuis himself aspires to do (see §5). The ideal of the optimum reappears in these prophetic moments as a meta-temporal, epoch-indifferent ideal; it now takes on the very structure of eternity.[8]

Hemsterhuis mentions this ideal of an omnitemporal optimum – or 'absolute optimum' (*B* 9.21, 59) – in his late letters, designating it the 'ideal

---

[7] That is, while Ayrault (1961: 1.489: see also Moenkemeyer 1975: 85) is generally right that Hemsterhuis' mysticism 'is insinuated rather than affirmed', these moments are the exception.

[8] Nevertheless, Socrates puts Diotima's achievement of an omnitemporal optimum somewhat into question by reducing Diotima to someone 'for whom the future is present' (*EE* 2.113; *OP* 548), that is, who ultimately reasserts the priority of the present. He does so, of course, from the perspective of a subject limited by the current state of organs, but nevertheless gestures towards the difficulty of maintaining a stable distinction between an optimum of the present and an optimum of eternity.

coexistence' produced by 'a faculty of the soul by which it can link the past, present, and future ... and make a whole' (B 2.21, 34). This faculty is the preserve of an 'eternal genius' who rises above 'the successiveness and divisibility of that relative [structure] we call time' and who thereby experiences 'the absolute unity of duration' and 'the identity of the I in all time' (B 9.28, 66; 9.18, 42).[9] Whereas the early Hemsterhuis' optimum of the present was 'disengaged from all idea of succession' through its refusal of temporal becoming and its reduction of the past and the future to the present, this late optimum encompasses the past, the present and the future as moments of eternity – no privilege is given to the present moment. The view-from-nowhere to which the geometrical method aspires (§4) makes a reappearance in a mystic key, as an experience of 'the eternal presence of duration and the true and too rare sensation *of really being*' (B 8.9, 35; see also B 3.61, 148). And this is ultimately what geometrical method means for Hemsterhuis – a way of describing reality *sub specie aeternitatis* without any commitment to a specific time or place; the geometrical method guarantees a neutrality that allows the philosopher to be everywhere and nowhere at the same time.

In one of his final letters to Gallitzin, Hemsterhuis makes explicit precisely the above distinction between the optimum of his early work, tied to a particular present – 'the expression of coexistence, either in place or time, [that] belongs only to time and place' – and an 'absolute optimum' structured around 'the unities of infinite space or eternal duration'. 'The word coexistence', he continues, strictly 'belongs to our present category alone', whereas the second optimum transcends any reliance on particular times and places and refuses to tie the past, the present and the future to them; instead, it transforms them into components of an eternal unity (B 9.33, 76). This opposition between the optimum of the present and the optimum of eternity is therefore one way to make sense of the turn in Hemsterhuis' thinking before and after 1775. The former ideal is dominant in the aesthetic, social and scientific ideals of the early letters, but the latter informs *Simon* and *Alexis*: it comprehends the entire system of times without

---

[9] Presupposed here is a metaphysical model of the relation between time and eternity, with 'duration' naming the quasi-chronological structure of eternity, as it were. That is, the late Hemsterhuis is close to Spinoza (and even may have had 'Spinoza's observations in mind') in opposing 'the majesty of duration' as a modality of 'eternal presence' to the dispersal, discontentment and disfiguration of temporal life (B 7.101, 270; Moretto 2005: 72–4). In this life, the subject stands between time and eternity – 'a human amphiboly swimming in duration and crawling in time' (B 9.33, 77; see also IN 178). It is important to stress, however, that Hemsterhuis' early work does not use 'duration' in this way (see EE 1.69; OP 120).

dissolving it, encompassing all ages – all perihelia – without nullifying their differences.

One of the goals of Hemsterhuisian philosophy is therefore to create subjects (readers) who can take up this eternal view-from-nowhere, comprehend all times and so experience 'a perfect conviction we can rarely enjoy in this life' which 'can take place only at moments when the soul is . . . [in] its natural state, not troubled by its attachment to the physical, by the disorders brought on by the moon, or by the stupidities which have followed from it' (B 5.59, 208). As he writes to Fürstenberg, this 'perfect conviction' is vouchsafed only to a few: 'I speak of people like Diotima, you and me, and a few others that resemble us, who not only believe, but have a sensation of an existence which cannot end' (B 12.72, 96). These are 'extraordinary souls', prone to 'internal sublime exaltations in which the physical plays no part', who 'reach this eternal present and touch it for some instants' and, by doing so, 'feel the prodigious difference between this eternal present and the past, present or future of this life' (B 7.101, 269–70). More generally, at its margins, Hemsterhuis' work practises a prophetic plasticity, skips between eras and makes itself equally at home in ancient Athens, contemporary Paris and the 'unknown lands' of the future. At such moments, Hemsterhuis is a writer of both the *archē* and the *eschaton*, a philosopher whose texts are equally imbued with the virtues of Greek sentiment, modern geometrical analysis and prophetic hope. At such moments, his texts present what lies *beyond the present*.

Conclusion

Four Characters in Search of a Philosophy

Much of this book has been dedicated to enumerating the various stylistic techniques deployed by Hemsterhuis in the wake of his poetic turn, as well as supplying some of his reasons for using them. There are many different ways such a list could be arranged. In this book, I have grouped these writing techniques and their justifications into three distinct, if interrelated studies of Hemsterhuis' post-1775 style. The first turned on his Platonism – that is, Hemsterhuis considers himself to be emulating Plato in his recourse to dialogue, the sublime and the sentimental, as well as in writing in a way that partakes of both analysis and poetry at the same time. The second study focused on Hemsterhuis' organology (a project that intervened in contemporaneous debates over perfectibility, fibre theory and the historicity of nature) as the ground for his late style, that is, for a style which is structured by analogic predication, which thematises plasticity and which uses the mythic and the figural to situate the reader in a revolutionary 'organic' history. The third study then interpreted Hemsterhuis' writing techniques through the lens of 'time-images'. It read the dialogues as a series of attempts to make temporality directly perceptible through irony, anachronism, genealogy, philosophical worlds, energetic language and a style of hope. I suggested that each of these devices exhibits a different configuration of the past, present and future in response to the twin orienting demands to become untimely and to write plastically.

1. Other taxonomies of Hemsterhuis' poetic turn are possible. For example, one might categorise it according to publications, since each of the four dialogues – *Sophyle*, *Aristée*, *Simon* and *Alexis* – exhibits these various stylistic devices in different combinations and for different ends. *Sophyle* contains less of the complex ironies of the later dialogues and, instead, is written in a way to foreground the popular and pedagogical functions of the dialogue form: it renders its philosophical arguments as accessible as possible to the

reader. Much like the *Meno*, the dialogue invokes a Socratic philosophy of good sense innate within everyone. *Aristée*, on the contrary, begins with a moment of obfuscation – a preface that constructs an elaborate fictional world, which is mirrored in Diocles' later invocation of the category of sentimental certainty and a mythic mode for communicating such a feeling. This shift from the popular to the esoteric is accelerated in *Simon*: it is a dialogue of indirection, asides and flamboyant set-pieces in which Hemsterhuis' distinctive practice of irony is worked out most fully. Finally, *Alexis* returns to a more austere structure, free from some of the more intricate fictions that frame *Aristée* and *Simon* but, in their place, a more direct confrontation with the poetry–philosophy relation takes place in both the content and the form of the dialogue. That is, the enthusiasm which, according to Diocles, grounds philosophical creativity is performed in a series of half-mythic, half-scientific attempts at narrating perfectibility.

Other taxonomies of Hemsterhuis' writing strategies are equally possible. One might catalogue them in terms of their effect on the reader: some devices are intended to alienate the reader (e.g., irony, anachronism, philological jokes); some are intended to educate the reader (e.g., myth, dialogue, accessible language); some are intended to energise the reader (e.g., the appeal to sentiment, a non-modern tone); and some are intended to historicise the reader's philosophical commitments (e.g., stories from an archaic past, prophecies). One might also categorise these same strategies in terms of the competing tendencies which pull Hemsterhuis' philosophy in different directions: there is the tendency to the popular and the tendency to the esoteric; the tendency to accessibility and the tendency to gibberish; the tendency to narrate the emergence of the present out of the past and the tendency to refuse any relation between past and present; the tendency to energetic language and the tendency to geometrically precise language – and, most generally, the tendency to analysis and the tendency to poetry.

Perhaps most interesting might be a taxonomy of Hemsterhuis' style according to dialogic personae. The characters of Hemsterhuis' late dialogues exemplify distinct features of his philosophical project – hence, their various encounters, arguments, alliances and conversions in these dialogues can be taken as a metaphilosophical commentary on the dynamics of his own thinking. This is an idea touched on in §7 with respect to Bakhtin's proposal that 'the heroes of the dialogue are ideologists' (1984: 111), that characters embody ideas not just in what they say, but in their comportment, tone and backstories. The dialogues are 'about' the social interactions of people committed to distinctive ways of life.

2. There are four personae (or 'ideologists') particularly worthy of note in the fictional world of the late dialogues: Socrates, Diotima, Hypsicles and 'the editor' of the prefaces to Aristée and Simon.

It has become clear that Hemsterhuis' Socrates exemplifies the ideal for the human subject *as currently constituted*. He is an ideal human, an ideal philosopher, an ideal moral agent, an ideal teacher and an ideal ironist. And this is because he possesses that harmony of the organs which is, for Hemsterhuis, a staging post on the way to virtue, wisdom and self-transcendence. Hemsterhuis' Socrates shows the reader how to perfect herself, how to make the most of her innate principle of perfectibility – both through his own example and through his pedagogical commitment to provoking all humans without exception into realising this perfectibility. And Socrates achieved this, according to Hemsterhuis, by means of playful conversation, ironic *meiosis* and *auxesis* and the refusal of dogmatic assertion.

The Diotima of *Simon*, on the contrary, plays the role of dogmatic foil to Socrates' irony. She is not shy of taking up a position of authority and speaking down to others from above. Diotima is defined as a mystic precisely on account of being *ahead* of us, of treading the path of perfectibility quicker than the rest of us – and perhaps even *too quickly*. That is, Diotima's speech is dangerous: its overly assertoric and occasionally hyperbolic exposition of psychological, metaphysical and moral truths is open to misinterpretation; it is all a little too doctrinal, too directly communicated to be pedagogically useful. Considering the present condition of humanity, more allowances for the reader are needed in the form of indirection and irony.

In *Alexis*, Hypsicles speaks from the past – and not just any past, but from the founding moment of our intellectual tradition, the moment when Pythagoras came to know those truths which have since grounded all Western scientific endeavour. Hypsicles speaks both myth and science at the same time – his language occupies a point of maximum semantic density, prior to the separation of *logos* from *mythos*. And not only does he speak from the past, he also speaks about the past – or, more precisely, about a past that is in the process of becoming the present and subsequently becoming the future. *Alexis* deploys all the resources of myth, allegory, science and rational reconstruction to make sense of an innate movement of perfectibility towards a better state. By mixing together these genres, the dialogue communicates what poetry alone or philosophy alone cannot – a tendency that cannot be fixed into one representational image or static concept but is precisely to be traced by way of its perpetual excess over any discursive container. Again, however, this is a risky communication strategy, one which can be dismembered (as Alexis does) into its separate, inadequate parts (absurd myths, on the one hand, and limited concepts, on the other). Hypsicles has need of a tactful reader who has managed to transcend the limitations of both the perihelion of sentiment (mere myth) and the perihelion of geometry (mere concept).

While Diotima and Hypsicles demand a lot from the reader, 'the editor' to the prefaces of *Aristée* and *Simon* requires very little, for he says too little and says it, moreover, in the antiquarian tone of someone who lacks tact and a feel for the past. The editor stands in a long tradition of philosophical representations of pedants who just don't get the philosophy, from Plato's Eryximachus and the Prudenzia of Bruno's *Ash-Wednesday Supper* to Jean Paul's 'stylicist' and the unnamed critic of Kierkegaard's *Philosophical Fragments*. Hemsterhuis' philosophical world requires a feeling for both the spirit and the letter of the past from his reader, but the editor confesses to understanding the letter alone. In other words, the editor's failings betray the need for better, more tactful, more untimely thinkers within modernity. Through his depiction of the editor Hemsterhuis spurs us on to become better readers (and so to interpret Diotima's and Hypsicles' excesses more tactfully).

3. Hemsterhuis situates Socrates at a midpoint between these three other personae. What is ideal about Socratic philosophising is ultimately its mediating role amidst the more extreme positions that other characters in the dialogues exemplify. Socrates is on his way to perfection without having yet gone too far into already accomplished perfection, as Diotima has. He lives in a classical past already torn (as modernity is) between competing demands of *mythos* and *logos*, rather than in the fullness of the archaic past, as Hypsicles does. He values precision (like the editor), but also conveys a tone that goes beyond its own time and speaks to all times (in a way that the editor does not).

To write Socratically (i.e., to write like a post-Newtonian Plato) is to inhabit this space constituted by the dynamic conjunctions and disjunctions that hold between characters, just as it is to inhabit a space constituted by conjunctions, disjunctions and disassociations between eras and modes of temporality. That is, the space of Hemsterhuis' poetic turn is also constituted between classical Greece and geometrical modernity, between Socrates and Newton, between analysis and poetry, between a hubristic present and a future or past of perfected organs, between the literal and the figurative, between the scientific and the mythic – between, most fundamentally, meiotic and auxetic practices, i.e., the ironic understatements of the fictional prefaces, on the one hand, and the dogmatic, literal exaggerations of Diotima's speech, on the other, between a bathetic present and the promise of a too-dazzling future of unprethinkable novelty.

Bibliography

Anderson, Lorin (1982) *Charles Bonnet and the Order of the Known*, Dordrecht: Reidel.
Anon. (1772) 'Lettre sur l'Homme et ses rapports', *Journal encyclopédique*, 15 September: 360–1.
Ayrault, Roger (1961) *La genèse du romantisme allemand*, 2 vols, Paris: Aubier.
Azadpour, Lydia and Daniel Whistler (2021) 'Polyp-Thinking in the Eighteenth Century', in Panayiota Vassilopoulou and Daniel Whistler (eds), *Thought: A Philosophical History*, London: Routledge, 148–61.
Baker, J. R. (1952) *Abraham Trembley: Scientist and Philosopher, 1710–1784*, London: Edward Arnold.
Bakhtin, Mikhail (1984) *Problems of Dostoevsky's Poetics*, trans. Caryl Emerson, Minneapolis: University of Minnesota Press.
Bell, David A. (1984) *Spinoza in Germany: From 1670 to the Age of Goethe*, London: Institute of Germanic Studies.
Binoche, Bertrand (2004a) 'Perfection, perfectibilité, perfectionnement', in Bertrand Binoche (ed.), *L'homme perfectible*, Seyssel: Editions Champ Vallon, 7–12.
Binoche, Bertrand (2004b) 'Les equivoques de la perfectibilité', in Bertrand Binoche (ed.), *L'homme perfectible*, Seyssel: Editions Champ Vallon, 13–36.
Blumenberg, Hans (1985) *The Legitimacy of the Modern Age*, trans. Robert M. Wallace, Cambridge, MA: MIT Press.
Blumenberg, Hans (1987) *The Genesis of the Copernican World*, trans. Robert M. Wallace, Cambridge, MA: MIT Press.
Böhm, Benno (1966) *Sokrates im achtzehnten Jahrhundert: Studien zum Werdegange des modernen Persönlichkeitsbewusstseins*, 2nd edn, Neumünster: Wachholz.
Böhme, Hartmut (2005) 'The Metaphysics of Phenomena: Telescope and Microscope in the Works of Goethe, Leeuwenhoek and Hooke', in

Helmar Schramm et al. (eds), *Collection, Laboratory, Theater: Scenes of Knowledge in the 17th Century*, Berlin: de Gruyter, 355–93.

Bohnen, Klaus (1981) 'Lessings Erziehung des Menschengeschlechts (§4) und Bonnets Palingenesie: Ein Zitat-Hinweis', *Germanisch-Romanische Monatsschrift* 31: 362–5.

Bonchino, Alberto (2014) *Materie als geronnener Geist: Studien zu Franz von Baader in den philosophischen Konstellationen seiner Zeit*, Paderborn: Ferdinand Schöningh.

Bonnet, Charles (1745) *Traité d'insectologie*, Paris: Durand.

Bonnet, Charles (1760) *Essai analytique sur les facultés de l'âme*, Paris: Philibert.

Bonnet, Charles (1762) *Considérations sur les corps organisés*, Amsterdam: Rey.

Bonnet, Charles (1779–83) *Œuvres d'histoire naturelle et de philosophie*, 8 vols, Neuchatel: Fauche.

Bonnet, Charles (2002) *La palingénésie philosophique*, ed. Christiane Frémont, Paris: Fayard.

Bonnet, Charles and Gabriel Cramer (1987) 'The Bonnet–Cramer Correspondence', in V. P. Dawson, *Nature's Enigma: The Problem of the Polyp in the Letters of Bonnet, Trembley and Reaumur*, Philadelphia, PA: American Philosophical Society, 239–43.

Bonnet, Charles and Abraham Trembley (1987) 'The Bonnet–Trembley Correspondence', in V. P. Dawson, *Nature's Enigma: The Problem of the Polyp in the Letters of Bonnet, Trembley and Reaumur*, Philadelphia, PA: American Philosophical Society, 189–238.

Bordoli, Roberto (2004) 'Teologia e filosofia in Hemsterhuis', in Luca Illeterati and Antonio Moretto (eds), *Frans Hemsterhuis e la cultura filosofica europea fra settecento e ottocento*, Trento: Verifiche, 123–36.

Bordoli, Roberto (2005) 'Predestination and Fatalism', in Claudia Melica (ed.), *Hemsterhuis: A European Philosopher Rediscovered*, Naples: Vivarium, 231–40.

Boulan, Emile (1924) *François Hemsterhuis: Le Socrate hollandais*, Paris: Arnette.

Bourdin, Jean-Claude (1999) 'Formes et écriture chez Diderot philosophe', in Annie Ibrahim (ed.), *Diderot et la question de la forme*, Paris: PUF, 17–36.

Bowler, Peter L. (1974) 'Evolutionism in the Enlightenment', *History of Science* 12: 159–83.

Brachin, Pierre (1952) *Le cercle de Münster (1779–1806) et la pensée religieuse de F. L. Stolberg*, Lyon: IAC.

Brummel, Leendert (1925) *Frans Hemsterhuis: Een philosophenleven*, Haarlem: H. D. Tjeenk Willink.
Bulle, Ferdinand (1911) *Franziskus Hemsterhuis und der deutsche Irrationalismus des 18. Jahrhunderts*, Leipzig: Spamer.
Burrell, David B. (1973) *Analogy and Philosophical Language*, New Haven: Yale University Press.
Cahen-Maurel, Laure (2017) *L'art de romantiser le monde: La peinture de Caspar David Friedrich et la philosophie romantique de Novalis*, Zürich: LIT Verlag.
Cahen-Maurel, Laure (2022) 'Philosophical Paths: The Legacy of Hemsterhuis's Dialogues in the Age of German Romanticism', in François Hemsterhuis, *Dialogues, 1778–1787*, ed. and trans. Jacob van Sluis and Daniel Whistler, Edinburgh: Edinburgh University Press, 22–43.
Cassirer, Ernst (1951) *The Philosophy of the Enlightenment*, Princeton: Princeton University Press.
Cheung, Tobias (2010) '*Omnis Fibra Ex Fibra*: Fibre Œconomies in Bonnet's and Diderot's Models of Organic Order', *Early Science and Medicine* 15.1–2: 66–104.
Cirulli, Franco (2015) *The Age of Figurative Theo-Humanism: The Beauty of God and Man in German Aesthetics of Painting and Sculpture (1754–1828)*, Dordrecht: Springer.
Coleridge, S. T. (1969) *The Friend*, vol. 1, ed. Barbara E. Rooke, London: Routledge.
Comay, Rebecca (2010) *Mourning Sickness: Hegel and the French Revolution*, Stanford: Stanford University Press.
Cometa, Michele (2005) 'Poetry and Catastrophe: The Romantic Tradition of Hemsterhuis's *Alexis ou de l'âge d'or*', in Claudia Melica (ed.), *Hemsterhuis: A European Philosopher Rediscovered*, Naples: Vivarium, 103–22.
Cooper, Andrew (2020) 'Force and Law in Kielmeyer's 1793 Speech', in Lydia Azadpour and Daniel Whistler (eds), *Kielmeyer and the Organic World*, London: Bloomsbury, 81–98.
Crary, Jonathan (1988) 'Techniques of the Observer', *October* 45: 2–35.
Croce, Benedetto (2017) *Aesthetic as Science of Expression and General Linguistic*, London: Routledge.
Curran, Andrew (2001) *Sublime Disorder: Physical Monstrosity in Diderot's Universe*, Oxford: Voltaire Foundation.
D'Acunto, Giuseppe (2005) '"*Vocabula sunt notae rerum*": The Origins of Language in Vico and Hemsterhuis', in Claudia Melica (ed.), *Hemsterhuis: A European Philosopher Rediscovered*, Naples: Vivarium, 3–18.

D'Alembert, Jean le Rond and Denis Diderot (eds) (2021) *Encyclopédie*, Chicago: ARTFL Encyclopédie Project; <http://encyclopedie.uchicago.edu>.

Danto, Arthur C. (1984) 'Philosophy as/and/of Literature', *Proceedings and Addresses of the American Philosophical Association* 58.1: 5–20.

Dawson, V. P. (1987) *Nature's Enigma: The Problem of the Polyp in the Letters of Bonnet, Trembley and Reaumur*, Philadelphia: American Philosophical Society.

De Booy, Jean (1956) 'Quelques renseignements inédits sur un manuscrit du *Rêve de D'Alembert*', *Neophilologus* 40: 81–93.

De Pater, Kees (1995) ''s Gravesande on Moral Evidence', in Marcel F. Fresco *et al.* (eds), *Frans Hemsterhuis (1721–1790): Quellen, Philosophie und Rezeption*, Munich: LIT Verlag, 221–42.

De Staël, Germaine (1814) *De l'Allemagne*, Paris: Nicolle.

Deleuze, Gilles (2008) *Proust and Signs*, trans. Richard Howard. London: Continuum.

Deleuze, Gilles (2013) *Cinema II: The Time-Image*, trans. Hugh Tomlinson and Roberto Galeta, London: Bloomsbury.

Deleuze, Gilles (2014) *Course on Rousseau, Sorbonne, 1959–60*, ed. and trans. Arjen Kleinherenbrink, Nijmegen: Radboud University; <https://deleuze.cla.purdue.edu/seminars/rousseau-and-bergson/lecture-01>.

Derrida, Jacques (1982) *Margins of Philosophy*, trans. Alan Bass, New York: Harvester Press.

Descartes, René (1985–91) *Philosophical Writings*, 3 vols, ed. and trans. John Cottingham *et al.*, Cambridge: Cambridge University Press.

Diderot, Denis (1916) *Early Philosophical Works*, trans. Margaret Jourdain, Chicago: Open Court.

Diderot, Denis (1955–79) *Correspondance*, 16 vols, ed. Georges Roth, Paris: Éditions de Minuit.

Diderot, Denis (1974) *Rameau's Nephew and D'Alembert's Dream*, trans. L. Tancock, London: Penguin.

Diderot, Denis (1975–) *Œuvres complètes* [DPV], 33 vols, ed. H. Dieckmann *et al.*, Paris: Hermann.

Diderot, Denis (1994–7) *Œuvres*, 5 vols, ed. Laurent Versini, Paris: Laffont.

Diderot, Denis and François Hemsterhuis (1964) *Lettre sur l'homme et ses rapports avec le commentaire inédit de Diderot*, ed. Georges May, New Haven: Yale University Press.

Diels, H. and W. Kranz (eds) (1951) *Die Fragmente der Vorsokratiker*, Berlin: Weidmann.

Dierik, A. P. (1997) 'Pre-Romantic Elements in the Aesthetic and Moral

Theories of François Hemsterhuis (1721–90)', *Studies in Eighteenth-Century Culture* 26: 247–71.
Dilthey, Wilhelm (1914–2005) *Gesammelte Schriften*, 26 vols, ed. Ulrich Herrmann *et al.*, Göttingen: Vandenhoeck & Ruprecht.
Drees, Martin (1995) '*Alexis* im *Hyperion*? Bemerkungen zu Hölderlins Hemsterhuis-Rezeption', in Marcel F. Fresco *et al.* (eds), *Frans Hemsterhuis (1721–1790): Quellen, Philosophie und Rezeption*, Munich: LIT Verlag, 527–43.
Ducheyne, Steffen (2014a) ''s Gravesande's Appropriation of Newton's Natural Philosophy, Part I: Epistemological and Theological Issues', *Centaurus* 56: 31–55.
Ducheyne, Steffen (2014b) ''s Gravesande's Appropriation of Newton's Natural Philosophy, Part II: Methodological Issues', *Centaurus* 56: 97–120.
Duflo, Colas (2003) *Diderot: philosophe*, Paris: Honoré Champion.
Engelen, Eva-Maria (1999) 'Der Begriff der Liebe in Hegels *Ästhetik* im Lichte der Vereinigungs-philosophie', *Hegel-Studien* 34: 115–34.
Fénelon, F. (1731) *Œuvres philosophiques, ou Démonstration de l'Existence de Dieu*, Amsterdam: Chatelain.
Feyerabend, Paul (1991) *Three Dialogues on Knowledge*, Oxford: Blackwell.
Forster, Georg (1791) *Ansichten vom Niederrhein, von Brabant, Flandern, Holland, England und Frankreich*, 3 vols, Berlin: Unger.
Franz, Michael (2012) *Tübinger Platonismus: Die gemeinsamen philosophischen Anfangsgründe von Hölderlin, Schelling und Hegel*, Tübingen: Francke.
Fresco, Marcel F. (1991) 'Hemsterhuis and Antiquity: How Greek Was He, This Frisian Socrates? (Some Preliminary Remarks)', *Zentrum für Niederlande-Studien* 1: 67–86.
Fresco, Marcel F. (1995a) 'Frans Hemsterhuis, ein niederländischer Philosoph von europäischer Bedeutung', in Marcel F. Fresco *et al.* (eds), *Frans Hemsterhuis (1721–1790): Quellen, Philosophie und Rezeption*, Munich: LIT Verlag, 35–61.
Fresco, Marcel F. (1995b) 'He Was Greek, This Frisian Socrates: From Cicero Back to Plato', in Marcel F. Fresco *et al.* (eds), *Frans Hemsterhuis (1721–1790): Quellen, Philosophie und Rezeption*, Munich: LIT Verlag, 93–149.
Fresco, Marcel F. (2003) 'Spinoza in der Sicht von Hemsterhuis", in Marcel F. Fresco and Klaus Hammacher, *Hemsterhuis und seine Stellungnahme zu Spinoza*, Delft: Eburon, 1–30.
Fresco, Marcel F. (2007) 'Die Fürstin und der Philosoph. Amalia, Hemsterhuis und ihre Zusammenarbeit', in Markus von Hänsel-Hohenhausen (ed.),

Amalie Fürstin von Gallitzin: Bedeutung und Wirkung, Frankfurt am Main: Frankfurter Verlagsgruppe, 193–222.

Frey, Christiane (2013) 'The Art of Observing the Small: On the Borders of the *subvisibilia* (from Hooke to Brockes)', *Monatshefte* 105.3: 376–88.

Friedlander, Paul (1970) *Plato: An Introduction*, trans. Hans Meyerhoff, Princeton: Princeton University Press.

Funder, Albert (1912) *Frans Hemsterhuis und die Ästhetik der Engländer und Franzosen*, Bonn: Hanstein.

Gaiger, Jason (2018) 'The Temporality of Sculptural Viewing in Hemsterhuis's *Lettre sur la sculpture*', *Sculpture Journal* 27.2: 225–50.

Gallitzin, Amalie (2015–17) *Lettres de Diotime à François Hemsterhuis*, 4 vols, ed. Jacob van Sluis *et al.*, Berltsum: self-published.

Geuss, Raymond (1994) 'Nietzsche and Genealogy', *European Journal of Philosophy* 2.3: 274–92.

Gobbers, W. (1963) *J.-J. Rousseau in Holland, een onderzoek naar de invloed van de mens en het werk*, Gand: Secretariaat van de Koninklijke Vlaamse Academie voor Taal- en Letterkunde.

Goethe, J. W. (1849) *Campaign in France in the Year 1792*, trans. Robert Farie, London: Chapman and Hall.

Gourinot, Michel (1986) 'Socrate était-il ironiste?', *Revue de métaphysique et de morale* 91.3: 339–53.

Grafton, Anthony (1990) *Forgers and Critics: Creativity and Duplicity in Western Scholarship*, Princeton: Princeton University Press.

Grucker, Émile (1866) *François Hemsterhuis: Sa vie et ses œuvres*, Paris: Durand.

Gründer, Karlfried (1955) 'Hamann in Münster', *Westfalen* 33: 74–91.

Haller, Albert von (1757) *Elementa physiologiæ corporis humani*, Lausanne: Marc-Michel Bousquet.

Hamann, J. G. (1955–75) *Briefwechsel*, 7 vols, ed. Walther Ziesemer and Arthur Henkel, Wiesbaden: Insel Verlag.

Hamann, J. G. (1967) *Socratic Memorabilia*, ed. and trans. James C. O'Flaherty, Baltimore: Johns Hopkins University Press.

Hammacher, Klaus (1971) *Unmittelbarkeit und Kritik bei Hemsterhuis*, Munich: Fink.

Hammacher, Klaus (1995a) 'Understanding Hemsterhuis', in Marcel F. Fresco *et al.* (eds), *Frans Hemsterhuis (1721–1790): Quellen, Philosophie und Rezeption*, Munich: LIT Verlag, 63–73.

Hammacher, Klaus (1995b) 'Hemsterhuis und seine Rezeption in der deutschen Philosophie und Literatur des ausgehenden achtzehnten

Jahrhunderts', in Marcel F. Fresco et al. (eds), *Frans Hemsterhuis (1721–1790): Quellen, Philosophie und Rezeption*, Munich: LIT Verlag, 405–32.

Hammacher, Klaus (1995c) 'Gegenwelten der Aufklärung: Der niederländische Philosoph Frans Hemsterhuis', in Marcel F. Fresco et al. (eds), *Frans Hemsterhuis (1721–1790): Quellen, Philosophie und Rezeption*, Munich: LIT Verlag, 611–33.

Hammacher, Klaus (2003) 'Hemsterhuis und Spinoza', in Marcel F. Fresco and Klaus Hammacher, *Hemsterhuis und seine Stellungnahme zu Spinoza*, Delft: Eburon, 31–41.

Hammacher, Klaus (2008) 'Rez.: Franz Hemsterhuis, *Lettres de Socrate à Diotime*, ed. Marcel F. Fresco', *Tijdschrift voor Filosofie* 70: 589–94.

Hartmann, Nicolai (1923) *Die Philosophie des deutschen Idealismus 1: Fichte, Schelling und die Romantik*, Berlin: de Gruyter.

Haym, Rudolf (1870) *Die romantische Schule: Ein Beitrag zur Geschichte des deutschen Geistes*, Berlin: Gärtner.

Hegel, G. W. F. (1999) *Aesthetics: Lectures on Fine Arts*, 2 vols, trans. T. M. Knox, Oxford: Clarendon Press.

Hegel, G. W. F. (2008) *Outlines of the Philosophy of Right*, trans. T. M. Knox, Oxford: Oxford University Press.

Hemsterhuis, François (1846–50) *Œuvres philosophiques*, 3 vols, ed. L. S. P. Meyboom, Leuwarde: Eekhoff.

Hemsterhuis, François (2001) *Wijsgerige Werken* [WW], ed. Michael John Petry, Leeuwarden: Damon.

Hemsterhuis, François (2007) *Lettres de Socrate à Diotime: Cent cinquante lettres du philosophe néerlandais Frans Hemsterhuis à la Princesse de Gallitzin*, ed. Marcel F. Fresco, Frankfurt am Main: Hänsel-Hohenhausen.

Hemsterhuis, François (2011–17) *Briefwisseling (Hemsterhuisiana)* [B], 13 vols, ed. Jacob van Sluis, Berlstum: self-published.

Hemsterhuis, François (2015) *Œuvres philosophiques. Edition critique* [OP], ed. Jacob van Sluis, Leiden: Brill.

Hemsterhuis, François (2021) *Œuvres inédits* [IN], ed. Jacob van Sluis. Berltsum.

Hemsterhuis, François (2022–) *The Edinburgh Edition of the Complete Philosophical Works of François Hemsterhuis* [EE], 3 vols, ed. and trans. Jacob van Sluis and Daniel Whistler, Edinburgh: Edinburgh University Press.

Herder, J. G. (1877–1913) *Sämmtliche Werke*, 33 vols, ed. Bernhard Suphan, Berlin: Weidmann.

Herder, J. G. (1977–2016) *Briefe*, 15 vols, ed. Günther Arnold et al., Weimar: Böhlaus.

Herder, J. G. (1993) *Against Pure Reason: Writings on Religion, Language and History*, ed. and trans. M. Bunge, Minneapolis: Fortress Press.
Hirzel, Rudolf (1895) *Der Dialog: Ein literarhistorischer Versuch*, 2 vols, Leipzig: Hirzel.
Hooke, Robert (1665) *Micrographia or, Some physiological descriptions of minute bodies made by magnifying glasses*, London: Martyn & Allestry.
Hösle, Vittorio (2006) *The Philosophical Dialogue: A Poetics and a Hermeneutics*, trans. Steven Rendall, Notre Dame: University of Notre Dame Press.
Ibrahim, Annie (1999) 'Diderot: forme, difforme, informe', in Annie Ibrahim (ed.), *Diderot et la question de la forme*, Paris: PUF, 1–15.
Ibrahim, Annie (2010) *Diderot: un matérialisme éclectique*, Paris: Vrin.
Ibrahim, Annie (2016) 'Diderot's Monsters, between Physiology and Politics', *Philosophy Today* 60.1: 125–38.
Illetterati, Luca (2005) 'The Eye and the Soul: Physics, Physiology and Psychology in Hemsterhuis's Optics', in Claudia Melica (ed.), *Hemsterhuis: A European Philosopher Rediscovered*, Naples: Vivarium, 123–40.
Ishizuka, Hisao (2006) 'Enlightening the Fibre-Woven Body: William Blake and Eighteenth-Century Fibre Medicine', *Literature and Medicine* 25.1: 72–92.
Israel, Jonathan (2007) *'Failed Enlightenment': Spinoza's Legacy and the Netherlands (1670–1800)*, Wassenaar: NIAS.
Israel, Jonathan (2011) *Democratic Enlightenment: Philosophy, Revolution, and Human Rights, 1750–1790*, Oxford: Oxford University Press.
Jacobi, F. H. (1994) *The Main Philosophical Writings and the Novel Allwill*, ed. and trans. George di Giovanni, Montreal: McGill-Queen's University Press.
Jean Paul (1973) *Horn of Oberon: J. P. Richter's School for Aesthetics*, trans. Margaret R. Hale, Detroit: Wayne State University Press.
Jorink, Eric and Ad Maas (2012) 'Introduction', in Eric Jorink and Ad Maas (eds), *Newton and the Netherlands*, Leiden: Leiden University Press, 7–12.
Jorink, Eric and Huib Zuidervaart (2012) '"The Miracle of Our Time": How Isaac Newton Was Fashioned in the Netherlands', in Eric Jorink and Ad Maas (eds), *Newton and the Netherlands*, Leiden: Leiden University Press, 13–66.
Jouary, Jean-Paul (1992) *Diderot et la matière vivante*, Paris: Messidor.
Kant, Immanuel (1996) *Religion and Rational Theology*, ed. and trans. Allen W. Wood and George di Giovanni, Cambridge: Cambridge University Press.
Kierkegaard, Søren (1962) *Philosophical Fragments*, trans. David Swenson and Howard V. Hong, Princeton: Princeton University Press.

Kierkegaard, Søren (1992) *The Concept of Irony with Continual Reference to Socrates*, ed. and trans. Howard V. Hong and Edna H. Hong, Princeton: Princeton University Press.

Kneller, Jane (2014) 'Sociability and the Conduct of Philosophy: What We Can Learn from Early German Romanticism', in Dalia Nassar (ed.), *The Relevance of Romanticism: Essays on German Romantic Philosophy*, Oxford: Oxford University Press, 110–26.

Koopman, Colin (2013) *Genealogy as Critique: Foucault and the Problems of Modernity*, Bloomington: Indiana University Press.

Kretsedemas, Philip (2017) 'What Is Genealogy?', *Genealogy* 1: 1–9.

Krop, Henri (2005) 'A Dutch *Spinozismusstreit*: The New View of Spinoza at the End of the Eighteenth Century', *Lias* 32: 185–211.

Krop, Henri (2009a) 'Der niederländische Newtonianismus', in Johannes Rohbeck and Helmut Holzhey (eds), *Die Philosophie des 18. Jahrhunderts: Frankreich und Niederlande*, Basel: Scheidegger & Spiess, 1098–106.

Krop, Henri (2009b) 'Frans Hemsterhuis', in Johannes Rohbeck and Helmut Holzhey (eds), *Die Philosophie des 18. Jahrhunderts: Frankreich und Niederlande*, Basel: Scheidegger & Spiess, 1170–82.

La Mettrie, J. O. (1796) *Œuvres philosophiques*, Berlin: Tutot.

Lacoue-Labarthe, Philippe and Jean-Luc Nancy (1975) 'Le dialogue des genres', *Poétique* 21: 148–75.

Lacoue-Labarthe, Philippe and Jean-Luc Nancy (1988) *The Literary Absolute: The Theory of Literature in German Romanticism*, trans. Philip Barnard and Cheryl Lester, Albany: SUNY Press.

Lang, Beryl (1990) *The Anatomy of Philosophical Style: Literary Philosophy and the Philosophy of Literature*, Oxford: Blackwell.

Le Doeuff, Michèle (1989) *The Philosophical Imaginary*, London: Continuum.

Leibniz, G. W. (1989) *Philosophical Essays*, Indianapolis: Hackett.

Lenhoff, S. G. and H. M. Lenhoff (1986) *Hydra and the Birth of Experimental Biology*, 2 vols, Pacific Grove: Boxwood Press.

Lessing, G. E. (2005) *Philosophical and Theological Writings*, ed. and trans. H. B. Nisbett, Cambridge: Cambridge University Press.

Loos, Waltraud (1995) 'Der Gesichtssinn als Organ der Weltbegegnung bei Frans Hemsterhuis', in Marcel F. Fresco et al. (eds), *Frans Hemsterhuis (1721–1790): Quellen, Philosophie und Rezeption*, Munich: LIT Verlag, 321–44.

Lope, H. J. (1990) 'Diderot et François Hemsterhuis', in Siegfried Jüttner (ed.), *Présence de Diderot*, Frankfurt am Main: Peter Lang, 152–70.

Lossky, Niklos (1931) 'Leibniz' Lehre von der Reinkarnation als Metamorphose', *Archiv für Geschichte der Philosophie* 40.2: 214–26.

Lotterie, Florence (2006) *Progrès et perfectibilité: un dilemme des Lumières françaises (1744–1814)*, Oxford: Voltaire Foundation.
Lovejoy, A. O. (1936) *The Great Chain of Being: A Study of the History of an Idea*, Cambridge, MA: Harvard University Press.
Lützeler, Heinrich (1925) 'Hemsterhuis und Novalis', *Neue Jahrbücher für Wissenschaft und Jugendbildung* 1: 212–21.
Mähl, Hans-Joachim (1994) *Die Idee des goldenen Zeitalters im Werk des Novalis: Studien zur Wesensbestimmung der frühromantischen Utopie und zu ihren ideengeschichtlichen Voraussetzungen*, Berlin: de Gruyter.
Marx, Jacques (1976) *Charles Bonnet contre les lumières, 1738–1850*, Oxford: Voltaire Foundation.
Matassi, Elio (1984) *Hemsterhuis. Istanza critica e filosofia della storia*, Naples: Guida.
Matazzi, Elio (2004) 'Il problema della bellezza nella *Lettre sur la sculpture* di F. Hemsterhuis e nella *Critica della facoltà di giudizio* di I. Kant', in Luca Illeterati and Antonio Moretto (eds), *Frans Hemsterhuis e la cultura filosofica europea fra settecento e ottocento*, Trento: Verifiche, 193–206.
Matazzi, Elio (2005) 'Beauty and Temporality in Hemsterhuis's *Lettre sur la sculpture*', in Claudia Melica (ed.), *Hemsterhuis: A European Philosopher Rediscovered*, Naples: Vivarium, 143–54.
Mazzocut-Mis, Maddalena (2005) 'Passion and Perfection in *Simon ou des facultés de l'âme*', in Claudia Melica (ed.), *Hemsterhuis: A European Philosopher Rediscovered*, Naples: Vivarium, 217–30.
McCabe, M. M. (2006) 'Form and the Platonic Dialogues', in Hugh H. Benson (ed.), *A Companion to Plato*, Oxford: Blackwell, 37–54.
McCormick, Peter (1987) 'Philosophical Discourses and Fictional Texts', in Anthony J. Cascardi (ed.), *Literature and the Question of Philosophy*, Baltimore: Johns Hopkins University Press, 52–74.
Melica, Claudia (2004) 'Dubitare, credere e sapere. Convinzione e sentiment in Hemsterhuis', in Luca Illeterati and Antonio Moretto (eds), *Frans Hemsterhuis e la cultura filosofica europea fra settecento e ottocento*, Trento: Verifiche, 11–46.
Melica, Claudia (2005) 'Astronomy and Mythology: Hemsterhuis on the Moon', in Claudia Melica (ed.), *Hemsterhuis: A European Philosopher Rediscovered*, Naples: Vivarium, 85–102.
Melica, Claudia (2007) 'Longing for Unity: Hemsterhuis and Hegel', *Bulletin of the Hegel Society of Great Britain* 55/56: 143–67.
Melzer, Arthur M. (2014) *Writing Between the Lines: The Lost History of Esoteric Writing*, Chicago: University of Chicago Press.

Moenkemeyer, Heinz (1975) *François Hemsterhuis*, Boston: Twayne.

Moenkemeyer, Heinz (1977) 'François Hemsterhuis: Admirers, Critics, Scholars', *Deutsche Vierteljahrsschrift für Literaturwissenschaft und Geistesgeschichte* 51.3: 502–24.

Montesquieu, Charles de (1989) *The Spirit of the Laws*, trans. Anne Cohler et al., Cambridge: Cambridge University Press.

Moretto, Antonio (2005) 'Hemsterhuis on Divisibility and Incommensurability', in Claudia Melica (ed.), *Hemsterhuis: A European Philosopher Rediscovered*, Naples: Vivarium, 67–84.

Morpurgo-Tagliabue, Guido (1987) 'Leggere Hemsterhuis', *Rivista di Storia della Filosofia* 42.1: 3–46.

Mortier, Roland (1997) 'Diderot et la fonction du geste', *Recherches sur Diderot et sur l'Encyclopédie* 23: 79–87.

Nancy, Jean-Luc (2002) *The Speculative Remark (One of Hegel's Bons Mots)*, trans. Céline Surprenant, Stanford: Stanford University Press.

Nancy, Jean-Luc (2008) *The Discourse of the Syncope: Logodaedalus*, trans. Saul Anton, Stanford: Stanford University Press.

Nassar, Dalia (2013) *The Romantic Absolute: Being and Knowing in Early German Romantic Philosophy, 1795–1804*, Chicago: University of Chicago Press.

Nehamas, Alexander (1985) *Nietzsche: Life as Literature*, Cambridge, MA: Harvard University Press.

Neuhouser, Frederick (2012) 'The Critical Function of Genealogy in the Thought of J.-J. Rousseau', *Review of Politics* 74.3: 371–87.

Niehaus, Irmgard (1998) 'Die Psychologie der Seelenvermögen als "Wissenschaft der Glückseligkeit"', in Petra Schulz and Erpho Bell (eds), *Amalia Fürstin von Gallitzin (1748–1806). Meine Seele ist auf der Spitze meiner Feder*, Münster: Ardey-Verlag, 84–91.

Nietzsche, Friedrich (1969) *On the Genealogy of Morals and Ecce Homo*, trans. Walter Kaufmann, New York: Vintage.

Niewöhner, Ulrich (1995) 'Comment Hemsterhuis reprenait l'idée de la glande pinéale, ou la fable médicale dans les réfutations du démocratisme cartésien', in Marcel F. Fresco et al. (eds), *Frans Hemsterhuis (1721–1790): Quellen, Philosophie und Rezeption*, Munich: LIT Verlag, 379–401.

Nightingale, Andrea (1995) *Genres in Dialogue: Plato and the Construct of Philosophy*, Cambridge: Cambridge University Press.

Nisbet, H. B. (2005) 'Lessing and Philosophy', in Barbara Fischer and Thomas Fox (eds), *A Companion to the Works of G. E. Lessing*, Cambridge: Cambridge University Press, 133–56.

Novalis (1960–2006) *Schriften*, 6 vols, ed. Paul Kluckhohn and R. H. Samuel, Stuttgart: Kohlhammer.
Partenie, Catalin (2009) 'Introduction', in Catalin Partenie (ed.), *Plato's Myths*, Cambridge: Cambridge University Press, 1–26.
Pascal, Blaise (1995) *Pensées*, trans. A. J. Krailsheimer, London: Penguin.
Pelckmans, Paul (1987) *Hemsterhuis sans rapports: Contribution à une lecture distante des Lumières*, Amsterdam: Rodopi.
Petry, Michael J. (1985) 'Hemsterhuis on Mathematics and Optics', in J. D. North and J. J. Roche (eds), *The Light of Nature*, Dordrecht: Springer, 209–34.
Petry, Michael J. (1995) 'Mathematics and the Geometrical Model', in Marcel F. Fresco et al. (eds), *Frans Hemsterhuis (1721–1790): Quellen, Philosophie und Rezeption*, Munich: LIT Verlag, 181–219.
Petry, Michael J. (2003a) 'Frans Hemsterhuis (1721–90)', in Wiep van Bunge et al. (eds), *Dictionary of Seventeenth- and Eighteenth-Century Dutch Philosophy*, vol. 1, London: Bloomsbury, 417–24.
Petry, Michael J. (2003b) 'Johann Friedrich Hennert (1733–1813)', in Wiep van Bunge et al. (eds), *Dictionary of Seventeenth- and Eighteenth-Century Dutch Philosophy*, vol. 1, London: Bloomsbury, 425–9.
Philipsen, Bart (1992) *Die List der Einfalt: Nachlese zu Hölderlins spätester Dichtung*, Munich: Fink.
Plato (1962) *Collected Dialogues*, ed. Edith Hamilton and Huntingdon Cairns, New Haven: Princeton University Press.
Poritzky, J. E. (1926) *Franz Hemsterhuis: Seine Philosophie und ihr Einfluss auf die deutschen Romantiker*, Berlin: Pätel.
Proust, Jacques (1981) 'Diderot et la philosophie du polype', *Revue des sciences humaines* 182: 21–30.
Ratcliffe, M. J. (2004) 'Abraham Trembley's Strategy of Generosity and the Scope of Celebrity in the Mid-Eighteenth Century', *Isis* 95.4: 555–75.
Reid, Thomas (1855) *Essays on the Intellectual Powers of Man*, ed. William Hamilton and James Walker, New York: Derby.
Rockhill, Gabriel (2010) *Logique de l'histoire: Pour une analytique des pratiques philosophiques*, Paris: Hermann.
Roe, Shirley A. (1981) *Matter, Life and Generation: Eighteenth-Century Embryology and the Haller–Wolff Debate*, Cambridge: Cambridge University Press.
Roger, Jacques (1963) *Les sciences de la vie dans la pensée française du XVIIIe siècle*, Paris: Armand Colin.

Rousseau, Jean-Jacques (1991) *Émile, or On Education*, ed. and trans. Allan Bloom, London: Penguin.

Rousseau, Jean-Jacques (2018) *The Discourses and Other Early Political Writings*, trans. Victor Gourevitch, Cambridge: Cambridge University Press.

Rowe, Christopher (1999) 'Myth, History, and Dialectic in Plato's *Republic* and *Timaeus-Critias*', in R. Buxton (ed.), *From Myth to Reason? Studies in the Development of Greek Thought*, Oxford: Oxford University Press, 251–62.

Salaün, Franck (2004) 'Diderot et le concept de perfectibilité', in Bertrand Binoche (ed.), *L'homme perfectible*, Seyssel: Editions Champ Vallon, 200–14.

Savioz, Raymond (1948) *La philosophie de Charles Bonnet de Genève*, Paris: Vrin.

Schelling, F. W. J. (1856–61) *Werke*, 14 vols, ed. K. F. A. Schelling, Stuttgart: Cotta.

Schiller, Joseph (1974) 'Queries, Answers and Unsolved Problems in Eighteenth-Century Biology', *History of Science* 12: 184–99.

Schlegel, A. W. (1964) *Kritische Schriften und Briefe*, 5 vols, ed. Edgar Lohner, Stuttgart: Kohlhammer.

Schlegel, Friedrich (1958–2002) *Kritische Ausgabe*, 35 vols, ed. Ernst Behler et al., Munich: Schöningh.

Sellars, John (2003) 'Simon the Shoemaker and the Problem of Socrates', *Classical Philology* 98.3: 207–16.

Shapin, Steven and Simon Schaffer (1985) *Leviathan and the Air-Pump: Hobbes, Boyle and the Experimental Life*, Princeton: Princeton University Press.

Söhngen, Frank (1995) 'Hemsterhuis in Context', in Marcel F. Fresco et al. (eds), *Frans Hemsterhuis (1721–1790): Quellen, Philosophie und Rezeption*, Munich: LIT Verlag, 263–97.

Sonderen, Peter C. (1996) 'Beauty and Desire: Frans Hemsterhuis' Aesthetic Experiments', *British Journal of the History of Philosophy* 4.2: 317–45.

Sonderen, Peter C. (2000) *Het sculpturale denken. De esthetica van Frans Hemsterhuis*, Leende: Damon.

Sonderen, Peter C. (2005) 'Passion and Purity. From Science to Art: Descartes, Spinoza and Hemsterhuis', in Claudia Melica (ed.), *Hemsterhuis: A European Philosopher Rediscovered*, Naples: Vivarium, 199–216.

Sonderen, Peter C. (2017) 'Where Theory and Artistic Practice Meet: The Art of Oscillation (on Hemsterhuis, Novalis and Now)', in Peter

C. Sonderen and Marijn de Langen (eds), *Theory – Arts – Practices*, Amsterdam: ArtEZ Press, 18–69.

Sonderen, Peter C. (2022) 'Hemsterhuis's Art and Aesthetics: Theories in the Making', in François Hemsterhuis, *Early Writings, 1762–1773*, ed. and trans. Jacob van Sluis and Daniel Whistler, Edinburgh: Edinburgh University Press, 3–22.

Spangler, Mai (1997) 'Science, philosophie et littérature: le polype de Diderot', *Recherches sur Diderot et sur l'Encyclopédie* 23: 89–107.

Spruit, Leen (2005) 'Hemsterhuis on Appearances and Immaterial Being', in Claudia Melica (ed.), *Hemsterhuis: A European Philosopher Rediscovered*, Naples: Vivarium, 49–66.

Starnes, Thomas C. (1987) *Christoph Martin Wieland: Leben und Werk*, 2 vols, Sigmaringen: Thorbecke.

Starobinski, Jean (1975) 'Le philosophe, le géomètre, l'hybride', *Poétique* 21: 8–23.

Stenger, Gerhardt (1999) 'L'ordre et les monstres dans la pensée philosophique, politique et morale de Diderot', in Annie Ibrahim (ed.), *Diderot et la question de la forme*, Paris: PUF, 139–58.

Strauss, Leo (1988) *Persecution and the Art of Writing*, Chicago: University of Chicago Press.

Sudhof, Siegfried (1973) *Von der Aufklärung zur Romantik: Die Geschichte des Kreises von Münster*, Berlin: Schmidt.

Sumi, Yoichi (1985) 'Traduire Diderot: style polype et style traduit', in A.-M. Chouillet (ed.), *Colloque international Diderot, 4–11 juillet, 1984*, Paris: Mélanges de la Bibliothèque de la Sorbonne, 255–60.

Sumi, Yoichi (2013) 'Traduire Diderot aujourd'hui', *Recherches sur Diderot et sur l'Encyclopédie* 48: 19–36.

Tavani, Elena (2005) 'Economy of Desire in Hemsterhuis', in Claudia Melica (ed.), *Hemsterhuis: A European Philosopher Rediscovered*, Naples: Vivarium, 155–98.

Tokarzewska, Monika (2015) 'Friedrich von Hardenbergs "moralische Astronomie"', *Athenäum: Jahrbuch der Friedrich Schlegel-Gesellschaft* 25: 41–78.

Tolstoy, Leo (1994) *What Is Art?*, trans. A. Maude, Bristol: Classical Press.

Trembley, A. (1986) *Memoirs Concerning the Polyps*, trans. S. G. Lenhoff, in S. G. Lenhoff and H. M. Lenhoff, *Hydra and the Birth of Experimental Biology*, vol. 2, Pacific Grove: Boxwood Press, 1–167.

Trop, Gabriel (2022) 'Hemsterhuis as Provocation: The German Reception of His Early Writings', in François Hemsterhuis, *Early Writings, 1762–1773*, ed. and trans. Jacob van Sluis and Daniel Whistler, Edinburgh: Edinburgh University Press, 36–54.

Trunz, Erich (ed.) (1971) *Goethe und der Kreis von Münster*, Münster: Aschendorff.

Van Bunge, Wiep (2018) *From Bayle to the Batavian Revolution: Essays on Philosophy in the Eighteenth-Century Dutch Republic*, Leiden: Brill.

Van der Hoeven, J. (1865) 'Drie Brieven van F. Hemsterhuis: Eene mededeeling betreffende de beoefening der natuurlijke historie in het midden der vorige eeuw', *Album der natuur* 14.1: 257–65.

Van Ruler, Johan Arie (2005) 'Sensing and Judging: Hemsterhuis, Empiricism and the Cartesian Legacy', in Claudia Melica (ed.), *Hemsterhuis: A European Philosopher Rediscovered*, Naples: Vivarium, 19–48.

Van Sluis, Jacob (1995) '*Gens et schola Hemsterhuisiana*: Franciscus Hemsterhuis between Friesland and Greece', in Marcel F. Fresco et al. (eds), *Frans Hemsterhuis (1721–1790): Quellen, Philosophie und Rezeption*, Munich: LIT Verlag, 75–89.

Van Sluis, Jacob (ed.) (2001) *Bibliotheca Hemsterhuisiana*, Leeuwarden: Damon.

Van Sluis, Jacob (2015) 'Mutual Affairs: Petrus Camper as Seen by His Friend François Hemsterhuis', in Klaas van Berkel and Bart Ramakers (eds), *Petrus Camper in Context*, Hilversum: Verloren, 91–110.

Van Sluis, Jacob (2022) 'Man in General and *Fagel* in Particular', in François Hemsterhuis, *Early Writings, 1762–1773*, ed. and trans. Jacob van Sluis and Daniel Whistler, Edinburgh: Edinburgh University Press, 23–35.

Vartanian, Aram (1950) 'Trembley's Polyp, La Mettrie, and Eighteenth-Century French Materialism', *Journal of the History of Ideas* 11.3: 259–86.

Verbeek, Theo (1995) 'Sensation et matière: Hemsterhuis et le matérialisme', in Marcel F. Fresco et al. (eds), *Frans Hemsterhuis (1721–1790): Quellen, Philosophie und Rezeption*, Munich: LIT Verlag, 243–62.

Vernière, Paul (1954) *Spinoza et la pensée française avant la Révolution*, Paris: PUF.

Vieillard-Baron, Jean-Louis (1985) 'Platonisme et antiplatonisme dans l'Aufklärung finissante Hemsterhuis et Fichte', *Archives de Philosophie* 48.4: 591–603.

Vieillard-Baron, Jean-Louis (1988) *Platonisme et interprétation de Platon a l'épochè moderne*, Paris: Vrin.

Vieillard-Baron, Jean-Louis (1995) 'Le Platonisme sans néoplatonisme de Hemsterhuis', in Marcel F. Fresco et al. (eds), *Frans Hemsterhuis (1721–*

1790): Quellen, Philosophie und Rezeption, Munich: LIT Verlag, 151–60.
Vlastos, Gregory (1991) *Socrates, Ironist and Moral Philosopher*, Cambridge: Cambridge University Press.
Voltaire (1878) *Œuvres complètes*, 52 vols, Paris: Garnier.
Vosskamp, Wilhelm (1992) 'Perfectibilité und Bildung. Zu den Besonderheiten des deutschen Bildungskonzepts im Kontext der europäischen Utopie- und Fortschrittsdiskussion', in Siegfried Jüttner and Jochen Schlobach (eds), *Europäische Aufkläruing(en). Einheit and nationale Vielfalt*, Hamburg: Meiner, 117–26.
Walzel, Oskar (1934) *Romantisches*, Bonn: Röhrscheid.
Weatherby, Leif (2016) *Transplanting the Metaphysical Organ: German Romanticism between Leibniz and Marx*, New York: Fordham University Press.
Whistler, Daniel (2022a) 'Forms of Philosophical Creativity: An Introduction to Hemsterhuis' Dialogues', in François Hemsterhuis, *Dialogues, 1778–87*, ed. and trans. Jacob van Sluis and Daniel Whistler, Edinburgh: Edinburgh University Press, 3–21.
Whistler, Daniel (2022b) 'Jacobi and Hemsterhuis', in A. Hampton (ed.), *Friedrich Jacobi and the End of the Enlightenment*, Cambridge: Cambridge University Press.
Whistler, Daniel (2022c) 'Post-Bonnetian Naturalism', in Luca Corti and Johannes Schülein (eds), *Life, Organism and Human Nature: Perspectives on Classical German Philosophy*, Dordrecht: Springer.
Wielema, Michiel R. (1989) 'Philosophy in the Netherlands in the Seventeenth and Eighteenth Centuries', *Rivista di Storia della Filosofia* 44.2: 353–63.
Wielema, Michiel R. (1993) 'Frans Hemsterhuis: A Philosopher's View of the History of the Dutch Republic', *Canadian Journal of Netherlandic Studies* 14.1: 109–17.
Wielema, Michiel R. (1995) 'Die christlich-platonische Hemsterhuis-Rezeption in den Niederlanden in der ersten Hälfte des 19. Jahrhunderts', in Marcel F. Fresco et al. (eds), *Frans Hemsterhuis (1721–1790): Quellen, Philosophie und Rezeption*, Munich: LIT Verlag, 573–85.
Wilson, Arthur M. (1972) *Diderot*, Oxford: Oxford University Press.
Wolfe, Charles (2014) 'On the Role of Newtonian Analogies in Eighteenth-Century Life Science', in Z. Biener and E. Schliesser (eds), *Newton and Empiricism*, Oxford: Oxford University Press, 223–61.
Wolz, Henry G. (1970) 'Philosophy as Drama: An Approach to Plato's Symposium', *Philosophy and Phenomenological Research* 30.3: 323–53.
Zammito, John H. (2003) '"The Most Hidden Conditions of Men of the

First Rank": The Pantheist Current in Eighteenth-Century Germany "Uncovered" by the Spinoza Controversy', *Eighteenth Century Thought* 1: 335–68.

Zuidervaart, Huib (2019) 'The Long Forgotten Relation between an English Binocular and a Dutch Philosopher: Frans Hemsterhuis (1721–1790) as Herschel's Precursor and Designer of Dollond's Achromatic Binocular Telescope', *Beiträge zur Astronomiegeschichte* 14: 123–89.

Index

(Names of characters in Hemsterhuis' dialogues are placed in quotation marks to differentiate them from historical figures.)

Adonis, 144, 146
Allamand, J. N. S., 15, 129, 178, 189
anachronism, 24, 33, 53–6, 92, 94, 97, 139, 235, 237, 245, 252, 265, 266; *see also* untimeliness
analogical Newtonianism, 41, 44, 136, 149
analogy, 18, 19, 31, 41, 43, 45, 108, 114, 120, 136, 138–9, 140–4, 148, 150, 151–2, 154, 169, 171, 175, 184, 186–7, 194, 208, 253, 257
analogy-thinking, 141
analysis, xiii, xiv, 19, 20–1, 27–8, 46, 52, 59–66, 68, 72–3, 74–5, 78, 106, 124, 186, 208, 229, 258, 262, 264, 265–6, 268
animal souls, 179
anomaly, doctrine of, 52–5
anonymous publication, 159
antiquarianism, 8, 32, 37–8, 83, 233–5, 237–8, 252, 268; *see also* erudition
Aquinas, T., 143
archaic, the, 8, 97, 148, 153, 155, 200–1, 235, 252–4, 260–2, 266, 268
Archimedes, 40, 53, 55, 149
'Aristophanes', x, 220
Aristotle, 34, 53, 60, 62, 143, 158, 232
arithmetic, 44, 47, 82
astronomy, 14, 28, 39, 41, 47–9, 110, 146–8, 150–2

atheism *see* Hemsterhuis, *Lettre sur l'athéisme*
atmosphere, 85–6, 201, 226, 248, 252; *see also* world-construction
attraction, 41, 48–9, 132, 136, 139, 150, 208–9
Augustine, 257–8
autoprosopis, 84
auxesis, 236, 240, 267–9

Bacon, F., 53, 84, 111
Bailly, J. S., 147
barbarous, the, 164–6, 199–200, 249, 251
Bentick, W., 15, 129, 178
Berkeley, G., 82, 122
Bildung, 126
Biran, M. de, xv
Blankenberg, F., 13
blessedness, 57, 261
Blumenbach, J. F., 41
Blumenberg, H., 109, 111–12, 116, 191, 236
Boeck, F. A., xvii
Bonnet, C., xiii–xiv, 60–5, 93–5, 97, 102–3, 115–16, 129–31, 132, 134, 143–4, 149, 151–3, 156, 172, 177–96
Bonnetism, 65, 167–8, 189
Boulan, E., xv, 11, 21, 203
bounty, 232, 236, 239

288   INDEX

Brummel, L., 11, 13, 82, 111, 143, 178, 188, 214, 216
Bruno, G., xii, 268
Buffon, G.-L., 41, 158, 165
Bulle, F., 11, 16, 27, 51, 66, 68–9, 73, 142, 208

Cahen-Maurel, L., 9, 78, 87, 143, 156, 196, 242, 259
Calvinism, 16; see also religion
Camper, P., 15, 36, 92, 110, 111, 151, 192–3
catastrophism, 48, 115, 145, 151, 191–3, 260; see also global revolution
catechism, 81–3
Caylus, Comte de, 15, 37, 102
celeritas see speed
ceremonial, the, 226–7
certainty *see* conviction
chain of being, 180, 182, 194
chain of reasons, 71, 176, 185–7, 194–6, 252
Charmus, 232, 234–5
childishness, 64, 81–2, 91, 223, 257
Christ, 48
Christianity *see* religion
Cicero, 8, 32–3, 75–6, 82
Clauberg, J., 142
Cleidemus, 232
clover leaf, 124–6
coexistence (of ideas), 78, 210, 211–2, 216, 230, 258, 263; see also optimum
Coleridge, S. T., xv
community, 241–3
compression, 215–8
conjecture, 27, 84, 90, 97, 109, 125, 148, 175–6, 184, 186–7, 195–6, 262
consumption, 115, 214, 221, 230
contingency, 111–12, 116, 119, 152, 155–6, 173–5, 184, 187, 190–1, 226, 230, 246, 260
conviction
   conviction in advance, 248, 257–9
   discursive conviction, 68, 70–2, 78, 143, 203, 257–9
   sentimental conviction, 67–73, 77–9, 92, 134, 155, 196, 204, 255–6, 258

Cousin, V., xv
Croce, B., xv

D'Alembert, J., 7, 16, 54, 166–7, 170, 215, 229
D'Holbach, P.-H., 17, 102, 224
Danto, A., xi–xii, 20
De Smeth, T., 16, 82, 216
De Staël, G., xvii
death, 134, 181, 193, 196
deduction *see* chain of reasons; conviction, discursive
déjà-lu, 249
déjà-vu, 201, 248–9
Deleuze, G., xiv, 161, 201, 248
Democritus, 53, 55, 86–7, 116, 149
Derrida, J., 10
Descartes, R., 59–61, 62–3, 79, 173, 204, 212, 223
Devil, 226, 236
dialogism, 23, 81–2, 84, 96
Diderot, D., xii, xiii–xiv, 16, 18, 48–9, 60, 64, 67, 80, 89, 92–3, 97, 101–3, 116, 119, 129, 134–5, 143, 149, 150, 156, 157–76, 180–5, 187, 190–3, 194, 196, 200, 211, 214–15, 216–17, 224, 229, 239, 249–50
Dilthey, W., xv, 27, 37, 159
Diogenes Laertius, 80, 232
Diotima (*Symposium*), 7, 86, 232
   Gallitzin as 'Diotima', 7, 11, 16, 22, 88, 264
'Diotima', 6–7, 84, 86–95, 96–7, 116, 117, 118, 123, 126, 133–4, 194, 232–4, 256, 261, 262, 267–9
discipleship, 17, 29, 80, 188–9
discursive reasoning *see* chain of reasons; conviction, discursive
diurnal rotation, 146
dormancy, 93, 115, 118, 120, 182, 185
dreams, 4, 89, 202, 246–52, 254, 257
duration, 205, 263

'Editor', 7, 147, 231, 233, 235–40, 252, 267–8
Egyptians, 8, 47, 56
electrizable souls, 79

INDEX

electricity, 41, 79, 119, 184
elite, the, 164, 166, 239
empathy, 209–10
empiricism, 112–14, 119–20, 191
encyclopedia, 7, 143, 157, 183, 195, 214–5, 229, 239–40
energy, 45, 79–80, 93, 130–1, 153, 168–70, 171, 216–7, 220, 228–30, 249–50, 256, 265–6
enthusiasm, 4, 9, 74, 79, 143, 241, 258, 266
Epictetus, 17
epigenesis, 178, 191
Erasmus, 33
erudition, 8, 32, 37–8, 232–5, 238, 252
esoteric writing, 20, 83, 91, 158–63, 165, 193–4, 239–42, 266
eternity, 55, 57, 78, 115, 140, 193, 207–8, 210, 255, 260, 262–3
Etruscans, 47
Euclid, 41, 42, 149, 45, 46, 60, 78
experimentation, xi, xiii, 4, 15, 41–2, 82, 84, 95, 103, 110, 124, 149, 177–9, 186, 187, 196, 205–6, 236, 244, 248–9, 257
expression, 5, 14, 161–2, 220–1, 240, 259
extra-terrestrial perfection, 132–4

fable, 3–4, 11, 59, 66, 69, 88, 147, 183
fabulation, 8, 175–6, 196, 234–5, 249
facilitas, 204, 212, 215, 218, 221
faculty psychology
   faculty-fusion, 258–9
   faculty-harmony, 124–6, 132, 138–9, 154, 164
Fagel, F., 12–13, 16, 23, 82, 123–5, 132, 164, 166, 210, 215–16
fallacy of the ephemeral, 175, 191, 196, 226, 260
Fénelon, F., 80, 112,
fibre-theory
   fibre physiology, 90–6, 116, 147, 149
   fibre psychology, 93–6
   special fibre theory, 93, 97, 117, 135
flirtation, 66
Fontenelle, B., 80, 175
forgery, 6, 8, 20, 233–5, 242

Fresco, M., 8, 11–12, 16, 20–22, 27, 28–9, 32–3, 36, 45, 51, 80, 83–4, 101, 120, 159, 178, 188, 190, 223, 236, 240
Fürstenberg, F. von, xv, 51, 53, 169, 195, 264
future truths, 256, 258

Gallitzin, A., x–xii, xiii, xv–xvi, xviii, 7, 11–12, 14–24, 31–2, 35–8, 39, 40, 51, 53–5, 56, 60–1, 64, 65–6, 70, 71, 74, 75–8, 81, 88, 91, 92, 95, 105, 121, 124–5, 139, 148–9, 153, 157, 163, 165–6, 169, 188–9, 195, 209, 216, 218, 220, 222, 227–8, 236, 239, 241, 243, 247, 250, 254, 255, 257, 258, 261, 263
Gallitzin, D., 17, 157, 166
Garve, C., xv
genius, 34, 37, 45, 54–5, 61, 77, 121, 143, 162, 166–7, 210, 214–16, 218–9, 263
geometrical spirit, 40, 43–6, 49–52, 123, 139, 167, 169
geometrical education, 43–4
gibberish, 91–2, 150, 165, 243, 249, 266; *see also* ridiculous
global revolution, 115, 171–2, 183–4, 185, 192–3, 261
Goethe, J. W., xv–xvii, 17, 35–7, 52–5, 105, 107–8, 169, 203, 212–3, 217, 234, 252
   Farbenlehre, 107–8
   Iphigenie auf Tauris, 36–7, 252
   Werther, 212–13, 216–17, 234
golden age, xiii, 8–9, 69, 131–2, 144–8, 150, 153, 155, 193, 200, 202, 229, 252–3, 254, 260–2
Grucker, E., 9, 12, 79, 125, 137, 254
Günderrode, K., xv

Haller, A., 41, 93
Halley, E., 147
Hamann, J. G., xii, xv, 14, 18, 241–2
Hamilton, W., xv
Hammacher, K., 5, 27, 33, 49, 50–1, 66–8, 73–4, 80, 82, 90–2, 102, 107, 125, 126, 134, 141, 142, 146, 147, 148, 187, 188, 219, 223, 250, 252

Hartmann, N., 16, 27, 71, 120, 137
Hegel, G. W. F., xv, xvii, 10, 144, 237
heliocentrism, 146
Helvétius, C. A., 17, 126
Hemsterhuis, F.
  Alexis, x–xi, xiii, 3–11, 12–15, 17, 19, 22, 23, 48, 56, 64, 69, 83–4, 101, 118, 131–2, 143, 144–7, 150–5, 192–3, 199, 200, 203–4, 221, 233, 237, 252–3, 258–61, 263, 265–8
  Alexis II, 139
  Aristée, xvi–xvii, 5, 6–7, 10, 11–13, 14, 19, 20, 22, 68–73, 83–4, 125–6, 134, 140, 155, 159, 196, 209, 221–2, 231–3, 236–40, 243, 255, 258, 263, 265–8
  biography, 11–18
  Description philosophique du caractère de feu monsieur F. Fagel, xvii, 13, 123–5, 216
  Lettre sur l'athéisme, xvi, 13, 94, 115, 122, 222–4
  Lettre sur l'Homme et ses rapports, xvi, 10, 12–13, 16, 18, 23, 41, 47–9, 54–5, 67, 70, 83, 92, 93, 115, 121, 132, 134–5, 141, 143, 149, 157–8, 160–6, 173, 193, 194, 210–12, 214–17, 239, 246, 250
  Lettre sur l'optique, 105–12, 114, 138, 151, 207
  Lettre sur la sculpture, xvii, 9, 10, 12–13, 19, 42, 56, 107, 204–8, 210, 213, 219–20, 229
  Lettre sur le fatalisme, 16, 95
  Lettre sur les désirs, xvi, 10, 12–13, 41, 190, 207–10, 226–7, 241
  Lettre sur les vertus et les vices, 89
  Lettre sur une pierre antique, 12
  reception history, xiv–xviii
  Simon, x, 6–7, 8, 10, 12–14, 19–20, 22, 27, 66, 74, 80–1, 83–4, 86, 88–91, 94–7, 116, 118, 123–6, 133–4, 140–1, 147, 199–200, 219–21, 231–5, 237–8, 240, 243, 256, 259, 261, 262–3, 265–8
  Sophyle, 10–14, 20, 22, 23, 38, 40–1, 63–4, 67, 70, 79, 81, 83, 91, 95,
112–13, 119, 120–1, 137, 141, 152, 159–60, 191, 195, 242, 253, 265
Hemsterhuis, T., 15, 33, 37, 142–3, 238
Hennert, J. F., 224
Hennings, J. C., 247
Herder, J. G., xv–xvii, 15, 27, 37, 190, 208, 212
Hesiod, 15, 146–8, 155, 260–2; *see also* golden age
Heusde, P. W. van, xv
Hevelius, J., 147
Hippocrates, 53–5, 149
historicity, 47–9, 112, 120, 127, 131, 134, 156, 202, 203, 221, 224, 226, 230, 265–6
Hölderlin, F., xv, xvii, 151
Homer, 17, 53, 54, 135
Hooke, R., 15, 111
Humboldt, W., xv
Hume, D., 83–4, 101
hyperbola, 210
hyperbole, 133–4, 154, 194, 267
hypermaterialism, 121–2, 137, 159–60
'Hypsicles', 5, 8, 84, 144–8, 150, 151, 153–5, 156, 252–3, 260–1, 267–8

idea, 107
imaginary, xi, 6, 66, 85, 252
imagination, the, 12, 60, 62–3, 66, 87–90, 92, 107–8, 115, 117, 124, 125, 138, 145, 154, 164, 169, 174, 186, 195, 216, 223, 228, 243, 246, 249, 251, 257, 258, 259
immaterialism, 65, 93, 120–2, 127, 160, 179
imposture, 240, 242–3
indirect realism, 117–18
indirection, 69–70, 79, 84, 90, 155, 240, 242, 253–4, 262, 266–7
inertia, 41, 48, 136, 139, 150, 208, 220
inexpressible, the, 251
insectification imperative, 109–10, 114–15, 122, 125, 138, 204, 207
introspection, 124, 242, 257
intuition, 43, 57, 70–1, 78, 109, 143, 187, 204 209, 212, 240, 258

irony, xviii, 27–8, 34, 62, 66, 75, 80, 83–4, 134, 165, 236–43, 265–6, 267
irrationalism, 27, 68, 73
Israel, J., 16, 27, 39, 159–60, 222, 224–5

Jacobi, F. H., xv–xvii, 13, 15, 27, 44–5, 69, 212, 222–3, 254
Jean Paul (Richter), 251–2, 268
Journal encyclopédique, 67, 158, 163
Jupiter *see* Zeus

Kant, I., xv, xvii, 14, 193, 196, 212
Kepler, J., 48–9, 132
Kierkegaard, S., xii, 83, 237, 240–2, 268
Krop, H., 13, 15, 213, 223–4

La Mettrie, J. O. de, 16–17, 102, 179
Lacoue-Labarthe, P., x, 9–10, 81, 84, 220–1, 254
Lavater, J. K., 220
Le Doeuff, M., 6
Le Sage, G.-L., 102, 188
legislation, 224–7, 230, 241
Leibniz, G. W., 53, 61, 62, 116, 130–1, 185, 251
Leiden University, 15, 178
Lessing, G. E., xv, xvi, 21, 90, 116, 129, 159–60, 222, 251
literal, the, 36, 41, 94, 96–7, 134, 147, 268–9
Locke, J., 49, 101, 113, 158
Longinus, 78
Lucian, 8, 33, 53, 80, 165, 167, 168, 217
Lucretius, 59–60, 62, 64
Lulofs, J., 15

Macpherson, J., 233–4
madness, 91–2, 165, 222, 226, 234
marriage, 22, 150, 225
materialist style, 64–6, 189
Maupertius, P. L., 147
mediation, 70, 116, 204, 207–9, 227, 246
meiosis, 236, 240–1, 267–9
Melica, C., xvii, 27, 146, 150, 256
Memory *see* recollection
Mendelssohn, M., xv–xvi, 159, 224
Merck, J. H., xvi

metaphor, 27, 49, 59, 66, 72,79, 94, 148, 150, 152, 162, 166, 194
metempsychosis, 31, 134, 267
Meyboom, L., 27, 188
Michelangelo, 206
mixture, xiv, 4, 33, 44, 57, 74–7, 126, 148, 150, 165, 168, 223, 225, 227, 232, 249, 267
'Mnesarchus', 80, 89, 219–20, 259
Moenkemeyer, H., xii, xv, 9, 21–2, 33, 49, 66, 68, 84, 86, 121, 125, 134, 143, 160, 196, 200, 216, 236, 252, 262
monologism, 4, 80–1, 194
monster, 56–7, 173–4, 223
Montaigne, M. de, 54, 116
Montesquieu, 37, 49, 84, 102, 147, 200
moon, 23, 51, 131–2, 145–7, 151, 264
moral evidence, 68, 73, 190; *see also* conviction, sentimental
moral organ, 18–19, 29, 64, 76–7, 82, 104, 115, 124, 131, 134–41, 151, 152–5, 162, 164, 166, 224–5, 246, 259
Münster Circle, xv, 17–18, 51, 101

Nancy, J.-L., x, xii, 9–10, 81, 84, 220–1, 254
narratival philosophy, 62–4, 94, 195; *see also* chain of reasons
Nassar, D., 103, 126, 137, 226
naturalism, 130–1, 135, 171, 181–3, 186, 190
neutralist model, 20–1,76
Newton, I., 38–41, 43, 44–5, 50, 52, 53, 59–60, 62, 121, 139, 142, 147, 268
Niethuis, 17–18, 254
Nietzsche, F., xii, 221
Nieuwentyt, B., 44, 68
Novalis, xv, xvii–xviii, 59, 70, 102–3, 105, 115, 126, 134, 137, 142,151–3, 211, 226, 227, 245, 258
novel, 21, 61, 63, 65, 186, 195, 216, 234

obscurity, 4, 8, 24, 63, 75–6, 83, 97, 134, 139, 147, 158, 161–4, 169–70, 213, 216–18, 223, 236
 epigrammatic obscurity, 217–8
 energetic obscurity, 217–8, 249

ocularcentrism, 140
Olympiodorus, 232
Olympus, 43, 69–70
omnitemporality *see* optimum
ontogeny, 172,184
optics *see* Hemsterhuis, *Lettre sur l'optique*
optimism, 111, 130, 223, 255
optimum
    aesthetic optimum, 205–7, 214, 219–20, 251
    omnitemporal optimum, 56–7, 139–40, 262–4, 268
    optimal form, 203, 214, 217–9, 221, 230–1, 240, 252
    scientific optimum, 210–12, 214
    social optimum, 209–10
Orion, 88, 118
ornament, xi–xii, 3–4, 9, 20, 76, 83, 148, 158

paradox of inquiry, 257–8
patriotism, 225
Pausanias, 234
pedagogy, 14, 28, 43, 81–3, 91,123–6, 128, 132, 138, 145, 155, 164, 220, 241, 265, 267
Pelckmans, P., 28, 123, 215, 246, 249, 252
perfectibility, 105, 119, 123–34, 154–5, 172, 184–5, 187, 190, 191, 193, 200, 201, 258, 259–61, 265–7
Perrault, C., 49
Perrenot, A., 17, 188, 234
personality, xvi, 259
Petry, M. J., 17, 21, 27–9, 40–4, 46–7, 102, 108, 142–3, 159, 224
Phaedo of Elis, 6, 232–3
philhellenism, 32–3, 54
philology *see* erudition.
Philopolis, 129–30; *see also* Bonnet, C.
Plato, x, xi–xii, xiii–xiv, xvi, xvii, 3, 5, 7, 8, 14, 17, 20, 21–3, 28–29, 31–5, 36, 38, 41, 50, 52, 53–4, 55, 62, 74–85, 86, 88, 91, 92, 142, 148, 149, 161, 167–8, 194, 199, 203, 232, 236–7, 239, 241, 242, 250, 251, 265, 268
    Alcibiades, 29
    Apology, 199

    Meno, 266
    Phaedrus, 7, 33, 78–9, 85, 92
    Protagoras, 86, 97
    Republic, 3–4, 29, 34, 74, 242
    Symposium, x, 31, 33, 35–6, 55, 80, 85, 86, 97, 236–7, 268
    Timaeus, 8, 33, 78, 89, 148
polyp, 15, 170–1, 175–6, 177–81, 183, 185–6, 189, 194
polyp-lice, 15, 177
polyp-style, 175–6, 185–6
Pope, A., xi, 33, 54
popularity, 20, 39, 81–3, 91, 154, 158, 199, 265–6
preformationism, 115, 178, 185, 191
prejudice, 6, 43–4, 53, 112–3, 146, 148, 154
premonition, 245, 248; *see also* prophecy
prison, 225
Prometheus, xvi, 86–91, 220
property, 225
prophecy, xvii, 27, 66, 134, 256–7, 260, 262, 264, 266; *see also* premonition
prosthesis, 103, 109–12, 115, 151–2, 184; *see also* telescope
Protagoras, 86
Pythagoras, 5, 51, 70, 128, 144–6, 153, 155, 267

quarrel between philosophy and poetry, xiii, 3–4, 10–11, 74
quarrel of the ancients and moderns, 49–50, 169, 203, 239

rapport, 33, 46, 103, 142–4, 148, 149–50, 170, 186–7, 190, 194–5, 204, 209, 211, 230, 258
recollection, 6, 8–9, 10, 14, 96, 123, 202, 234, 248–9, 262
recollection-image, 201, 248
religion, 13, 16, 27, 42, 48, 65, 69, 131, 139, 157, 161–2, 181, 209, 223–5, 227
resurrection, 181
revolution *see* global revolution
ridiculous, 90–6, 133–4, 150, 165, 194, 249; *see also* gibberish

Roche, S. de la, xvi
Romans, 15, 223
Rousseau, J.-J., v, xii, xiii, 3–4, 16, 17, 37, 63–5, 71, 125, 127–30, 131–2, 167, 185, 193, 199–201, 220, 229–30, 254
   Discours sur les sciences et arts, 3–4, 101, 200
   Discours sur l'origine et les fondements de l'inégalité, 101, 127, 129, 200–1, 229–30
   Émile, 16, 63, 71, 199
Royal Society, 73

Sappho, 32
satyr, 56
Saunderson, N., 135, 173
Schelling, F. W. J., xv, xvii, 151
Schlegel, A. W., xv, xvii–xviii, 152, 157
Schlegel, F., xv, xvi–xviii, 9, 14, 31, 41, 83, 105, 116, 126, 161, 207, 215, 240
Schleiermacher, F. D. E., xv, 37
Schlosser, J. G., xv, 190
schola Hemsterhuisiana, 15, 32
Scythian, 199–200, 243
self-consciousness, 131, 136–7, 139
semiotics *see* sign
sentimental certainty *see* conviction, sentimental
sentimental spirit, 47–9, 51, 55, 139, 169, 221, 249
's Gravesande, W., 15, 40, 41–2, 44, 63, 68, 102, 142, 190
shadow, xi, 8–9, 252–4
Shaftesbury, A., xii
sigh, 69–70, 258
sight *see* vision
sign, xiv, 13, 75–6, 79, 131, 142, 145, 148–50, 154, 170, 184, 211–2, 217, 228–9, 248, 249–51, 258
   primitive signs, 75–6, 211–12, 228, 250
Simon the Shoemaker, 80, 232
simultaneity *see* coexistence (of ideas); optimum
sketch, 206, 212–5
sociability, 28, 80–1, 226–7, 230, 240–2
social contract, 136–7

Socrates, x, 5, 7, 17, 28–9, 31–5, 38–9, 42, 50, 52, 59, 60–4, 74, 80, 85, 97, 123–5, 128, 132, 139, 165, 168, 199, 232, 236–7, 239, 240–2
'Socrates', x, 80, 84, 86–7, 96–7, 116, 133, 199–200, 219–21, 233, 234–5, 262, 267–8
Solon (*Timaeus*), 8
Sonderen, P., 7, 9, 18, 35, 37, 41–2, 111, 115, 135–6, 143, 205–6, 214, 217, 220
Sophists, 34, 60, 62
speed, 114–15, 118, 204, 206, 212, 214–15, 218, 221
Spinoza, B., xvi, 44–5, 62, 121, 149, 159–60, 195, 222, 223–4, 251, 263
state of nature *see* social contract
Stein, C. von, xvi
sterility, 245, 254
St-Evremont, C. de, 49
Stolberg, L., xv
Strauss, L., 159, 163, 242
stylicist, 251–2, 268
sublime, xvi, 9, 38, 54, 74–80, 94, 145, 153–5, 204, 210, 228, 249, 252, 257, 264, 265
succession, 57, 75, 78, 200, 203–4, 207–8, 218, 220, 263
syllogism *see* conviction, discursive
Symphilosophie, 22
synthesis, 51, 78, 106–8, 150, 229, 258
system, 6, 14, 21, 38–9, 43–5, 61, 62–3, 70, 72, 81, 168, 182, 214, 234

Tacitus, 217
tact, 37–8, 43, 45–7, 48, 71, 79, 97, 123, 139, 143–4, 147, 149, 167, 169–70, 195, 204, 207, 209, 236, 238–9, 241–2, 252, 258–9, 268
taste, 38, 53–4, 78, 115, 168, 235, 251
'Telecles', 232
telescope, 13, 16, 18, 41, 106, 109–12, 114, 140, 151–3, 184, 191
   binocular telescope, 13, 16, 18, 110–11
text-asylum, 254, 257
Theon of Alexandria, 232
Tolstoy, L., xv

tone, xi, 11–12, 36–8, 45, 49, 54–6, 61, 64, 66, 79–80, 82, 84, 86, 88, 93–4, 109, 111, 143, 147, 158, 161–5, 166–7, 168, 187, 196, 229, 231, 235, 238–9, 245, 252, 254, 255–6, 260, 266, 268
touch, 117, 120, 122, 134, 138, 140, 142, 219–20
transformism, 172–3, 182–5, 192–3
Trembley, A., 15, 177–81, 186, 188
Trop, G., xvii, 122, 161, 251
Tyrannicide, 35

uncanny, 163, 248, 250
untimeliness, xii, 36–7, 53–7, 74, 86, 139, 163, 165, 169, 200, 202, 221, 230, 231, 235, 239, 243, 250, 254, 265, 268; *see also* anachronism

Van Bunge, W., xv, 28, 32, 49, 101, 131, 242
Van Sluis, J., xv, xviii, 8, 11, 15, 21, 42, 91–2, 111, 159, 188, 190, 199, 215, 236
vase experiment, 41–2, 205–6, 208
vehicle of action, 116–18, 141
velleity, 87, 89, 117, 124, 135, 162, 217, 259
Verbeek, T., 121–2, 159–60
Vereinigungsphilosophie, xvii
Vernière, P., 159–60

Vieillard-Baron, J.-F., xiv, 21, 29, 32–3, 34, 52, 142, 246
view-from-nowhere, 43, 46, 57, 219, 263–4
vignette, 9
virtuality, 54, 89, 200–1, 203, 218, 248–50, 252, 254, 259–61
vision, 13, 69, 105–12, 116–17, 134–5, 138–41, 142, 152, 175, 189, 207, 219, 220
Volland, S., 171
Voltaire, 16, 49–50, 63, 101, 158, 165, 167–8, 200

Weatherby, L., xiv, 102–3
web, 142, 196
whatifery, 175, 184, 192
Whiston, W., 147
Wieland, C., xv–xvi, 190
Wielema, M., xii, xv, 11, 16, 21, 225
Winckelmann, J. J., 31–2
Wolfe, C., 41
Wolff, C., 64, 251
world-construction, 85–7, 248, 251–4
world-image, 201, 246
writing under persecution *see* esoteric writing
Wyttenbach, D., 32

Zeus, 6, 8, 9, 43–6, 87–8
zoophyte, 179–80